ONE POTATO, TWO POTATO

ONE POTATO, TWO POTATO

300 RECIPES FROM SIMPLE TO ELEGANT — APPETIZERS, MAIN DISHES, SIDE DISHES, AND MORE

ROY FINAMORE

WITH MOLLY STEVENS

HOUGHTON MIFFLIN COMPANY

BOSTON   NEW YORK   2001

Library of Congress Cataloging-in-Publication Data
Finamore, Roy.
 One potato, two potato : 300 recipes from simple to elegant—appetizers, main dishes, side dishes, and more / Roy Finamore and Molly Stevens.
  p. cm.
 Includes index.
 ISBN 0-618-00714-8
 1. Cookery (Potatoes) I. Stevens, Molly. II. Title.

 TX803.P8 F56 2001
 641.6'521—dc21   2001026373

Printed in the United States of America
Designed by Marysarah Quinn
Food styling by Rori Spinelli-Trovato
Prop styling by Roy Finamore

RRD/CRA   10 9 8 7 6 5 4 3 2 1

The author is grateful for permission to reprint the following recipes:
"Shepherd Potatoes" from *My Mexico* by Diana Kennedy, copyright © 1998 by Diana Kennedy. Used by permission of Clarkson Potter/Publishers, a division of Random House, Inc.
"Little Potato Knishes" and "Potato Kugel" from *Jewish Cooking in America* by Joan Nathan, copyright © 1994, 1998 by Joan Nathan. Used by permission of Alfred A. Knopf, a division of Random House, Inc.
"Tom Colicchio's Potato-Leek Soup" from *Think Like a Chef* by Tom Colicchio, copyright © 2000 by Tom Colicchio. Photographs copyright © 2000 by Bill Bettencourt. Foreword copyright © by Danny Meyer. Used by permission of Clarkson Potter/Publishers, a division of Random House, Inc.
"Simplest Potato Soup" and "Soupy Stewed Potatoes" from *Vegetarian Cooking for Everyone* by Deborah Madison, copyright © 1997 by Deborah Madison. Used by permission of Broadway Books, a division of Random House, Inc.
"Smashed Potato Salad" from *Jim Fobel's Big Flavors* by Jim Fobel, copyright © 1995 by Jim Fobel. Used by permission of Clarkson Potter/Publishers, a division of Random House, Inc.
"Hungarian Potato Stew" and "Hungarian Potato Casserole" from *The Hungarian Cookbook* by Susan Derecskey. Text copyright © 1972 by Susan Derecskey. Illustrations copyright © 1972 by Harper & Row Publishers, Inc. Reprinted by permission of HarperCollins Publishers, Inc.
"Squid with Potatoes" from *Essentials of Classic Italian Cooking* by Marcella Hazan, copyright © 1992 by Marcella Hazan. Used by permission of Alfred A. Knopf, a division of Random House, Inc.
"Martha Stewart's Mashed Potatoes" from *The Martha Stewart Cookbook* by Martha Stewart, illustrations by Rodica Prato, copyright © 1995 by Martha Stewart Omnimedia, L.L.C.; illustrations copyright © 1995 by Rodica Prato. Used by permission of Clarkson Potter/Publishers, a division of Random House, Inc.
"Nancy Barr's Potato Cake" from *We Called It Macaroni* by Nancy Verde Barr, copyright © 1990 by Nancy Verde Barr, illustrations copyright © 1990 by Kathe Helander. Used by permission of Alfred A. Knopf, a division of Random House, Inc.
"Sweet Potatoes with Horseradish" from *The New Southern Cook* by John Martin Taylor, copyright © 1995 by John Martin Taylor. Used by permission of the author.
"Potatoes in Beer" from *Simple French Food* by Richard Olney, copyright © 1974, 1992 by Richard Olney. Used by permission of Hungry Minds, Inc.
"Arequipeña Potatoes" from *The Art of South American Cooking* by Felipe Rojas-Lombardi, copyright © 1991 by Felipe Rojas-Lombardi. Reprinted by permission of HarperCollins Publishers, Inc.

For my grandmothers, Anne Gorman and Anna Finamore
—R.F.

For my father
—M.S.

ACKNOWLEDGMENTS

Thanks first must go to Marian Young and Tom Pearson. Marian tasted eagerly and often, offered encouragement and sage guidance, and never missed a chance to inject humor while she washed yet another sinkful of dishes. Tom tasted willingly too, and tested and shopped and shopped some more. Together, they opened their house in Virginia to me and Molly for marathons of potato cooking. Their generosity is extraordinary, and it is impossible to imagine this book without them.

Thanks to my buddy Kelly Bugden for the beautiful photographs. And to Rori Spinelli-Trovato for making the food look so tasty. And to the very dear Marysarah Quinn, thank you for enthusiasm, advice, and the perfectly elegant design.

My thanks to Susan Simon for your company on many mornings at the Greenmarket, for props, and for the potato salad recipe.

Many friends and colleagues were helpful and enthusiastic along the way. I'm grateful to Leigh Ann Ambrosi, Jean Anderson, Mario Batali, Tom Colicchio, John Derian, Jessie Duff-McLaurin, Lily Genis, Charles Gold, Jimmy Gross, Martha Holmberg, Pam Krauss, Bill Leritz, Barbara Marks, Laura Simon, Christopher Monte Smith, Rebecca Staffel, Martha Stewart, Zanne Stewart, John Martin Taylor, Carole Walter, Peri Wolfman, and Cathy Young. All of you have made valued contributions.

Samia Ahad, my e-mail friend, has been particularly kind and generous.

My sister Marie, sister-in-law Donna, and their families were enthusiastic supporters from the beginning; David Rossler is an eager kitchen assistant and budding cook; and I thank them all.

Thank you to my folks for innumerable kindnesses.

Thank you, Rux Martin, for rising to the challenge of editing an editor with such grace and aplomb, for being available for every phone call, for fighting back when you needed to, and for conceding when you felt it right. Thank you as well to the cheerfully efficient Lori Galvin-Frost and the delightful Deb DeLosa. There is also the unnamed legion of supporters any author hopes for in a publishing house. Please know, friends at Houghton, that I appreciate your efforts on my behalf.

Throughout it all has been Molly Stevens—coming through with her quietly cheerful voice on the phone and through e-mail. Best, not surprisingly, were the days we spent together in the kitchen. Molly is a pearl beyond price.

And Pat Adrian: well, Pat is the best.

I am in debt to you all. And I am lucky beyond words to count you all as friends and advisers.

—Roy

A big sweeping thanks to all the various friends, colleagues, and acquaintances who have put up with my endless queries, shared their ideas and favorite recipes, and, most important, gathered around my table to taste and critique a relentless number of potato dishes. It would have been no fun at all without your support.

I am indebted to the many chefs and cookbook authors whose recipes and research have taught me so much about the incredible versatility and properties of the venerable potato—many of their names appear in the bibliography. In particular, Chef Robert Barral took the time to help me to unravel the mystery of *pommes soufflées,* and Randall Price kept me laughing (via e-mail) through it all. Thank you both.

Thanks to my editors and friends at *Fine Cooking* (Martha Holmberg, Susie Middleton, Sarah Jay, and Amy Albert), who encouraged me from the start and remained patient when I disappeared for weeks on end into this book.

A warm thank-you goes to Marlene Holtan for graciously sharing her magnificent home with me any time I travel to New York. I echo Roy in his tribute to Marian and Tom for letting us take over their kitchen in Virginia, and for welcoming me into their tight circle of friendship without hesitation.

Much of the joy in working on this book came from converting our entire vegetable garden to a potato patch, and thanks go to the folks at Wood Prairie Farm in Bridgewater, Maine, for the excellent seed potatoes and their helpful advice.

I am perpetually grateful to Mark for his good company, for tasting almost every recipe I have ever developed, for willingly enduring my erratic schedule, and for believing in me—sometimes more than I do myself.

And lastly, my greatest thanks go to Roy, who dreamed up this whole project and invited me into it. I have been enriched by your acumen, by your friendship, and by your approach to cooking and to books about cooking. You spoil me.

—Molly

CONTENTS

INTRODUCTION

As I was beginning to work on this book, I got a call from my friend Laura on Nantucket. Laura is usually calm, and the tone of her voice was alarming. Someone, she said, had raided her root cellar and stolen most of her baking potatoes. These weren't grocery-store spuds. Laura is a dedicated gardener who spends untold hours planning what will go into the potato bed, sometimes trying something new, often relying on the varieties that have served her well over the years. Like nutty Rose Golds—perfect with just a little butter. And Red Garnets, which caramelize deliciously in pancakes. And German Butterballs—the perfectly round, golden-fleshed heirloom variety that's so tasty in a salad or a rough mash. And Sierra bakers, her greatest pride. As I listened to her, I made all the appropriate noises, but to tell the truth, I'd coveted her potatoes myself.

Luckily, though, I don't have to resort to theft for superlative potatoes. I live in New York City, not far from the Union Square Greenmarket. There, in the beginning of July, New Jersey farmers bring the first potatoes of the year: just-pulled Yukon Golds and Reddales with wispy skin so delicate that a good scrub is enough to remove it. Bill Leritz comes a few weeks later, bringing his crop of Augustas and Estimas and a few other heirlooms from his farm in Sugarloaf, New York. Depending on the day of the week and what farmers are selling, there can be more than twenty varieties to choose from. Molly grows her own in her Vermont garden and calls to let me know when she's pulled the first ones and how she's cooked them. To us, it's not a meal without potatoes, whether great heirlooms or plain old supermarket russets.

In each culture where it has appeared, the adaptable potato has been appropriated, stolen, and, inevitably, embraced. Potatoes are international and immensely important—second only to rice as a food crop. And unlike rice, potatoes find their way easily and elegantly into every course of a meal.

The conquistadores found the potato cultivated in the Andes. Sixteenth-century Peruvians freeze-dried this important staple, spreading the potatoes out in the frigid night air, then stomping them like grapes to rid them of moisture, repeating the freeze and the stomp over the course of several days. Potatoes preserved in this way can last up to ten years, and to this day Peruvians continue the practice. Such potatoes are difficult to find in the United States, but there's no reason we can't make such Peruvian dishes as Arequipeña Potatoes, a toothsome casserole of diced potatoes with a chile buried in its heart.

Perhaps as a curiosity, perhaps as a serious attempt to introduce a new food crop, the potato was taken to Spain in the late 1500s. While it had its admirers ("a delicacy to the Indians and a dainty dish even for the Spaniards," according to one source), it was slave food. For hundreds of years, France turned its back on the potato. "However it is prepared," Diderot wrote in the late 1700s, "this root is tasteless and starchy. One would not include it among the agreeable foods, but it does provide plentiful and sufficiently healthful nourishment for men who do not require more than sustenance." Flash forward to the present, where the consumption of potatoes in France outstrips that of bread.

Regardless that many considered the potato a poison (Sicilians would write down the name of an enemy, attach it to a potato, and bury it in hopes that the victim would die), that it was said to promote lust, that the plant itself was thought ugly, it spread across Europe. The Irish adopted it, indeed relished it, well in advance of the rest of the Continent. And in Ireland it was not simple peasant food; rich and poor alike ate their praties. Dishes created in early Irish kitchens remain popular today, colcannon being a prime example. This mix of potatoes and kale—whipped until fluffy, baked until piping hot, with a well of melted butter—was certainly known in the 1700s.

Credit for making the potato fashionable in France has long been given to Antoine-Auguste Parmentier, a servant to Louis XVI. It began with the flower of the plant, which he induced the king to wear. Marie Antoinette soon asked for some so she might be similarly adorned. Before long, the French were planting fields of potatoes and guarding them from the peasants who stole them at night.

However the potato has traveled the world, what has resulted is a wealth of recipes. Baked, the potato can be passed with a dipping sauce as an hors d'oeuvre. A potato might be the way you thicken a soup, the secret in a chocolate cake, a meal in itself. You can fry them, boil them, steam them, braise them, bake them; and you can slice, dice, chop, and mash. Much the same applies to the sweet potato, culinary cousin but no botanical relative to the potato. The world is there for inspiration, and they are ready to step in for every part of a meal.

As we surveyed our subject, we set a few ground rules. First, and most important, was to record recipes for the dishes we most love to eat. That's not an easy task when potatoes are your world. Much as we relish the flavor of a freshly dug potato, which needs only to be boiled for a few moments and eaten with good salt, we have found many other ways to make potatoes the center of a meal. Take home fries or hash brown potatoes, add a poached egg, and that's lunch or dinner. Molly raids the refrigerator to find ingredients to make a stuffed baked potato for herself in the middle of the day. I make gnocchi for company, as I have ever since I was a kid, when my grandmother taught me how. Through Diana Kennedy, an author I'm privileged to work with and who has been called the Julia Child of Mexican cooking, I learned that tiny whole potatoes can be served with drinks. My good friend the late cookbook author

Richard Sax helped me re-create the potato doughnuts I remembered from my childhood. Molly applied her classic French training to re-creating dishes as extravagant as potatoes cooked in cream and as elegant as Pommes Anna.

We also wanted to figure out what potato was best for what (for guidelines, see page 17). We tried mashing waxy potatoes, for example, knowing—instinctively—that their starch was wrong for that dish. The result is that we can give you hints about what to do when a waxy potato is all you have in the house and you want a mash, as well as tell you the best variety for perfect mashed potatoes.

As we worked on the book and told friends about it, the response was always, "Oh, everyone loves potatoes." We hope so. More, we hope that our own enthusiasm excites you.

POTATO PRINCIPLES

Possibly the most important lesson to learn about potatoes is that they are not created equal. At even the most bare-bones supermarket, you will find side-by-side bins of round red potatoes, long white thin-skinned potatoes, yellow-fleshed Yukons, and the large rough-skinned russets. And, if you're lucky enough to live near a farmers' market, there you will likely see an even greater array of colors, shapes, and sizes, which can cause the uninitiated to scratch their heads and ask, "Which potato do I choose?" The answer to that question lies in knowing a few things about the basic character of potatoes.

Nutritionally, all potatoes fall into the category of complex carbohydrates, with only small amounts (less than 10 percent) of protein. In cooking terms, complex carbohydrates are known as starches, and it is the type and quantity of starch in any given potato that matter to the cook. Basically, potato varieties are divided into three categories: high-starch potatoes, low-starch potatoes, and, in between, medium-starch potatoes. These differing levels of starch affect the way a potato cooks.

HIGH-STARCH POTATOES

The most common high-starch potatoes, also known as *mealy*, or *floury*, potatoes, are russets, or Idahos. These familiar potatoes are characterized by a dry and delicate texture that readily crumbles when cooked and quickly absorbs any liquids and seasonings. This dry texture is what makes these starchy potatoes the first choice for both baking and frying. When baked, their large starch granules swell up and separate, becoming ethereally light and fluffy. When cut into sticks and fried, high-starch potatoes become crisp on the outside and light on the inside, because what little moisture there is inside is quickly forced out as the fries sizzle in hot fat.

Another prized attribute of high-starch potatoes is that they are thirsty enough to absorb all the rich cream and butter that you care to add without becoming cloying or heavy. For this reason, you'll find them used in many luxurious casseroles and gratins, where the potatoes and other ingredients meld into a soft and unctuous dish. Starchy potatoes are also great for mashing, because their floury texture renders them smooth, not lumpy.

When simmered or boiled, these dry-textured, starchy potatoes want to take up all the liquid around them and fall apart into a soft mush. Whether this is a good or a bad thing depends on what you're after. When you are making rustic soup and want the starch to thicken it, high-starch potatoes are the answer. Cut into small chunks and simmered, they will soften and eventually collapse, lending a creamy thickness to the broth. If, however, you want the potatoes to hold their shape for something such as a salad or sauté, choose another kind.

Added to breads or desserts, a bit of mashed potato produces an incomparably tender dough. Since potatoes contain no gluten (a protein found in flour that becomes elastic and tough when kneaded or mixed), they soften the dough, making it moist, supple, and subtly sweet.

LOW-STARCH POTATOES

Often referred to as *waxy,* or *boiling,* potatoes, or often, mistakenly, as *new* potatoes (see page 17 for the real explanation of "new"), low-starch potatoes have a higher moisture content, a denser texture, and thinner skin than the high-starch potatoes. The most familiar of the waxy low-starch varieties are round red potatoes and white boiling potatoes. Waxy potatoes are the first choice for recipes where you want the potatoes to hold their shape and have a little tooth to them. Think of potato salads and hash browns. They are also the ones to choose when boiling or steaming, not only because they hold a clean shape but because they tend to have intrinsic flavor rather than being a vehicle for other flavors. Since their texture is more dense and moist, low-starch potatoes will not absorb as much dressing in a salad or as much liquid when simmered, so choose them when you want integrity of flavor and texture. Waxy potatoes also find their way into chowders, other chunky soups, and stews, where their firm texture will hold up even after a long simmer.

Small round walnut-sized waxy potatoes are sometimes sold as *creamer* potatoes. This description applies to their moist, creamy interior—perfect left whole and boiled, simmered, or roasted.

Not only do waxy potatoes have less starch than the mealy varieties, but they have a slightly different kind of starch. When cooked, the starch granules in waxy potatoes don't swell up and separate as much, but instead remain close and dense. (Waxy potatoes contain more of a starch known as amylopectin. If you think of pectin, which is what makes jelly jell, you'll have a sense of why these starches hold the potatoes together even when cooked until tender. Because of this, waxy potatoes are not fluffy enough for baking, and they have an unpleasant tendency to turn gluey when overworked—for example, by an overzealous masher or blender for a pureed soup. If you want to make mashed potatoes and you have only waxy ones around, the best approach is to smash them coarsely (skins on, if you want) with just a bit of olive oil or butter—and stop there. Although they won't soak up loads of gravy, they will have excellent flavor.

Low-starch potatoes are a good choice for roasting because of their creamy, dense interior. Since lower starch means higher sugar, and sugar browns faster than starch, when they are cut up into smallish chunks, their surfaces get wonderfully crisp and brown—just the way they should be. If you are roasting potatoes under a large roast or chicken, however, you may want to choose a starchier potato that will absorb more of the drippings—waxy potatoes won't soak up as much of the other flavors as drier varieties will.

Waxy potatoes make lousy French fries for two reasons. First, their high moisture content leaves them limp, not crisp. Second, because of their higher sugar content, the fries get browned on the outside before they are fully cooked inside.

MEDIUM-STARCH POTATOES

These potatoes have a starch content that falls, not surprisingly, somewhere in between the mealy and waxy varieties. Probably the most familiar medium-starch potatoes in markets today are the *white all-purpose* potatoes and the *yellow-fleshed* varieties, such as Yukon Gold. Despite the moniker "all-purpose," these medium-starch potatoes are not as good for baking and frying as the high-starch varieties, but they can be called into service just about everywhere else. The greatest attributes of the medium-starch potatoes are their creamy texture and, when it comes to the yellow varieties, their rich, almost nutty flavor. In the recipes that follow, you'll find medium-starch potatoes in everything from salads and gratins to mashes and braises. When cooked, they become wonderfully soft, without disintegrating the way a mealy potato would. In salads, they hold their shape yet are soft and creamy without being waxy, and they absorb more dressing and seasoning than a low-starch potato. Mashed or baked, they won't be as light and fluffy as russets, but they are good in their own right.

A FEW FAVORITE VARIETIES

With more than a thousand varieties of potatoes grown worldwide, it would be impossible, and fairly useless, to attempt an exhaustive list. Instead, here are the ones you are most likely to see in the market, along with some perhaps less familiar that are worth seeking out.

NEW POTATOES *New* is perhaps one of the more confusing terms used to categorize potatoes. To begin with, *new* does not refer to any specific variety of potatoes but rather to any potato that is young and freshly dug. To best understand new potatoes, it helps to know a bit about the life cycle of a potato plant. Potatoes are tubers, which means that they grow underground attached to the roots of a green leafy plant. When the plant blossoms early in the season, this indicates that the tubers have begun to form, and it is at this point that the first new potatoes can be dug. These young potatoes are always small, with fragile, papery, flaking skins that are somewhat ragged-looking—

TWO QUICK TESTS FOR STARCHINESS

When you boil or bake a potato, one quick look is all you need to determine if it's high- or low-starch. if the potato looks dry and fluffy, it's starchy; if it's dense and moist, it's waxy. It would be nice, however, to know the starch content *before* you begin to cook. A simple test is to cut a raw potato in half with a large chef's knife: if there is a lot of white residue on the blade and if the potato seems to cling to the knife, it's starchy. If the potato leaves little residue on the blade and falls away from the knife without clinging, it's most likely waxy.

From a more scientific point of view, low-starch potatoes have a high solid content and low moisture content, while the inverse is true for the high-starch varieties. If you want to estimate the starch content of any particular variety of potatoes, here's a test from the food-science guru Shirley Corriher: put the potatoes in a brine of 1 cup of salt and 11 cups of water. Those that float contain less starch.

For both these tests, keep in mind that the starch content of all potatoes deteriorates as the tubers sit in storage. So, if you use the knife test in April on a russet potato that was dug in October, the starch may be less apparent.

their tougher more protective skins grow later in the season. True new potatoes are only to be found in the late spring and summer, and the best place to shop for them is at farm stands or farmers' markets. These potatoes have a high moisture content and a delicate sweet flavor—their starches are not yet fully developed. They cook more quickly than mature potatoes, and the best way to appreciate them is simply boiled or steamed with a dot of sweet butter or a drizzle of olive oil. They also roast up nicely and love a shower of fresh summer herbs. Since new potatoes have not been "cured"—a process in which the tubers are left in the ground after their foliage dies back or are kept in a controlled environment to toughen their skins and dry so that they can be stored without rotting—expect these fragile treasures to last only a week or two.

You will often see small red or white supermarket potatoes labeled "new." Keep in mind that once they sit around for more than fifteen days, they have lost all the characteristics that made them new. If you can't easily rub the skin off the potato with your thumb, it's not a real new potato.

And, finally, some authors and chefs refer to any freshly dug potato as new—no matter whether the potato is a young, thin-skinned one pulled from the ground in the early summer or a full-grown specimen unearthed only after the leafy plant has died back in the fall. While the latter may not technically be called new, we treasure these as much as we do any early-season potato. The bottom line is, whether you want to call them new or freshly dug, the best-tasting potatoes you will ever find are those that make it into your kitchen soon after leaving the ground.

The inverse of new or freshly dug potatoes are the storage potatoes that fill our supermarket bins from November through June, when fresh ones are not available. Storage potatoes have thicker skins to protect them from spoilage during the winter. While we certainly rely on storage potatoes for many of the recipes in the book, anyone who really loves potatoes needs to seek out at least a pound or two of freshly dug new potatoes at the next opportunity. We guarantee you'll get hooked.

RED POTATOES Sold year-round in most markets, red-skinned potatoes are our most common waxy variety. Sometimes called *Red Bliss*, or *Red Pontiac*, red potatoes are typically on the small side. Reds have a nice creamy texture and slightly nutty flavor that make them good for salads, roasting, braising, and simmering, and other places where you want a dice to stay diced without cooking to mush.

LONG WHITE POTATOES Another supermarket standby, these elongated, almost flat potatoes are sometimes called *California whites,* or *long California whites.* They have a rather thin, slightly yellowish skin and medium to low starch content. Use them in gratins, salads, and braises and for roasting.

MAINE POTATOES Rounder than long whites, and with a slightly thicker tan skin, these white potatoes have a medium starch content, making them a good all-purpose spud. Sometimes called *Kennebecs,* Eastern potatoes, and *chef's potatoes,* Maine potatoes lack the sweetness of red potatoes, but they are a reliable workhorse for salads, roasts, braises, and other dishes where you want a potato to hold its shape. They also make a decent mash, although a bit less fluffy than some.

RUSSETS These hardy potatoes earned their common name with their rugged, thick brown skins. They are also known as *Russet Burbank* (named after Luther Burbank, who developed the variety), *Idaho* (although they are grown in many other states), and even just *baking potatoes.* The ultimate high-starch potatoes, russets are the first choice for making fries and baking. They are a favorite for gratins and casseroles in which you want the potatoes to soften completely and absorb all the other ingredients, and they are good tucked under a large roast to soak up the drippings as the meat cooks. Russets also make incomparably light and fluffy mashed potatoes.

ALL-PURPOSE POTATOES When we refer to all-purpose potatoes, we mean to direct you to the bins of white potatoes that you find in the supermarket next to the russets and the reds. No matter if they are Maine potatoes or long white potatoes, these common medium-starch varieties are good roasted, boiled, and sautéed, and in all sorts of gratins and pancakes.

YELLOW-FLESHED POTATOES The first yellow-fleshed potato to go mainstream was the *Yukon Gold.* These medium-starch potatoes have a rich flavor and unmistakably yellow-gold flesh. Creamy enough to make fantastic mashed potatoes that tend to want a bit less butter and cream than the starchier russets, the yellow-fleshed varieties also hold their shape well enough to be excellent for sautéing and for some salads. Another yellow-fleshed variety that is gaining ground is *Yellow Finn.*

HEIRLOOM POTATOES Growers and produce suppliers use the term *heirloom* to describe the ever-expanding range of potato varieties now found in specialty markets, catalogs, and farmers' markets. With their charming names, skin colors ranging from pale pink to deep purple, some speckled and some swirled, and all sorts of odd and even shapes, they are too numerous to list. The best thing to do is to find what you can in your area and try them. No matter which you choose, you'll find that they have real potato flavor, be it sweet or nutty or buttery. Most have medium or low starch content. We recommend cooking them simply — maybe simmered in water and served with a pat of butter and some salt and pepper — so you can really appreciate their taste. Later, you may want to try them steamed, mashed, or roasted. Since the skins tend to be thin and tender, it's rarely worth the bother to peel them — and besides, some of the smaller varieties are so knobby as to make peeling a chore.

Heirloom potatoes are the closest we get to the original wild potatoes first discovered in South America. They haven't been crossbred and hybridized by growers for bigger sizes, tougher skin, and longer storage capability. As a result, heirlooms tend not to keep very well, so eat them in season, not long after you bring them home. Most heirloom potatoes tend to be on the small size — some as tiny as marbles, others closer to a baseball. Many are referred to as fingerlings, because their wobbly, knobby shapes resemble somewhat exaggerated fingers.

Some of our particular favorites are *German Butterball* (a relatively large late-season variety with amazing buttery flavor); *French Fingerling* (creamy, dense, waxy red-skinned variety with pale flesh, also called *Nosebag*); *Desiree* (rosy skin with golden flesh and a sweet flavor); *Ruby Crescent* (pink skins with pale yellow flesh and delicate flavor); *La Ratte* (a French variety, sometimes called *La Reine,* and a favorite for its rich flavor and creamy texture); *Ozette* (a delicious fingerling with ivory-colored flesh and pale skin); *Bintje* (a medium-sized yellow-fleshed potato with good, moist flesh); and *All Red* (a low-starch variety with real red skin and a pale pink interior).

BLUE OR PURPLE POTATOES These extraordinary-looking vegetables really fall under the same umbrella as heirloom potatoes; in fact, some of the first Peruvian potatoes were indeed deep blue. Their initial appeal in markets and restaurants began, perhaps, as a mere curiosity, but blue potatoes have a distinct flavor and a fine texture that deserves recognition. The blue color ranges from an almost purple-black to a paler lavender tint. Their moist, waxy flesh is great for making salads, roasting, boiling, and even mashing. Their skins do tend to be rather thick and tough, so you need to peel them (after boiling is easiest) for salad and mashes. Try to find the *True Blue* and *All Blue*. Others have unevenly colored flesh, which doesn't affect the taste—they're just not very pretty.

SWEET POTATOES

Botanically speaking, a sweet potato is not related to the potato, but since they share many preparations (gratins, mashes, baked, and such), we have included them here. Sweet potatoes are often confused with yams (see page 433)—another case of mistaken identity. Unlike potatoes, which grow primarily in northern cold climates (Maine, Canada, Idaho, and northern California, for instance), sweet potatoes are happier in the more temperate South.

The rough, dry skin of sweet potatoes ranges from pale brown to almost purple, and the inside runs from soft yellow to garnet. Sweet potatoes can be as small as 6 ounces to as large as 1 pound. They come to market in the winter months and are sweetest at that time. Some cooks claim that the ones with the pointy ends are the sweetest, but we've yet to find proof of this. Instead, shop for the sweet potatoes with the tautest skins that are the heaviest for their size. If they are wrinkled or at all soft, move on.

BUYING POTATOES

If you are lucky enough to live near a farmers' market, shop there. You will find a greater variety of better-tasting potatoes that have not had to travel thousands of miles to get to you.

Look for potatoes with smooth, unbroken skin. With the exception of new potatoes, which will have feathered, papery skin, all potatoes should have tight, even skin. At farmers' markets, you'll find potatoes still covered with dirt. This is a good thing, as it means that they weren't run through an abusive mechanical washer.

Avoid potatoes with cracks or blemishes, or any that show evidence of having been mauled by a spade—they will spoil more quickly. Squeeze the potatoes—or try to. They should be firm and not yielding. If they are at all spongy, soft, or wrinkled, they are old and beginning to rot.

Do not buy potatoes tinged with green. This green appears just under the skin when the potatoes have been exposed to light, and it contains solanine, a mildly toxic alkaloid (solanine was actually once used to treat epilepsy). Although you can peel away the layer of green, it's better just to avoid potatoes with signs of it.

Another sign that potatoes have been improperly stored is sprouting. This indicates that their starches will have begun to convert to sugars, something that makes them taste decidedly wrong. In addition, the sprouts themselves contain solanine and are therefore toxic.

STORING POTATOES

Keep potatoes in the dark, keep them low to the ground, and keep them cool. The ideal temperature for storing potatoes is around 50 degrees, but since few of us have well-ventilated root cellars, this is a problem. The best place for potatoes is a deep drawer or in a basket inside a cabinet. Do not be tempted to put them in the refrigerator. If you do, the starches will begin to convert to sugar and the potatoes will not taste right. The sugars will also cause them to brown too quickly when fried or sautéed and absorb less liquid in gratins and braises, ultimately causing problems in your recipes. Since exposure to light (whether natural or artificial) is what turns potatoes green, they need to be in the dark. A brown paper bag is better than nothing.

PEELING AND SCRUBBING

The decision to peel or scrub a potato is based on a few factors: the type of potato, the recipe, and personal preference. For instance, russets, with their leathery skins, are almost always peeled before being sliced for a gratin or mashed into a puree. These same tough skins, however, provide the perfect sturdy jacket to hold all the fillings of a twice-stuffed potato. For salads with low- and medium-starch potatoes, we sometimes leave the skins on, sometimes peel them. It all depends on the style of the salad: casual, keep the skin; more refined, peel it. Some nutritionists would tell you about all the nutrients in the peel of any vegetable, but we confess to putting a higher priority on flavor and aesthetics than grams of fiber. In the recipes that follow, we've specified our preference for peeled or scrubbed, but feel free to go your own way.

There are legends about the tedium of peeling potatoes. We quite disagree. There's something wonderfully restorative about feeling the weight of the potato in one hand, holding your favorite peeler in the other, and quickly and deftly stripping the skin to reveal the pristine, moist flesh beneath. But to really enjoy peeling potatoes, first get a good peeler. I like the Y-shaped peelers because they strip a wider swath, but Molly prefers the old-fashioned swivel peeler because she likes the way you can use the pointed tip to dig out any eyes or blemishes. Whichever peeler you choose, make sure that it's sharp. If it struggles or cuts a ragged peel, toss it out and get a new one. Before you peel any potatoes, give them a quick rinse. Otherwise, any dirt on the surface will end up all over your hands and the potatoes themselves. Hold the potato firmly in one hand and draw the peeler across the surface in a smooth continuous motion. A rapid back-and-forth scraping wastes energy and takes forever. Don't peel over the garbage can, because if the spud slips—and one is bound to—you'll have to go fishing through the trash.

As for scrubbing, it too is easy if you have the right tool: a stiff-bristled vegetable brush, not a "scrubby" that you use on dishes and the stove and everything else. Depending on the variety, you'll need to rub more or less vigorously. For older, thick-skinned storage potatoes, you can scrub pretty hard without tearing the skin, but be more gentle with newer, freshly dug potatoes, or you'll end up scraping off all the skin before you know it.

SOAKING

Most every cook knows that a peeled or cut-up potato will turn brown if left to sit on the counter for any time. Certain enzymes inside the potato that react with oxygen as soon as you cut into the potato cells cause this. Starchy potatoes, such as russets, tend to turn brown more quickly than waxy varieties, but this is a problem for all potatoes. In truth, the problem is mostly cosmetic, but fortunately, it is easy enough to avoid.

The most obvious solution is to peel or cut up the potatoes right before you are ready to cook. But if you are trying to get ahead and prep the ingredients in advance—or if you suddenly get called off task—just drop the peeled potatoes into a bowl of water. As long as the water is deep enough to cover all the potatoes, it will keep them out of contact with the air and thus prevent them from discoloring. The more potatoes, the more water, and the bigger the bowl—if they are too crowded, they will begin to turn, even underwater. You're safest if you slip the bowl into the refrigerator if you are planning on waiting more than a half-hour or add ice cubes as the water starts to warm to room temperature.

If you do plan to soak and chill potatoes for any length of time, you should understand that after several hours in a cold environment, the starches will begin to convert to sugars, affecting the way the potatoes cook, since sugars brown more quickly than starches. This is not a real problem in the late summer and fall, since freshly harvested potatoes have the highest starch content. As the potatoes sit in storage, however, their starches naturally begin to convert to sugars. When working with late-season potatoes in the spring and early summer, be especially careful not to soak and chill them for more than a few hours or their sugar content will become so high that they will tend to brown quickly or even burn before cooking all the way through.

Soaking potatoes can also wash away some of their starch, so be careful how you do it. For gratins and soups, for example, when the recipe relies on the potato's starch as a thickener, soaking can cause problems. If you do want to get a jump on your preparation, peel the potatoes and soak them whole, but leave the final dicing or slicing until the last minute, lest you wash that needed starch away.

You'll also find recipes (chips and fries, and some of the fried cakes) where you want to rid the potato of excess starch. For these dishes, the cut-up, sliced, or diced potatoes will need a long soak or should be rinsed several times.

Regardless of why you're soaking potatoes, be sure to drain them well and dry them thoroughly before you add them to butter or oil. Water in a deep fryer is terribly dangerous—it will splatter and pop—and a wet or even damp potato will not brown when you're sautéing or panfrying.

BOILING

For many recipes (hash browns, home fries, mashes, salads), the first step to preparing the potatoes is to boil them, but don't take the term *boil* too literally. The action of boiling is simply too violent for most foods (dried pasta being a notable exception), and potatoes are no different. They should be cooked at a steady simmer, with the surface of the water bubbling evenly but not so vigorously as to buffet them around in the pot.

DRAINING POTATOES

We suggest that you drain potatoes that have been cooked in their jackets on a rack set in the sink. Here's why. A couple of things happen when you dump boiled potatoes into a colander. First, chances are the tender potatoes on the bottom will get crushed or broken. But, more important, as you leave them there to "cool," the potatoes on the bottom of the pile steam and overcook, and they all take much longer than necessary to cool. Drain them in a single layer, with space around them, and your potatoes will be beautiful.

We use wire racks, the kind used to cool cakes and cookies. You can also find baskets that fit over your sink.

COOKING TIMES

We've deliberately not given cooking times in many recipes for three reasons. First, different-sized potatoes cook at different rates. If you have chosen 8 small potatoes to make up a pound, these will cook more quickly than 3 large potatoes. Likewise, if you cut a potato into 1/4-inch bits, these will cook in much less time than 2-inch chunks. Second, different varieties cook at different rates. Finally, old storage potatoes take longer to cook than freshly dug potatoes.

We've noticed another thing about storage potatoes. Late in the season (from March through July), high- and medium-starch potatoes just aren't as thirsty as they are when they're at their peak because their starch content decreases during storage. The same holds for potatoes that have been refrigerated or otherwise improperly stored. What that means for the cook is that cooking times will vary in those recipes where you expect potatoes to absorb liquids, in particular, some of the braises and gratins. So give them additional time, and if the potatoes are being particularly obstreperous, spoon out some liquid.

The best guideline for cooking potatoes is to cook similar-sized and similar varieties together. Check for doneness with a skewer or needle (see page 131). And if you tend to space out in the kitchen, as we are both known to do, set a timer for short intervals to call you back to the stove.

NOTES FOR THE COOK

PORTION SIZES

How, you ask, does a pound and a half of potatoes serve 4 to 6 people? Well, listen. A lot of these recipes are rich with butter and cream and cheese. We find them pretty filling. And we also find it a lot more satisfying to take a smaller portion than to load up on a reduced-fat alternative.

HEATING YOUR OVEN

We turn the oven on a good 20 minutes before we need it to make sure it's fully heated.

GREASING PANS AND BOWLS

If a recipe calls for a greased pan, chances are we've used olive oil, but it doesn't make much difference. Use a neutral-flavored oil for the bowl when you're making bread, though. A buttered pan is just that: buttered. If there's no mention of greasing the pan, you don't need to grease it.

SALT

We both keep a bowl of coarse salt on the stove, and we're both salt junkies, with boxes of kosher salt and different sea salts stashed in the pantry. About the only kind of salt we don't keep is the stuff known as table salt, because we find it overprocessed and pretty awful-tasting.

Kosher salt is our choice for everyday cooking. It's easiest to pinch and it sprinkles easily—we salt by feel and taste, for the most part, measuring only when we're baking, so using a salt that doesn't stick to our fingers is important to us.

Sea salts are great to use when you want to accent a special salty flavor right before serving. The coarse stuff has bigger crystals than kosher, so you get a bit of crunch. If you find them too big for sprinkling over your fries, get a salt mill from any decent kitchen-supply shop. Fine sea salt is wonderful for baking.

PEPPER

Neither Molly nor I owns a can of preground pepper, and we wouldn't have one even if it were given away with a box of tea. You've heard this before, but the flavor and aroma of pepper is a fleeting thing. The only thing to do is grind it yourself. We usually have two mills going: one for white pepper and another for black. Tellicherry peppercorns are our black pepper of choice.

CRACKING PEPPER Use a mortar and pestle if you have one. Or put the peppercorns on the counter and crack them with the bottom of a small, heavy saucepan. Hold the handle and the opposite rim and apply as much pressure as you can while you rock the pot back and forth over the peppercorns.

HERBS

Yes, we like fresh, but sometimes you want the flavor of a dried herb (dried tarragon in a vinaigrette, say), and we rarely use fresh oregano. We also like chopping herbs right before we add them to whatever dish we're making for the brightest flavor. Here are some of our favorites:

PARSLEY It's always flat-leaf, which is sometimes called Italian. We don't mind a few tender stems chopped in with the leaves.

MINT We like peppermint or black mint, but there's nothing wrong with spearmint. Leaves only; the stems are tough and bitter. The flowers are nice for garnish.

BASIL Leaves only. Avoid basil that has gone to seed; the leaves are never as sweet.

DILL We chop it with a chef's knife, not snip it with scissors, and we use the flowers when we can find them.

OREGANO We don't have much use for the fresh stuff. The thing about the dried is that different varieties vary wildly in taste. I like Mexican and Mediterranean.

BAY There's nothing to compare with the flavor of fresh bay leaves, and there are few things more difficult to find. For dried leaves, we prefer Turkish.

SPICES

Ground spices don't keep forever, so refresh your supplies periodically.

Some whole spices—cumin, mustard, fennel, and coriander seeds, are good examples—pay you back with beautiful perfume when you toast them. To do this, pour the spices into a small dry skillet and cook over medium heat until they are fragrant and beginning to darken. Shake the pan often during the 2 or 3 minutes that this takes, and then get them out of the skillet right away so they don't burn.

CARAWAY If you want caraway to give you its best flavor, crush it with the side of a chef's knife or the back of a spoon before you add it to whatever you're making.

NUTMEG There is no reason whatsoever to use the preground stuff.

BUTTER

Unsalted butter has a sweeter, fresher taste, so that's what we use. You'll be adding salt anyway, right?

SOFTENED When we call for "softened butter," it means *just* softened: we've taken the butter out about 20 minutes before we need it (less if the kitchen's hot). Softened butter should still feel cool to the touch, and if you squeeze it gently, you'll leave a slight impression.

ROOM TEMPERATURE We use this term to describe butter that's been sitting on the counter a lot longer. It may have started to slump; think about butter that you could spread easily on very soft bread without it tearing, and that's room-temperature butter. But butter that's starting to melt and get oily should go back into the refrigerator to firm up some.

CLARIFIED BUTTER

As much as we love its sweet flavor, there is one great disadvantage to cooking with a knob of butter. When you heat it to the high temperature you want for panfrying, the milky part of the butter speckles and burns. (This is because these milk solids are actually proteins, and they burn at a lower temperature than the pure butterfat.) In addition, most butter contains at least 20 percent water, which will sizzle and spatter when very hot.

You have two options if you want to sauté or fry food in butter without having it smoke and burn. The first is simply to use a mix of oil (which has a higher smoke point) and butter. You won't get as much buttery flavor, but you'll get some. The second solution is to make clarified butter—removing both the milk solids and the water, leaving only the pure, clear butterfat—which is simple enough to do.

CLARIFYING BUTTER Drop 1 or 2 sticks of butter into a small saucepan. The larger the amount of butter, the easier the task, and leftover clarified butter keeps for months (it lasts longer than whole butter). Heat the butter over medium heat. As the butter melts, a good deal of foam will rise to the surface. Continue cooking until this foam subsides and the milk solids coagulate and fall to the bottom of the pan, about 10 minutes. The butter should be very clear and you will be able to see the residue on the bottom of the pan. For light-tasting clarified butter, stop cooking at this point. If you continue to heat it, the residue will begin to brown. Once this happens, you have gone beyond clarified butter and made ghee, that staple of the Indian kitchen, which works just as well for sautéing with the added advantage that it has a mild toasty flavor.

For the clearest clarified butter, strain it through a very fine sieve, a few thicknesses of cheesecloth, or even a coffee filter. We admit that sometimes we don't bother to strain the butter but simply decant it by pouring the clear butter off the residue. Store leftover clarified butter in a jar in the refrigerator. Two sticks of butter will give you about 3/4 cup of clarified.

OLIVE OIL

As you'll see from the recipes, we like the flavor of olive oil, and in fact, our everyday oil is extra-virgin. But not all extra-virgins are created equal. You can find reasonably priced extra-virgin olive oil that will be flavorful and aromatic and not so dear that you gulp when you pour out a quarter-cup. So try a bunch and find an inexpensive extra-virgin for cooking and a finer one to use to finish dishes. If a recipe calls for extra-virgin, pull out the good stuff. It's there as a flavoring.

Be careful, though, with olive oil in the food processor. The action of the metal blade has a tendency to turn the oil bitter.

VEGETABLE OIL

We like corn oil for cooking and for plain dressings. Peanut oil is what we use when we're deep-frying, because it has the highest smoke point, but we think its flavor is a bit too definite for a sauté. Canola's fine; soybean's not (we think it tastes fishy).

AROMATICS (ONIONS, CARROTS, AND GARLIC)

Unless we've told you different, 1 onion or carrot or garlic clove listed in the ingredients means 1 medium. Yes, we all have our own ideas of what medium means, but a slight variation in size won't really make a difference. In fact, that's what makes cooking fun.

Aromatics should be peeled before you chop them.

BACON

If you're lucky enough to have a source for local bacon, straight from the farmer, pay the extra money for it. If not, look for thick-cut bacon at a butcher's or a good supermarket. We developed and tested these recipes with meaty, thick-cut bacon.

EGGS

They're always large.

If you're poaching eggs to serve on hash and you want to use jumbos, fine. But if you substitute extra-large, one for one, for large in something like a cake recipe, you're going to have trouble, because it's just too much egg and you're changing the ratio of dry to wet ingredients.

It's easier to separate eggs when they're cold, but whites should be brought to room temperature for whipping if you want the highest volume.

MILK AND CREAM

Whole milk's what we keep in our refrigerators (we don't drink it; we just cook with it). You can use what you have on hand as long as you realize that low-fat milk will give you results less creamy than ours.

Heavy cream, light cream, half-and-half—we use them all, and they're pretty much interchangeable in these recipes, unless the cream is whipped (heavy only for that). Use what you have on hand, and if you can find cream that has not been ultrapasteurized, please, please buy it.

TOMATOES

In some of our recipes, the tomatoes are canned; the rest of the time, they're ripe summer tomatoes. We don't use those hard pink impostors from the grocery store.

PEELING AND SEEDING TOMATOES Easy enough to do for those times when you don't want skin or slippery seeds in your food. Bring a deep saucepan of water to a boil, and fill a bowl with ice water. Cut out the core of the tomato and score an X in the other end of the tomato (that way, the water can infiltrate the tomato from both sides). Lower the tomato into the water (when you're doing more than one, keep them in a single layer) and watch for the skin to start to peel back from either end. This should happen quickly, 60 to 90 seconds (faster if the tomato is truly ripe). Lift it out with a slotted spoon, drop into the ice bath to cool, then slip off the skin. If the skin's tenacious, give it a second dip in boiling water, but be careful not to cook the flesh.

If you're peeling just one or two tomatoes, you can spear them on a fork and hold them over a gas flame until the skin blisters all over.

To seed, cut the tomato across the equator and squeeze gently. You'll need to pry a bit with your finger to encourage the seeds out of their home. Then give an extra squeeze to rid the tomato of excess juice.

WHITE WINE AND VERMOUTH

Many of our recipes call for just a few tablespoons of dry white wine, and some days we do have an open bottle knocking around. But we certainly don't open a new bottle so we can add a few sips to a dish. That's when we turn to dry vermouth. We like its herby perfume, and vermouth's slightly higher alcohol content means you can keep it around for a while in the refrigerator.

APPETIZERS &

FIRST COURSES

POTATOES ROASTED IN SALT

No proportions here, just a method. The potatoes come out of the salt all wrinkly and amazingly tender. Once the salt has cooled down, you can pack it into a jar and reuse it for roasting several times. Just add more salt when you need it.

There is no more elegant way of serving these potatoes than slicing them in half and topping with a dollop of sour cream and as much caviar as you dare. If this isn't going to be a beluga evening, go for salmon roe. Or try any of the dips and sauces (pages 36–40) that follow this recipe. You can even, should you care to, use any of the composed butters in the chapter on boiled potatoes (pages 483–485).

Coarse salt
Small red-skinned or heirloom potatoes, scrubbed

Heat the oven to 400 degrees.

Spread a layer of salt in a deep baking dish or casserole large enough to hold the potatoes in a single layer. Put the potatoes in the dish and cover completely with more salt.

Roast the potatoes for 50 to 60 minutes, or until tender. Poke them with a skewer or the tip of a small knife to check. Dump the potatoes out onto a tray and knock off the salt.

Slice the potatoes in half and move them to a serving dish (placing them on a bed of salt is pretty). Top them in the kitchen if you want, or pass with a dipping sauce.

PAULA WOLFERT'S POTATOES BAKED
IN SEA SALT

An enameled cast-iron cocotte (Dutch oven) with a tight-fitting lid is essential for this dish. Paula's salt of choice is sea salt from the Ile de Ré in France, but a combination of any coarse sea salt and kosher salt will be fine.

Wash and dry 1½ pounds small red-skinned potatoes. Spread 1½ cups sea salt in the bottom of the cocotte and sit the potatoes on top in a single layer. Cover and bake in a 450-degree oven for 45 minutes to 1 hour. Take off the cover and let the potatoes sit for 5 minutes. Brush off the salt and serve. This is enough to serve 6 to 8 for cocktails.

FETA SPREAD

My friend Julie Chadwick asked for something simple that she could spread on salt-roasted potatoes. It's easy for her to find feta in her grocery store in Mississippi. Try varying the herbs, using oregano or marjoram or another strong herb; just keep the total amount at a tablespoon.

8 ounces feta
1 garlic clove, chopped
1 teaspoon chopped fresh rosemary
2 teaspoons chopped fresh thyme
1/4 cup olive oil

Put all the ingredients in the bowl of a food processor. Hit the pulse button a few times, until the mixture is smooth. Scrape into a bowl. Spread on hot salt-roasted potatoes.

BLUE CHEESE DIP

MAKES ABOUT 1 CUP

Put this out with Saratoga Chips (page 314) or Sweet Potato Chips (page 317) or spread it on roasted potatoes. You could also turn leftovers into a quick salad dressing by whisking in some oil and red wine vinegar.

1 garlic clove, peeled
Coarse salt
4 ounces blue cheese
1/3 cup sour cream
1/3 cup mayonnaise
2 tablespoons dry vermouth
1 teaspoon Worcestershire sauce
2–3 shots of Tabasco sauce, or to taste
Milk (optional)

Smash the garlic with the side of your knife, add a pinch of salt, and keep on chopping and mashing to make a smooth puree. Scrape it off the board and into a small mixing bowl. Crumble in the cheese; add the sour cream, mayonnaise, vermouth, Worcestershire, and Tabasco. Stir well and taste for Tabasco and salt. If the dip is thicker than you like, thin it down with a little milk.

This will keep for 4 to 5 days in the refrigerator, but let it sit on the counter for about 30 minutes before serving.

SALMON SPREAD

Here's another topping for salt-roasted potatoes and a variation to turn it into a dip for chips. It couldn't be easier. And you can use either the spread or the dip on a baked potato.

    If your store sells trimmings from smoked salmon, buy them for this recipe. There's no point in spending extra money for beautiful slices of salmon when they are going to end up in the food processor.

3 ounces smoked salmon (sliced or trimmings)
8 ounces cream cheese, at room temperature
Grated zest and juice of 1 lemon
Coarse salt and freshly ground black pepper

    Put the salmon in the bowl of a food processor and hit the pulse button a few times to chop it. Add the remaining ingredients and pulse until the spread is smooth.

    Scrape it into a bowl and serve with hot salt-roasted potatoes.

VARIATION
SALMON DIP

To turn this into a dip, add $1/2$ cup sour cream along with the other ingredients after you've chopped the salmon. This makes about $1^1/2$ cups.

CILANTRO DIPPING SAUCE

This, like the parsley sauce that follows, is yet another accompaniment for salt-roasted potatoes. "Double-dipping" encouraged.

1 large garlic clove, sliced
1/2 green bell pepper, chopped
1 1/2 cups cilantro leaves
2/3 cup extra-virgin olive oil
3 tablespoons white wine vinegar
Coarse salt

Hit the "on" button of your food processor and drop in the garlic slices (it's a quick way of chopping garlic; it doesn't work if the garlic is in the bowl when you turn the machine on). The garlic will fly to the sides of the bowl. Scrape the sides and add the bell pepper and cilantro. Hit the pulse button a few times to chop coarsely. Then hit the "on" button again and quickly pour in the oil. Turn off the machine as soon as you've added the oil; if you process it too much, it will turn bitter. Transfer the sauce to a bowl, stir in the vinegar, and taste for salt.

You should serve this the day you make it; the flavors will flatten if kept overnight.

PARSLEY DIPPING SAUCE

Not everyone's a fan of cilantro, so here's an alternative to the sauce on page 39. You can make this as *picante* as you like by adjusting the amount of chile. But please leave in the seeds.

You'll notice that both this dipping sauce and the one before it call for extra-virgin olive oil. It's worth it here, but be aware that if you overprocess the oil, the sauce will turn bitter.

1 teaspoon cumin seeds
2 large garlic cloves, sliced
1½ cups flat-leaf parsley (leaves only)
1–2 serrano chiles, minced
½ cup extra-virgin olive oil
1 tablespoon sherry vinegar
Coarse salt and freshly ground black pepper

Crush the cumin seeds with the flat of a large knife and put them in the food processor. Hit the "on" button and drop in the garlic. Once the garlic is chopped, scrape it from the sides of the bowl and add the parsley and chiles. Hit the pulse button a few times to start chopping, then turn the machine on and quickly pour in the oil. Turn the machine off as soon as you've added the oil. Scrape the sauce into a bowl, and stir in the vinegar and salt and pepper (this does need salt to wake it up, so don't be shy).

This should be served the day it's made. Don't refrigerate it—it will taste dull.

OVEN-FRIED POTATO CHIPS

You can make as few or as many of these as you like, so I'm just giving you the method. These are beautiful chips, long and straight and flat. A mandoline is mandatory here—see page 443.

These work best if you make one baking sheet of them at a time. Choose small potatoes and peel and cut only as much as will fit on the sheet. The chips don't come out right if you cut them in advance or cover the potatoes in cold water.

Olive oil
Russet potatoes
Fine sea salt

Heat the oven to 275 degrees.

Cut a piece of parchment to fit a baking sheet, line the pan with it, and brush it completely but very lightly with oil.

Peel a potato, trim it top and bottom to make a nice shape and, using a mandoline, slice it lengthwise as thin as possible. Lay the slices side by side on the baking sheet and sprinkle lightly with salt. Brush another sheet of parchment lightly with oil and place it oiled side down on the potatoes. Bake for 30 minutes, or until golden.

VARIATION
OVEN-FRIED POTATO CHIPS WITH LEMON OIL

You can flavor the chips lightly with lemon. Put $1/4$ cup olive oil in a small pan with the grated zest of 1 lemon. Turn the heat to low; when the oil bubbles, turn it off. Let the oil infuse for 30 minutes before you use it to brush the parchment.

ROASTED POTATO SKINS

Remember these? Overloaded bar food from the '70s and '80s? While the restaurant version is often deep-fried and then piled high with bacon, melted cheese, and sour cream, we like ours so you can still taste the crunchy roasted potato skin underneath a few select ingredients. Here are a few of our favorite variations, but you can certainly invent your own. Use the insides of the potatoes to make croquettes or one of the potato cakes or tortas (see the index), or to thicken a soup or stew.

4 russet potatoes (each about 3/4 pound), scrubbed
Toppings (pages 43–44)

Heat the oven to 350 degrees.

Place the potatoes on the center oven rack and bake until tender enough that you can easily make an indentation by squeezing, 60 to 70 minutes. About halfway through baking, prick the skins in a few spots with a fork to allow steam to escape.

Let the potatoes cool on a rack for at least an hour. (The skins tend to tear if you try to prepare them when the potatoes are still warm.)

Heat the oven to 450 degrees.

Slice each potato lengthwise in half and scoop out most of the flesh, leaving a 1/4-to-1/3-inch layer of flesh on the skin—just enough to keep the skins from being too flimsy. Using a very sharp knife or scissors, cut the skins lengthwise into 1-inch-wide strips. Ordinarily, you will get 3 strips from each potato half.

Arrange the strips close together, skin side down, on a baking sheet. Brush them with olive oil or melted butter, according to the topping recipe. Scatter the topping onto the skins (avoid overloading—this makes the skins hard to eat and less crisp). Roast until browned and very crisp, 18 to 20 minutes.

Serve hot. You may want to dollop sour cream on the hot skins—especially the bacon and Jack ones.

TOPPINGS

PARMESAN POTATO SKINS

$1/4$ cup olive oil
Pinch of cayenne pepper (optional)
$1/3$ cup freshly grated Parmesan
Coarse salt and freshly ground black pepper

Line the skins up on a baking sheet so they are very close together but not over-lapping. Brush with the olive oil. Stir the cayenne into the cheese. Sprinkle the skins with the cheese and season with salt and pepper. Roast as directed on the facing page.

CURRIED POTATO SKINS

1 teaspoon curry powder
4 tablespoons ($1/2$ stick) unsalted butter
Coarse salt and freshly ground black pepper

Heat the curry powder in a small dry skillet over medium heat until fragrant, about 2 minutes. Give it a stir once or twice. Turn off the heat. Cut the butter into the pan and let it melt.

Line the skins up on a baking sheet so they are very close together but not overlapping. Brush the tops with the curry butter and season with salt and pepper. Roast as directed on the facing page.

BACON AND JACK CHEESE
POTATO SKINS

Don't overcrisp the bacon, or it will burn in the oven.

4 tablespoons (½ stick) unsalted butter, melted
Coarse salt and freshly ground black pepper
4 slices bacon, lightly cooked and chopped
½ cup shredded Monterey Jack (about 2 ounces)

Line the skins up on a baking sheet so they are very close together but not over-lapping. Brush the tops with the butter and season with salt and pepper. Scatter with the bacon and cheese. Roast as directed on page 42.

SAUSAGE, FONTINA, AND
FENNEL SEED POTATO SKINS

¼ cup olive oil
Coarse salt and freshly ground black pepper
3 ounces Italian sausage, casings removed
½ cup shredded fontina (about 2 ounces)
1½ teaspoons fennel seeds

Line the skins up on a baking sheet so they are very close together but not over-lapping. Brush the tops with the olive oil and season with salt and pepper. Break the sausage into small bits. Fill the skins with the sausage and cheese. Sprinkle on the fennel seeds and roast as directed on page 42.

SHEPHERD POTATOES

What could be more fun than serving tiny bite-sized potatoes that you can pick up with your fingers or skewer with a pick with cocktails? This recipe from Mexican cooking authority Diana Kennedy is a winner. Rux Martin, my editor, has discovered what a standout this dish is: it's the star wherever she takes it.

You can use little red potatoes, but this is also an opportunity to showcase waxy heirloom potatoes. Look for the smallest you can find. If they're large, cut them down to size. And while you can adjust the number of serranos in the dish, never, never seed them.

2 tablespoons olive oil
1 pound very small waxy potatoes, scrubbed and dried
Coarse salt
1/3 cup chopped white onion
1 garlic clove, minced
3 serrano chiles, minced
1/2 cup coarsely chopped cilantro leaves
3 tablespoons fresh lime juice

Heat the oil over medium-high heat in a heavy skillet large enough to hold the potatoes in one layer. Add the potatoes and a good pinch of salt and fry them, shaking the pan occasionally, until the skins wrinkle and begin to brown.

Add the onion, garlic, and chiles and cook for 3 minutes. Add the cilantro and lime juice and cook, stirring, for another minute, or until very fragrant. Pour in 1 cup water and bring to a boil. Reduce to a simmer and cook, uncovered, for 20 to 25 minutes, until the liquid has just about been absorbed.

Scrape into a bowl and let cool to room temperature before serving.

ROASTED SWEET POTATO DIP WITH TAMARIND AND LIME

This is a very pretty dip, with a beautiful color and surprisingly exotic flavor with the tang of tamarind and the lime. Serve with toasted pita wedges, tortilla chips, red pepper slices—whatever your heart desires.

Both the tamarind and the sambal oelek are available by mail-order from Kalustyan's, 123 Lexington Avenue, New York, NY 10016; (212) 685-3451. You can also find them in many Asian markets. Be sure to use brick tamarind; the prepared paste is usually sour.

1 pound sweet potatoes
One 2-inch hunk of tamarind
1/2 cup plain yogurt
2 tablespoons fresh lime juice, or more to taste
1/2 teaspoon sambal oelek (hot chile paste)
Coarse salt

Heat the oven to 450 degrees.

Place the sweet potatoes on a sheet of foil to catch any drips and roast them until very tender, about 45 minutes.

While the potatoes cook, cover the tamarind with boiling water and let it soften. Push as much of it as you can through a coarse wire sieve. Discard the tough bits remaining in the sieve.

When they are cool, peel the sweet potatoes and drop them into a mixing bowl. Use a fork to mash them into a coarse puree. Then, using a wooden spoon, beat the puree until somewhat smooth.

Stir in 1 heaping tablespoon of the tamarind pulp, the yogurt, lime juice, and chile paste. Taste for salt and seasoning, adding more lime juice if desired. The dip can be covered and kept in the refrigerator for 2 days. Check the seasoning again before serving, and serve at room temperature.

ARTICHOKE AND POTATO NIBBLE

MAKES ABOUT 5 DOZEN HORS D'OEUVRES

This is a handy dish to know about. You can make it ahead, even a day ahead, and serve it at room temperature. It's a category of recipe that classifies as vintage these days. We like it with classic American orange cheddar.

$1/2$ pound white potatoes, scrubbed
Coarse salt
2 tablespoons unsalted butter
1 small onion, finely chopped
Freshly ground black pepper
1 garlic clove, minced
4 large eggs
1 (14-ounce) can artichoke hearts, drained and coarsely chopped
8 ounces orange cheddar, shredded (about 2 cups)
2 tablespoons chopped flat-leaf parsley
$1/4$ teaspoon Tabasco sauce

Put the potatoes in a saucepan, cover with water by at least an inch, add a good pinch of salt, and bring to a boil. Reduce the heat to medium, cover partway, and cook until the potatoes are tender. Drain the potatoes on a rack set in the sink and let cool.

Heat the oven to 325 degrees. Butter an 8-inch square baking dish.

When the potatoes are cool, peel and cut them into $1/3$-inch dice.

Heat the butter in a medium skillet over medium heat. Add the onion, season with salt and pepper, and cook until translucent, about 7 minutes. Add the garlic and cook for another minute or so more, until you can smell it. Remove from the heat.

Crack the eggs into a large mixing bowl and beat them with a fork until well mixed. Stir in the sautéed onions. Add the diced potatoes, artichokes, cheese, parsley, and Tabasco sauce and stir to combine. Season with salt and pepper.

Scrape the mixture into the baking dish and bake until it has set like a quiche—puffed at the sides and a little jiggly in the center—about 25 minutes.

Allow to cool for at least 30 minutes before cutting into 1-inch squares. The nibble is easiest to cut if it is completely cool. It tastes just as good at room temperature as it does warm from the oven.

SALT COD AND GARLIC PUREE
(BRANDADE DE MORUE)

MAKES ABOUT 3 CUPS; SERVES 8 TO 10

Brandade is heady stuff—dense and creamy, with a hint of garlic and a mild taste of salt cod. When it originated in the French province of Languedoc, brandade was a simple puree of salt cod and olive oil. Later, as the recipe moved north and abroad, cooks began adding potatoes and a bit of milk or cream to mellow the taste—a smart move.

We serve brandade as an hors d'oeuvre, spread on triangular croûtes (see the facing page). It's also good as a first course, served warm on small plates and sprinkled with croutons, or you can make it into a whole supper by topping it with a poached egg.

1 pound salt cod
3/4 pound russet potato (1 large potato), peeled and cut into chunks
Coarse salt
1 garlic clove, minced
1/2 cup extra-virgin olive oil, heated
1/3–1/2 cup light cream or milk, heated
Freshly ground white pepper

Put the cod in a large plastic container with a tight-fitting lid. Fill the container with cold water and snap on the lid. Put it in the refrigerator and let soak for 2 days, changing the water at least twice a day. (The lid is to contain the fish smell.)

Drain the cod, put it into a large nonreactive pot (stainless steel is fine), and cover with fresh cold water. Bring just to a simmer over medium heat; immediately lower the heat and cook gently—that means lazy bubbles—until tender, 12 to 15 minutes. Boiling, or even overzealous simmering, will toughen the fish. Drain and let cool slightly.

Meanwhile, put the potato in a saucepan, cover with water by at least an inch, add a good pinch of salt, and bring to a boil. Reduce the heat to medium, cover partway, and cook the potato until very tender. Drain and put the potato through a ricer or mash with a hand masher; keep warm.

When the cod is just cool enough to handle, pick through it to remove any bones or bits of skin. Return it to the pot and flake it into very small pieces with a fork. The more thoroughly you flake the fish, the smoother the puree will be. For an especially smooth puree, you can chop the fish very quickly in the food processor, being careful to use only a few on-and-off pulses and diligent about not turning it to mush.

Use a sturdy wooden spoon to stir the mashed potatoes into the flaked fish. Add the garlic and stir to combine. Working vigorously, stir in the olive oil a bit at a time. After all the olive oil has been incorporated, begin adding the cream a few tablespoons at a time, beating with the wooden spoon as you go, until the puree resembles a sturdy, creamy version of mashed potatoes. You may not need all of the cream. Season with salt and pepper.

Serve warm or at room temperature.

FRIED TRIANGULAR CROÛTES

Choose a loaf of fine-crumbed white bread. Slice it into 1/4-inch-thick slices. Trim off the crusts and cut each slice in half on the diagonal to form 2 triangles. Heat 1/4 inch olive oil, clarified butter, or a mix of butter and vegetable oil in a large skillet over medium heat. Fry the bread, turning once, until golden and crisp, about 1 minute per side. Drain on paper towels. These are best served right away.

GREEK POTATO-GARLIC DIP
(SKORDALIA)

MAKES ABOUT 2 CUPS

Slather this thick, robust Greek potato-garlic puree on crostini (see the facing page) or crusty bread as a great start to a meal. It's a close kin to aïoli, so you can also put it out to accompany vegetables or seafood (grilled or poached or fried). Sometimes skordalia is made with almonds or bread. Is it a surprise that we prefer the potato version?

If you have a large enough mortar and pestle, now's the time to use it. Otherwise, employ the back of a wooden spoon to mash the warm boiled potatoes one at a time and then to incorporate the oil.

1 pound small white or all-purpose potatoes, scrubbed
Coarse salt
3–4 garlic cloves, peeled
1/2–3/4 cup extra-virgin olive oil
2–4 tablespoons fresh lemon juice
Warm water or chicken stock for thinning (optional)

Put the potatoes in a saucepan, cover with water by at least an inch, add a good pinch of salt, and bring to a boil. Reduce the heat to medium, cover partway, and cook until the potatoes are very tender. Drain the potatoes on a rack set in the sink and leave them there to cool somewhat.

Meanwhile, pound the garlic and 1 teaspoon salt into a smooth paste, either in a mortar with a pestle or on a cutting board with the side of a chef's knife. Transfer the paste to a bowl—wooden is best.

When the potatoes are cool enough to handle but still rather warm, peel them and add them one at a time to the garlic, crushing them completely with the pestle or spoon as you go. Continue until you have a smooth puree.

Dribble in the olive oil a bit at a time, working the puree until each bit is incorporated before adding more oil, until you have a creamy puree. The amount of oil that the potatoes will absorb depends on their texture, character, and age.

Season with lemon juice to taste. Taste for salt—you may not need any more. The sauce should be thick enough to hold up a spoon, but if you prefer a looser sauce, stir in a bit of warm water or stock.

Serve right away, or cover loosely and keep at room temperature for several hours. The dip can also be covered and refrigerated for a day or two; just be sure to let it return to room temperature before serving. If any oil puddles on the surface, stir it back in.

CROSTINI

Heat the oven to 350 degrees. Slice a baguette on the diagonal into ⅓-inch-thick slices.

Arrange the slices on a baking sheet and bake, turning once halfway through, until crusty and beginning to brown around the edges, about 15 minutes. You may want to finish them with a brush of extra-virgin olive oil or a rub on the crust with a cut clove of garlic—or both. Serve immediately.

ROASTED GARLIC SKORDALIA

Molly's friend Daphne Zepos, the cheese expert, told us about this. It sounded like a good idea at the time, and it remains so. Roasting the garlic makes the taste mellower. The cloves should get creamy, not caramelized. Serve with croûtes (see page 51).

$^1/_2$ head garlic, cloves broken apart but not peeled, plus 1 garlic clove, peeled
$^1/_2$–$^3/_4$ cup extra-virgin olive oil
Coarse salt and freshly ground black pepper
1 pound small white potatoes, scrubbed
1–2 tablespoons fresh lemon juice
Warm water or chicken stock for thinning (optional)

Heat the oven to 350 degrees.

Put the unpeeled garlic on a square of foil. Drizzle with 1 teaspoon of the oil, season with salt and pepper, and fold up the foil to form a neat little packet. Roast for about 30 minutes, until the garlic is very soft but not caramelized. Carefully open the foil and let the garlic cool.

Put the potatoes in a saucepan, cover with water by at least an inch, add a good pinch of salt, and bring to a boil. Reduce the heat to medium, cover partway, and cook until the potatoes are very tender. Drain the potatoes on a rack set in the sink and let cool a bit.

Meanwhile, pound the raw garlic with 1 teaspoon salt into a smooth paste, either in a mortar with a pestle or on a cutting board with the side of a chef's knife. Transfer the paste to a bowl—a wooden one is best.

Using scissors or a sharp knife, cut the tips off the roasted garlic cloves and squeeze the pulp into the bowl. Smash to combine with the raw garlic. Drizzle any excess oil from the foil packet into the bowl with the garlic.

When the potatoes are just cool enough to handle but still rather warm, peel them and add them one at a time to the garlic, crushing each one completely with the pestle or spoon as you go. Continue until you have a smooth puree.

Dribble in the remaining olive oil a bit at a time, working the puree until each bit is incorporated before adding more oil, until you have a creamy puree. The amount of oil that the potatoes will absorb depends on their texture, character, and age.

Season with lemon juice to taste. Taste for salt—you may not need any more. The sauce should be thick enough to hold up a spoon, but if you prefer a looser sauce, stir in a bit of warm water or stock.

Serve right away, or keep (covered loosely) at room temperature for several hours. The sauce can also be covered and refrigerated for a day or two, just be sure to let it return to room temperature before serving; any puddled oil should be stirred back in.

ASPARAGUS AND POTATO FRITTATA

A frittata is Italian, kin to the French omelet. When this cools to room temperature, you can cut it into smaller pieces to pass with drinks. Make a sandwich with leftovers (on Italian bread, and dress some lettuce with oil and vinegar to go on the sandwich).

3/4 pound russet or yellow-fleshed potatoes, peeled and cut into
   1/8-inch-thick slices
1/4 cup olive oil
Coarse salt and freshly ground black pepper
1 pound asparagus
1 tablespoon unsalted butter
6 large eggs
1/2 cup milk
1/4 cup freshly grated Pecorino

Heat the oven to 350 degrees. Oil a gratin dish or casserole large enough to hold the potatoes in two layers.

Put one layer of potatoes in the dish, drizzle with about 1/2 tablespoon of the oil, and season with salt and pepper. Repeat, layering the remaining potatoes, another 1/2 tablespoon oil, and salt and pepper. Bake for 30 to 35 minutes, turning the potatoes once about halfway through the cooking. The potatoes should be cooked through, and some of them will be browned, with nice crusty edges. Remove from the oven; leave the oven on.

Trim the asparagus and peel it if it's thick. Cut it into 1-inch lengths. Heat 1 tablespoon of the oil in a large ovenproof skillet over medium-high heat until it shimmers. Add the asparagus and some salt and pepper and cook, stirring frequently, for 2 to 3 minutes, until the asparagus starts to brown. Add the butter, reduce the heat to medium, and cook until the asparagus is tender, about 7 minutes.

Scrape the potatoes and whatever oil is left into the skillet with the aspara-gus—make sure to get any bits of potato stuck to the dish—and add the remaining 2 tablespoons or so oil. Let it all get hot.

Beat the eggs, milk, and cheese together with a fork—you want them com-bined, not light and frothy.

Increase the heat to medium-high and pour in the eggs. As the eggs begin to set, scrape them with a spatula toward the center of the pan, allowing the uncooked eggs to run down to the bottom of the pan. Continue to cook until the eggs have pretty much set, 4 to 5 minutes; the frittata will still look uncooked on top, but it will have a shape.

Slide the skillet into the upper third of the oven and bake for 20 minutes, or until very puffed and golden. Let it cool for a bit, and serve it right from the skillet.

POTATO PORCINI FRITTATA

MAKES ONE LARGE OMELET

This is rustic cooking and eating. Cut the frittata into squares or triangles to serve with drinks or slice into wedges for a first course. It's also great picnic food, because it's equally tasty at room temperature and hot. Just make sure to let it cool before you wrap it, lest it get soggy.

1/2 pound yellow-fleshed potatoes, peeled and cut into 1/3-inch dice
Coarse salt
1/4 cup olive oil
1/2 pound porcini or other wild mushrooms, sliced
Freshly ground black pepper
1 shallot, minced
6 large eggs
1/2 cup milk
1/4 cup freshly grated Pecorino
2 tablespoons chopped flat-leaf parsley

Put the potatoes in a saucepan, cover with cold water by at least an inch, add a good pinch of salt, and bring to a boil. Cook for 3 minutes, then drain.

Meanwhile, heat the oven to 350 degrees.

Heat a large ovenproof skillet over medium-high heat. Add 1 tablespoon of the oil, heat it until it shimmers, and add the mushrooms. Season with salt and pepper. Cook the mushrooms, stirring once in a while, until tender, about 5 minutes. If the mushrooms begin to stick, add a tablespoon of water, but be sure to cook it away. You want the mushrooms to be dry when they're done. Scrape the mushrooms into a bowl, wipe out the skillet, and return it to medium heat.

Add the remaining 3 tablespoons oil to the skillet and heat it until it slides across the pan. Add the shallot and cook for about a minute, so it softens. Add the potatoes and cook, turning with a spatula once or twice, until tender with bits of crisp crust, about 5 minutes. Stir in the mushrooms and cook to heat them through and blend the flavors.

Meanwhile, beat the eggs, milk, and cheese together with a fork—you want them combined, not light and frothy.

Increase the heat to medium-high and pour in the eggs. As the eggs begin to set, scrape them with a spatula toward the center of the pan, allowing the uncooked eggs to run down to the bottom of the pan. Continue to cook until the eggs have pretty much set, 4 to 5 minutes; the frittata will still look uncooked on top, but it will have a shape.

Slide the skillet into the upper third of the oven and bake for 20 minutes, until very puffed and golden. Let it cool for a while, then sprinkle with the parsley and serve it right from the skillet.

SPANISH POTATO OMELET
(TORTILLAS DE PATATA)

MAKES ONE 9-INCH OMELET

Not to be confused with Mexican tortillas, this is one of the truly great tapas of Spain and cousin to the Italian frittata. It's an omelet, and such a good one. You can cut it into squares or wedges, serve it warm or at room temperature or even cold, put it out with drinks, or have it for lunch. Leftover, it makes a great sandwich.

While I've given two variations of this recipe on the next page, that's not the end of the story. Play with other combinations of flavors.

Yes, you can make this in a well-seasoned heavy skillet with sloping sides, but your life will be a lot easier if you use nonstick.

5 large eggs
Coarse salt
Potatoes for Tortillas de Patata (page 62), prepared either by stovetop
    or by oven method and still hot
3 tablespoons olive oil (reserved oil, if you used the stovetop technique
    for the potatoes)

Crack the eggs into a large bowl, add a pinch of salt, and beat them lightly with a fork. Add the hot cooked potatoes, pushing down to make sure they're completely covered by the eggs, and let sit for 15 to 20 minutes.

Spoon 2 tablespoons of the oil into a 9-inch nonstick skillet and turn the heat to medium-high. When the oil begins to smoke, add the eggs and potatoes. Press down with the back of a flexible spatula so no bits of potato stick out, and cook, shaking the pan frequently, until the bottom browns, about 5 minutes. Push the edges of the tortilla in with the back of your spatula, then slide the tortilla out onto a plate.

Spoon the remaining 1 tablespoon oil into the skillet and heat until it starts to smoke. Cover the tortilla with another plate, flip it over, and slide it back into the skillet. Press down with the spatula again and tidy up the edges, pushing in with the back of the spatula. Keep shaking the pan, and cook until the second side is browned, about 4 minutes this time. Again slide it out onto a dish, invert it, and slip it back into the pan—you don't need more oil. Press down and neaten the edges. Cook for a minute, then flip it one last time.

Slide the tortilla out onto a clean plate and let it cool for at least 10 minutes before you cut it.

VARIATIONS

SPANISH POTATO OMELET WITH HAM AND MINT

Add 3 ounces finely chopped prosciutto or Black Forest ham, 1 garlic clove, minced, and 2½ teaspoons chopped fresh mint to the eggs when you beat them.

SPANISH POTATO OMELET WITH PARSLEY AND GARLIC

Add 2 garlic cloves, minced, and 3 tablespoons chopped flat-leaf parsley to the eggs when you beat them.

POTATOES FOR TORTILLAS DE PATATA

According to Spanish cooking authority Penelope Casas, the classic technique for preparing potatoes to be used in a tortilla is the stovetop simmering-in-oil method. It does make a tasty, almost unctuous potato, but boy, does it use a lot of oil. So I'm also offering an oven method, one that I think results in an equally tasty potato. I've adapted both techniques from Casas.

3/4 cup olive oil if using stovetop method, about 3 tablespoons if using oven method
1–1 1/4 pounds russet potatoes, peeled and sliced 1/8 inch thick
Coarse salt
1 small onion, very thinly sliced

STOVETOP METHOD: Pour the oil into a 9-inch skillet and heat it over medium heat until it shimmers. Carefully slip in a layer of potatoes, sprinkle with salt, and scatter with some of the onion. Repeat the layering until you've added all the potatoes and onion, then reduce the heat to medium-low. Cook gently, flipping the potatoes with a spatula from time to time, until very tender and just starting to break apart. This will take 20 to 35 minutes, depending on the age of the potatoes and just how you interpret "medium-low."

Drain the potatoes in a colander set over a bowl. Reserve the oil to use making the tortilla. Pat the potatoes dry with paper towels and proceed immediately with the tortilla recipe (see page 60).

OVEN METHOD: Heat the oven to 350 degrees. Use some of the oil to grease a 1 1/2-quart gratin dish. Put in a layer of potatoes, sprinkle with salt, and scatter with some of the onion. Drizzle with oil. Repeat the layering until you've used all the potatoes and onions. Bake for 30 minutes, turn the potatoes with a spatula, and bake for another 15 minutes, or until the potatoes are tender (some will have started to brown at the edges). Proceed immediately with the tortilla recipe (see page 60), or one of the variations.

BAKED CLAMS

Too often, baked clams are blobs of gummy bread crumbs baked in a shell, concealing any morsel of clam. Not here. These are clammy and light and briny, with potatoes to soak up the clam juice. Not a bread crumb in sight.

I like these big—hence chowder clams. If you can't find them, though, you can substitute 2 dozen littlenecks. Use your knife skills and make the tiniest dice you can of the potatoes and chorizo.

12 chowder clams, well scrubbed
$1/3$ pound yellow-fleshed potatoes, cut into tiny dice
Coarse salt
2 ounces chorizo or prosciutto, cut into tiny dice
1–2 tablespoons olive oil
2 whole scallions, minced
2 tablespoons chopped flat-leaf parsley
Grated zest of 1 lemon
Pinch of cayenne pepper (optional)

Heat the oven to 350 degrees.

Shuck the clams into a strainer set over a bowl so you can capture the clam juice. Clean the shells and coarsely chop the clams. Set aside.

Put the potatoes in a small saucepan and cover with water by an inch. Add a pinch of salt, bring to a boil, and cook until tender. Drain well, turn into a bowl, and roughly mash about half the potatoes with a fork.

Heat a small skillet over medium heat. Add the chorizo and 1 teaspoon of the oil and cook until browned, 4 to 5 minutes.

Add the clams and chorizo to the potatoes and stir in the scallions, parsley, zest, and cayenne, if using. Stir in $1/4$ cup of the clam juice. Fill the clamshells, place on a baking sheet, and drizzle with the remaining olive oil.

Bake until heated through and beginning to brown, about 8 minutes. Serve hot.

CRAB PUFFS

I'm not going to kid you: these are fussy, something you make when you want to show off or because you love the process of cooking.

Dauphine potatoes are cream puff paste (*pâte à choux*) combined with potato. They have a lot of uses. But mixed with crab—what, please, could be wrong with that? You pass these with drinks before dinner, or make everyone sit at the table, and serve them proudly as a first course.

Make sure to read the note at the end of the recipe before frying the puffs.

FOR THE DAUPHINE POTATOES
1 medium russet potato (about 3/4 pound), scrubbed
1/2 cup all-purpose flour
4 tablespoons (1/2 stick) cold unsalted butter
Coarse salt and freshly ground white pepper
Freshly grated nutmeg
2–3 large eggs

FOR THE CRAB
6 ounces (about 1 cup) fresh crabmeat, picked over
1/4 cup finely diced red bell pepper
2 teaspoons Worcestershire sauce
1 teaspoon Old Bay or crab boil seasoning

Vegetable oil for frying
All-purpose flour for dredging
2 large eggs, beaten with 2 teaspoons water
1 cup fresh bread crumbs
Lemon-Caper Mayonnaise (page 66)

Heat the oven to 400 degrees.

FOR THE POTATOES: Bake the potato until tender when pressed with your fingertips, about 1 hour. Keep the potato warm as you prepare the pastry.

Have the flour in a cup and a wooden spoon ready.

Cut the butter into bits and put it in a small saucepan with 1/2 cup water. Season with salt (at least 1/2 teaspoon), pepper, and some nutmeg. Bring to a boil over medium-high heat. When the butter is melted and the water is bubbling wildly, dump in the flour all at once and stir vigorously with your wooden spoon. It will be a sloppy mess, so be careful, but it will quickly form a ball. Keep beating and the ball will tighten, then become glossy, and you will see a film on the bottom of the pot—now you're there. At most, this will take 2 minutes. Take it off the heat right away.

Take a breath and leave this paste to cool for a few minutes. Then crack an egg into it. Stir it to amalgamate the egg into the paste (it's ugly at this stage, but the egg *will* go into the paste), then beat the dickens out of it. Repeat with another egg. Depending on how well you dried the paste on the stove, you may need only 2 eggs. Check the consistency by lifting a spoonful of dough from the pan. The dough should slowly fall from the spoon back into the pot. If it sticks to the spoon, beat the third egg to mix the white and yolk, then stir it in a bit at a time until the dough is soft enough to fall from the spoon.

Cut the baked potato in half and scoop the pulp into a ricer. Rice the potato directly into the paste, and stir it in. Taste for salt and pepper.

FOR THE CRAB: Toss the crab and bell pepper together in a big bowl. Season with the Worcestershire and the Old Bay or crab boil seasoning. Stir in the dauphine potatoes. Check it for salt and pepper and refrigerate for an hour or two—this makes the dough a bit easier to handle.

Heat 2 to 3 inches of oil in a deep fryer or large heavy saucepan to 360 degrees.

Set out three shallow bowls for breading the crab puffs: one bowl of flour, a second with the 2 beaten eggs, and a third filled with the bread crumbs. Drop the crab mixture by the tablespoonful into the flour. Using your hands, shape it into small cakes or balls. (We tend to prefer flatter cakes, but balls are pretty stacked on a cocktail tray.) One by one, transfer the crab puffs, patting off any excess flour, to the egg. Coat on all sides, lift out and let any excess egg drip off, then roll in the bread crumbs to coat.

You want to fry the crab puffs in batches so as not to crowd the pan and lower the temperature of the oil too much. Fry them until deeply golden and cooked through, about 5 minutes. Remove with a slotted spoon and drain on a wire rack set over a baking sheet. It's a good idea to cut into one puff from the first batch to be sure that it is indeed cooked through before continuing.

Serve right away, or keep warm in a low oven for up to 20 minutes. You can also fry the crab puffs a few hours in advance and reheat them in a 350-degree oven for 10 to 15 minutes.

Serve with the Lemon-Caper Mayonnaise.

NOTE: One of the secrets of good fried food, learned from the Southern cooking authority John Martin Taylor, is that the food must be dry and the breading or coating should only be applied just before frying. If the crab puffs sit for too long after being breaded, they will leak moisture into the coating, which will cause them to split open during frying. If you need to get ahead and hold foods in the refrigerator after they've been coated, be certain to give them a second coating of bread crumbs before you fry.

LEMON-CAPER MAYONNAISE

MAKES ABOUT 1¾ CUPS

This relative of tartar sauce is here so you can dip the crab puffs into it, but it's delicious on fried or broiled fish too.

1½ cups mayonnaise
6 tablespoons capers, rinsed and chopped
1 tablespoon grated lemon zest
3 tablespoons fresh lemon juice
1 tablespoon Dijon mustard
Coarse salt and freshly ground black or white pepper

Stir together all the ingredients. Taste for seasoning, and refrigerate until you need it.

RUSTIC POTATO AND GOAT CHEESE TART

This can be a first course or be served in tiny wedges with drinks before dinner. Or it can be a lunch, with a big salad of ripe tomatoes drizzled with oil.

1 cup all-purpose flour
Coarse salt
8 tablespoons (1 stick) cold unsalted butter, cut into bits
1 small red onion, sliced into very thin rounds
1/2 pound red-skinned potatoes, scrubbed and very thinly sliced
1 teaspoon chopped fresh rosemary
Freshly ground black pepper
3–4 ounces fresh goat cheese
1 tablespoon olive oil

Put the flour in a bowl and add a good pinch of salt. Stir with a fork. Add the butter and toss it in the flour, then cut it into the flour with a pastry cutter or your fingers. You want something that looks like very coarse oatmeal, with some larger bits of butter. Add 1 tablespoon of ice water, toss the pastry with a fork, and continue adding water (a little at a time) and tossing and stirring with the fork until the pastry comes together. You may need as much as 4 tablespoons water. Gather the pastry into a ball, then form it into a disk on a lightly floured countertop. Wrap it in plastic and refrigerate for 30 minutes.

Heat the oven to 350 degrees and line a baking sheet with parchment.

Flour the countertop lightly and roll the pastry out into a 12-to-13-inch circle. Transfer the pastry to the baking sheet. Fold in about 1/2 inch of the pastry and make a decorative edge. Scatter about half the onion over the pastry. Arrange the potatoes in slightly overlapping concentric circles—take your time to make it look nice. Scatter with the rest of the onion, separated into rings, and the rosemary. Sprinkle with pepper. Crumble the cheese over the top and drizzle with the oil.

Bake for 40 to 45 minutes. The crust should be well browned and the cheese golden brown. Serve hot or at room temperature.

PIEROGI

These Polish dumplings are a great first course—five or six of them nestled in each bowl and glistening with buttery cream. But you can also serve them as an hors d'oeuvre; see the variations.

Some cooks add a cup of farmer cheese or sautéed onion to the filling, but we like them made with plain butter-enriched mashed potatoes. If you happen to have leftover mashed potatoes, you'll need 1½ cups—just be sure that they are smooth and well seasoned.

FOR THE DOUGH
1 large egg
1½ tablespoons unsalted butter, melted and cooled
1 teaspoon coarse salt
2½ cups all-purpose flour

FOR THE FILLING
1 pound white potatoes, peeled
Coarse salt
3 tablespoons unsalted butter, softened

FOR THE SAUCE
5 tablespoons unsalted butter
1 pint sour cream
1½ tablespoons poppy seeds

1 tablespoon vegetable oil

FOR THE DOUGH: Combine ¾ cup warm water, the egg, butter, and salt in a standing mixer fitted with the paddle (or in a large bowl if you don't have a standing mixer). Add the flour and beat on low speed until combined. Increase the speed to medium-low and continue to work the dough until uniform and elastic, about 4 minutes. Turn the dough out onto a lightly floured board and knead it for a minute, or until smooth. (If mixing by hand, beat well with a wooden spoon until combined. Turn the dough out onto a lightly floured surface and knead by hand for about 7 minutes, until smooth.) Cover with plastic wrap and let rest for 1 hour.

FOR THE FILLING: Put the potatoes in a saucepan, cover with water by at least an inch, add a pinch of salt, and bring to a boil. Reduce the heat to medium, cover partway, and cook until the potatoes are very tender. Drain.

Return the potatoes to the pan, set over medium heat, and dry the potatoes for a minute or two, shaking the pan and stirring so they don't stick. Remove from the heat. Mash with a hand masher or wooden spoon. Using a fork, whip in the butter and salt to taste. Let cool to room temperature.

Cut the dough in half. Set 1 piece aside, covered, and roll the other out as thin as possible on a lightly floured surface. You should end up with a circle about 15 inches in diameter. Cut rounds from the dough with a 3-inch cookie cutter. Gather up the scraps into a ball, for rerolling later. Spoon a heaping teaspoon of mashed potatoes into the center of each circle and fold the dough over into a half-moon. Pinch the edges to seal or, for a more decorative finish, press the edges together using the tines of a fork. The dough should seal under the pressure of your fingers, but if it seems too dry, brush the edges with water before folding. Arrange the pierogi on a flour-dusted towel, and continue with the remainder of the dough and filling. The pierogi can be made ahead, covered, and refrigerated for up to 8 hours.

Just before serving, make the sauce: Melt the butter in a small saucepan over medium-low heat. Whisk in the sour cream and heat until smooth but not boiling. Stir in the poppy seeds, and keep warm while you cook the pierogi.

Bring a large pot of salted water to a boil. Add the oil. Cook the pierogi, in batches so as not to overcrowd the pot, until tender, 3 to 4 minutes. Remove each batch with a skimmer. Drain and put into a warm serving bowl while you finish cooking the rest. Toss the cooked pierogi with the sour cream sauce and serve in shallow bowls.

Brown butter also makes a good sauce for potato pierogi. Heat 8 tablespoons (1 stick) unsalted butter in a skillet over medium heat. Once the foam subsides, reduce the heat to medium-low and watch the butter carefully. It is done when the white bits in the melted butter turn golden brown and the butter smells nutty and toasty. Immediately remove from the heat, toss with the cooked pierogi, season with salt, and serve.

To serve pierogi as an hors d'oeuvre, boil the dumplings earlier in the day. At cocktail time, heat a few tablespoons of vegetable oil in a skillet over medium-high heat until it starts to shimmer. Add the pierogi and fry until lightly browned and crisp, flipping to cook both sides, about 6 minutes total. Drain briefly on paper towels and serve warm, with a bowl of sour cream for dipping.

SAMOSAS FILLED WITH POTATOES AND PEAS
(ALOO SAMOSAS)

MAKES 16 SAMOSAS

Samosas, little packets filled with nicely spiced diced potatoes, then fried to a crisp, are best eaten right away, but they can be reheated in the oven by dropping them back in the deep fryer. We've adapted this from a recipe by the Indian cooking expert Julie Sahni.

FOR THE FILLING

1 pound yellow-fleshed potatoes, scrubbed

Coarse salt

2 tablespoons vegetable oil

1 teaspoon coriander seeds

$1/2$ teaspoon mustard seeds

1 teaspoon grated fresh ginger

1 small red onion, minced

$1/2$ cup frozen green peas, thawed

1 teaspoon garam masala (available in Indian markets)

$1/4$ teaspoon cayenne pepper, or to taste

1 tablespoon fresh lemon juice

FOR THE DOUGH

$1^1/4$ cups all-purpose flour, plus more for sealing and rolling out

$1/8$ teaspoon baking soda

$1/2$ teaspoon coarse salt

$1/4$ cup vegetable shortening or lard

2 tablespoons plain yogurt

Peanut oil for frying

Cilantro-Mint Chutney (page 75) or other favorite chutney

START THE FILLING: Put the potatoes in a saucepan. Cover with water by at least an inch, add a good pinch of salt, and bring to a boil. Reduce the heat to medium, cover partway, and cook until the potatoes are tender. Drain the potatoes on a rack set in the sink and let them cool.

MEANWHILE, FOR THE DOUGH: Combine the flour, baking soda, and salt in a bowl. Drop the shortening or lard into the bowl and, using your fingertips, rub it into the flour bit by bit until the dough resembles coarse cornmeal, with no large lumps of shortening.

Thin the yogurt with $1/4$ cup water, and add this a little at a time to the dough, mixing with your fingertips until the dough comes together. You may not need all of the yogurt-water mixture.

Form the dough into a ball and knead it with the palm of your hand until it is soft, smooth and no longer sticky, about 5 minutes. Shape into an 8-inch log, wrap in plastic, and let rest for at least 15 minutes. The dough can be refrigerated for up to 24 hours, but bring it back to room temperature before rolling out.

FINISH THE FILLING: Peel the potatoes and cut them into dice the size of the peas. Heat the oil and coriander and mustard seeds in a skillet over medium-high heat until the seeds are fragrant and beginning to pop, about 1 minute. Add the ginger and onion and cook until soft, another 2 to 3 minutes. Add the diced potatoes and cook, stirring often, until evenly seasoned and starting to brown.

Transfer the mixture to a bowl and stir in the peas, garam masala, cayenne, lemon juice, and about $1^1/4$ teaspoons salt to taste. Let the filling cool completely.

SHAPE THE SAMOSAS: Make a slurry for sealing the dough by stirring together 2 tablespoons flour and 3 tablespoons water in a small bowl. Set this aside while you roll out the dough.

Cut the dough into 8 equal pieces—each piece will make 2 samosas. One at a time, flatten each piece into a disk; keep the rest covered while you are working. Roll each flattened piece into a thin 6-inch round. Cut the round into 2 half-moons.

Lift 1 half-moon and wrap it into a cone shape, so that the very center of the straight side of the half-moon becomes the bottom tip of the cone and the rounded part becomes the top opening of the cone. Dip your finger into the slurry and run it along the seam where the edges of the cone come together. Overlap them by about $1/4$ inch and squeeze gently to seal.

Holding the cone open in one hand, spoon 2 heaping tablespoons of filling into it. Smear a bit more slurry along the top edges and pinch together to seal. Set the filled samosa on a dry plate or waxed paper while you shape the rest.

Heat the oven to 200 degrees.

Heat at least 3 inches of oil in a deep pan or deep fryer to 350 degrees. Drop the samosas into the oil in batches and cook, turning frequently, until golden brown on all sides, about 5 minutes. Drain each batch on a cooling rack set over a baking sheet, then keep warm in the oven while you fry the rest. Serve warm with the chutney.

CILANTRO-MINT CHUTNEY

Fresh and spicy relishes like this are known in India as chutneys. The walnuts give the chutney a bit of body—other nuts such as almonds or pine nuts will do. Leftovers are particularly tasty spooned over boiled potatoes, or even basmati rice.

1 cup lightly packed cilantro leaves and tender stems
1/2 cup lightly packed mint leaves
1/4 cup chopped walnuts
2 garlic cloves
2–3 jalapeño or serrano chiles, coarsely chopped
1/3 cup fresh lemon juice
1 tablespoon light brown sugar, dissolved in 2 tablespoons warm water
Coarse salt

Grind the cilantro, mint, nuts, garlic, and chiles in a food processor or blender until you achieve a rough paste. Add the lemon juice and dissolved sugar and process until smooth. Transfer to a small bowl and season with salt to taste. Serve immediately, or cover and refrigerate for up to 2 days.

LITTLE POTATO KNISHES

Big, doughy knishes turn up everywhere in New York City these days: on the street and in refrigerator cases in delis. These, which I've adapted from a recipe in Joan Nathan's *Jewish Cooking in America,* have a much more delicate pastry, one that bakes up crisp rather than soft.

We cut these into small slices before baking so they're just a mouthful or two.

The filling is especially delicious. You might even want to serve it as a mash with pot roast.

FOR THE FILLING
2 tablespoons vegetable oil or schmaltz (see page 428)
2 large onions, sliced
Coarse salt
1–1¼ pounds russet potatoes, peeled and cut into chunks
1 large egg
¼ cup chopped flat-leaf parsley
Freshly ground black pepper

FOR THE PASTRY
1 large egg
¼ cup vegetable oil, plus additional for brushing
2 tablespoons white vinegar
Coarse salt
2 cups all-purpose flour

FOR THE FILLING: Heat the oil or schmaltz in a skillet over medium-low heat until it slides across the pan. Add the onions and a pinch of salt and toss to coat the onions with the fat. Cover and cook, stirring a few times, for about 20 minutes, until the onions are completely limp. Take off the cover, increase the heat to medium-high, and cook, stirring often, until the onions brown, 15 to 20 minutes more.

Meanwhile, put the potatoes in a saucepan, cover with cold water by at least an inch, add a good pinch of salt, and bring to a boil. Cover partway, lower the heat to medium, and cook until the potatoes are tender. Drain and return the potatoes to the pan. Bring them back to the heat and dry them, shaking the pan and stirring, until they are floury. Mash them with a hand masher until they're smooth.

Beat the egg in a small bowl, then pour most of it into the potatoes; you want to reserve about 1 tablespoon for the glaze. Add the onions and parsley, season well with salt and pepper, and beat the mash with a wooden spoon until light and well mixed. Put the filling out of the way while you make the pastry.

FOR THE PASTRY: Crack the egg into a mixing bowl, add the oil, vinegar, a pinch of salt, and 1/2 cup cold water, and beat with a fork until frothy. Add 1 cup of the flour and mix with a fork until smooth. Add the rest of the flour gradually and work it in with your hands until you have a firm, smooth dough that is only very slightly sticky. Cover the pastry with a towel and leave it to rest for 30 minutes.

Heat the oven to 375 degrees and brush two cookie sheets with oil.

Cut the pastry in half and roll each piece into a 12-by-6-inch rectangle on a lightly floured surface. Rip four 18-inch lengths of waxed paper off the roll. Center each piece of pastry on a piece of waxed paper, cover with a second piece, and let sit for 15 minutes.

Now comes the fun part: uncover a piece of pastry and, working from the center, stretch it out to the size of the waxed paper (about 10 by 18 inches).

Position the pastry with a long side facing you and spread the lower third with half of the potato filling. Brush the exposed pastry with vegetable oil, then roll it up as you would a jelly roll. The waxed paper is an invaluable tool for this; lift it up and away from you, and the pastry will practically roll itself. Cut each roll into 16 pieces. Push in any filling that has squeezed out, pinch the cut edges closed, and neaten them up. Place on the baking sheets.

Combine the reserved 1 tablespoon egg with 1 tablespoon water and brush all the knishes with it.

Bake for 40 to 45 minutes, until nicely browned. Reverse the sheets about halfway through baking so they brown evenly. Let the knishes cool for about 20 minutes before you serve them; directly from the oven, the filling will be searingly hot.

SOUPS

POTATO PRINCIPLES
CHOOSING POTATOES FOR SOUP

To get the right result, choosing the proper potato for soup matters as much as technique.

For chowders and other chunky soups, the best potatoes are waxy low-starch varieties such as Superior, Kennebec, Red Bliss, and other white and red-skinned potatoes. The firm texture of these potatoes will hold up even after an hour-long simmer, so you will have tender whole cubes or chunks when the soup is done. At the same time, these lower-starch spuds do shed just enough starch to thicken the broth slightly.

For rustic soups that rely solely on the starch from potatoes to thicken them, the best potatoes are high-starch russets or medium-starch Yukon Golds. As they simmer, these mealy textured potatoes break down and absorb the stock or water to make a soup that's thick and almost creamy. Once fully cooked, starchy potatoes are soft enough to turn into a coarse puree by simply stirring or mashing with a hand masher.

For pureed soups, the choice of potato is more a matter of personal preference. Once fully cooked, most any variety will turn into a smooth puree when run through a food mill or blender. There are, however, a few things to keep in mind. Russets have a greater amount of starch and will therefore thicken a greater quantity of liquid. At the same time, because of the nature of their starch, which differs slightly from that in a waxy spud, russets are less likely to turn gluey or overly sticky when pureed.

Waxy potatoes do have a tendency to turn gummy and pastelike, especially when overworked in a high-speed blender. There are, however, occasions when we like the sweeter, less earthy flavor of a white potato. With them, it's best to use a food mill, because the gentle mechanical action is less apt to turn the potatoes to glue. If you do choose a blender, just be careful to work in small batches and not to overprocess the soup.

CLASSIC VICHYSSOISE

We like our vichyssoise with plenty of leeks and a mix of cream and whole milk. Any white or low-starch potato works best here, although Molly once made it with yellow-fleshed Yukons by mistake; the color was a bit less alabaster than normal, but the flavor and texture were perfect.

4 tablespoons (1/2 stick) unsalted butter
4 cups thinly sliced leeks (white part only of 4–5 leeks)
Coarse salt and freshly ground white pepper
1 1/2 pounds white or russet potatoes, peeled and thinly sliced
4 cups Chicken Stock (page 85)
1 1/2 cups heavy cream
1 cup milk
2 tablespoons chopped fresh chives

Melt the butter in a soup pot over medium heat. Add the leeks and season with salt and pepper. Stir to coat the leeks with butter, cover, and cook, stirring occasionally, until the leeks are tender and fragrant, 8 to 10 minutes. Do not let the leeks brown.

Add the potatoes, stir, and cook for a few minutes. Pour in the stock, cover partway, and bring to a boil. Reduce the heat to a simmer and cook until the potatoes are very tender, about 20 minutes. Let the soup sit for 5 minutes or so.

Puree the soup in a blender—you'll probably have to do this in two batches. Be sure to vent the blender so the lid doesn't pop off and splatter hot soup over you and your walls. Or, to be safe, put it through a food mill.

Rinse out the soup pot and strain the soup through a fine sieve back into the pot. Stir in 1 cup of the cream and the milk and bring to a simmer over medium heat. Season with salt and pepper and cook for a minute or two. Let the soup cool just a bit at room temperature, then cover and chill thoroughly. (If you leave the soup uncovered, it will form a thick skin.)

Take the soup out of the refrigerator about 15 minutes before you're going to serve it. You want it chilled but not icy-cold.

There are two ways to finish this soup: The more classic is to stir in the remaining ½ cup heavy cream just before serving, ladle the soup into bowls, and sprinkle with chives. But what we like is to whip the remaining cream just until it mounds softly, ladle the chilled soup into bowls, drop a spoonful of cream in the center of each, and sprinkle with the chives.

CLEANING LEEKS

Here's a fast way to prepare leeks for soup, to make sure they're free of sand: Trim off the roots and the tough green parts (we use the tender green parts except in vichyssoise, where a pale color is important). Halve the leeks lengthwise and cut into thin half-moons. Put the leeks in a big bowl and cover with cold water. Swirl them around a few times, then leave them for a few minutes. Lift the leeks out into a colander — don't pour: you'll just redistribute the dirt. If there's a lot of grit left in the bowl, rinse it out and repeat the process, but one quick bath is usually enough.

MODERN VICHYSSOISE

SERVES 4 TO 6

We skip the straining, use less stock and butter, and substitute yogurt for the cream to make a lighter version of the classic.

2 tablespoons unsalted butter
4 cups thinly sliced leeks (white part only of 4–5 leeks)
Coarse salt and freshly ground white pepper
1½ pounds white or russet potatoes, peeled and thinly sliced
2 cups Chicken Stock (page 85) or water
¾ cup milk, plus more if needed (low-fat is okay here)
¾ cup plain yogurt
2 tablespoons chopped fresh dill

Melt the butter in a soup pot over medium-low heat. Add the leeks and season with salt and pepper. Stir to coat the leeks with butter, cover, and cook, stirring occasionally, until the leeks are softened, about 10 minutes. Do not let the leeks brown.

Add the potatoes, stir, and cook for another few minutes. Pour in the stock plus 2 cups water. Cover partway and bring to a boil. Reduce the heat to a simmer and cook until the potatoes are very tender, about 20 minutes. Let the soup sit for about 5 minutes.

Ladle the soup into a blender and puree it until smooth; you'll want to do this in batches, and be sure to vent the blender so the lid doesn't pop off and splatter hot soup. Or just put the soup through a food mill.

Rinse out the soup pot and return the soup to it. Add the milk and bring to a simmer over medium heat. Season with salt and pepper and cook for a minute or two. Let the soup cool just a bit at room temperature, then cover and chill thoroughly.

Stir the yogurt and dill into the chilled soup. Taste for salt and pepper. If the soup is too thick, add a bit more milk. Ladle the soup into bowls and serve.

CHICKEN STOCK

Since chicken stock needs to simmer slowly for several hours, we often make a double or even triple batch and then freeze it in 2- or 4-cup containers, making it handy to defrost for a particular recipe. We don't salt stock; it's easier to control the level if we hold off adding salt until we're using it. I buy big bags of backs and necks and small bags of chicken feet, which make incredible stock. But if these are not available, just buy the cheapest cuts you can find—probably legs and thighs.

1½–2 pounds chicken parts (see note above)
2 onions (pull off the loose papery skin), quartered
1 large bay leaf
5–6 sprigs flat-leaf parsley

Rinse the chicken and put it into a stockpot. Turn the heat to medium and cook the chicken for about 5 minutes. Add the onions, cover, and cook until the chicken has started to steam and gotten very juicy. This should take about 10 minutes—stir once or twice so the chicken doesn't brown.

Toss in the bay leaf and pour in 2 quarts water. Slowly bring to a simmer, skimming occasionally to get rid of the goop that rises to the surface, and cook at a very gentle simmer for 2½ to 3 hours. Add the parsley after the first hour. Be careful not to let the stock boil or even simmer too vigorously as it cooks—this would result in a cloudy, greasy-tasting stock. Strain and cool.

The simplest way to get the fat off the surface is to chill the stock. The fat will solidify on the surface, making it a cinch to scrape off and discard. Decant the stock into smaller containers for freezing (for up to 6 weeks) or refrigerate and use within 2 to 3 days.

SUMMER VICHYSSOISE

There's a time in early summer when leeks have been sitting in storage for too long. But that doesn't mean you don't have a taste for a chilled oniony potato soup. This variation on the classic is meant for just those days.

Fat red scallions have been turning up at more farmers' markets these days, but you can also use spring onions. And sure, regular scallions will do in a pinch, but they won't have as much flavor as the other two choices.

4 tablespoons ($\frac{1}{2}$ stick) unsalted butter
4 cups chopped red scallions or spring onions, with some of the greens (about 4 bunches)
Coarse salt
1 pound white or yellow-fleshed potatoes, peeled and thinly sliced
5 cups Chicken Stock (page 85)
3 cups loosely packed fresh basil leaves
1 cup heavy cream
Freshly ground white pepper
1 cup thinly sliced radishes for garnish

Melt the butter in a soup pot over medium heat. Add the scallions or onions and a pinch of salt, stir, and cover. Sweat the scallions or onions until limp and tender, stirring once or twice, about 5 minutes. Add the potatoes and stock and bring to a boil, then reduce to a simmer and cook until the potatoes are tender, about 20 minutes. Remove from the heat and let the soup cool for a bit, say, 5 to 10 minutes.

Stir the basil leaves into the soup, then puree in batches in a blender or food processor. The soup will still be hot enough to erupt in the blender, so small batches are in order, and don't snap the lid on tightly, or it may explode.

Rinse out the soup pot and pour the soup back in. Stir in the cream and bring the soup to a simmer over medium-low heat. Cook for about a minute, then check for salt and add pepper. Let the soup cool for a bit, then cover it and chill it thoroughly.

Take the vichyssoise out of the fridge about 15 minutes ahead of serving. Ladle the soup into bowls and strew each serving with radishes.

CHILLED POTATO AND SORREL SOUP

This springtime soup was inspired by a mid-May walk through New York City's Union Square Greenmarket, where Molly and I found a chef leading a tour and describing sorrel to his eager acolytes as being "like lemon trapped in green." And, in fact, the sharp, lemony tang of sorrel is a fine foil for mellow potatoes. Sorrel turns an unfortunate drab color when it's cooked, but there's enough cream here to render it pastel.

3 tablespoons unsalted butter
1½ cups chopped spring onions (both green and white parts)
Coarse salt
1¼ pounds white potatoes, peeled and thinly sliced
Freshly ground white pepper
4 cups Chicken Stock (page 85)
½ pound sorrel, stems removed (6–8 cups loosely packed)
1½ cups heavy cream or half-and-half

Melt the butter in a soup pot over medium heat. Add the onions and a pinch of salt and cook, stirring occasionally, until soft but not at all browned, about 8 minutes. Add the potatoes, season with salt and pepper, stir, and cook for a minute or two. Pour in the stock and bring to a boil. Reduce the heat to medium-low, cover partway, and cook until the potatoes are falling apart, 20 to 25 minutes.

Set aside a small handful of sorrel leaves for garnish, and add the rest to the soup. Stir and cook for 2 to 3 minutes, until the sorrel wilts completely. Let the soup sit for about 5 minutes.

Ladle the soup into a blender (in batches) and puree until smooth, remembering to vent the blender to mitigate the volcano effect. Clean the pot, pour in the soup, and stir in the cream. Correct the seasoning and refrigerate the soup until well chilled, at least 2 hours.

Set the soup out on the counter for about 15 minutes to take the chill off before serving. Taste again for seasoning, since the cold will mute the flavors some.

Ladle the soup into bowls. Cut the reserved sorrel leaves into thin shreds and float a few on each serving.

TOM COLICCHIO'S POTATO-LEEK SOUP

This soup has so much going for it. Tom Colicchio—chef-owner of Gramercy Tavern and Craft restaurant in New York City—adds the liquid gradually, as you would with risotto. The result is that the potatoes keep their shape better, so the soup is more chunky than creamy. And with the short cooking time, the soup has a cleaner, more potatoey taste. Let it sit for a while and it will thicken, and then you have a superb side dish for short ribs or a thick steak.

1 tablespoon olive oil
1/4 pound sliced bacon, diced
4 cups thinly sliced leeks (white and pale green parts of 3–4 leeks)
Coarse salt and freshly ground black pepper
3 cups Chicken Stock (page 85)
2 pounds russet potatoes, peeled and cut into 1/3-inch dice
2 tablespoons unsalted butter
3 tablespoons chopped fresh chives

Put the oil and bacon in a wide saucepan or a soup pot over medium heat and cook until the bacon has started to brown but is not crisp. Check to see how much fat your bacon has rendered. You want just about 3 tablespoons, so spoon off any excess. Add the leeks, season with salt and pepper, and stir well. Cook until the leeks are limp, about 10 minutes.

While the leeks are cooking, bring the stock to a simmer in a separate pot.

Add the potatoes to the leeks and cook for 3 to 5 minutes, or until they just begin to soften and are good and hot. Reduce the heat to medium-low and pour in enough stock to cover the bottom of the pan, about 1/2 cup. Bring it to a simmer, stir, and then add another 1/2 cup of stock. Again bring the stock to a full simmer, then stir in another 1/2 cup of stock. Continue this process of stirring in stock and bringing it to a simmer until you have added all the stock.

Once all the stock is added, continue simmering the soup until the potatoes are tender. From the time you ladle in the first bit of stock, the soup should take about 15 minutes. Add the butter and stir slowly to incorporate it. Stir in the chives, taste for salt and pepper, and serve immediately.

(If you want to serve this as a side, cover it and let it sit until it thickens.)

POTATO-CELERY SOUP
(AARDAPPELSOEP)

This is a reworking of an old Michigan Dutch receipt: plain, simple, and nourishing. Substituting a half cup or so of cream for some of the milk adds a satisfying richness and is likely truer to the recipe's early days, when top cream would have been ladled off the top of a jug of milk.

There's a lot of celery here, and peeling it does make a difference. Just scrape along the outside of the stalks with a vegetable peeler to get rid of the strings.

2 pounds russet potatoes, peeled and cut into 1-inch chunks
1 large onion, chopped
2 cups peeled and diced celery (about 5 stalks)
Coarse salt and freshly ground black pepper
2$\frac{1}{2}$–3 cups milk or a mix of milk and cream
2 tablespoons cold unsalted butter

Put the potatoes, onion, and celery in a soup pot. Add 2 to 3 cups cold water, enough to just cover the vegetables, and season with salt and pepper. Bring to a boil over medium-high heat, cover partway, and reduce to a gentle boil. Cook until the potatoes are tender and beginning to fall apart, 20 to 25 minutes.

Remove from the heat and mash the potatoes in the pot with a hand masher. It's fine to leave the potatoes a bit coarse to give the soup a chunkier texture.

Return the soup to the heat and stir in enough milk to reach a good pourable consistency. Bring to a simmer over medium heat and taste for salt and pepper. Ladle the soup into large soup bowls, and float slivers of butter on top of each serving.

POTATO SOUP
WITH CUCUMBER

Use a medium-starchy potato for this. Yellow-fleshed potatoes like German Butterballs have incredible flavor, and their color makes the soup look more like buttermilk. Kennebecs, though, will also work. The finished soup doesn't keep or reheat very well at all, I'm sad to say. The cucumbers get too soft and slimy. But you can make the potato part well in advance.

2 pounds medium-starchy potatoes, such as German Butterball or Maine, peeled and cut into chunks
Coarse salt
1 cup milk
1 cup heavy cream
2 large cucumbers, peeled, seeded, and cut into $1/3$-inch dice
1 small sweet onion, such as Vidalia, peeled
2 tablespoons chopped fresh mint

Put the potatoes in a saucepan and add 4 cups water and a pinch of salt. Bring to a boil, reduce the heat to medium, and cook, uncovered, until the potatoes are very tender, about 30 minutes. Put the potatoes and cooking water through a food mill fitted with a medium disk.

Clean out the pot and return the puree to it. Add the milk and cream and bring to a simmer. Cook for a minute or two. You can prepare the recipe ahead to this point and keep it covered in the refrigerator overnight. Just bring it back to a simmer before proceeding.

Add the cucumbers and simmer for 3 to 5 minutes, until the cucumbers are heated through but still have texture. Grate the onion into the soup (use the large holes of a box grater and do it right over the pot so you get all the juice). Stir in the mint, taste for salt, and serve.

SUMMER SQUASH AND POTATO SOUP

This soup couldn't be quicker to throw together, and it's the kind of thing that makes converts of zucchiniphobes.

1 tablespoon unsalted butter
1 medium onion, chopped
3/4 pound Leida or other green summer squash, scrubbed and cut into 1/3-inch dice
1 1/2 pounds yellow-fleshed potatoes, peeled and cut into 1/3-inch dice
Coarse salt and freshly ground black pepper
1 bay leaf
1 cup heavy cream
1 or 2 whole scallions, minced

Melt the butter in a saucepan over medium heat. Add the onion and cook until it begins to brown, about 10 minutes. Add the squash and cook for 2 minutes, stirring once or twice. Add the potatoes, salt and pepper, bay leaf, and 4 cups water. Bring to a boil, reduce to a simmer, cover partway, and cook until the potatoes are very tender, 15 to 20 minutes.

Put the soup through the fine disk of a food mill. Rinse out the pan and return the soup to it. Add the cream, bring to a simmer, and cook for a minute or so to heat through. Taste for salt and pepper, and serve garnished with the scallions.

CARROT AND POTATO SOUP

This delicious variation on the great theme of cooking potatoes and a vegetable in water, pureeing, and then enriching with cream has great color and even better flavor. You can give it a further boost by roasting the carrots. Drizzle them with a little oil, sprinkle with salt, and put them in a 400-degree oven for 30 minutes while the potatoes are cooking. Then add them to the pot for the last 20 minutes.

1 teaspoon unsalted butter
3 slices bacon, chopped
1 shallot, minced
1 pound Superior or other white potatoes, peeled and cut into $1/2$-inch chunks
1 pound carrots, cut into $1/3$-inch slices
Coarse salt
1 cup heavy cream
2 tablespoons chopped fresh chives or flat-leaf parsley

Heat the butter in a wide saucepan over medium heat. Add the bacon and cook until it browns and crisps. Remove the bacon with a slotted spoon and drain it on paper towels.

Add the shallot to the fat in the pan and cook until softened and just starting to brown, about 2 minutes. Add the potatoes and carrots and a good pinch of salt. Stir and cook for a minute or two. Pour in 5 cups water and bring to a boil. Reduce the heat to medium, cover partway, and cook until the potatoes and carrots are falling apart, about 50 minutes.

Put the soup through a food mill fitted with the medium disk. Rinse out the pan and return the soup to it. Stir in the cream and bring to a simmer. Taste for salt. Ladle into bowls and serve, scattered with the bits of the browned bacon and the chives.

CREAM OF RED PEPPER AND POTATO SOUP

Luxurious, smooth, elegant. And what a beautiful color this soup has. For a downtown version, place a few ounces of fresh crabmeat or cooked lobster in the center of each bowl.

1 tablespoon olive oil
1 pound red bell peppers (2–3 peppers), cored, seeded, and chopped
    into 1-inch pieces
1 cup chopped leeks (white and pale green parts)
2 garlic cloves, minced
1/2 teaspoon sweet paprika
Pinch of cayenne pepper
Coarse salt and freshly ground black pepper
1 pound waxy potatoes, peeled and cut into 1/2-inch chunks
1 cup light cream

Heat the olive oil in a wide soup pot over medium heat until it slides across the pan. Add the bell peppers, leeks, garlic, paprika, cayenne, and salt and pepper. Reduce the heat to medium-low and cook gently, stirring from time to time, until the vegetables begin to give up some of their liquid but are not at all brown, about 5 minutes. Add the potatoes and continue to cook for another 5 minutes.

Add 4 cups water, cover partway, and bring to a boil. Reduce the heat to a simmer and cook until the vegetables are very tender, 20 to 30 minutes.

Let the soup cool for 5 minutes, then work it through a food mill to eliminate all the pepper skins. Stir in the cream and then strain the soup through a fine-mesh sieve. (Skipping this last step will give you a soup of equally fine flavor but with a much less luxurious texture.) Rinse out the pot and pour the soup into it. Return the soup to the heat and bring it to a simmer. Taste for seasoning. Transfer to a soup tureen (use your best-looking one—this soup deserves it) and serve warm.

POTATO-HORSERADISH SOUP

You find soups like this in the north of Italy. With long, slow cooking, the cream turns ivory, the horseradish mellows, and the potatoes cook down into a smooth, thick amalgam. You add more horseradish at the end to wake up the soup.

All-purpose potatoes are fine. Not surprisingly, yellow-fleshed ones will give you an even richer color. Do not—listen to me here— trim away any of the fat from the prosciutto.

$^{1}/_{2}$ pound fresh horseradish, peeled
1 teaspoon unsalted butter
2 ounces prosciutto, minced
1$^{1}/_{2}$ pounds all-purpose potatoes, peeled and cut into $^{1}/_{2}$-inch chunks
6 cups Chicken Stock (page 85)
2 cups heavy cream
Coarse salt
1 heaping teaspoon poppy seeds
1 tablespoon minced scallion

Grate the horseradish on the fine side of a box grater (or do it even more quickly with a rasp; see page 493). Reserve 3 or 4 tablespoons to add at the end of cooking; you should have about $^{1}/_{2}$ cup, loosely packed, remaining.

Melt the butter in a soup pot over medium heat. Add the prosciutto and cook, stirring gently, until it begins to render its fat, about 5 minutes. Add the potatoes, the $^{1}/_{2}$ cup horseradish, the stock, cream, and a good pinch of salt. Bring to a simmer and cook gently, stirring occasionally and scraping down the sides of the pot, for 2 hours.

Just before serving, season the soup with the reserved horseradish and salt to taste. Ladle the soup into warmed soup cups or bowls and garnish with a stripe each of poppy seeds and scallion.

SIMPLEST POTATO SOUP

Adapted from a recipe from cookbook author Deborah Madison, this is one of the most fundamental and delicious soups you can ever make. It's a good choice when you want to show off any favorite specialty potatoes, but in a pinch, yellow-fleshed will be just fine. Since bay leaves are the only seasoning, it's worth getting good, richly flavored Turkish bay leaves just for this soup.

2 tablespoons unsalted butter
2 onions, finely chopped
3 small bay leaves
Coarse salt
2 pounds German Butterballs or any medium-starch potato, scrubbed, halved, and
    thinly sliced
3 tablespoons chopped flat-leaf parsley
Freshly ground black pepper

Melt the butter in a soup pot or wide saucepan over medium-low heat. Add the onions, bay leaves, and a pinch of salt and cook, stirring occasionally, until the onions are soft and very fragrant, about 7 minutes.

Increase the heat to high, add the potatoes and a generous teaspoon of salt, and cook quickly, shaking or stirring to prevent sticking, until the potatoes begin to brown in spots, about 10 minutes. Pour in 1 cup water and bring to a boil. Scrape the bottom of the pot with a wooden spoon to dissolve any caramelized bits, and add another 6 cups cold water. Bring to a boil, reduce to a simmer, and cook, partway covered, until the potatoes are very tender, 25 to 30 minutes. Let the soup cool for 5 minutes.

Remove the bay leaves. Ladle one-third of the solids into a blender or food processor and puree until smooth. (Remember to vent the lid so the soup doesn't erupt and splatter.) Return the puree to the pot. Add the parsley, pepper to taste, and salt if needed, and serve.

SERVING SUGGESTIONS

Slice a baguette into thin rounds and toast lightly. Brush with olive oil and top each with a bit of grated Parmesan. Bake in a 375-degree oven until the cheese melts, about 10 minutes. Pass the croutons to be dropped into individual bowls of the soup.

Alternatively, this soup is lovely with a dollop of crème fraîche.

RUTABAGA-POTATO SOUP

SERVES 4 TO 6

Let's pause for a moment to sing the praises of the rutabaga: its elegant color, the tang it brings to the table. Here, combined with potato, it is the star of an elegant soup. Try it and you may, as Molly's sister did, swear there's cream in it. Yellow potatoes enhance the color, but you can substitute all-purpose.

Use the best ham you can find—something like imported Black Forest—although you can skip it if you want to go vegetarian. But frizzle the leeks; they're worth the effort.

3 tablespoons unsalted butter
$1/4$ pound best-quality smoked ham, cut into $1/4$-inch dice
1 cup sliced leeks (white and pale green parts only)
$1^{1}/4$ pounds rutabaga, quartered, peeled, and thinly sliced
$1/2$ pound yellow-fleshed potatoes, peeled and cut into $1/2$-inch chunks
1 small sprig rosemary
Coarse salt and freshly ground black pepper
$1/2$ cup dry white wine or dry vermouth
4 cups Chicken Stock (page 85) or water
Frizzled Leeks (page 101)

Melt 1 tablespoon of the butter in a soup pot over medium heat. Add the ham and cook, stirring a few times, until sizzling and beginning to brown, 4 to 5 minutes. Remove the ham with a slotted spoon and set aside. Don't fret if a few bits of ham remain in the pot—they'll add flavor to the soup.

Add the remaining 2 tablespoons butter and the leeks to the pot. Cook, stirring occasionally, until the leeks are wilted and tender, about 7 minutes. Add the rutabaga, potatoes, and rosemary and season with salt and pepper. Increase the heat to high, pour in the wine, and let it cook down by about half, about 3 minutes. Add the stock and bring to a boil. Reduce the heat to medium, cover partway, and simmer until all the vegetables are very tender, 20 to 30 minutes.

Remove the rosemary and let the soup cool for 5 minutes.

Puree the soup in batches in a blender (remember to vent the lid, or the soup will erupt and splatter). Wipe out the pot, pour in the soup, and return it to the heat. Stir in the ham to heat through, and taste for seasoning.

Ladle the hot soup into bowls, garnish each with a mound of Frizzled Leeks, and serve.

FRIZZLED LEEKS

I love the flavor and texture of this garnish and frizzle leeks to scatter on mashes and steaks and chops too. If you like height on your plate, make a bunch of these and go wild.

Trim the root and tough green from a leek and cut the white and pale green lengthwise in half. Slice each half into 2-inch lengths, then into fine (1/16-inch) julienne. Wash well and dry thoroughly with paper towels.

Heat 2 inches of vegetable oil in a heavy pan. When it's moderately hot, about 325 degrees, dredge the leeks lightly in flour, shaking them in a strainer to remove any excess flour. Drop half the leeks into the oil and fry just until golden, about 2 minutes. Scoop them out with a spider or slotted spoon, drain on paper towels, and sprinkle with coarse salt. Repeat with the remaining leeks. Serve soon after frizzling.

CELERIAC, FENNEL, AND POTATO SOUP

Fennel gives this soup a Mediterranean flavor, and it's remarkably light for something made with winter vegetables. We prepare it with stock or with water; you could even do it with milk.

1 fennel bulb
2 tablespoons olive oil
1 cup chopped leeks (white and pale green parts)
1/2 teaspoon crushed fennel seeds
Coarse salt and freshly ground black pepper
1 tablespoon Pernod or Ricard
1 knob (about 3/4 pound) celeriac (celery root), peeled and cut into 1/2-inch chunks
3/4 pound Maine or all-purpose potatoes, peeled and cut into 1/2-inch chunks
6 cups Chicken Stock (page 85) or water, or a combination

Cut away the fennel branches; reserve a small handful of the feathery greens for garnish. Cut the bulb in half and then slice very thin.

Heat the oil in a soup pot over medium-high heat until it shimmers. Add the leeks, sliced fennel, fennel seeds, and salt and pepper to taste, and cook until the vegetables are wilted and tender, about 7 minutes. Add the Pernod and cook for another minute. Add the celeriac, potatoes, and stock, and bring to a boil. Reduce the heat to medium, cover partway, and simmer until the celeriac and potatoes are tender. Let cool for 5 minutes.

Transfer the soup in batches to a blender and puree until smooth (remember to vent the lid so the soup doesn't erupt). Wipe out the pot and return the soup to it. Bring it back to a simmer; taste for seasoning. Ladle into warm soup bowls and garnish with the reserved fennel fronds.

DOCTORED CANNED STOCK

We're the type of cooks who keep containers of stock in the freezer. But there are also times when we need something quick. This is a simple way of getting more flavor into canned stock. It works equally well with chicken and beef stock and is easily doubled, tripled, or quadrupled.

1 (14½-ounce) can low-sodium broth
2 shallots, halved but not peeled (you can substitute small onions)
1 sprig thyme
1 teaspoon unsalted butter

Combine the ingredients in a small saucepan and bring to a simmer. Reduce the heat to low and simmer very gently for 20 to 25 minutes. Discard the solids.

OLD-FASHIONED POTATO SOUP

SERVES 4 TO 6

If you're looking for a simple, down-home, stick-to-your-ribs potage, you've found it. This is a slightly refined version of a peasant classic, where you would throw whatever you have on hand into a pot and leave it simmering at the back of the stove until everything was cooked really well.

Add and subtract to the list of vegetables according to your larder. No celery, but parsnips in the bin? Fine. This tastes best the next day or even the day after. Maybe you should double the recipe as long as you're cooking?

1 bay leaf
1 onion, peeled
2 whole cloves
1 small smoked ham hock (about 1/2 pound)
1 pound Maine or other white potatoes, peeled and cut into 1/2-inch dice
2 carrots, cut into 1/2-inch dice
1 celery stalk, cut into 1/2-inch dice
1 small turnip, peeled and cut into 1/2-inch dice
2 garlic cloves, minced
Coarse salt and freshly ground black pepper
3 cups shredded savoy cabbage (about 1/2 head)

Stick the bay leaf onto the onion, using the cloves as tacks. Put the onion and ham hock in a soup pot and add enough cold water to cover them, at least 2 quarts. Bring to a boil over high heat, cover partway, and reduce the heat. Simmer gently for 45 minutes, then skim any cloudy bits that have risen to the surface.

Add the potatoes, carrots, celery, turnip, and garlic to the pot, along with 1 1/2 teaspoons salt and 1/2 teaspoon pepper. Continue to simmer, covered partway, until the ham is beginning to fall from the bone and the vegetables are almost tender, 20 to 25 minutes.

Using a meat fork, remove the ham and onion from the soup. Set the ham aside to cool a bit, and discard the onion. Add the cabbage to the soup and simmer until tender, about 10 minutes more.

As soon as you can handle the ham hock, strip away the skin, fat, and bone and cut the meat into small bits.

Return the ham pieces to the soup. Taste for seasoning—this soup wants lots of freshly ground black pepper—and serve.

POTATO AND ARUGULA SOUP

Baby arugula will give you the most delicate soup; the adult greens will be bolder. But experiment: try Red Russian kale, mizuna, or tatsoi. Just be diligent in removing the stems. And as long as you're making this your own, try chorizo, andouille, or even kielbasa instead of the Italian sausage.

1/2 pound sweet Italian sausage
1 tablespoon plus 1 teaspoon olive oil, plus more for serving
1 large shallot or small red onion, minced
2 1/2 pounds all-purpose potatoes, peeled and cut into 1/3-inch dice
6 cups Chicken Stock (page 85) or water
Coarse salt
Crushed red pepper
1/2 pound arugula

Heat a small skillet over medium-high heat. Add the sausage and 1 teaspoon of the oil and brown the sausage on all sides. Reduce the heat to low, cover, and cook until the sausage is cooked through, about 10 minutes. Remove the skillet from the heat.

Spoon the remaining 1 tablespoon oil into a large saucepan. Add the shallot and cook over medium heat until translucent, about 3 minutes. Add the potatoes, stock, salt, and a good pinch of crushed red pepper and bring to a boil. Cook until the potatoes are tender, 15 to 20 minutes.

Meanwhile, cut the arugula into thin strips (if you're using infant greens, just tear the leaves in half). Thinly slice the sausage.

When the potatoes are tender, remove the pot from the heat and mash with a hand masher; you want a relatively smooth soup, but with some small chunks of potato. Return the soup to a boil and stir in the arugula and sausage. Cook for 5 minutes to heat through, taste for salt and pepper, and transfer to a tureen. Drizzle with olive oil and serve.

POTATO, PARSNIP, AND CHEDDAR SOUP

You have Iowa farm-country comfort food here. Not too thick, not gooey and supercheesy like some cheese soups, but just right. It's a good winter after-sledding or after-skiing soup.

1½ pounds russet potatoes, peeled and cut into ½-inch dice
½ pound parsnips, peeled and cut into ½-inch pieces
2 small carrots, sliced into ⅛-inch rounds
1 onion, chopped
4 cups Chicken Stock (page 85) or water
Coarse salt and freshly ground black pepper
4 tablespoons (½ stick) unsalted butter
¼ cup all-purpose flour
1½ cups milk, warmed
6 ounces sharp cheddar, shredded (about 1½ cups)

Combine the potatoes, parsnips, carrots, onion, and stock in a soup pot. Season with salt and pepper and bring to a boil over high heat. Cover partway, reduce the heat to medium, and simmer until the vegetables are very tender, about 30 minutes.

Meanwhile, melt the butter in a heavy saucepan over medium heat. Whisk in the flour and cook for a minute or two. Gradually whisk in the milk and let the mixture simmer gently, whisking often, until slightly thickened, 3 to 5 minutes. Reduce the heat to low and slowly stir in the cheese. Do not let the mixture boil, but keep it warm until the soup is ready.

Pour the milk-cheese mixture into the soup and stir to incorporate. Taste for salt and pepper. Transfer to a soup tureen and ladle it up.

WILD MUSHROOM AND POTATO SOUP

SERVES 4 TO 6

We adapted this fine Spanish soup, with its deep mushroom flavor and pleasant sherry accent, from Spanish cooking authority Penelope Casas. If you have the time, do make the mushroom stock; adding it deepens the mushroom flavor even more. And if you have them, use Estimas or German Butterballs.

3/4 pound wild or specialty mushrooms (such as shiitake, oyster, chanterelle, morel, porcini, portobello, or cremini)
1/4 cup olive oil
1 large shallot, finely chopped
1 garlic clove, minced
1 1/2 teaspoons fresh thyme leaves or 1/2 teaspoon dried
Coarse salt and freshly ground black pepper
2 tablespoons dry sherry
2 plum tomatoes, peeled, seeded, and chopped (see page 30)
3/4 pound yellow-fleshed potatoes, peeled and cut into 1/3-inch dice
6 cups Chicken Stock (page 85) or Beef Stock (page 115)
2 tablespoons chopped flat-leaf parsley

If you are using shiitake or other mushrooms with tough stems, trim off the stems and place them in a small saucepan. Cover with cold water and simmer for 30 minutes to make a quick little mushroom stock to add to the soup.

Meanwhile, trim any other types of mushrooms as necessary and cut into 1/3-inch dice.

Heat 2 tablespoons of the oil in a soup pot over medium-high heat until it shimmers. Add half of the mushrooms and cook, stirring, until they release their liquid and begin to brown in spots, about 7 minutes. Remove to a bowl. Add the remaining 2 tablespoons oil to the pot and cook the remaining mushrooms in the same way. When the second batch of mushrooms is cooked, return the first batch, with their juices, to the pot, add the shallot, garlic, thyme, and some salt and pepper, and cook for another minute.

Stir in the sherry and tomatoes, bring to a boil, and cook for 2 to 3 minutes. If you've made the mushroom stock, strain and add it along with the tomatoes.

Add the potatoes and stock. Bring to a boil, cover partway, and reduce the heat to a gentle simmer. Cook until the potatoes are tender, 25 to 35 minutes.

Stir in the parsley and taste for salt and pepper. Ladle into warm soup bowls and serve.

KALE, POTATO, BEAN, AND LINGUIÇA SOUP

Our version of the Portuguese soup *caldo verde* is earthy and gutsy and bright with the colors of tomatoes, kidney beans, and kale. This recipe makes a big batch, so you can serve it to a crowd. But it also keeps very well; like a stew, it might even be better the next day.

2 teaspoons olive oil, plus more for serving
1/2 pound linguiça or chorizo, cut into 1/2-inch chunks
1 large onion, chopped
2 garlic cloves, minced
3/4 pound red-skinned potatoes, scrubbed and cut into 1/2-inch chunks
1 bay leaf
Coarse salt and freshly ground black pepper
1 small bunch kale, stems removed and coarsely chopped (about 4 very
   generous cups)
1 (14 1/2-ounce) can tomatoes, drained and chopped, or 1 3/4 cups peeled,
   seeded, and chopped ripe tomatoes (see page 30)
1 (15-ounce) can kidney or pinto beans, drained and rinsed, or
   1 1/2 cups cooked beans

Put the oil and linguiça in a heavy soup pot over medium-high heat. Cook until the sausage renders some of its fat and begins to shrink up, 4 to 5 minutes. Remove the sausage with a slotted spoon to a bowl.

Add the onion to the pot and cook, stirring, until it's limp and the edges are starting to turn golden, 5 to 7 minutes. Stir in the garlic and cook for a few minutes more, until it's fragrant. Add 1 cup cold water, stirring with a wooden spoon to dissolve any caramelized bits on the bottom of the pot. Add the potatoes, bay leaf, and 7 more cups cold water. Season with salt and pepper and bring to a boil. Reduce to a simmer, cover partway, and cook for 10 minutes.

Add the kale and continue to simmer until the kale and potatoes are tender but not falling apart, 10 to 15 minutes more.

Add the tomatoes, beans, and sausage and continue to simmer for another 8 to 10 minutes. Correct the seasoning and serve in wide soup bowls. The soup will really sing if you drizzle each bowl with a thread of fruity olive oil.

If you are serving this on the second day, make sure you have plenty of broth. Add water to thin the soup as necessary and simmer for about 10 minutes.

SICILIAN POTATOES AND DITALINI

You can just about stand a spoon up in this rustic soup. It's hearty and comforting, real peasant food, and a great lunch for a raw, rainy day.

Sicilians would start this with water and a bouillon cube and then add water with the pasta. As for the pasta, I use Barilla. The timing will be different with other brands, so check. But whatever brand you choose, make sure it's imported: the American stuff gets mushy. You can make this soupier by adding more stock with the pasta.

1 red onion, chopped
2 tablespoons olive oil, plus more for serving
1 1/4 pounds yellow-fleshed potatoes, peeled and cut into 1/4-inch dice
Pinch of cayenne pepper
Coarse salt
3 cups Chicken Stock (page 85)
1 cup ditalini
2 tablespoons chopped flat-leaf parsley
1/4 cup freshly grated Pecorino

Put the onion and oil in a wide saucepan and turn the heat to medium. Cook until the onion has softened and the edges are just starting to turn golden, about 10 minutes. Add the potatoes, cayenne, and a good pinch of salt and cook, stirring once or twice, for about a minute. Add 2 cups of the stock and bring to a boil. Reduce to a simmer, cover, and cook until the potatoes are tender. The potatoes will drink up some of the stock, so stir once in a while and add some warm water if the pan is dry.

Once the potatoes are cooked, add the ditalini and the remaining 1 cup stock. The liquid should just about cover the other ingredients; add some warm water if you need it. Bring to a boil, then cover the pan, turn off the heat, and let sit for 15 minutes, until the pasta is al dente.

Stir in the parsley and Pecorino, taste for salt, and serve in deep bowls. Pass a cruet of olive oil at the table. You'll want a good drizzle of it.

SHALLOT AND POTATO SOUP GRATINÉE

SERVES 6

Inspiration came from a Normandy creamy shallot and potato soup recipe, which we twisted into a version of the bistro favorite, French onion soup. Slicing all those shallots takes a little time and may make you weep. The russets melt lovingly into the soup. Bread? Find a crusty country loaf, with a diameter just about the size of your soup bowls.

3 tablespoons unsalted butter
1 pound shallots, thinly sliced (about 4 cups)
Coarse salt and freshly ground black pepper
1 cup dry white wine
1 pound russet potatoes, peeled, quartered, and cut into ⅛-inch-thick slices
6 cups Chicken Stock (page 85), Beef Stock (page 115), or water
Six ⅓-inch slices country bread, lightly toasted
4 ounces Gruyère, finely shredded (about 1 cup)

Melt the butter in a soup pot over medium-low heat. Add the shallots, season with salt and pepper, and cook, stirring to prevent sticking, until they are very soft and beginning to brown, 30 to 35 minutes.

Increase the heat to medium-high, add ½ cup of the wine, and bring to a boil. Stir to dissolve any caramelized bits on the bottom of the pot and cook until the wine is reduced by at least half, about 5 minutes. Repeat with the remaining ½ cup wine.

Add the potatoes and stock and bring to a boil. Reduce the heat to medium-low, cover partway, and simmer gently until the potatoes are very tender.

Heat the oven to 425 degrees.

Taste the soup for salt and pepper. Arrange ovenproof soup bowls on a sturdy baking sheet and ladle the hot soup into them. Float a slice of bread in each bowl and top with cheese. Slide the baking sheet into the oven and bake until the cheese is melted and beginning to bubble, about 10 minutes. Serve right away.

BEEF STOCK

If you happen to have a bottle of dry white wine open, use wine in place of some of the water to deglaze the pan.

2–3 pounds meaty beef shanks, cut into $1^1/_2$-inch pieces
1 large onion (skin on), chopped
1 carrot, scrubbed and chopped
1 celery stalk, chopped
4 whole garlic cloves, skins on
4–5 sprigs thyme
4–5 sprigs parsley
1 bay leaf
6–8 black peppercorns

Heat the oven to 400 degrees. Lightly oil a large roasting pan and dump in the bones. If they don't all fit in a loose single layer, use two pans (a rimmed baking sheet will do in a pinch). Roast, turning with tongs once or twice, until they are browned, about 45 minutes, and transfer to a deep stockpot.

Pour the excess fat off from the roasting pan and set the pan over your largest burner. If the pan's really big, set it over two burners. Heat over medium heat and add about $^1/_2$ cup cold water—enough to cover the bottom of the pan generously. Bring the water to a boil, stirring and scraping with a wooden spoon until you have dissolved all of the caramelized browned bits from the bottom of the pan. Pour the water into the stockpot. Add the vegetables to the stockpot. Tie the herbs and peppercorns together in a piece of cheesecloth to make a little packet and toss it in the pot. Fill the pot with $2^1/_2$ quarts of cold water (enough to cover the bones) and set over medium heat. Gently bring to a simmer and let it bubble gently for 4 to 5 hours. Skim the surface often and add more water anytime the bones are not completely covered. Don't let the stock boil, this will make it muddy-tasting and cloudy.

Strain, discard the solids, and chill. Scrape the fat from the surface of the chilled stock before using. Refrigerate for up to 4 days or freeze for up to 4 months.

POTATO AND
MEATBALL SOUP

The potatoes in this recipe are grated so they will melt away, thickening the soup and giving it body and richness without cream. It's the starch that does it, hence russets. And, yes, you *can* make 40 meatballs from just half a pound of ground meat. Two of them, snuggled together in a soupspoon, make a toothsome mouthful.

Stock is important here. Please use homemade.

2 tablespoons olive oil
1 onion, chopped
6 cups Chicken Stock (page 85) or Beef Stock (page 115)
Coarse salt and freshly ground black pepper
One 1/2-inch-thick slice Italian bread, crust removed
1/4 cup milk or cream, warmed
1 ounce (about 2 slices) prosciutto, minced
1 large egg yolk
2 garlic cloves, minced
2 teaspoons minced fresh sage
1/2 teaspoon grated lemon zest
1/4 cup chopped flat-leaf parsley
1/2 pound ground veal or pork
1 pound russet potatoes

Combine the oil and onion in a heavy soup pot and cook over medium-low heat until the onion is soft, about 7 minutes. Add the stock and bring to a simmer. Season with salt and pepper, turn off the heat, and cover.

Meanwhile, rip the bread into pieces, put it in a small bowl with the milk, and let it soak until it's mush—squeeze it once or twice—at least 15 minutes.

Combine the prosciutto, egg yolk, garlic, sage, lemon zest, and 2 tablespoons of the parsley in a large bowl. Season with 1/2 teaspoon salt and a bit of pepper. Squeeze most of the milk from the soaked bread and add the bread to the bowl (discard the milk). Stir everything together until very well mixed. Crumble in the ground meat and mix with your hands just until the mixture is well combined; overwork it, and you'll end up with little bullets instead of tender meatballs.

Bring the stock back to a simmer over medium heat. Drop a small pinch of the meatball mixture into the stock and simmer until it's cooked through, about 3 minutes. Taste for salt and pepper and correct the mixture if it needs it.

Once the seasoning is correct, shape the rest of the mixture into tiny meatballs about the size of a big marble. This will be easier if you keep your hands damp, so have a bowl of warm water handy. You should end up with about 40 meatballs.

When all the meatballs are shaped, drop half the batch into the simmering stock and simmer until just cooked through, 3 to 5 minutes. Remove them to a bowl with a slotted spoon and cook the second batch. Add those to the others in the bowl.

Once all the meatballs are cooked, peel the potatoes and grate them fine on a mandoline or the large holes of a box grater. Don't use the food processor for this; the shreds will be too long and thick, and they won't melt as they should. Add the potatoes to the stock and bring to a boil. Cover partway, reduce the heat to a simmer, and cook until the potatoes have dissolved and thickened the soup, about 12 minutes.

Return the meatballs to the soup, along with any accumulated juices, add the remaining 2 tablespoons parsley, and taste for salt and pepper. Once the meatballs are heated through, ladle the soup into wide soup bowls and serve.

PEANUT SOUP

Molly came up with this New World spin on a spicy West African peanut stew. The tomatoes balance the richness of the peanut butter and give the soup a pleasant rosy hue.

Be certain to get natural peanut butter—no sugar, no additives. We garnish with dry-roasted peanuts because we like them, but plain roasted will work fine.

2 tablespoons vegetable oil
1 large onion, chopped
2 garlic cloves, minced
1/2 teaspoon cayenne pepper, or more to taste
3/4 pound russet potatoes, peeled and cut into 1/2-inch chunks
Coarse salt and freshly ground black pepper
3 cups Chicken Stock (page 85) or water
1 (28-ounce) can whole plum tomatoes with their juice
3/4 cup smooth natural peanut butter (with no sugar)
1/4 cup roasted peanuts, chopped
3 tablespoons finely chopped scallions

Put the oil and onion in a heavy soup pot over medium heat and cook until the onion is limp, about 7 minutes. Add the garlic and cayenne and cook for about a minute longer, until the garlic is fragrant. Stir in the potatoes and season with salt and pepper. Cook for another minute.

Add the stock and tomatoes. Bring to a boil, cover partway, and lower the heat to medium. Cook, stirring occasionally, until the potatoes are very tender. Let the soup sit for 5 minutes.

Puree the soup in batches in a blender or food processor—remember to vent the lid. Clean the pot, pour in the soup, and return it to low heat. Whisk in the peanut butter until smooth and bring to a simmer. Taste for salt and cayenne.

Ladle the soup into cups and sprinkle with peanuts and scallions.

ROASTED CORN CHOWDER

SERVES 4 TO 6

Should you care to, you can make this soup into a vegetarian dish by cutting out the bacon and adding another tablespoon of oil or butter. Yukon Golds or Yellow Finns give the best color, but you can substitute russets.

3 ears corn, shucked
Coarse salt
3 tablespoons olive oil
4 slices bacon, chopped
1 large white onion, chopped
4 sprigs thyme
1 sprig oregano
1 sprig flat-leaf parsley
2 pounds yellow-fleshed potatoes, peeled and cut into $1/3$-inch dice
Freshly ground white pepper
1 cup heavy cream
4 scallions, green part only, chopped

Heat the oven to 400 degrees.

Cut the kernels from the corn and toss them on a baking sheet with some salt and 1 tablespoon of the oil. Roast the corn, stirring once in a while, for 15 to 20 minutes, until well browned.

Put the remaining 2 tablespoons oil and the bacon in a saucepan over medium heat. Cook, stirring occasionally, until the fat has rendered and the bacon is beginning to brown. Add the onion. Cook until browned, about 15 minutes.

Tie the herb sprigs into a bundle with kitchen string and add to the saucepan, along with the potatoes, salt and pepper to taste, and 5 cups water. Bring to a boil, reduce to a simmer, cover partway, and cook until the potatoes are very tender.

Stir in the roasted corn and simmer for 5 minutes. Stir in the cream and bring to a simmer. Cook for at least a minute. Discard the herb bundle, taste for salt and pepper, and serve garnished with the scallions.

CLAM CHOWDER

We're of the tomato school of clam chowder—no milk or cream. Our recipe does say to peel the celery, but if you don't mind the strings, leave them unpeeled. Otherwise, run a vegetable peeler along the outside to remove the strings before you dice.

2 onions, diced
3 tablespoons olive oil
4 carrots, cut into $1/4$-inch dice
2 celery stalks, peeled and cut into $1/4$-inch dice
1 pound red-skinned potatoes, scrubbed and cut into $1/4$-inch dice
1 (28-ounce) can whole Italian plum tomatoes, lightly drained and
    coarsely chopped
3 cups Fish Stock (page 122)
Coarse salt
Pinch of crushed red pepper
1 bay leaf
1 cup dry white wine
Several sprigs thyme
12 chowder clams (or 3 dozen cherrystones), well scrubbed

Put the onions and 2 tablespoons of the olive oil in a stockpot over medium-low heat and cook gently until the onions are translucent, about 7 minutes. Stir in the carrots and celery and cook for 2 to 3 minutes. Add the potatoes, tomatoes, stock, salt to taste, crushed red pepper, and bay leaf. Increase the heat to medium-high and bring to a boil, then reduce the heat and simmer until the vegetables are tender, 20 to 25 minutes.

Meanwhile, put the wine, thyme, and clams in a saucepan. Bring to a boil, cover, and steam the clams, removing them as they open. Let the clams cool a bit, then pour any clam juices in the shells back into the steaming liquid, remove the clams from their shells, and coarsely chop them. Place them in a bowl, drizzle with the remaining 1 tablespoon olive oil, and cover them to keep warm.

Pour the clam-steaming liquid into the soup, leaving behind any grit and the thyme sprig. (If you want to be fussy, strain the liquid through some dampened paper towels or a dampened coffee filter first.)

To serve the chowder, remove the bay leaf, stir in the clams and taste for salt. Heat for about a minute, and then dish it up.

FISH STOCK

You'll never get the fresh, sweet flavor of homemade fish stock in any store-bought version. Really, the hardest part about making your own might be finding fish frames. Use bones and heads only from mild white fish, ideally flounder or sole. If you don't have a helpful fishmonger who will sell you bones, see if you can buy chunks of white fish cut up for chowder, and substitute those.

1 pound fish frames with heads
1 sprig thyme
2 sprigs flat-leaf parsley
1 bay leaf
1 tablespoon unsalted butter
1 small onion, sliced
1 cup chopped fennel stalks (optional)
1 small leek, white and pale green parts, chopped
1 small celery stalk, chopped
1/2 cup dry white wine
5 or 6 black peppercorns

Thoroughly rinse the fish frames, removing any gills, guts, skin, or traces of blood. Drain. Break or chop them into 2-to-3-inch pieces. Tie the thyme, parsley, and bay leaf together with a piece of kitchen string.

Melt the butter in a large saucepan over medium heat. Add the onion, fennel (if using), leek, and celery and cook until partly softened, about 7 minutes. Add the fish frames, stir, and cook until lightly fragrant, about 5 minutes.

Pour in the wine and bring to a simmer. Add 3 1/2 cups cold water, the herb bundle, and the peppercorns. Bring slowly to a simmer, skimming as needed, and cook at a simmer for 30 minutes. Strain. Fish stock is best used the day it is made.

POTATO AND SALT PORK CHOWDER

Here's a simple New England farmhouse soup. Blanching the salt pork for a few minutes mellows its flavor so it doesn't take over the whole soup, and you'll find that it won't smoke either when you brown it. Vermont common crackers—also called Montpelier crackers—are our soup cracker of choice, but if you must, make do with oyster or soda crackers.

$1/4$ pound salt pork, rind removed, cut into $1/3$-inch dice
1 large onion, chopped
1 teaspoon fresh thyme leaves or $1/2$ teaspoon dried
2 tablespoons all-purpose flour
$1^1/2$ pounds waxy potatoes, peeled and cut into $1/3$-inch dice
Coarse salt and freshly ground black pepper
2 cups Chicken Stock (page 85) or water
$2^1/2$–3 cups milk, as needed
Soup crackers

Put the salt pork in a medium saucepan filled with cold water. Bring to a boil and cook for 4 minutes. Drain.

Transfer the pork to a heavy soup pot and cook over medium heat until it renders its fat and browns, about 7 minutes. Add the onion and thyme and cook until the onion is soft, about 7 minutes. Stir in the flour and cook, stirring, for a minute longer. Add the potatoes, season with salt and pepper, and pour in the stock and 2 cups of the milk. Bring to a boil, cover partway, and reduce to a simmer. Cook, stirring occasionally, until the potatoes are tender.

Add $1/2$ to 1 cup milk as needed to adjust the consistency. Heat and taste for salt and pepper. Ladle into warm soup mugs or bowls and pass a basket of soup crackers.

SALADS

MOM'S POTATO SALAD

SERVES 6

This is the potato salad I grew up with. My mother makes it for backyard cookouts, when cousins from out of town are stopping by for lunch, and at Christmas (to go with ham sandwiches in the early evening). It's about as simple a salad as they come, but here's the thing: aunts, cousins, and the whole family have the recipe and they make it all the time, and still, all of them agree that my mom's is the best. Hands down.

You can replace the garlic powder with fresh garlic if you dare, but then it won't be Mom's salad. And you'll notice I don't call for freshly ground black pepper. Well, that's not what Mom uses.

2–2¼ pounds red-skinned or white potatoes
Coarse salt
2 large eggs, hard-cooked (see page 127)
Garlic powder
Black pepper
1 cup Hellmann's (or Best Foods) mayonnaise

Place the potatoes in a large saucepan, cover with cold water by at least an inch, add a good pinch of salt, and bring to a boil. Cover partway, reduce the heat to medium, and cook until the potatoes are tender. Drain on a rack set in the sink and leave the potatoes there to cool completely.

Peel the potatoes and cut them into uneven chunks, somewhere between ⅓ and ½ inch. Drop them into a mixing bowl.

Chop the eggs, then mash them into little bits with a fork. Scrape the eggs into the potatoes, and add a few shakes of garlic powder, some salt, and a very little pepper. Fold in the mayo. I love eating this right away. Mom always serves it chilled.

HARD-COOKED EGGS

Tender whites, bright yolks still a bit moist in the center—these are hallmarks of a hard-cooked egg that's done properly. Treat an egg wrong, and you end up with rubbery whites and that nasty green ring around the yolk.

You'll read conflicting instructions in just about every cookbook, and you just might have your own ideas, but here's how we've been making them. Cook only as many as you need (we don't much care for hard-boiled eggs if they've been sitting in the refrigerator).

Put the eggs in a saucepan and cover with water. Don't crowd them; they want room. So if you need a lot, use several pans. Bring the water just to a boil over medium to medium-high heat. Once it starts to bubble, turn the heat to the lowest possible setting and set the timer for 8 minutes.

When the timer goes off, turn off the heat and drain off the water. Now give the pan two or three vigorous shakes, which will crack the shells and release any noxious fumes (ever peeled an egg and smelled sulfur?). Cover with cold water, drain, and cover again with cold water. Let the eggs cool completely in the water before you peel them.

CREAMY HEARTLAND POTATO SALAD
WITH CUCUMBER

This is a true heartland salad, very creamy, with exactly the right balance of sweet and sour. I make it with the heirloom Estima potatoes from Bill Leritz's Fox Hill Farm, but it's great with any yellow-fleshed or white potato.

The recipe comes from Bridget DeClerk, who works at New York's Union Square Greenmarket. She said she didn't know where her mom got the recipe, but she suspected her grandmother came up with it on their North Dakota farm.

FOR THE SALAD AND GARNISH
1¹/₂–2 pounds yellow-fleshed potatoes, scrubbed
Coarse salt
¹/₄ cup chopped cucumber (peel and seed the cucumber first)
¹/₄ cup finely chopped green bell pepper
1 whole scallion, chopped
4 large eggs, hard-cooked (see page 127)
¹/₄ cup sliced radishes

FOR THE DRESSING
¹/₄ cup cider vinegar
¹/₄ cup sugar
1 teaspoon ground mustard
Coarse salt and freshly ground black pepper
2 large eggs
1 cup mayonnaise

FOR THE SALAD: Put the potatoes in a large saucepan, cover with cold water by at least an inch, add a good pinch of salt, and bring to a boil. Cover partway, reduce the heat to medium, and cook until the potatoes are tender. Drain on a rack set in the sink and leave the potatoes there to cool completely.

Peel the potatoes and cut them into 1/3-inch dice. Drop them into a mixing bowl, separating the cubes as you go. Add the cucumber, bell pepper, and the scallion. Chop 2 of the hard-cooked eggs and add them too.

FOR THE DRESSING: Combine the vinegar, sugar, mustard, and salt and pepper to taste in a small saucepan with 1/4 cup water. Stir to dissolve the sugar, and bring it to a boil.

Whisk the eggs well in a small bowl and slowly pour in the boiling vinegar, whisking all the time. Scrape this back into the pan and return to medium-low heat. Cook, stirring constantly, until the dressing thickens and coats the back of a spoon, about 3 minutes. Scrape it back into the bowl and whisk in the mayonnaise.

Pour the dressing over the salad and fold to combine it all well. Chill it for at least an hour.

Serve the salad garnished with the remaining 2 hard-cooked eggs, sliced, and the radishes.

RED POTATO SALAD WITH MUSTARDY MAYONNAISE

When my pal Susan Simon had a takeout business in New York's East Village, her A-list, uptown clients sent down for this salad by the gallon. It's easy to see why once you taste it.

SERVES 4 TO 6

1¹/₂–1³/₄ pounds red-skinned potatoes, scrubbed
Coarse salt
2 celery stalks, peeled and finely diced
¹/₂ cup finely diced green bell pepper
3 whole scallions, finely chopped

FOR THE MAYONNAISE
1 large egg
1 heaping tablespoon grainy mustard
Coarse salt and freshly ground black pepper
²/₃ cup corn oil

Place the potatoes in a large saucepan, cover with cold water by at least an inch, add a good pinch of salt, and bring to a boil. Cover partway, reduce the heat to medium, and cook until the potatoes are tender. Drain on a rack set in the sink and leave the potatoes there to cool completely.

Once the potatoes are cooled, cut them into ¹/₂-inch chunks and drop them into a mixing bowl. Add the celery, bell pepper, and scallions.

FOR THE MAYONNAISE: Crack the egg into your food processor and add the mustard and salt and pepper to taste. Hit the "on" button; once the egg is frothy, start pouring in the oil in a slow, thin stream, adding it all, until you have a nice, fairly thick mayonnaise.

Scrape the mayonnaise into the mixing bowl and fold the salad together with a big rubber scraper. You can serve this right away or refrigerate it for up to 2 days.

POTATO PRINCIPLES
TESTING BOILED POTATOES
FOR DONENESS

Boiled potatoes have a tendency to get waterlogged and soggy. For breads and some soups, that doesn't matter, but sometimes you need to take more care. The easiest way to avoid overcooking is to boil the potatoes in their jackets and to be careful how you test them for doneness.

Your first impulse will likely be to take out a fork and stick it into the potato. Don't. You'll poke the skin full of holes and invite water inside. Some cooks use the tip of a sharp knife. That's fine if you're testing surface doneness, but to check the center, you'll end up putting a big slice in the potato. Skip the knife.

We've found that the best tool for the job is a long, thin skewer or a larding needle. Both are long enough so you don't have to get your hand too close to the boiling water, and they make just a tiny hole, so water invasion is minimal. Resurrect yours from the back of the utility drawer or visit a kitchen supply shop and make this minor but oh-so-worthwhile investment.

SMASHED POTATO SALAD

This Southern-style salad is just right with barbecue, fried chicken, a burger, or deep-fried turkey.

The salad needs resting time in the refrigerator. Make it early in the day or even the day before. The hot mixed pickles are the kind that come in jars from the grocery; you can use the sweet mix if you prefer. I've adapted this from a recipe by Jim Fobel in his award-winning book *Big Flavors*.

3 pounds russet potatoes, scrubbed
Coarse salt
3 large eggs, hard-cooked (see page 127)
$1/2$ cup mayonnaise
2 tablespoons spicy brown mustard
1 tablespoon sugar
1 tablespoon cider vinegar or sherry vinegar
$1/2$ teaspoon hot paprika
$1/2$ cup finely chopped hot mixed pickles
2 whole scallions, minced
$1/3$ cup chopped flat-leaf parsley
2 tablespoons chopped roasted red pepper (see note) or pimiento
 (make it easy on yourself and use the stuff from a jar)
Freshly ground black pepper

Place the potatoes in a large saucepan, cover with cold water by at least an inch, add a big pinch of salt, and bring to a boil. Cover partway, reduce the heat to medium, and cook until the potatoes are tender. Drain on a rack set in the sink and leave them to cool to room temperature.

To make the dressing, peel the eggs and coarsely chop them, then mash them thoroughly with a fork. Scrape them into a small bowl and add the mayo, mustard, sugar, vinegar, paprika, pickles, scallions, parsley, roasted pepper, and salt and pepper to taste (be generous with the salt). Stir to mix well.

Peel the potatoes and cut them into chunks. Drop them into a big mixing bowl as you go. Use a hand masher or the side of a big spoon to smash the potatoes: you want a texture that's more rustic than nicely cubed potatoes but not as smooth as a mash. Scrape in the dressing and stir well.

The salad will seem dry at this stage; don't worry. It comes together perfectly as it chills. Cover with plastic and refrigerate for at least 3 hours, or overnight. Serve cold.

NOTE: Peppers taste great roasted on an open flame, but you can also make them in the oven.

For the flame method, turn on a gas burner and set the pepper in it. Char it all over, turning with tongs, so the skin is black and blistery.

For the oven method, heat the oven to 350 degrees. Place the pepper on a baking sheet or a piece of aluminum foil and cook for about 30 minutes, until the skin has blistered and browned in spots.

Either way you cook the pepper, seal it up in a bag (traditional is brown paper, but plastic does work) for 15 to 20 minutes to steam. Rub off the skin with your fingers or paper towels—never wash it off, never—and tear the pepper open. Pull off the stem and seed pod, trim away the veins, and you're ready to go.

TOMATO POTATO SALAD
WITH LEMON MAYONNAISE

SERVES 4 TO 6

This salad is best served right after you make it, with potatoes that have never been chilled. But it's easy enough to have the potatoes, tomatoes, and mayonnaise ready and just combine them before dinner.

Salting concentrates the flavor of the tomatoes, and it removes excess liquid from them too, so the salad won't be watery.

4 ripe tomatoes, seeded and diced
Coarse salt
2 pounds yellow-fleshed potatoes, scrubbed

FOR THE LEMON MAYONNAISE
1 large egg yolk
Grated zest and juice of 1 lemon
Coarse salt and freshly ground black pepper
$1/4$ cup olive oil
$3/4$ cup corn oil

2 heaping tablespoons finely sliced fresh mint or basil

Place the tomatoes in a colander, sprinkle with salt, and set in the sink or over a plate for an hour or so.

Put the potatoes in a saucepan, cover with cold water by at least an inch, add a good pinch of salt, and bring to a boil. Cover partway, reduce the heat to medium, and cook until the potatoes are tender. Turn the potatoes out onto a rack set in the sink and leave them to cool in a single layer.

FOR THE MAYONNAISE: Put the yolk in a medium bowl (a deep one if you have it). Add the zest and some salt and pepper. Whisk to combine. Whisking constantly, start adding the olive oil in little drips. Once the mayonnaise has begun to take shape, you can then add the corn oil a bit more quickly, but take your time. It will be very thick. Beat in the lemon juice and taste for salt and pepper.

Peel the potatoes, cut them into $1/3$-inch dice, and put in a bowl. Shake the colander with the tomatoes to get rid of the last drops of liquid and add the tomatoes to the potatoes. Fold in the mayonnaise and mint. Serve right away.

LOBSTER AND POTATO SALAD WITH TARRAGON

Here's a happier version of the classic French potato salad known as
salade à la Russe. The original includes a mix of diced vegetables bound
together with a very thick mayonnaise; this one uses fresh tarragon
to flavor the mayonnaise and omits the diced carrots, turnips, and
pickled tongue of the classic.

Ruby Crescent potatoes give a nice rosy color to the salad, but
any small creamer potato will do. For a real summer luncheon salad,
line the plates with Bibb lettuce.

1¼ pounds Ruby Crescent or small creamer potatoes
Coarse salt
½ pound green beans, topped, tailed, and cut into 1½-inch pieces (or substitute
    fresh sugar snaps, but leave them whole)
1 red bell pepper, cored, seeded, and diced
½ pound fresh-cooked lobster meat (picked from about 2½ pounds lobsters)
Freshly ground black pepper
¼ cup heavy cream
⅓ cup mayonnaise
1½ teaspoons chopped fresh tarragon

Put the potatoes in a saucepan, cover with cold water by at least an inch, add a
good pinch of salt, and bring to a boil. Reduce the heat to medium, cover partway, and cook until the potatoes are tender. Drain the potatoes on a rack in the
sink and let them cool in a single layer.

Bring another pot of salted water to a boil and drop in the beans. Boil until
just tender, about 4 minutes. Just before draining the beans, drop the diced red
pepper into the water for 20 to 30 seconds. (This takes just the slightest bit of
crunch off the pepper dice so they blend better with the other salad ingredi-

ents.) Drain the beans and peppers and rinse them immediately with plenty of cold running water. Drain again and then dump onto a clean towel to dry.

When the potatoes are at room temperature, peel them. It may seem a bit of work to peel these little potatoes, but you're making a fancy French salad. Cut the potatoes into bite-sized pieces and drop them into a bowl.

Chop the lobster meat into bite-sized pieces and add to the potatoes. Add the beans and peppers, season very lightly with salt and pepper, and toss to combine.

Whisk the heavy cream until it is just a bit frothy and beginning to thicken. Whisk in the mayonnaise. Add the tarragon and season with salt and pepper.

You have two options for serving here. You could pour the dressing over the salad and toss to dress, or since the salad is so pretty and colorful as is, you may want to serve it plain and pass the dressing in a sauceboat. We sometimes spoon the salad onto a bed of Bibb lettuce leaves and nap the dressing over the top. Once the salad is dressed, serve it. Undressed, it can be chilled for several hours.

RED POTATO SALAD
WITH CAPERS AND DILL

This zesty salad makes a fine alternative to boiled potatoes as a side for salmon or other fish. In place of the rich sour cream normally used, we've used yogurt, which is lower in fat, draining it first to get a thicker, creamier texture.

²/₃ cup plain yogurt
1¹/₂ pounds smallish red potatoes, scrubbed
Coarse salt
2 tablespoons mayonnaise or sour cream
2 teaspoons Dijon mustard
2 tablespoons fresh lemon juice
Freshly ground black pepper
2 large eggs, hard-cooked (see page 127) and coarsely chopped
4–5 whole scallions, chopped
3 tablespoons capers, rinsed and drained
1 cucumber, peeled, seeded, and chopped
1 heaping tablespoon chopped fresh dill

Spoon the yogurt into a fine sieve and set it over a bowl to drain for 2 to 3 hours. (If you don't have a fine sieve, line a strainer with paper towels.)

Put the potatoes in a saucepan, cover with cold water by at least an inch, add a good pinch of salt, and bring to a boil. Reduce the heat to medium, cover partway, and cook until the potatoes are tender. Drain the potatoes on a rack set in the sink and leave them to cool.

Whisk the drained yogurt in a large salad bowl with the mayonnaise, the mustard, and lemon juice. Season with salt and pepper.

Cut the potatoes in halves or quarters, depending on their size. Add them to the dressing, along with the eggs, scallions, capers, cucumber, and dill. Stir to combine. Taste for salt and pepper.

Chill for an hour or so before serving. Serve within a day of being made.

CRESS AND POTATO SALAD

This is a good winter salad. You can make the potato portion ahead and keep it covered in the refrigerator, but don't dress the greens until right before you're ready to serve.

To make your own crème fraîche, combine 1 cup heavy cream with 2 tablespoons buttermilk. Cover and leave in a warm spot in the kitchen for at least 6 hours, until it's very thick. It will keep for about a week in the refrigerator.

1 pound waxy potatoes, scrubbed
Coarse salt
Generous 1/2 cup paper-thin radish slices
1/2 cup crème fraîche
4 teaspoons Dijon mustard
About 4 cups trimmed watercress
2 tablespoons olive oil
1 tablespoon fresh lemon juice
Freshly ground black pepper

Put the potatoes in a saucepan, cover with cold water by at least an inch, add a good pinch of salt, and bring to a boil. Cover partway, reduce the heat to medium, and cook until the potatoes are very tender. Drain on a rack set in the sink and allow to cool in a single layer.

Peel the potatoes and cut them into 1/3-inch dice. Transfer to a mixing bowl and add the radishes. Whisk the crème fraîche and mustard together and scrape into the potatoes. Toss well.

Toss the watercress with the oil, lemon juice, and salt and pepper. Pile the greens on a platter, mound the potatoes on top, and serve.

SOUR CREAM AND CARAWAY POTATO SALAD

The sour cream and caraway make this potato salad a great accompaniment to roast pork. There's no reason to think of potato salad as just picnic food, right?

1½ pounds yellow-fleshed potatoes (new, if possible), scrubbed
Coarse salt
3 slices bacon
¼ cup very thinly sliced radishes
2 scallions, white parts only, minced

FOR THE DRESSING
1 teaspoon caraway seeds
½ cup sour cream
⅓ cup mayonnaise
2 teaspoons cider vinegar
½ teaspoon sugar
Coarse salt and freshly ground black pepper

2 large eggs, hard-cooked (see page 127), for garnish (optional)

Put the potatoes in a large saucepan, cover with cold water by at least an inch, add a good pinch of salt, and bring to a boil. Cover partway, reduce the heat to medium, and cook until the potatoes are tender. Drain on a rack set in the sink and leave the potatoes there to cool.

While the potatoes are cooking, fry the bacon until very crisp; drain it on paper towels.

Peel the potatoes and cut them into ⅓-inch cubes. Drop them into a mixing bowl, separating any that stick together as you go. Crumble in the bacon and add the radishes and scallions.

FOR THE DRESSING: Crush the caraway seeds slightly with the flat of a knife or in a mortar; transfer to a bowl. Whisk in the remaining ingredients and scrape the dressing into the mixing bowl.

Fold the salad and dressing together and let sit for at least 30 minutes.

If you want, garnish the salad with wedges of hard-cooked eggs. This will keep for up to 2 days, but bring it out of the refrigerator at least 30 minutes before serving.

SOUR CREAM POTATO SALAD WITH HAM

SERVES 6

The sour cream dressing gives this salad an appealingly sharp edge.
You should experiment with variations for the ham. Black Forest is
wonderful here, but so too is country ham and even smoked turkey.
But boiled ham just won't cut it.

2 pounds yellow-fleshed potatoes, scrubbed
Coarse salt
1/2 pound good smoked ham (see note above)
3 large eggs, hard-cooked (see page 127)
2 whole scallions, minced
1 small white onion, minced
2 tablespoons chopped roasted red pepper (see page 133) or
    pimiento (use the jarred stuff)
2 tablespoons chopped flat-leaf parsley
Freshly ground black pepper
3/4 cup sour cream
2 tablespoons white wine vinegar
2 tablespoons Dijon mustard
1 tablespoon fresh lemon juice

Put the potatoes in a large saucepan, cover with cold water by at least an inch,
add a good pinch of salt, and bring to a boil. Cover partway, reduce the heat to
medium, and cook until the potatoes are tender. Drain on a rack set in the sink
and leave them there to cool to room temperature.

Peel the potatoes and cut them into medium chunks. Drop them into a
mixing bowl as you go, separating any that stick together. Cut the ham into
matchsticks and add it to the potatoes. Coarsely chop the eggs and add them,
along with the scallions, onion, roasted pepper, parsley, and some salt and pepper. Toss.

Whisk the sour cream, vinegar, mustard, lemon juice, and salt and pepper to taste in a small bowl until smooth. Scrape it into the salad, fold it in with a big rubber scraper, and let the salad sit for 30 minutes.

You can make this in advance and refrigerate it, but let it come to room temperature before you serve it.

PINK POTATO SALAD

This is a very simple salad with great flavor. The beets bleed into the dressing and dye it a shocking, vibrant color. Use any waxy potato here. And don't throw those beet greens away. Use them in a green salad if they're young and tender, or sauté them in butter and season with salt, pepper, and a splash of vinegar.

4 beets
Coarse salt and freshly ground black pepper
Olive oil
1–1 1/2 pounds new red-skinned potatoes, scrubbed
3/4 cup sour cream
2 tablespoons chopped fresh dill
1/2 teaspoon grated lemon zest

Heat the oven to 400 degrees.

Trim the greens from the beets, leaving an inch or two of stem. Scrub the beets well, then put them on a large piece of heavy-duty aluminum foil (or a couple of layers of regular-weight foil). Sprinkle with salt and pepper and drizzle with olive oil. Wrap the beets in the foil, sealing securely, and bake until tender, about 1 hour. When the beets are done, open the foil packet (careful: they're hot) and let the beets cool slightly.

Meanwhile, put the potatoes in a large saucepan, cover with cold water by at least an inch, add a big pinch of salt, and bring to a boil. Cover partway, reduce the heat to medium, and cook until the potatoes are tender. Drain on a rack set in the sink and let the potatoes sit there until they're just cool enough to handle. Both the beets and the potatoes should still be pretty warm when you dress them.

Peel the potatoes if you like and cut them into 1-inch pieces. Drop the pieces into a mixing bowl. Peel the beets (the skins should slip right off; use paper towels if you don't want to dye your fingers) and cut them into pieces the same size as the potatoes. Add the beets to the potatoes. Spoon in the sour cream, add 1 tablespoon of the dill, the lemon zest, and salt and pepper. Fold thoroughly, and let cool. Cover the salad and chill for about 1 hour before serving.

Garnish with the remaining 1 tablespoon dill. This salad doesn't keep particularly well; use it within a day for maximum impact.

POTATO SALAD
WITH SWEET PICKLES AND BUTTERMILK DRESSING

SERVES 6

The dressing for this salad was inspired by the classic sauce gribiche, in which hard-cooked egg yolks are sieved and used in place of raw yolks to make a mayonnaise-style dressing. Buttermilk lightens and makes it tangy.

It's great with ribs or other barbecue, with hamburgers or hot dogs. It's at its finest when made at least 2 hours ahead, so it's a good picnic salad. We like it with homemade bread-and-butter pickles.

2 pounds Yukon Gold or white potatoes, scrubbed
Coarse salt
2 large eggs, hard-cooked (see page 127)
1 tablespoon white wine vinegar
1 tablespoon juice from the pickle jar
2 teaspoons Dijon mustard
1/2 cup vegetable oil
1/2 cup buttermilk
Freshly ground black pepper
1 small bunch radishes, trimmed, and coarsely grated (about 1 cup)
1/3–1/2 cup chopped sweet pickles
3 tablespoons chopped flat-leaf parsley

Put the potatoes in a saucepan, cover with cold water by at least an inch, add a big pinch of salt, and bring to a boil. Reduce the heat to medium, cover partway, and cook until the potatoes are just tender. Drain the potatoes on a rack set in the sink.

Separate the yolks from the whites of the hard-cooked eggs. Chop the whites and drop them into a mixing bowl. Push the yolks through a fine-mesh sieve into a food processor. Add the vinegar, pickle juice, and mustard and process into a paste. With the machine running slowly, drizzle in the oil until the dressing is smooth and well homogenized. Pour in the buttermilk in the same manner, and season with salt and pepper.

When the potatoes are cool enough to handle, peel and cut them into bite-sized chunks. Drop the potatoes into the mixing bowl with the egg whites and pour in the dressing. Toss to combine.

Add the radishes, pickles, and parsley and toss again. Season to taste. Cover and refrigerate for at least 2 hours so the potatoes absorb the flavors of the dressing.

Just before serving, toss again and taste for seasoning.

HERB GARDEN POTATO SALAD

Please, please experiment with this recipe and make it your own. It's a French-style salad—the potatoes are sprinkled with wine while they're still hot and later dressed with vinaigrette flavored with lots of fresh herbs. Use what you have on hand or what you like best.

Here are a few guidelines: use waxy or medium-starch potatoes (no russets); alter the acid in the vinaigrette as you like but keep the acid-to-oil ratio; use discretion with tough herbs like rosemary and strong herbs like tarragon; and keep the parsley constant.

1 1/2 pounds white potatoes, scrubbed
Coarse salt
3 tablespoons dry white wine or dry vermouth

FOR THE VINAIGRETTE
1 teaspoon Dijon mustard
2 tablespoons red wine vinegar
Coarse salt and freshly ground black pepper
3 tablespoons olive oil

1/3 cup chopped mixed fresh mint and basil
1/3 cup chopped flat-leaf parsley
Freshly ground black pepper

Put the potatoes in a large saucepan, cover with cold water by at least an inch, add a big pinch of salt, and bring to a boil. Cover partway, reduce the heat to medium, and cook until the potatoes are tender. Drain on a rack set in the sink.

As soon as the potatoes are cool enough to handle (it's best if you do this sooner rather than later, so hold them in a towel), peel them and slice them into rounds that are about ⅓ inch thick; spread them out in a bowl and sprinkle them with some of the wine as you go. Let cool completely.

FOR THE VINAIGRETTE: Combine the mustard and vinegar with salt and pepper to taste in a small bowl. Gradually whisk in the oil to make an emulsion.

Add the herbs to the potatoes and season with salt and pepper. Pour in the vinaigrette and fold thoroughly, trying to break as few of the slices as possible (some damage is inevitable). Leave this to sit on the counter for 30 minutes before serving.

This salad will keep for a day or so, but it's not meant to be served cold. If you've refrigerated it, let it come back to room temperature.

VARIATION

To send you on your way experimenting, here's another combination of herbs and dressing. Use yellow-fleshed potatoes instead of white. For the mixed herbs, use a combination of thyme, lemon thyme, and chives. Substitute lemon juice for the vinegar in the dressing, and add about 1 teaspoon grated lemon zest.

RED POTATO SALAD WITH BACON AND CHIVES

SERVES 4

The touch of honey and cider vinegar in the dressing works great with the crispy, smoky bacon. We found inspiration in a recipe by California chef John Ash when we made this salad. John finishes the salad by crumbling in a few ounces of Maytag Blue cheese.

1½ pounds red-skinned potatoes, scrubbed
Coarse salt
1 shallot, minced
1 teaspoon Dijon mustard
1 teaspoon honey
1 teaspoon grated lemon zest
2 tablespoons cider vinegar
6 tablespoons olive oil
Freshly ground black pepper
2 tablespoons chopped fresh chives
4 slices bacon, cooked till crisp and crumbled

Put the potatoes in a saucepan, cover with cold water by at least an inch, add a good pinch of salt, and bring to a boil. Reduce the heat to medium, cover partway, and cook until the potatoes are tender. Drain the potatoes and leave them to cool in a single layer on a rack set in the sink.

Combine the shallot, mustard, honey, lemon zest, and vinegar in a salad bowl. Whisk in the oil and season with salt and pepper.

When the potatoes are cool, peel and cut them into fork-sized chunks. Drop them into the bowl with the dressing and toss. Season with salt and pepper.

Chill the salad for an hour or so.

Just before serving, sprinkle the salad with the chives and bacon. (The salad can be made a day in advance, but add the chives and bacon only at the last minute.)

WARM POTATO SALAD WITH OLIVES AND LEMON

Russets are about the only kind of potato that won't work in this salad. Yellow Finns make a great-looking salad, but this is also a good place to use heirlooms like Ruby Crescents or Desirees or Red Golds. Don't peel them; just cut them in half (cut fingerlings lengthwise) once they're cooked.

$1^{1}/_{2}$ pounds yellow-fleshed potatoes, scrubbed
Coarse salt
2 tablespoons dry vermouth
$^{1}/_{2}$ cup Kalamata olives, pitted
2 red scallions, bottoms with some green, chopped (you can substitute
    4 whole regular scallions)
1 lemon
Freshly ground black pepper
2 tablespoons olive oil
Coarse sea salt

Put the potatoes in a saucepan, cover with cold water by at least an inch, add a good pinch of salt, and bring to a boil. Cover partway, reduce the heat to medium, and cook until the potatoes are tender. Drain on a rack set in the sink and let the potatoes sit until just cool enough to handle. You need them warm, so proceed quickly and use a towel to protect your hand if you need to.

Peel the potatoes and cut into thick slices, about $^{1}/_{2}$ inch. As you finish each one, put it in a mixing bowl and sprinkle with some of the vermouth. Add the olives and scallions and grate in the zest of the lemon. Cut all the white pith from the lemon and use a small sharp knife to cut the lemon segments from between the membranes. Add the lemon segments to the salad. Season with pepper and drizzle in the olive oil.

Transfer the salad to a serving platter and sprinkle with sea salt. Let it sit for 20 minutes or so, and serve.

GERMAN POTATO SALAD

SERVES 6

This is a real favorite. The warm potatoes are dressed with stock and left to sit and drink it up. The salad is unctuous with the bacon fat, offset by a little bit of vinegar.

Go to the butcher and get slab bacon for this. You want it meaty, and you want it sliced thick.

2¹/₂ pounds Charlottes or other yellow-fleshed potatoes, scrubbed
Coarse salt
¹/₂ pound best-quality bacon, chopped
1 onion, chopped medium-fine
¹/₂ cup Beef Stock (page 115)
Freshly ground black pepper
1 tablespoon red wine vinegar
3–4 tablespoons chopped flat-leaf parsley
3 or 4 radishes, thinly sliced (optional)

Put the potatoes in a saucepan, cover with cold water by at least an inch, add a good pinch of salt, and bring to a boil. Reduce the heat to medium, cover partway, and cook until the potatoes are tender. Drain the potatoes on a rack in the sink and leave to cool briefly in a single layer.

Just before the potatoes are done, cook the bacon in a skillet over medium heat until browned. Remove the bits with a slotted spoon—leave the fat in the skillet—and combine the bacon with the onion in a small bowl. Bring the stock to a simmer in a small saucepan.

Peel the potatoes while they're still hot (hold them in a towel if you have to). Thinly slice them, and layer in a wide bowl. Once you have a layer of potatoes, season with salt and pepper and strew some of the bacon and onion on top. Keep repeating the layering. When you've finished, heat the bacon fat and pour it over the potatoes.

Add the vinegar to the stock and pour it over the potatoes. Toss gently, trying not to break up the potato slices too much. Let the salad sit for 15 minutes or so, until it absorbs the dressing.

Sprinkle with the parsley, garnish with the radishes if desired, and serve. This really needs to be warm, or at least at room temperature. If you have leftovers that you've refrigerated, let them sit out for at least 45 minutes before serving.

POTATOES AND STRING BEANS

Make sure to cook the beans all the way through. They should be very tender, not at all crunchy; after all, this is Grandma cooking of the Italian-American brand. This salad should be served icy-cold.

1 pound red-skinned potatoes, scrubbed
Coarse salt
3 garlic cloves
3/4 pound mixed green and wax beans, topped, tailed, and cut into 1-inch lengths
1/4 cup olive oil
3 tablespoons red wine vinegar
2 large eggs, hard-cooked (page 127) and sliced
Freshly ground black pepper

Put the potatoes in a pot, cover with cold water by at least an inch, add a good pinch of salt and 1 of the garlic cloves, and bring to a boil. Reduce the heat to medium, cover partway, and cook until the potatoes are very tender. Drain the potatoes on a rack in the sink; discard the garlic.

Meanwhile, bring a few cups of water to a boil. Add the beans and salt and cook until the beans are very tender, 8 to 10 minutes. Drain them, dump them into a bowl of ice water for a minute or so, and drain well. Dry the beans on paper towels.

Cut the potatoes into chunks while they are still warm. Cut the remaining 2 garlic cloves into the thinnest slices possible.

Combine the potatoes with the garlic, beans, oil, vinegar, eggs, and pepper. Toss well, check the salt and pepper, cover, and chill for at least 2 hours before serving.

MOLDAVIAN POTATO SALAD WITH FETA

SERVES 4

We adapted this vibrant, gutsy, and very pretty salad from *Please to the Table* by Anya von Bremzen. The feta and dill offer a great contrast to the mild potatoes.

1½ pounds small red or white waxy potatoes, scrubbed
Coarse salt
¼ cup olive oil, plus more as needed
1 small garlic clove, minced
Freshly ground black pepper
4 whole scallions, chopped
½ cup crumbled feta
⅓ cup chopped Kalamata olives
2 tablespoons chopped fresh dill
1 tablespoon red wine vinegar

Put the potatoes in a saucepan, cover with cold water by at least an inch, add a good pinch of salt, and bring to a boil. Reduce the heat to medium, cover partway, and cook until the potatoes are tender. Drain the potatoes on a rack set in the sink and let cool slightly in a single layer.

As soon as the potatoes are cool enough to handle, peel and cut into ½-inch pieces. Drop them into a mixing bowl and pour on the olive oil. Add the garlic, season with salt and pepper, and toss gently to combine. Be careful not to break up the potatoes.

Once the potatoes have cooled to room temperature, add the scallions, feta, olives, dill, and vinegar. Season with salt and pepper. If the salad appears dry, add a bit more olive oil.

Serve at room temperature, or cover with plastic and refrigerate overnight. Let the salad sit out for about 20 minutes before serving.

SICILIAN POTATO SALAD
(INSALATA COTTA CLASSICA)

SERVES 4 TO 6

Inspiration here comes from cooking teacher Anna Tasca Lanza, in the heart of Sicily. It's really the kind of dish that you make with whatever vegetables are freshest. Peas would be nice, or sliced artichoke bottoms, and so would a mix of green and wax beans. The whole onions cooked with the potatoes are a pleasant surprise, since they mellow. This is a case where a fresh herb won't taste the same: get the best dried oregano you can find (I like Mediterranean).

3 tablespoons red wine vinegar
1 teaspoon dried oregano
Coarse salt and freshly ground black pepper
$^1\!/_4$ cup plus 1 teaspoon olive oil
1 pound fava beans in the pod
$^1\!/_2$ pound green beans
1$^1\!/_2$ pounds new potatoes (red-skinned or yellow-fleshed), scrubbed
2 red onions, washed but left unpeeled
$^1\!/_4$ cup chopped fresh herbs (such as flat-leaf parsley, basil, and thyme)

Combine the vinegar and oregano with salt and pepper in a bowl and whisk in $^1\!/_4$ cup of the olive oil until emulsified. Let the dressing sit while you prepare the salad.

Bring a small pot of water to a boil while you pop the favas from their pods. Drop the favas into the water and blanch them for about a minute. Drain them and run them under cold water, then slip them from their tough skins into a little bowl. Drizzle them with the remaining 1 teaspoon oil.

Top and tail the green beans, halve them, and slice them in half the long way. They call this "Frenching," and while it may seem fussy, it actually means you're less likely to encounter raw green beans in your salad. Bring a pot of water to a boil, salt it, and drop the beans in bit by bit, so you don't lower the temperature of the water too abruptly. Boil the beans until tender, 6 to 7 minutes. Drain them, run them under cold water, and dry them well on a kitchen towel or paper towels.

Meanwhile, put the potatoes and onions in a pot, cover with cold water by at least an inch, add a good pinch of salt, and bring to a boil. Cover partway, reduce the heat to medium, and cook until the potatoes are very tender. Drain on a rack set in the sink and leave them there until they're barely cool enough to handle.

Peel the potatoes—hold them in a towel if you need to—and cut them into cubes, say, 1/3 inch. Drop them into a mixing bowl. Peel the onions and cut them into wedges. Add the onions to the bowl, along with the favas and green beans. Give the dressing another whisk to freshen it, then drizzle it over the salad. Fold in the dressing, then add the herbs and fold again. Try not to break up the potatoes too much.

Let the salad sit for about 30 minutes, and serve it warm. It really doesn't benefit from refrigeration.

POTATO SALAD WITH TOMATOES AND CAPERS
(INSALATA PANTASCA)

SERVES 4 TO 6

Insalata pantasca is the potato and tomato salad of Pantelleria, a small, poor island near Sicily that is famous for its capers. Big, fat capers, full of flavor and packed in salt. Like any local recipe, this has as many variations as there are cooks. The fish that you would find in the Pantelleria salad, however, is something you can't locate in this country. I like sardines in it; you might try something different, such as smoked trout.

You wouldn't find yellow-fleshed potatoes on the island, but I love their flavor in this salad. The more traditional choices would be whites, or red-skinned—something on the waxy side.

1½ pounds yellow-fleshed potatoes, scrubbed
Coarse salt
1 pint cherry tomatoes, halved (quartered if very large)
1 small red onion, thinly sliced
⅓ cup oil-cured black olives, pitted and halved
2 tablespoons salted capers, well rinsed and drained
⅓ cup chopped flat-leaf parsley
Pinch of crushed red pepper
1 teaspoon dried oregano
¼ cup olive oil
1 (3.75-ounce) can sardines in olive oil (see note above)

Put the potatoes in a pot, cover with cold water by at least an inch, add a good pinch of salt, and bring to a boil. Cover partway, reduce the heat to medium, and cook until the potatoes are tender. Drain on a rack set in the sink and leave them there until cool enough to handle.

Peel the potatoes and cut them into $1/3$-inch cubes. Drop them into a mixing bowl, separating the cubes as you go. Add the tomatoes, onion, olives, capers, parsley, and crushed red pepper. Toss gently. Crumble the oregano over the top, pour in the oil, and toss gently.

Transfer the salad to a large serving dish. Drain the sardines and blot them with paper towels, them arrange them over the salad. Let this sit for 30 minutes, and serve it at room temperature.

POTATO SALAD
WITH PASSATA

Passata—the dressing for this salad—is the purest of tomato sauces, just fresh tomatoes and a bit of salt, cooked until softened, then strained and cooked down until it makes a sauce. You will have some leftover *passata*. Use it on spaghetti, with a drizzle of extra-virgin olive oil and some torn basil leaves.

If you can find heirloom varieties of cherry tomatoes at your farmers' market, by all means buy them for the salad.

FOR THE PASSATA
3 pounds plum tomatoes
Coarse salt

1½ pounds red-skinned potatoes, scrubbed
Coarse salt
½ pint cherry tomatoes, halved
1–2 tablespoons extra-virgin olive oil
2 tablespoons chopped fresh chives

FOR THE PASSATA: Break the plum tomatoes in half and put them in a saucepan with a good pinch of salt. Cover partway and cook over medium-high heat until the tomatoes have collapsed and softened, about 25 minutes. Stir and scrape the bottom so the tomatoes don't stick.

Put the tomatoes through a food mill fitted with the fine disk, wipe out the pan, and return the tomato puree to it. Cook over medium heat, stirring occasionally, until thickened and reduced almost by half, about 45 minutes.

Put the potatoes in a saucepan, cover with cold water by at least an inch, add a good pinch of salt, and bring to a boil. Cover partway, reduce the heat to medium, and cook until the potatoes are very tender. Drain the potatoes on a rack set in the sink and allow to cool slightly in a single layer.

Smear about ½ cup of the passata on a serving platter. Slice the potatoes (peel them if you care to) and layer them over the sauce. Spoon 1 cup of the passata over the potatoes. Be casual about it—you're not icing a cake. Scatter the cherry tomatoes over the potatoes. Drizzle with the oil and garnish with the chives.

The salad can sit for a couple of hours before serving. It wants to be at room temperature.

POTATO AND CHICKPEA SALAD
WITH TAMARIND DRESSING

(CHAAT)

Refreshing and exciting may be the best words to describe this Indian salad from cooking teacher Samia Ahad. Bring it out at a picnic, or let it dress up a simple roast chicken.

The recipe calls for all-purpose potatoes, but there's no reason you can't make it with heirloom varieties.

3/4 pound all-purpose potatoes, scrubbed
Coarse salt
1 (3-inch) hunk of tamarind

FOR THE SPICED SALT
3 tablespoons cumin seeds
1 tablespoon black peppercorns
1 tablespoon coarse salt

1 (19-ounce) can chickpeas, drained and rinsed
1 plum tomato, chopped
1 small onion, chopped
3 green chiles, minced
2 tablespoons chopped cilantro leaves

Put the potatoes in a saucepan, cover with cold water by at least an inch, add a pinch of salt, and bring to a boil. Cover partway, reduce the heat to medium, and cook until the potatoes are tender. Drain on a rack set in the sink and leave them there to cool completely.

Break up the tamarind and put it in a heatproof bowl. Pour in 1/2 cup boiling water and let it sit for about 15 minutes to soften. Push as much of the pulp as you can through a coarse wire sieve (scrape off what's clinging to the outside) and discard what's left in the strainer.

FOR THE SPICED SALT: Heat a small skillet over high heat until it's good and hot. Add the cumin seeds and toast them until light brown and fragrant. Pour them into a spice grinder or mortar, add the peppercorns, and reduce to a fine powder. Pour into a small jar, add the salt, and shake well to combine. (This will keep, tightly covered, for months.)

Peel the potatoes and cut them into $1/2$-inch cubes. Combine with the chickpeas, tomato, onion, chiles, and cilantro.

Measure out 3 tablespoons of the tamarind pulp and stir in 1 tablespoon spiced salt. Scrape this dressing over the salad and toss it well.

You can serve this right away, but it will taste even better if you let it sit for 30 minutes or so.

SALADE NIÇOISE

The constants of salade niçoise are the tomatoes, olives, anchovies, and a garlic-based vinaigrette. From there, you can pretty much take this where you want. For us, boiled baby potatoes are mandatory. Canned tuna (packed in olive oil), blanched green beans, and hard-cooked eggs are also favorites. Other possibilities are artichoke hearts, red bell peppers—roasted or raw—and fresh herbs such as tarragon, basil, or parsley. Just keep in mind that in the words of British food writer Elizabeth David, a salade niçoise "should be a rough country salad, rather than a fussy chef's concoction."

This makes a fine first course; it's also plenty for a lunch or light supper.

FOR THE DRESSING
1 garlic clove, minced
1 tablespoon Dijon mustard
3 tablespoons white or red wine vinegar
Coarse salt and freshly ground black pepper
3/4 cup olive oil

FOR THE SALAD
1 pound small red potatoes, scrubbed and halved or quartered, depending on size
Coarse salt
1 pound green beans, topped and tailed
1 large head Boston or Bibb lettuce, leaves separated
2 (6-ounce) cans oil-packed tuna, drained and flaked
2 ripe tomatoes, cut into wedges
3 large eggs, hard-cooked (see page 127) and cut into wedges
6–10 anchovy fillets
2 tablespoons capers, rinsed and drained
1/2 cup niçoise or other good-quality black olives

FOR THE DRESSING: Whisk the garlic with the mustard and vinegar in a small bowl. Season with salt and pepper. Gradually begin whisking in the olive oil, a few drops at a time, until the dressing starts to thicken. Continue whisking, pouring in the oil in a slow, steady stream. Taste for salt and pepper.

FOR THE SALAD: Put the potatoes in a large saucepan, cover with cold water by several inches, and add a good pinch of salt. Cover partway and bring to a boil; reduce the heat to medium and cook until the potatoes are tender. Remove the potatoes with a slotted spoon and place on a rack set in the sink to cool.

Return the cooking water to high heat and bring back to a boil. Plunge the beans into the water and cook until bright green but still crisp, about 3 minutes. Drain and refresh under cold water. Drain again. Lay on towels to dry.

There are two ways to serve this salad: arranged on individual plates or composed on a large platter for a buffet. Either way, you want to place the elements in neat heaps, alternating the red-skinned potatoes with the green beans, the red tomatoes with the white and yellow eggs, and so forth. Finally, the whole thing gets garnished with the anchovies, olives, and capers.

First, line the plates or platter with lettuce. Drizzle with a bit of dressing. Toss the potatoes and beans separately with enough dressing to just coat them. Arrange them on top of the lettuce. Put the tuna into a bowl and season it with a few tablespoons of dressing. Spoon it onto the salad. Arrange the tomato wedges and eggs on the salad. Garnish with the anchovies, capers, and olives. Drizzle with a little more dressing and serve. Pass the remaining dressing at the table.

FRESH TUNA SALAD WITH POTATOES AND HERBS

SERVES 4

This is a looser, uncomposed version of a salade niçoise, with fresh tuna rather than canned. You want whole leaves of herbs for this salad. A mix of basil and parsley alone is nice, but celery leaves add a little bite.

1 pound fresh tuna
Coarse salt and freshly ground black pepper
12 basil leaves
5 tablespoons olive oil
1 pound red-skinned potatoes, scrubbed
1 tablespoon dry white wine or dry vermouth
1 1/2 cups mixed fresh basil, flat-leaf parsley, and celery leaves
2 teaspoons Dijon mustard
2 tablespoons white wine vinegar
1 red bell pepper, roasted (see page 133) and cut into strips
6 anchovy fillets
2 large eggs, hard-cooked (see page 127) and cut into wedges
1 ripe tomato, cut into wedges

Sprinkle the tuna with salt and pepper. Place on a plate, cover with the basil leaves, drizzle with 2 tablespoons of the oil, and leave it to marinate for about 30 minutes, turning it over once or twice.

Put the potatoes in a saucepan, cover with cold water by at least an inch, add a good pinch of salt, and bring to a boil. Reduce the heat to medium, cover partway, and cook until very tender. Drain the potatoes on a rack in the sink.

While the potatoes are still warm, cut them into chunks, place in a mixing bowl, and drizzle with the wine.

Heat a cast-iron stovetop grill pan over high heat. Brush the basil off the tuna and sear the tuna for 1 1/2 minutes on each side. Cut the tuna into chunks and add to the potatoes, along with the herbs.

Combine the mustard, vinegar, and salt and pepper to taste in a small bowl. Whisk in the remaining 3 tablespoons olive oil.

Add the vinaigrette to the salad, toss well, and pile it on a serving platter. Garnish prettily with the roasted pepper, anchovies, eggs, and tomato.

ROASTED POTATO AND ASPARAGUS SALAD

This salad started with my sister Marie, who hates mayonnaise and loves lemony vinaigrette. Her version features boiled potatoes, and she adds canned artichoke hearts. Me, I like this variation, with everything roasted. But you'll see how adaptable it is.

1½ pounds yellow-fleshed potatoes, peeled
1 large red onion
3 tablespoons olive oil
Coarse salt and freshly ground black pepper
1 pound asparagus, trimmed

FOR THE VINAIGRETTE
1 tablespoon minced shallot
1 garlic clove, minced
1 teaspoon Dijon mustard
3 tablespoons fresh lemon juice
Coarse salt and freshly ground black pepper
¼ cup olive oil

Heat the oven to 400 degrees.

Cut the potatoes in half lengthwise, then into ½-inch slices. Halve the onion, then cut it into ½-inch slices. Toss the potatoes and onion with 2 tablespoons of the olive oil and salt and pepper to taste on a baking sheet (there's no reason to dirty a bowl). Bake for 15 minutes, turn over with a spatula, and bake for another 15 minutes, or until the potatoes are tender (the tip of a knife will easily pierce them) and starting to brown.

Meanwhile, if the asparagus stalks are thick, you might want to peel them. Cut them into 2-inch lengths, toss with the remaining 1 tablespoon olive oil and some salt and bake them on a second sheet along with the potatoes. They will take about 20 minutes to roast.

MEANWHILE, FOR THE VINAIGRETTE: Combine the shallot, garlic, mustard, lemon juice, and salt and pepper in a bowl. Gradually whisk in the oil to make an emulsion. Or, if you want a very creamy and smooth dressing, make it in a mini food processor.

When the vegetables are done, scrape them into a mixing bowl and toss with 3 tablespoons of the vinaigrette while they're still hot. Let the salad sit for 30 minutes or so.

Taste for salt and pepper, check to see if you need or want more dressing, and serve. I think this is best at room temperature on the day it's made. But if you have leftovers, take them out of the refrigerator 45 minutes before you eat them.

GRILLED POTATO SALAD

If you want this salad to truly shine, you need *new,* meaning young, freshly dug potatoes, but any smallish red-skinned spuds will do as long as you parboil them first. Cut them into 1-inch chunks and boil in salted water for 4 to 5 minutes, until they start to soften. Real new potatoes don't need to be precooked.

1½ pounds baby new potatoes, scrubbed and halved (unless tiny)
3 tablespoons olive oil, plus more as needed
2 teaspoons fresh thyme leaves
Coarse salt and freshly ground black pepper
3 small red onions (about 1 pound), cut into ½-inch rounds

FOR THE VINAIGRETTE
1 teaspoon Dijon mustard
3 tablespoons white wine vinegar
Coarse salt and freshly ground black pepper
6 tablespoons olive oil

½ cup chopped mixed fresh herbs (choose from flat-leaf parsley, tarragon, dill, chervil, basil, and/or chives)

Prepare a grill and bank the coals to one side; you want a cooler area to grill the potatoes and onions.

Toss the potatoes with 2 tablespoons of the oil, the thyme, and salt and pepper. If the potatoes are so small as to risk slipping through the grill grate, slide them onto skewers. Stick the onion rounds with toothpicks to secure them so the rings don't separate during grilling. Brush the onions with the remaining 1 tablespoon oil and season with salt and pepper. Grill the potatoes and onions on the cooler area of the grill, turning occasionally, until browned on the outside and very tender inside, 10 to 15 minutes

MEANWHILE, FOR THE VINAIGRETTE: Whisk together the mustard, vinegar, and salt and pepper to taste in a medium bowl. Slowly whisk in the olive oil and taste for seasoning.

When the vegetables are done, remove the toothpicks from the onions, and slip the potatoes off the skewers if you used them. Toss the onions and potatoes with the vinaigrette until well coated. Toss with the herbs and taste for salt and pepper. Serve warm or at room temperature.

MUSSELS AND POTATOES

Here's a good first-course salad, one to make ahead and leave out covered on the counter until dinnertime. Using the reduced mussel liquor packs the potatoes with flavor. As with any salad, the better the potato, the better the flavor. Larger medium-starch heirlooms (like Estimas and French Fingerlings) shine here, but if they're not available, use whites or yellow-fleshed.

1 celery stalk, finely chopped
1 small onion, thinly sliced
1 small carrot, minced
3 tablespoons olive oil
Coarse salt
1 cup dry vermouth or dry white wine
2 pounds mussels, scrubbed and debearded
1½ pounds potatoes (see note above), scrubbed
1 teaspoon grated lemon zest
1 tablespoon fresh lemon juice
Freshly ground black pepper
¼ cup flat-leaf parsley leaves

Put the celery, onion, and carrot in a wide saucepan. Add 1 tablespoon of the oil and a pinch of salt and cook over medium heat until the vegetables are softened and just starting to become golden at the edges, about 7 minutes. Pour in the vermouth, increase the heat to medium-high, and bring to a boil. Add the mussels, cover, and cook until the mussels open, about 3 minutes. Scoop the mussels out with a slotted spoon and let them cool. Strain the broth through a fine sieve into a bowl (discard the solids) and let the broth sit for a few minutes to settle.

Rinse out the pan and pour most of the broth back in, leaving any grit behind. Bring it to a boil over high heat and reduce it by half.

Meanwhile, put the potatoes in a saucepan, cover with cold water by at least an inch, add a good pinch of salt, and bring to a boil. Cover partway, lower the heat to medium, and cook until the potatoes are just tender. Drain on a rack set in the sink. Peel the potatoes immediately—hold them with a kitchen towel or paper towels—and set them back on the rack. Once you've peeled them all, cut them into $1/3$-inch dice and drop them into a mixing bowl. Drizzle the potatoes with 5 tablespoons of the reduced mussel broth and fold gently.

Remove the mussels from their shells and add to the potatoes. Spoon in the remaining 2 tablespoons olive oil, the lemon zest and juice, a few grinds of pepper, and the parsley. Fold again, trying not to break up too many of the potatoes, and let sit for 30 minutes before serving.

SPICY GREENS WITH ROASTED POTATOES, STRING BEANS, AND HEIRLOOM TOMATOES

SERVES 4

There are a lot of flavors going on here: the nuttiness of the potato, the acid of the tomato, the bite of the peppery greens, and the tang of the dressing. It all comes together under the influence of a poached egg with its runny golden yolk.

This is a salad to make at the height of summer, when unusual greens and heirloom potatoes and tomatoes are in the markets, but it's too fine a combination to pass up if you can't find exotics. (See the variations.)

3/4 pound small heirloom potatoes (Austrian or Ruby Crescents, Nosebags, German Butterballs, and La Ratte are all good choices), scrubbed and dried
Olive oil
Coarse salt
1/2 pound green beans, topped and tailed

FOR THE VINAIGRETTE
1 teaspoon minced shallot
1/4 teaspoon dried tarragon
2 tablespoons sherry vinegar
Coarse salt and freshly ground black pepper
1/4 cup olive oil

4 handfuls spicy greens (wild watercress, red mustard, baby arugula, dandelion)
1 cup ripe currant and cherry tomatoes (try for a mix of red, yellow, and orange)
4 large eggs, poached (see page 176)

Heat the oven to 350 degrees.

Put the potatoes on a baking sheet, drizzle them with olive oil, sprinkle with salt, and toss them with your hands. Bake until they give when you pinch them, 30 to 40 minutes.

Meanwhile, bring a pot of water to a boil, add the beans and a pinch of salt, and cook, uncovered, until the beans are crisp-tender, about 7 minutes. Drain, run them under cold water, and drain again. Put the beans on a towel to dry.

FOR THE VINAIGRETTE: Combine the shallot, tarragon, vinegar, and salt and pepper to taste in a small bowl. Whisk in the oil little by little to make an emulsion.

Combine the potatoes, beans, and greens in a mixing bowl and toss well with the vinaigrette. Divide among four salad plates. Nestle the tomatoes into the salads (cut any larger ones in half for easy eating) and top each plate with a poached egg. Serve right away, and pass the salt and pepper.

VARIATIONS

You can substitute red-skinned potatoes for the heirlooms. Scrub them well and cut them into chunks. Roast them as instructed above, with oil and salt; they should take about 40 minutes.

You can make the salad with just one green, like arugula.

To improve the flavor of less-than-primo cherry tomatoes, heat a teaspoon of olive oil in a small skillet over high heat and sauté the tomatoes for 2 to 3 minutes, until the skins are glistening and the tomatoes are heated through.

POACHING EGGS

We like poached eggs and potatoes. We love sticking a fork into the soft white, then breaking the wall of the buttery yolk and seeing it run into a potato salad or corned beef hash. And we don't restrict them to breakfast or brunch, either. Potatoes and eggs are often our choice for an easy supper.

The real key to pretty poached eggs is getting truly fresh eggs. As eggs sit in your refrigerator (or in the case at the supermarket), the whites get thinner and runnier and the yolks get flatter. So, if you can, buy fresh eggs for poaching.

Heat about 3 inches of water in a deep skillet or saucepan. Add a good splash—a tablespoon or two—of white vinegar (this helps the white cling to the yolk), and bring to a simmer over medium-high heat. Crack the eggs into separate custard cups or coffee cups.

When the water is just simmering, stir it several times so it is swirling, hold the rim of each cup against the water, and slip the egg from its cup into the water, so that the eggs are side by side but not touching. You should be able to fit 4 to 6 eggs in a 10-inch skillet. Lower the heat so that the water is just barely moving—if it boils or even simmers too vigorously, the eggs will become tough and may break apart.

When the white is set and opaque but the yolk still soft, about 4 minutes, lift the eggs, one by one, from the water with a slotted spoon and slide them onto a cloth or paper towel to drain for a few seconds. If you are terribly fussy about presentation, you may want to trim off any runaway bits of egg white with a small knife. Carefully slide the eggs off the towel and onto plates to serve.

If you must poach eggs ahead or for a crowd, you can hold them in a bowl of cold water for several hours in the refrigerator. Just slide them back into a bath of simmering water for a few seconds to reheat.

PAM'S PICNIC SALAD

My colleague Pam Krauss, who runs the cookbook program at Clarkson Potter, threw this salad together with stuff from the refrigerator. It's a fine one.

SERVES 4 TO 6

1½ pounds yellow-fleshed or white potatoes, scrubbed
Coarse salt
1 pound kielbasa
1 tablespoon grainy mustard
¼ cup sherry vinegar
Freshly ground black pepper
5 tablespoons olive oil
2 large eggs, hard-cooked (see page 127) and coarsely chopped
1 small red onion, chopped
2 tablespoons fat capers, rinsed and drained
½ cup or so cooked green beans cut into 1-inch lengths
2 tablespoons chopped flat-leaf parsley

Put the potatoes in a large saucepan, cover with cold water by at least an inch, add a good pinch of salt, and bring to a boil. Cover partway, reduce the heat to medium, and cook until the potatoes are tender. Drain on a rack set in the sink and leave them there to cool slightly.

Meanwhile, heat a ridged stovetop grill pan over medium-high heat until quite hot. Slice the kielbasa lengthwise in half and grill until heated through. Or steam for 8 to 10 minutes. Cut into ¼-inch slices and keep warm.

Whisk the mustard and vinegar together in a large bowl with some salt and pepper. Gradually whisk in the oil to make an emulsion. Then add the eggs, onion, and capers and mix very well. The egg yolks will melt into the dressing.

Cut the potatoes into nice-sized chunks while still warm (Pam doesn't peel them) and add them to the dressing, with the kielbasa and beans. Toss well.

Transfer the salad to a nice bowl or platter, sprinkle with the parsley, and serve warm or at room temperature.

ROASTED SWEET POTATO SALAD WITH ORANGE MARMALADE DRESSING

Sweets can be used to make some pretty good salads. This is sort of a cross between a chutney and a Waldorf salad. Serve small portions as a colorful and spirited condiment or accompaniment to roast pork, grilled meats, or sandwiches. You need marmalade made with Seville oranges for this salad.

1½–1¾ pounds sweet potatoes, peeled and cut into ⅓-inch chunks
1 tablespoon vegetable oil
Coarse salt
⅓ cup pecans, chopped (walnuts would be okay too)
1 teaspoon grated orange zest
½ cup fresh orange juice
⅓ cup sultana raisins (or golden raisins)
3 tablespoons bitter-orange marmalade
1 or 2 celery stalks, peeled and chopped
1 green apple, cored and chopped
2 heaping tablespoons mayonnaise

Heat the oven to 400 degrees.

Spread the sweet potato chunks on a large baking sheet. Drizzle with the oil, season with salt, and toss with your hands to coat. Roast, turning once or twice with a spatula, until tender and just starting to brown, about 25 minutes.

Pour the pecans onto a smaller baking sheet, spread them out, and toast lightly in the oven, about 5 minutes, while the potatoes roast.

Combine the orange zest, juice, and raisins in a small saucepan over medium heat. Simmer until the raisins are softened and the juice has reduced to only a few tablespoons, about 10 minutes. Remove from the heat and stir in the marmalade.

When the potatoes are cooked, transfer them to a large bowl. Add the celery, apple, and pecans and toss to mix. Add the mayonnaise to the orange and raisin mixture and stir to combine. Pour this dressing over the potatoes and toss gently. Taste for salt.

Serve immediately, or chill for an hour or two. This salad tastes best within a few hours of preparation.

SWEET POTATO SALAD
WITH CURRIED RED PEPPER
RELISH

What a beautiful mix of colors and textures and flavors you'll find in this salad. It's a snap to make if you've planned ahead and canned the relish.

1½–1¾ pounds sweet potatoes
¼ cup olive oil
Coarse salt
1 cup Curried Red Pepper Relish (page 181)
3 whole scallions, chopped
2 tablespoons chopped flat-leaf parsley

Heat the oven to 400 degrees.

Peel the potatoes and cut them into ½-inch cubes. Dump them on a baking sheet and toss with 1 tablespoon of the oil and some salt. Roast until the potatoes are tender and starting to brown, flipping them once with a spatula, about 25 minutes. Let the potatoes cool to room temperature.

Put the potatoes in a mixing bowl with the relish, scallions, parsley, and the remaining 3 tablespoons oil. Toss well and taste for salt. Let the salad sit for 30 minutes before you serve it.

VARIATION

You can boil the sweets if you care to. Put the cubed potatoes in a saucepan with a copious amount of cold water and a pinch of salt. Bring to a boil and cook until just tender, about 8 minutes. Drain, refresh in cold water, and drain again. Dry the potatoes well on paper towels.

CURRIED RED PEPPER RELISH

You can cut this recipe in half, which would be just enough for the salad recipe, or you can make the full amount and serve what's left with steaks and chops—or, what may be the most clever, double it and follow the instructions in a reliable canning book to preserve the relish so you have it on hand when you want it.

2 large red bell peppers, cored, seeded, and diced
1 red onion, chopped
1 jalapeño or other hot pepper, minced
1/3 cup sugar
2 teaspoons Madras curry powder (medium-hot)
1 teaspoon mustard seeds
1 teaspoon celery seeds
2/3 cup sherry vinegar

Combine all the ingredients in a saucepan and bring to a boil, stirring at the beginning to dissolve the sugar. Reduce the heat and simmer for 15 minutes, until the peppers are tender.

You can use it now, or store it, covered, in the fridge for a week.

MAIN DISHES

YOUNG CHICKEN STUFFED
WITH POTATOES AND SHIITAKE

SERVES 2

Diced potatoes mixed with wild mushrooms are used to stuff a tender, juicy chicken. Add a salad or some simply sautéed bitter greens, and you've got dinner tête-à-tête.

1/2 pound yellow-fleshed potatoes (such as Carola), scrubbed and cubed
Coarse salt
1/2 pound shiitake mushrooms
2 tablespoons unsalted butter
2 tablespoons olive oil
1/4 cup finely chopped shallot
1 teaspoon fresh thyme leaves
Freshly ground black pepper
1/4 cup dry vermouth or dry white wine
Several sprigs thyme and rosemary
1 (2 1/2-to-3-pound) chicken

Heat the oven to 400 degrees.

Put the potatoes in a large saucepan, cover with cold water, add a good pinch of salt, bring to a boil, and cook for 3 minutes. Drain the potatoes on a rack set in the sink.

Remove the stems from the mushrooms and save for another use (see note). Cut the mushrooms into pieces about the size of the potato cubes, or a bit bigger.

Heat the butter and 1 tablespoon of the olive oil in a large skillet over medium heat. Add the shallot and cook for a few minutes, until it softens. Add the shiitake and a sprinkling of salt and cook, stirring from time to time, until tender, 3 to 4 minutes. Add the potatoes, thyme leaves, and a grind or two of pepper. Cook for a minute or so, then add the vermouth and cook, stirring, until it has almost evaporated, about 1 minute. Check the seasonings and set aside to cool.

Carefully stick some thyme and rosemary sprigs under the skin of the chicken (carefully, so you don't tear the skin). Season inside and out with salt and pepper and rub with the remaining 1 tablespoon olive oil. Place some additional herb sprigs in the bottom of a large cast-iron skillet. Place the chicken on top of them and stuff the cavity and neck end with the potatoes and mushrooms. If your chicken hasn't come with a lot of neck skin, put the extra stuffing in a small baking dish and cover with foil to bake with the chicken.

Roast the chicken for 30 minutes. Add 1/2 cup water to the pan and roast for another 30 minutes, basting once or twice (but leave it alone for the last 10 minutes). Allow the chicken to rest for 15 minutes before carving.

NOTE: If you feel like being fussy, finely chop the shiitake stems in a food processor and sauté them in 1 tablespoon butter until nicely browned and tender. Salt and pepper to taste, then stuff this mixture under the skin of the chicken with the herbs.

ROAST CHICKEN ON A BED OF POTATOES AND FENNEL

SERVES 4

Roasted underneath chicken, vegetables take on a wonderful savory flavor. Fennel adds a sweet taste, while lemon gives a sharp edge. A quick brine of the chicken keeps it moist. Molly roasts the chicken on a jelly-roll pan so that the vegetables have plenty of room to brown up around the edges; you could also use the bottom of the oven broiler pan. The vegetables that are hidden under the chicken have a more braised quality, while those around the edges of the pan get crispy brown and caramelized. It's a great one-dish meal.

3/4 cup coarse salt, plus more for seasoning
1/2 cup sugar
3 1/2 pounds bone-in chicken breasts and/or thighs
1 1/2 pounds russet or all-purpose potatoes, scrubbed and cut
   into 3/4-to-1-inch wedges
2 small or 1 large fennel bulb, trimmed and cut into 3/4-inch wedges
3 tablespoons olive oil
2 tablespoons fresh lemon juice
1/2 tablespoon dried oregano
Freshly ground black pepper

Fill a deep bowl with 6 cups water. Add the salt and sugar and stir to dissolve. Add the chicken to the brine, adding more water if necessary to just cover the chicken pieces. Set a plate or lid on top to keep the chicken submerged. Refrigerate for 1 1/2 to 2 hours.

Heat the oven to 400 degrees.

Combine the potatoes and fennel on a jelly-roll pan or low-sided roasting pan. The pan should be large enough so the vegetables have plenty of space to brown; if they're too crowded, they'll stew instead of roast. Toss the vegetables with the olive oil, lemon juice, oregano, and some salt and pepper. Roast for 15 minutes.

Meanwhile, drain the chicken; rinse and pat the pieces dry. Using poultry shears, trim the ends of the rib bones from the breast to make a more compact shape (these end bits have very little meat, but they are worth saving for stock). If the breasts are large, cut each in half crosswise to make a more manageable serving. Trim any excess fat from the chicken pieces, leaving all the skin intact. Season with pepper.

After they have roasted for 15 minutes, toss the vegetables with a spatula and arrange the chicken pieces on top. Roast, flipping the exposed vegetables once more partway through cooking, until the chicken is nicely browned and the juices run clear, about 25 minutes for breasts and 35 minutes for thighs. If you're roasting a mix of breasts and thighs, just pull out the breasts and cover them with foil while the thighs finish roasting. Serve hot.

A HEN WITH GOLDEN "EGGS"

A hen, gently poached, is nestled on a large platter in a nest of phyllo straw and surrounded by golden duchess potato "eggs." This is not, I'm afraid, the kind of dish you attempt after a long day at work, but it is fun when you have the time to play and want to show off a little. As Alice B. Toklas said, "It's an amusing way to present a chicken"— and a truly delicious one.

1 (4½-to-5-pound) chicken
2 tablespoons unsalted butter
1 onion, coarsely chopped
1 leek, sliced
1 carrot, sliced
1½ cups dry white wine
Coarse salt
2 sprigs tarragon
1 sprig thyme
1 sprig flat-leaf parsley
1 bay leaf

FOR THE "EGGS"
Duchess Potatoes (page 402)
Scant ½ teaspoon ground turmeric (optional)
Melted butter for shaping and brushing

FOR THE "NEST"
6 sheets phyllo

FOR THE SAUCE
2 tablespoons unsalted butter

2 tablespoons all-purpose flour
1 sprig tarragon
1/4 cup heavy cream
1 teaspoon fresh lemon juice, or to taste
Coarse salt and freshly ground white pepper

Remove the excess fat from the neck and tail of the chicken, and truss the bird with kitchen string.

Melt the butter in a pot large enough to hold the chicken, over medium heat. Add the onion, leek, and carrot and cook until the vegetables have begun to soften, about 6 minutes. Remove from the heat and add the wine and a pinch of salt.

Tie the tarragon, thyme, parsley, and bay leaf together with kitchen string into a small bundle and add to the pot. If you have the giblets, add the neck and gizzard to the pot as well. Discard the liver (or save for another recipe); it would turn the broth cloudy. Place the chicken in the pot and add enough cold water to cover it.

Set the pot over medium heat and slowly bring the water to a very gentle simmer. Expect it to take 30 to 40 minutes to reach poaching temperature. Skim any goopy scum that rises to the top as the water heats up.

Once lazy bubbles begin to appear on the surface of the water, monitor the temperature carefully so that the chicken poaches, not boils—you want lazy bubbles, not a rapid simmer, which would toughen the bird. Continue to poach the chicken until the juices from the thigh run clear when pierced with a meat fork. The timing depends on the size of the chicken and the temperature at which it cooks, but expect it to take anywhere from 1 to 1³/₄ hours from when the water first reached poaching temperature. You can also test for doneness by wiggling a leg to see if it feels loose in the joint.

FOR THE "EGGS": While the chicken is cooking, prepare the Duchess Potatoes; if you want to have truly "golden" eggs, add the turmeric to the potatoes when you beat in the butter and eggs.

Rub your hands with a bit of melted butter and gently shape a ball of potato to imitate a hen's egg. Repeat with the remaining potatoes, arranging the eggs on a buttered baking sheet. Finally, brush the tops with a bit of melted butter; set aside.

FOR THE "NEST": Heat the oven to 350 degrees. Roll the phyllo into a loose roll and slice it crosswise into 1/4-inch strips. Unravel the strips and loosely drop them onto several baking sheets. Don't pile the phyllo too deep, or it will not crisp well. Bake until the phyllo is crisp and just starting to brown, 10 to 15 minutes. We like to bake some lighter and some darker to have a more natural straw color. Remove the phyllo from the oven and increase the temperature to 400 degrees.

When the chicken is cooked, lift it from the broth, tent it with foil, and set it in a warm spot to rest while you bake the potatoes and make the sauce.

Bake the duchess potatoes until golden and slightly puffed, 20 to 30 minutes.

MEANWHILE, FOR THE SAUCE: Strain the broth and measure out 1 3/4 cups for the sauce. (Save the remainder to use for soups and braises.) Melt the butter in a saucepan over medium heat. Whisk in the flour and cook, whisking, for a minute or two, until thick and bubbling. Whisk in the broth and bring to a simmer. Add the tarragon. Simmer, stirring to prevent sticking, until thickened and smooth, about 10 minutes. Add the cream and continue to simmer for another 10 minutes. Remove the tarragon and season with the lemon juice and salt and pepper.

To serve, pull out your largest platter. Arrange the phyllo straw on it to simulate a nest. Set the chicken in the center and nestle the golden eggs all around. Nap some of the sauce over the breast of the chicken, and triumphantly carry the entire ensemble to the table. Serve some of the phyllo straw, a few eggs, and a tender portion of chicken to each person, passing the remaining sauce at the table.

CHICKEN CHILI WITH A QUILTED SWEET POTATO CRUST

This chili has lots of juice to be sopped up by the sweet-potato-and-cheddar biscuits. You'll need to let the chili cool to room temperature before trying to weave the biscuit dough into a lattice on top. If you can't spare the time, simply stamp the biscuits into rounds, diamonds, or even stars. But the quilt is rather pretty.

The biscuit dough may take more or less buttermilk, depending on how moist the sweet potatoes are.

2 tablespoons vegetable oil
1/2 pound chorizo, cut into 1/4-inch slices
1 large onion, chopped
4 garlic cloves, minced
1–2 jalapeño or serrano chiles, minced (seed them if you must)
1 tablespoon chili powder, or to taste
1 teaspoon ground cumin
1 teaspoon dried oregano
2 pounds boneless, skinless chicken thighs, cut into bite-sized pieces
Coarse salt and freshly ground black pepper
2 bell peppers, preferably 1 red and 1 green, cored, seeded, and chopped
1 (28-ounce) can whole peeled tomatoes, with their juice
3 cups cooked kidney beans (or two 15-ounce cans, drained and rinsed)
1–1 1/2 cups beer, stock, water, or bean cooking water, as needed
Splash of red wine vinegar (about 2 teaspoons)

FOR THE BISCUITS
2 cups all-purpose flour
1 tablespoon light brown sugar
2 teaspoons baking soda
1 teaspoon baking powder

continued

³/₄ teaspoon coarse salt
Freshly ground black pepper
6 tablespoons (³/₄ stick) unsalted butter, cut into small bits and very cold
¹/₂ cup shredded cheddar (about 2 ounces)
3 tablespoons chopped fresh chives
1 cup leftover mashed sweet potato, chilled
About ¹/₂ cup buttermilk, as needed

Heat the oil in a large wide saucepan over medium heat. Add the chorizo and cook, stirring once or twice, until nicely browned on both sides, about 5 minutes. Transfer the sausage to a bowl and return the pan to the heat.

Add the onion and cook until translucent, about 7 minutes. Stir in the garlic, jalapeño, chili powder, cumin, and oregano and cook until fragrant, about 2 minutes. Add the chicken, season with salt and pepper, and stir until all the pieces are coated with spices. Stir in the bell peppers, then add the tomatoes. Bring to a simmer and cook for 20 minutes. Give the chili a stir from time to time with a wooden spoon, and break up the tomatoes as they become tender.

Stir in the beans and the sausage. Add a bit of beer or stock if the chili appears too thick or threatens to stick. Ultimately, this should be rather loose. Simmer until the chicken and vegetables are tender, another 20 minutes. Add the vinegar and taste for salt and pepper.

Pour the chili into a large (3-quart) baking dish—a deep 9-by-13-inch pan works nicely. If you plan on creating a quilted (or lattice) biscuit top, allow the chili to cool to room temperature. If you're going to stamp out rounds of biscuit dough, you can set them on top while the chili is still hot.

Heat the oven to 375 degrees.

FOR THE BISCUITS: Put the flour, sugar, baking soda, baking powder, salt, and pepper in a mixing bowl and whisk together. Add the butter and, using your fingertips, rub it into the flour until the dough resembles coarse oatmeal. Add the cheese and chives and toss to combine. Add the sweet potato and work it in, still using your fingertips. Stir in just enough buttermilk—use a fork—to make a soft but not wet dough; the amount will depend on how moist the sweet potato was.

Dump the dough onto a lightly floured surface and pat it out to $1/2$ inch thick. If you are making a lattice crust, cut the dough into 3/4-inch-wide strips and weave them loosely on top of the chili. Alternatively, stamp out shapes with a cookie cutter and arrange the biscuits on top of the chili, leaving an inch or so between each. Lightly brush the tops of the biscuits with buttermilk. If you have leftover biscuit dough, shape it into individual biscuits and bake alongside the chili until lightly browned, about 20 minutes.

Bake the potpie until the biscuits are well browned and the chili is bubbling up between them, about an hour. Be sure to let the biscuits brown very well; otherwise, you risk their being undercooked on the bottom. Serve in deep bowls with a bit of biscuit topping on each one.

CHICKEN WITH POTATOES, GRANDMA-STYLE

SERVES 4

My grandmother Anna Finamore was Italian, so Grandma-style means Italian-style to me. You may not have an Italian grandmother, but make this and pretend that you do. It's juicy, the potatoes end up packed with flavor, and it's the kind of dish that just yells Sunday supper. The cherry peppers give it a nice hit of heat, and they're the ingredient that sets the dish apart. Don't skimp on them. You will find them in jars in the pickle section of your grocery store.

You can make the dish in a roasting pan, but I learned to cook it in a cast-iron skillet, and I still think there's no better piece of equipment.

1 (3-pound) chicken, excess fat removed
3 hot cherry peppers, stemmed, seeded, and torn into pieces
1 large onion
Coarse salt and freshly ground black pepper
1 teaspoon dried thyme
Olive oil
Red wine vinegar
1/2 cup dry white wine or dry vermouth
1 1/2 pounds yellow-fleshed or all-purpose potatoes

Loosen the skin along the breast and the backbone of the chicken and slip pieces of the hot pepper (about half of them) under it. Try not to tear the skin.

Peel the onion and cut off 2 rather thick slices. Put them in a large cast-iron skillet. Cut the rest of the onion into very large chunks.

Season the cavity of the chicken with salt and pepper and 1/2 teaspoon of the dried thyme. Stick the onion chunks in the cavity, with the rest of the hot peppers. Rub the chicken liberally with olive oil and the rest of the thyme, and salt and pepper it all over. Tuck the wings under the chicken and place it on the onion slices in the skillet. Drizzle it with some vinegar and let it sit at room temperature for about an hour.

Heat the oven to 400 degrees.

Roast the chicken for 30 minutes, then pour the wine over it. Roast for another 30 minutes, basting two or three times, or until the juices run clear.

Meanwhile, peel the potatoes and cut them into slices about 1/3 inch thick. Put them in a saucepan, cover with cold water by at least an inch, add a pinch of salt, and bring to a boil. Drain the potatoes right away and leave them in a colander on the stove so they don't get cold.

When the chicken is done, spear the cavity with a large fork and hold the chicken, cavity down, over the skillet. Scoop out the onion and peppers into the skillet, and let the juices drain into it too. Then let the chicken rest, under a tent of aluminum foil, while you finish the potatoes.

Increase the oven temperature to 450 degrees. Stir the onion in the pan to break up the pieces. Add the potatoes and stir to coat with the pan juices. Roast for about 20 minutes, stirring several times. The potatoes should be tender and browned and look juicy.

Carve the chicken and serve surrounded by the potatoes, peppers, and onion.

CHICKEN, POTATO, AND PEPPER STEW

SERVES 4 TO 6

We find the combination of chicken and potatoes irresistible. This stew is almost a soup, with pieces of chicken and potatoes set in an elegant broth. Serve it in wide soup dishes and make sure soup spoons are part of the setting.

1 tablespoon olive oil
1 (3-pound) chicken, cut into serving pieces
Coarse salt and freshly ground black pepper
1½ pounds yellow-fleshed potatoes, peeled and cut into large chunks
4 tablespoons (½ stick) unsalted butter
3 red bell peppers, cored, seeded, and coarsely chopped
3 ripe plum tomatoes, coarsely chopped
1 cup dry white wine
1 cup Chicken Stock (page 85)
Pinch of saffron
1 teaspoon grated orange zest
2½–3 pounds spinach, stems removed and well washed

Heat the oil in a large skillet set over medium-high heat. Season the chicken pieces with salt and pepper and brown them lightly on all sides. Remove the chicken to a plate.

Add the potatoes and 1 tablespoon of the butter to the skillet. Sprinkle in a bit of salt and pepper. Cook, stirring occasionally, until the potatoes begin to brown on their edges, 7 to 8 minutes. Add the bell peppers and tomatoes, season with salt and pepper, and cook for a minute. Pour in the wine and bring to a boil. Be sure to scrape the bottom of the pan to release any browned bits left from the chicken and potatoes.

Once the stew is boiling, pour in the stock and crumble in the saffron. Nestle the chicken into the liquid. Bring it again to a boil, then reduce to a simmer, cover, and cook gently for 45 minutes, or until the chicken is cooked and the potatoes are tender. Stir in the orange zest and check the seasoning.

Meanwhile, bring a large pot of water to a boil. Add a big pinch of salt and the spinach. Bring to a boil and cook for a minute or two, until the spinach is completely wilted. Drain, refresh the spinach with cold water, drain again, and squeeze out the excess moisture.

Just before you are ready to serve the stew, melt the remaining 3 tablespoons butter in a skillet over medium-low heat. Add the spinach and toss it in the butter until heated through. Check for salt and pepper.

Divide the spinach among your soup dishes, making a pile in the middle of each. Ladle in the stew to surround the spinach (with lots of broth), and serve.

COLOMBIAN POTATO AND CHICKEN STEW
(AJIACO)

SERVES 10 TO 12

What a great party dish this is, and perfect for late-summer entertaining, when all the heirloom potatoes are available.

Jean Anderson published a recipe for this national dish of Colombia in *Jean Anderson Cooks.* She adapted it for grocery-store potatoes, but *ajíaco* (you pronounce it *ah-YAH-co*) should showcase as many different kinds of potatoes as you can lay your hands on. You want russets, which will melt and provide the thickening, creamy red-skinned potatoes for texture, heirlooms for flavor and color. I try to use at least eight different potatoes when I make this stew.

Use the list below as a guide and adapt it to the potatoes you can find. You need a total of 5½ pounds. Yes, this is a big stew. The potatoes can all be prepared well in advance; just keep them covered with cold water and drain them before you add them to the kettle.

1 (7½-to-8 pound) chicken (or two 4-pound chickens)
3 quarts Chicken Stock (page 85)
2 large onions, chopped
10 whole scallions, chopped
8 black peppercorns
2 bay leaves
3 or 4 sprigs thyme
10–12 sprigs cilantro
1 pound russet potatoes, peeled and cut into ½-inch cubes
1 pound white potatoes, peeled and cut into ½-inch cubes
1 pound Kennebec (or other Maine) potatoes, peeled and cut into ½-inch cubes
½ pound Yellow Finn potatoes, scrubbed and cut into ½-inch cubes

8 small True Blue (or other purple) potatoes, scrubbed

8 small Red Norland potatoes, scrubbed and halved

8 Ruby Crescent potatoes, scrubbed and halved

8 La Ratte potatoes, scrubbed and halved

Coarse salt

4 ears corn, shucked

$\frac{1}{2}$ cup heavy cream

$\frac{1}{4}$ cup capers, rinsed and drained

$\frac{1}{4}$ cup chopped cilantro

Freshly ground black pepper

FOR SERVING

Heavy cream

Capers

Chopped cilantro

Diced avocado

Put the chicken in a kettle with the stock, onions, scallions, and peppercorns. Tie the bay leaves, thyme, and cilantro sprigs together with a bit of kitchen string and add to the pot. Bring to a boil, cover partway, reduce the heat to low, and simmer very gently for 1$\frac{1}{2}$ hours.

Take the chicken out of the pot and let it sit until it's cool enough to handle, then discard the skin and bones and cut the meat into big chunks. Skim the fat from the stock and discard the herb bouquet. You can do this the day ahead, refrigerating the stock and chicken separately once they've cooled down.

Bring the stock back to a boil and add all the potatoes and salt to taste. Wait a few minutes for the stock to return to a boil, then cover partway, lower the heat to medium, and cook for 1 hour.

Cut each ear of corn into 4 pieces and add to the kettle, along with the chicken. Simmer for 40 minutes.

At this point, many of the potatoes will have disappeared into the stew, thickening it nicely. Add the cream, capers, and chopped cilantro and check for salt and pepper. Ladle the stew out into a big tureen.

Serve the *ajiaco* in wide bowls, and pass more cream, capers, and cilantro at the table, as well as diced avocado.

CHICKEN, ARTICHOKE, AND EGGPLANT PIE
WITH A POTATO CRUST

SERVES 6

You'll be surprised how tasty and seductive this pie is. We've adapted the recipe from one by Mediterranean cooking authority Paula Wolfert.

Chicken thigh meat is essential here.

1³/₄–2 pounds russet potatoes or Yukons, peeled
1 large eggplant (about 1 pound), cut into 1-inch cubes
3 tablespoons olive oil
Coarse salt and freshly ground black pepper
1 (9¹/₂-ounce) box frozen artichoke hearts, defrosted and drained
8 tablespoons (1 stick) unsalted butter, clarified (see page 28)
1¹/₄ pounds boneless, skinless chicken thighs, cut into 1¹/₂-inch pieces
2 garlic cloves, minced
3 tablespoons chopped fresh chives
2 tablespoons chopped flat-leaf parsley
2 teaspoons chopped fresh thyme
1 tablespoon fresh lemon juice

Heat the oven to 375 degrees.

Use a knife or mandoline to slice two-thirds of the russets into rounds just under ¹/₈ inch thick. Slice the remaining potatoes lengthwise into long thin slices, again just under ¹/₈ inch thick. Dump all the slices into a large bowl and cover with cold water while you prepare the filling.

Dump the eggplant cubes onto a rimmed baking sheet. Drizzle with the olive oil, season with salt and pepper, and toss to distribute evenly. Roast, turning the eggplant with a spatula a few times, until just tender and beginning to brown, about 35 minutes. Transfer the eggplant to a large mixing bowl, and turn the oven up to 400 degrees.

Trim any leaves from the artichoke hearts, leaving just the meaty part of the hearts.

Heat 2 tablespoons of the clarified butter in a medium skillet over medium-high heat. Season the chicken pieces with salt and pepper. When the butter is hot, add half the chicken and sear it quickly, turning once, about 30 seconds per side. Transfer the chicken to a plate and continue with the remaining chicken.

When all the chicken is seared, add another tablespoon of butter to the skillet and then add the artichokes. Cook, stirring, until just beginning to brown, 2 to 3 minutes. Return the chicken to the skillet, along with any juices, and cook for a minute or two to combine the flavors. Add the chicken and artichokes to the eggplant and toss to combine. Season with the garlic, chives, parsley, thyme, lemon juice, and salt and pepper and toss again. Set aside.

Butter a tarte tatin dish or other heavy 10-to-11-inch round ovenproof dish (a deep cast-iron skillet also works well). The pie gets presented in the pan it's cooked in, so choose something you'd like to carry to the table.

Drain the potatoes and pat them dry. Dry out the bowl as well, and return the slices to it. Toss the potatoes with the remaining 5 tablespoons clarified butter and a touch of salt and pepper.

Cover the bottom of the ovenproof dish with an overlapping layer of the round potato slices; make sure that you have enough round slices left over to cover the top of the pie. Line the sides of the dish with the lengthwise slices, skinny ends pointing into the dish so the slices hang partway over the sides.

Spoon the filling into the dish. Fold the overhanging slices over the filling, and then cover the filling with the remaining rounds in a decorative overlapping pattern. Butter a sheet of foil and cover the pie.

Choose a heavy flat lid that will just fit inside the rim of the baking dish. (If you don't have the proper lid, you can set a heavy stone or other weight in a round cake pan and set it on top.) Press down on the lid to compact the pie, and, with the lid in place, slide the pie into the oven and bake for 25 minutes.

Press down again to compress the pie and then remove the lid and the foil, being careful not to lift off any potato slices. Continue to bake, uncovered, for 25 to 30 additional minutes. The top should be nicely browned and crisp. If not, brush with a bit of additional butter and slide under the broiler for a few minutes.

Let sit for at least 5 minutes, then serve directly from the baking dish, scooping out portions of the filling and the potatoes with a large spoon.

ROAST GOOSE WITH POTATO, JERUSALEM ARTICHOKE, AND SAUSAGE STUFFING

SERVES 6 TO 8

Great things happen here. The sausage perfumes the goose, and the potatoes and artichokes absorb some of the juices from the bird. Thanks to the folks at *Cook's Illustrated* for the roasting method.

Please, please save the fat you pour out from the pan. It's delicious, it keeps forever, and you can use it to fry potatoes or to season hearty winter greens or to make a roux for a sauce or gravy.

1 (10-to-12-pound) goose
1 tablespoon olive oil
1 pound sweet Italian sausage, casings removed
3/4 pound Jerusalem artichokes, peeled and cut into 1/3-inch dice
1 1/2 pounds russet potatoes, peeled and cut into chunks
Coarse salt
Freshly ground black pepper
1 teaspoon fennel seeds

Remove the excess fat from the goose and hack off the first joint of the wings. Lift up the skin at the neck cavity and cut out the wishbone: you need a small sturdy knife for this task. Reserve the wing tips and wishbone for stock, along with the neck and giblets. Prick the goose all over with a trussing needle.

Bring a large stockpot of water to a boil. Immerse the goose in the boiling water for 3 to 4 minutes, until "goose pimples" appear. If your pot isn't large enough, you may need to do this in two steps, first one end of the goose, then the other. Use heavy kitchen towels to avoid splashing yourself. Remove the goose from its bath, dry it well, and let it rest on a rack for at least an hour. If you want even crisper skin, refrigerate the bird, uncovered, for up to 2 days.

Heat the oven to 325 degrees.

Heat the olive oil in a skillet over medium-high heat. Crumble in the sausage meat and cook, stirring to break it up, until well browned. Remove from the heat and stir in the Jerusalem artichokes.

Put the potatoes in a large saucepan, cover with cold water by at least an inch, add a good pinch of salt, and bring to a boil. Reduce the heat to medium, cover partway, and cook for 10 minutes. The potatoes should be fairly tender, but you should feel some resistance when you poke them with a skewer. Drain and return the potatoes to the pot. Mash them roughly with a hand masher or the edge of a heavy metal spoon—you want there to be plenty of lumps. Combine with the sausage mixture and season with salt, a generous amount of pepper, and the fennel seeds.

Stuff the goose (both body and neck cavities) while the stuffing is still warm. If you happen to be the type who likes to truss, truss the openings closed. Otherwise, use cocktail picks to make sure the openings are securely closed. Season the goose liberally with salt and a few grinds of pepper.

Place the goose breast side down on a rack set in a roasting pan and roast for 1½ hours. Remove from the oven, carefully lift out the rack with the goose on it and set it on a baking sheet. Pour off the fat into a metal bowl. Turn the goose breast side up on the rack and return to the pan. Roast for about another 1¼ hours. The skin will puff up some and the thigh meat will feel spongy.

Lift the rack and goose back onto the baking sheet and slip it back into the oven. Save the rest of the fat and deglaze the pan if you're making gravy. Increase the oven temperature to 400 degrees and roast the goose until it's well browned and the skin is crispy. Let it rest for 30 minutes before carving.

Pour off the remaining fat from the roasting pan and use the browned bits left in the pan as the base for your favorite gravy.

Spoon the stuffing into a bowl, carve the goose, and serve.

RABBIT ROASTED WITH POTATOES

Simple and rustic, this is an Italian country dish. After its long soak in wine perfumed with juniper, the rabbit becomes incredibly flavorful, and the long cooking ensures it will be fork-tender. Have a loaf of bread on the table, and perhaps some grilled peppers and zucchini. If you have a nice large terra-cotta baking dish, you could make the rabbit in that and bring it to the table.

1 rabbit, cut into serving pieces
2 cups hearty red wine (such as a Chianti)
10 juniper berries, crushed
2 shallots or 1 small red onion, finely chopped
1 carrot, finely chopped
1 celery stalk, finely chopped
1 garlic clove, cut into slivers
4 or 5 sprigs rosemary
1 lemon
Olive oil
1¼ pounds very small new potatoes, scrubbed
Coarse salt and freshly ground black pepper

Place the rabbit in a bowl. Add the wine, juniper berries, shallots, carrot, and celery, cover, and refrigerate for 8 hours or so.

Remove the rabbit from the marinade and pat the pieces dry. Discard the marinade. Use the point of a knife to poke gashes in the rabbit and stick in slivers of garlic and bits of 1 rosemary sprig. Place the pieces in a baking dish. Grate the zest of the lemon over the rabbit, then juice the lemon over the pieces. Add the remaining rosemary to the pan. Drizzle with olive oil and let it sit for about an hour.

Heat the oven to 400 degrees.

If the potatoes aren't very small, halve them. Scatter the potatoes around the rabbit, drizzle it all well with olive oil, and season with salt and pepper. Bake, turning the rabbit and potatoes once or twice, until the rabbit is very tender and the potatoes browned, 45 to 50 minutes. Serve from your nice baking dish or transfer to a platter.

SUNDAY LAMB
WITH PROPER ROAST POTATOES

This combination—a big roast and very crusty potatoes—is about as British as you can get. Bring out the good china.

Ask your butcher to bone and tie the lamb, and be sure to take home the bones. (Ask to have them cut into 4-inch pieces.) I'm giving you the lamb stock recipe here even though you don't need it until you have leftovers for Shepherd's Pie (page 208).

What, you say, is a proper roast potato? One with a serious crust and a creamy interior. These potatoes cook longer than you would imagine, but it's the only way to make them "proper."

1 leg of lamb (7–9 pounds), boned and tied (bones reserved)
1 large garlic clove
4 large sprigs rosemary
Olive oil
1 lemon
Coarse salt and freshly ground black pepper

FOR THE LAMB STOCK
Bones from the leg
1 large onion
1 carrot, chopped
1 tablespoon tomato paste
8 black peppercorns

FOR THE POTATOES
6 tablespoons fat (duck or goose, or bacon drippings; vegetable oil in a pinch)
2½–3 pounds russet potatoes, peeled and cut into large (about 2-inch) chunks
Coarse salt
1 tablespoon all-purpose flour or cornmeal

Put the lamb in a roasting pan. Cut the garlic into slivers. Stab the lamb all over with a paring knife, and insert a garlic sliver into each slit. Break up the rosemary into pieces about 1½ inches long and stick these bits in with the garlic or into holes of their own: space these out evenly over the lamb, and leave bits of garlic and rosemary sticking out, so it ends up looking like a hedgehog. Drizzle with the olive oil. Grate the zest from the lemon and combine it with about 2 teaspoons salt. Squeeze the lemon over the lamb, then rub with the zest-salt mixture and pepper to taste. Let sit on the counter for about 1 hour.

MEANWHILE, FOR THE LAMB STOCK: Heat the oven to 400 degrees.

Put the bones in a stockpot and roast them for about 25 minutes. Cut the onion into large pieces (no need to peel it, just pull off the loose papery skin) and add it to the pot, with the carrot. Stir as well as you can and roast for another 10 minutes.

Move the pot to the stove and add 6 cups cold water, the tomato paste, and the peppercorns. Bring to a boil, then simmer gently for 1 hour. Strain and cool. Use some of this as a gravy for the lamb, or put it all in the refrigerator for Shepherd's Pie (page 208). This makes about 1 quart.

When you're ready to start the roast, heat the oven to 425 degrees.

Roast the lamb on the bottom rack (you need the top for the potatoes) for 1 hour, or until it registers 130 to 135 degrees on an instant-read thermometer. Let it rest, tented with foil, for 15 minutes before carving.

MEANWHILE, FOR THE POTATOES: About 5 minutes after you've put the lamb into the oven, put the fat for the potatoes in a shallow roasting pan and slip it into the oven to heat while the potatoes parboil. The pan and oil must be searingly hot.

Put the potatoes in a pot, cover with cold water by at least an inch, add a big pinch of salt, and bring to a boil. Once the water's boiling, cook for 3 minutes, then drain the potatoes well and return them to the pot. Hold the lid on and shake the pot with brio to soften up all the edges of the potatoes. Sprinkle in the flour, give the pan another shake or two, and stir to coat the potatoes.

Drop the potatoes into the hot fat (being careful not to spatter) and stir them. Roast for 30 minutes, then turn with tongs, and roast for another 30 minutes. The potatoes will be golden brown and crispy, and if you've timed it right, they will be done when you've finished carving the lamb.

SHEPHERD'S PIE

Yeah, this is leftovers, but pretty glorious leftovers. This recipe uses lamb, but you could make an equally woodsy stew with beef, top it with the mashed potatoes, and bake. If you're preparing this with beef, use Doctored Canned Stock (see page 103).

You can put the dish together a day ahead and leave it covered in the refrigerator overnight before baking.

1 quart Lamb Stock (page 206)
$1/4$ cup all-purpose flour
10 ounces pearl onions, peeled
1 teaspoon chopped fresh thyme
$1/2$ ounce dried porcini mushrooms
$1/2$ cup red wine
$1 1/4$–$1 1/2$ pounds leftover roast lamb
$1 1/2$ cups very small peas (frozen are fine)
Coarse salt and freshly ground black pepper
$1 1/2$ pounds russet potatoes, peeled and cut into chunks
4 tablespoons ($1/2$ stick) plus 2 teaspoons unsalted butter
$3/4$ cup milk, heated
1 large egg yolk

Bring the stock to a boil in a large saucepan over medium heat. Make a slurry by whisking the flour with about $1/4$ cup water until completely smooth. Whisk the slurry into the stock and bring it back to a boil, whisking to discourage lumps. Add the onions and thyme, bring to a simmer, and cook gently for 30 minutes.

Heat the oven to 350 degrees.

While the sauce is simmering, soak the porcini in the wine, start the potatoes (see below), and cut the lamb into small pieces, about $1/3$-inch dice.

Put the potatoes in a large saucepan, cover with cold water by at least an inch, add a good pinch of salt, and bring to a boil. Cover partway, reduce the heat to medium, and cook until the potatoes are very tender.

Lift the mushrooms out of the wine, chop them, and add them to the sauce. Pour in most of the wine, leaving behind any grit. Stir in the meat and bring to a simmer. Add the peas and taste for salt and pepper. Pour the stew into a 2½-quart casserole (or a deep 8-inch square pan).

Drain the potatoes, return them to the pot, and dry them over heat, stirring and shaking the pan so they don't stick or burn.

Mash the potatoes with a hand masher or hand mixer, then beat in 4 tablespoons of the butter. Beat in the milk in three additions, whipping vigorously with a wooden spoon (or the hand mixer) after each addition. Beat in the yolk and salt and pepper to taste.

Spread the potatoes over the stew, going right to the edges of the pan to seal it in. Smooth the surface, then rub the potatoes with the remaining 2 teaspoons butter. Make a decorative pattern in the potatoes with a fork. Bake the pie for 20 to 25 minutes, until piping hot. (Or store, covered, in the refrigerator for up to a day before baking—in which case, it will need 40 to 50 minutes in the oven.) Serve hot.

LAMB CHOPS AND SLICED POTATOES WITH GARLIC AND VINEGAR SAUCE

SERVES 4

I've tinkered with this Spanish regional dish from cookbook author Penelope Casas, finishing the chops and potatoes together, rather than separately, as in the original. Use a large shallow casserole for the potatoes; mine is about 14 inches round and made of terra-cotta. It seems too big, but it actually helps when the potatoes have room around them. And, I know, it looks like there is a staggering amount of garlic in this dish. Don't worry: it's just right, but I wouldn't serve this to someone who wasn't a fan of the stuff.

12 garlic cloves, minced (about 3 tablespoons)
3 tablespoons sherry vinegar
1/2 cup Chicken Stock (page 85)
1 1/2 pounds yellow-fleshed or white potatoes, peeled and cut into 1/8-inch-thick slices
3 tablespoons olive oil
Coarse salt and freshly ground black pepper
8 small rib lamb chops, 1 inch thick (about 2 pounds)

Combine the garlic, vinegar, and stock and let sit for at least 2 hours.

Heat the oven to 350 degrees. Oil a large shallow casserole (see note above).

Arrange half the potatoes in a layer in the casserole—take the time to make them look nice, since you will serve them right from this dish, drizzle with about 1/2 tablespoon of the oil, and season with salt and pepper. Repeat the process: nice-looking layer of potatoes, oil, salt and pepper. Cover the dish with foil and bake for 30 minutes. If you haven't already, take the chops out of the refrigerator. Season them with salt and pepper.

After 30 minutes, remove the foil from the potatoes and spoon in half the garlic sauce. Bake for 10 minutes, then start the chops. Heat the remaining 2 tablespoons oil in a large skillet over medium-high heat until the oil is shimmering. Add the chops and brown them, about 2 minutes per side. Pour in the rest of the garlic sauce and reduce the heat to low. Cook for 5 minutes, turning the chops once.

Add the chops to the casserole and spoon in any sauce from the skillet. Bake for 5 minutes more to meld the flavors and finish the chops (they should be medium-rare). Serve this right from the casserole.

BOULANGER POTATOES WITH PORK

If you lived in a cottage in rural France and didn't have an oven, you would prepare the dishes for your meal, then take them to the bakery for baking. The friendly baker would lend you the use of his oven after all the bread was done. Dishes like a casserole of potatoes would go on lower levels and roasts would go on top, the drippings seasoning the potatoes.

There's no reason now to borrow an oven, but also no reason not to nestle a roast on top of potatoes so the juices can flavor them.

1–2 garlic cloves, minced
2 tablespoons chopped fresh thyme
Coarse salt and freshly ground black pepper
2 tablespoons olive oil
1 (5-pound) boneless pork loin roast
2 tablespoons unsalted butter
2 large onions, halved and very thinly sliced
2 red bell peppers, cored, seeded, and thinly sliced
2 pounds russet potatoes, peeled and thinly sliced
10 juniper berries, crushed
1 cup dry white wine
1 cup Chicken Stock (page 85)

Combine the garlic, 1 tablespoon of the thyme, salt, pepper, and olive oil to make a loose paste. Rub this into the pork and set aside for 30 minutes to an hour.

Heat the oven to 350 degrees.

Put the butter and onions into a large skillet over medium heat. Add a pinch of salt and cook until the onions are limp and beginning to color, about 10 minutes. Spread the onions in the bottom of a large (3-quart) casserole.

Toss the peppers and potatoes with the remaining 1 tablespoon thyme, juniper berries, and salt and pepper. Layer this over the onions and pour in the wine and stock. Top with the roast and cover with aluminum foil. Bake for 30 minutes.

Remove the foil and continue to roast until the pork is done (about 160 degrees), about another 30 minutes. Let the pork rest for 10 to 15 minutes. Carve the pork and serve with the potatoes.

PORK CHOPS BRAISED IN MILK WITH FINGERLINGS AND FENNEL

There's a classic Italian dish, bolognese pork braised in milk, that provided inspiration for our casserole. When you simmer pork in milk, the meat comes out tender and mild and the milk is transformed into a deeply delicious and unctuous sauce. Firm-fleshed fingerlings hold up to the long cooking, but a waxy variety would also do.

2 tablespoons olive oil
4 center-cut bone-in pork chops, about ¾ inch thick
Coarse salt and freshly ground black pepper
All-purpose flour for dredging
1 tablespoon unsalted butter
1 fennel bulb, trimmed and sliced
1 onion, sliced
2 garlic cloves, chopped
1 teaspoon fennel seeds, lightly crushed
¼ cup dry white wine or dry vermouth
1 bouillon cube (any kind—your choice)
1 pound fingerling potatoes, scrubbed and cut into 1-inch pieces
About 2 cups milk

Heat the olive oil in a heavy lidded pan that is wide enough to accommodate the chops in one layer. Season the chops on both sides with salt and pepper. Dredge them in the flour, shake off the excess, and brown over medium-high heat for about 4 minutes per side. Remove the chops to a plate for now.

Reduce the heat to medium and add the butter to the pan. Add the fennel and onion and season with salt and pepper. Cook, stirring a few times, until soft and beginning to brown, about 5 minutes. Add the garlic and fennel seeds and cook for another minute. Pour in the wine and bring it to a simmer. Add the bouillon cube and crush it up and stir to dissolve.

Settle the chops onto the fennel and onions and tuck the potatoes in around them. Pour in the milk; there should be enough to not quite cover the chops. Cover the pan with a sheet of foil and then set the lid snugly in place. Reduce the heat to low and simmer gently until the pork is fork-tender and the potatoes are cooked through, 45 to 50 minutes. Lift the lid once or twice during cooking to check that the liquid is simmering gently.

If there is too much liquid left when the pork is ready, you can lift out the meat and potatoes while you simmer the liquid to reduce. Serve warm, scooping out plenty of the thick cooking liquid for each serving of pork and potatoes.

SCALLOPED POTATOES
WITH SAUSAGE AND PEPPERS

This is one sturdy casserole, a stick-to-your-ribs wintertime dish. And the combination of Italian sausage, peppers, and homey scalloped potatoes is about as American as you can get.

I like it juicy, but you can try it with russets, which will soak up more of the liquid in the casserole.

2 tablespoons olive oil
1 pound sweet Italian sausage, casings removed
2 onions, thinly sliced
1 large red bell pepper, cored, seeded, and cut into $1/3$-inch strips
1 large green bell pepper, cored, seeded, and cut into $1/3$-inch strips
Coarse salt
2 garlic cloves, minced
1 teaspoon dried oregano, preferably Mexican
Pinch of crushed red pepper
1 cup canned tomatoes, with their juices
1 3/4 pounds all-purpose or russet potatoes
1/4 cup all-purpose flour
1/2 cup freshly grated Pecorino or Parmesan
Freshly ground black pepper
2 cups half-and-half

Heat the oil in a large heavy skillet over medium heat until shimmering. Crumble in the sausage and cook, stirring and breaking up the meat with the side of your spoon, until it loses its pink color. Spoon off all but about a tablespoon of the fat.

Add the onions and bell peppers, season with salt, and cook, stirring frequently, until the vegetables are soft, about 10 minutes. Add a tablespoon or two of water if the pan dries out and the vegetables start to stick. Add the garlic and cook for about 1 minute, until fragrant. Then add the oregano, crushed red pepper, and tomatoes. Stir and break up the tomatoes with the side of your spoon and cook until very thick, about 7 minutes. Remove from the heat.

Heat the oven to 350 degrees. Grease a 3-quart casserole.

Peel the potatoes and cut them into 1/8-inch-thick slices. Combine the flour with 1/4 cup of the cheese.

Place one-third of the potatoes in a layer in the casserole. Season with salt and pepper and sprinkle with half the flour mix. Spoon on half of the sausage and peppers. Again, layer potatoes, with salt and pepper, the rest of the flour mix, and the rest of the sausage and peppers. Top with a layer of potatoes and season with salt and pepper. Pour in the half-and-half and cover the casserole with aluminum foil. Bake for 45 minutes.

Uncover the casserole and push the potatoes down with a spatula or the back of a spoon to submerge them. Sprinkle with the remaining 1/4 cup cheese and bake for another 40 minutes or so. The top of the casserole will be a rich brown, the potatoes easily pierced with a knife, and the dish will be very juicy. Let it rest for at least 20 minutes before serving.

SWEET POTATO PUFF WITH CHILE-RUBBED PORK CUTLETS

SERVES 6

This is a pretty dish and a fine combination—a casserole filled high with sweet potatoes, with the cutlets jutting out. The fieriness of the chile is tamed by the sweetness of the puff, and the colors—that contrast of golden orange and browned red—are worth looking at.

Powdered chile de árbol is available in many Latin markets or by mail from Kitchen Market, 218 Eighth Avenue, New York, NY 10011; (212) 243-4433.

FOR THE PORK
1 garlic clove
$^1/_2$ teaspoon coarse salt
$^1/_2$ teaspoon black peppercorns
1 tablespoon powdered chile de árbol
2 pounds boneless pork loin roast

FOR THE PUFF
$1^1/_2$ pounds sweet potatoes, baked
$^3/_4$ teaspoon chopped fresh thyme
1 tablespoon balsamic vinegar
3 large eggs, separated
$^1/_3$ cup heavy cream
Coarse salt and freshly ground black pepper
1 shallot, thinly sliced

2 tablespoons olive oil
$^3/_4$ cup dry red wine
2 tablespoons unsalted butter

FOR THE PORK: Crush the garlic, salt, and peppercorns together in a mortar and pestle. Stir in the chile de árbol.

Cut the pork into 6 slices and pound them to half their original thickness between sheets of plastic wrap. Rub the dry chile marinade into both sides of the cutlets and let them sit, covered, at room temperature for about an hour.

FOR THE PUFF: Heat the oven to 400 degrees. Grease a 2-quart gratin dish.

Peel the sweet potatoes and mash them coarsely with a fork in a mixing bowl. Add the thyme, vinegar, egg yolks, cream, and salt and pepper to taste. Beat this well.

In a separate bowl, whip the egg whites with a pinch of salt to stiff peaks. Fold the whites into the sweet potatoes, gently but thoroughly, and spoon the puff into the dish. Scatter the top with the slices of shallot and bake for 30 minutes, until puffed up and golden in spots.

Meanwhile, heat the olive oil in a large skillet over medium-high heat. Cook the cutlets (it's likely you will need to do this in two batches) until nicely browned on both sides (about 8 minutes total cooking time for each batch). Keep the cutlets warm while you prepare the sauce.

Pour off most of the fat from the pan and add the wine. Cook over medium-high heat until reduced to about 1/4 cup. Add the butter, in a couple of pieces, and tilt the pan back and forth to incorporate the butter into the sauce.

Stick the cutlets into the puff at an angle, drizzle with the sauce, and serve.

POTATO AND CHORIZO STEW

Top-quality chorizo is the sausage of choice here, but there's no reason you can't try others, like andouille or even kielbasa. Just make sure it's the best you can find. I've adapted this regional Spanish dish from the authority, Penelope Casas.

3 tablespoons olive oil
1^1/$_2$ pounds chorizo, cut into ^{1}/$_3$-inch slices
2 onions, finely chopped
2 red bell peppers, cored, seeded, and finely chopped
2 green bell peppers, cored, seeded, and finely chopped
6 garlic cloves, minced
2 bay leaves
Coarse salt
3 pounds small red-skinned potatoes, scrubbed and cut in half
1 teaspoon sweet paprika
5 cups Chicken Stock (page 85)
1 dried chile or crushed red pepper to taste
8 black peppercorns
3 tablespoons chopped flat-leaf parsley
Freshly ground black pepper

Heat the oil in a large heavy pot over medium-high heat. Add the chorizo and brown it on both sides. Remove the chorizo with a slotted spoon. Add the onions, bell peppers, about a third of the garlic, and the bay leaves. Season with salt and cook for 2 minutes. Reduce the heat to low, cover, and cook for 15 minutes.

Bring the heat up to medium, add the potatoes and chorizo, and cook for 2 minutes. Sprinkle with the paprika and stir well. Pour in the stock, add the chile and peppercorns, and bring to a boil. Reduce to a simmer and cook for 20 minutes.

Meanwhile, make a paste of the remaining garlic and the parsley (you can use a mortar and pestle or a mini food processor, or just chop them together on a board).

Add the garlic paste to the stew at the end of the 20 minutes' cooking and continue to simmer for another 15 minutes, or until the potatoes are tender. Cover and let the stew sit for about 5 minutes, then taste for salt and pepper and serve.

LYONNAIS SAUSAGE AND WARM POTATO SALAD
WITH LENTILS

This old French country dish is ideal for New Year's revelry. Lentils, rounds of sausage, and potato are all coin-shaped, hence lucky eating as the year starts.

For the potato, you want something firm that won't fall apart when you slice it. Yellows are the potato of choice, but try heirlooms too. The sausage should be semi-cooked, what is called a *saucisson à cuire* in France. Other good choices are garlic sausage (available from Dartagnan by calling 1-800–327–8246), kielbasa, or cotechino.

Francis Amunatégui, a distinguished French gastronome and journalist, writes of this dish in deeply emotional terms. "The appearance," he says, "of a hot sausage with its salad of potatoes in oil can leave nobody indifferent. . . . It is pure, it precludes all sentimentality, it is the Truth."

FOR THE DRESSING
3 tablespoons chopped shallots
1/4 cup dry white wine or dry vermouth
2 tablespoons red wine vinegar
1 tablespoon Dijon mustard
1/2 cup olive oil
Coarse salt and freshly ground black pepper

FOR THE SALADS
1 tablespoon olive oil
1 small onion, finely chopped
1 small carrot, diced

222   ONE POTATO, TWO POTATO

I cup lentils (preferably French green—Le Puy—but brown will do),
    picked over and rinsed
Coarse salt
1½ pounds yellow-fleshed or white potatoes, scrubbed
¾–1 pound saucisson (see note above)
Freshly ground black pepper

FOR THE DRESSING: Whisk the shallots, wine, vinegar, and mustard together in a small bowl. Gradually whisk in the oil to make an emulsion. Season with salt and pepper.

FOR THE SALADS: Heat the olive oil in a medium saucepan over medium heat. Add the onion and carrot and cook, stirring once or twice, until they're just beginning to soften, about 4 minutes. Add the lentils and enough cold water to cover by a good inch. Add a pinch of salt and slowly bring to a boil. Reduce the heat to a simmer and cook gently until the lentils are tender but not mushy, 20 to 25 minutes. Drain (you may want to reserve the broth for soup), and toss the lentils with 3 tablespoons of the dressing. Set aside.

Meanwhile, put the potatoes in a saucepan, cover with cold water by at least an inch, add a good pinch of salt, and bring to a boil. Reduce the heat to medium, cover partway, and cook until the potatoes are tender. Drain the potatoes on a rack set in the sink.

Prick the sausage with a fork and put it in a pot full of cold water. Bring to a simmer and poach gently until heated through. The timing will depend on the type of sausage: expect a fully cooked kielbasa to be ready in about 8 minutes; some of the partially cured sausages may take quite a bit longer.

As soon as the potatoes are cool enough to handle, peel and slice into ¼-inch-thick rounds. Transfer to a mixing bowl and toss gently with 5 to 6 tablespoons of the dressing. Taste for seasoning, adding more dressing if you like.

Toss the lentils again, adding more dressing if they need it. Arrange the potatoes and lentils on a large serving dish; season with pepper. Slice the sausage and place the slices down the center of the dish. Serve warm.

HUNGARIAN POTATO STEW
(KRUMPLI PAPRIKAS)

In *The Hungarian Cookbook,* where I discovered this recipe, Susan Derecskey admits to breaking one of those unwritten rules of the good hostess. She serves peasant dishes to company. But when the dish is as appealing as this homey stew, who can blame her?

Follow her example and make this stew for friends. Susan serves it with rye bread (a must), and a salad (cucumber would be my preference), or pickles (but why not both?). Beer is the beverage of choice.

Yellow-fleshed potatoes make the best-looking and -tasting stew. Get loose frankfurters from your butcher (don't even think of skinless). Or experiment with other sausages like weisswurst or kielbasa. That kind of substitution might shock Susan, so don't tell.

1/4 cup vegetable oil
1 large onion, thinly sliced
1 teaspoon paprika
1/4 teaspoon caraway seeds, crushed
Coarse salt
3 pounds yellow-fleshed potatoes, peeled, halved lengthwise, and
   cut into 1/4-inch slices
4 frankfurters, cut into 1/2-inch-thick slices

Heat the oil in a wide saucepan over medium heat until it moves easily across the pan. Add the onion and cook until softened, translucent, and beginning to brown at the edges, about 8 minutes. Add the paprika, caraway, and salt to taste and cook, stirring, for about 30 seconds. Pour in 1/2 cup water and stir. Add the potatoes and stir to coat them well, then add enough water, say, 2 cups, to just about cover them. Bring to a boil, then reduce to a simmer, cover, and cook gently for 15 minutes.

Strew the frankfurter slices over the top of the stew and cover the pan again. Cook for another 10 minutes or so, until the potatoes are tender and the franks hot and plumped. Taste for salt—please make sure to put enough salt in this—and serve it in bowls.

SCANDINAVIAN BOILED DINNER

(ROTMOS)

SERVES 4 TO 6

This is a traditional Swedish supper dish, a Scandinavian boiled dinner. The difference from the Italian or French version is that the meats are sent to the oven to brown and the simmering liquid is used to cook potatoes and turnips, which are then mashed together. It's a simple, hearty dish, with more flavor than you might expect. Try it some autumn night when there's a chill in the air.

The best potato for this might just be a Yukon Gold, but it's worth trying with a Maine potato like a Kennebec.

2–2½ pounds boneless pork shoulder
2–2½ pounds beef short ribs, cut into 2-rib sections
2 bay leaves
1 onion, peeled
4 whole cloves
Coarse salt and freshly ground black pepper
1½ pounds rutabaga or turnips, peeled and cut into 1-inch chunks
1¾ pounds all-purpose potatoes, peeled and cut into 2-inch chunks
2 tablespoons unsalted butter
3–4 tablespoons heavy cream
1 teaspoon sugar

Put the meats in a small kettle or stockpot and cover them with cold water. Bring to a boil and skim off the scum that rises to the surface. Stick the bay leaves onto the onion, using the cloves as tacks. Add it to the pot, cover partway, and simmer for 1¾ to 2 hours—a gentle simmer, just the laziest of bubbles.

Heat the oven to 350 degrees.

Transfer the meats from the broth to a roasting pan or cast-iron skillet.

Season with salt and pepper and roast for 30 minutes, or until browned.

While the meats roast, add the rutabaga to the meat broth and boil for 15 minutes. Add the potatoes and boil for 20 to 30 minutes, until the potatoes and rutabaga are both tender.

Drain the potatoes and rutabaga and return them to the pot. Mash with a hand masher—this should be a rustic mash, with some recognizable bits of rutabaga—and beat in the butter. Beat in the cream by the tablespoon, adding just enough to moisten the mash, then add the sugar and salt and pepper to taste.

Pile the mash in the center of a platter and surround with the short ribs and slices of pork shoulder. Serve this right away, while it's piping hot.

LEMONY VEAL SHANKS
WITH GARLIC AND POTATOES

SERVES 4

All unctuous and meaty, with the good lip-smacking sauce that braised veal shanks create—this is comforting food. The dish may seem to have a lot of garlic, but all of its heat cooks away, leaving just a nice sweetness that balances against the sharp lemon zest and the coriander seeds.

Go with a waxy potato; you want it to hold its shape.

3 tablespoons olive oil
4 veal shanks, about 1½ inches thick
Coarse salt and freshly ground black pepper
All-purpose flour for dredging
2 onions, thickly sliced
1 tablespoon coriander seeds, lightly crushed
1 small head garlic, separated into cloves, peeled, and chopped
Zest of 1 lemon, cut into strips and minced
1 cup dry white wine
1 cup Chicken Stock (page 85) or water
1 pound small new potatoes, peeled (cut in half if larger than 2 inches
   in diameter)

Heat the oven to 350 degrees.

Heat the olive oil in a Dutch oven or deep lidded flameproof casserole. Season the shanks on both sides with salt and pepper. Dredge them in the flour, shake off the excess, and brown over medium-high heat for about 5 minutes per side. Set the shanks on a plate.

Add the onions and coriander to the pot and cook, stirring a bit, until the onions are soft and golden, about 7 minutes. Add the garlic and lemon zest and cook a minute longer. Settle the shanks on top of the onions and pour in the wine and stock. Bring to a simmer. Cover the pot with a sheet of foil and then set the lid snugly in place. Slide into the oven and bake for 1 hour.

Remove the lid and add the potatoes to the pot, tucking them alongside the veal shanks to submerge them in the cooking liquid as best you can. Cover, return to the oven, and continue to bake until the veal is incredibly tender and the potatoes are cooked through, 35 to 45 minutes more.

If there is too much liquid left when the veal is ready, you might want to lift out the meat and potatoes from the pot and set them aside while you simmer the liquid for 5 to 10 minutes to reduce it. Serve warm.

VENISON AND POTATO STEW COOKED IN A PUMPKIN

SERVES 4 TO 6

Yes, yes, this is on the fussy side. But presenting a stew in a pumpkin really does dress up a homely dish. The easiest way to proceed is to start by baking the pumpkin in a large low casserole that will look good on the table. That way you needn't worry about transferring it from a baking sheet.

You can make the stew well in advance, even the day before. Just bring it to a simmer before you put it into the pumpkin. But you shouldn't cook the pumpkin much more than $1\frac{1}{2}$ hours before filling it with the stew, or it will start weeping and you run the risk of its collapsing.

1 (9-to-10-pound) cheese pumpkin (see note)
2 tablespoons olive oil
1 pound boneless venison, cut into 1-inch cubes
Coarse salt and freshly ground black pepper
1 large onion, minced
1 red or yellow bell pepper, cored, seeded, and minced
1 garlic clove, minced
2 tablespoons brandy
4 plum tomatoes, peeled, seeded, and chopped (see page 30)
2 cups Beef Stock (page 115)
1 bay leaf
1 sprig rosemary
2 or 3 sprigs thyme
1 pound sweet potatoes, peeled and cut into $\frac{1}{3}$-inch-thick pieces
1 pound German Butterball or other yellow-fleshed potatoes, peeled and cut into $\frac{1}{3}$-inch pieces
$\frac{1}{2}$ cup dried currants

Heat the oven to 350 degrees.

Cut a lid from the pumpkin and remove the strings and seeds. Replace the lid and put the pumpkin in a large shallow casserole or on a rimmed baking sheet. Bake the pumpkin until it's just tender, about 45 minutes; check it with a skewer or a small sharp knife.

Start the stew while the pumpkin bakes: Heat the oil in a large ovenproof casserole, like an enameled cast-iron cocotte or Dutch oven, over medium heat. Add the venison, season with salt and pepper, and cook, turning, until nicely browned. Remove the meat with a slotted spoon and put it in a bowl. Add the onion, bell pepper, garlic, and salt and pepper to taste to the pot and cook until all the vegetables have softened, 5 to 7 minutes.

Return the venison and any of its juices to the pot, pour in the brandy, and cook for a minute or two. Add the tomatoes and stock and bring to a simmer. Tie the bay leaf, rosemary, and thyme together with kitchen string and add to the pot. Cover and simmer very gently for 1 hour. (You can also cover and bake it at 350 degrees for an hour.)

Stir all the potatoes into the stew, cover again, and simmer until the potatoes are tender, 30 to 35 minutes. Stir in the currants.

Ladle the stew into the pumpkin, replace the lid, and bake for 30 minutes. Serve the stew in bowls, and be sure to scrape some of the pumpkin flesh into each serving.

NOTE: I love the flavor and look of cheese pumpkins, but I find them only at farmer's markets. Any pumpkin, really, will do.

LEEK AND POTATO MEATBALLS

SERVES 4 TO 6 (MAKES ABOUT 12 MEATBALLS)

We found this dish, called *albóndigas di Prasa,* in Claudia Roden's *The Book of Jewish Food,* and adapted it. The yogurt and cilantro sauce that follows is a great accompaniment, but you might want to put out a very simple tomato sauce instead. These are really more patties than meatballs, but whatever you call them, they're superb. You can also shape them into bite-sized meatballs, fry, and serve them on tooth-picks as cocktail snacks with the sauce for dipping.

1$^1/_2$ tablespoons unsalted butter
2 cups chopped leeks (white and pale green parts)
Coarse salt and freshly ground black pepper
$^1/_2$ pound white potatoes, boiled
2 large eggs
$^1/_2$ teaspoon ground coriander
$^1/_4$ teaspoon ground cumin
$^1/_2$ pound ground pork or beef
Vegetable oil for frying
All-purpose flour for dredging
Yogurt-Cilantro Sauce (facing page)

Melt the butter in a skillet over medium-low heat. Add the leeks and season with salt and pepper. Cook, loosely covered, until wilted and tender, about 10 minutes.

Peel the potatoes and rice them into a mixing bowl. Lightly beat 1 of the eggs and add to the bowl, with the leeks, coriander, cumin, $^1/_2$ teaspoon salt, and pepper to taste. Stir with a wooden spoon until well combined, then crumble in the ground beef. Toss with your hands and mix until just smooth and combined. If you overwork a meat mix like this one, you will end up with hock-ey pucks instead of tender patties. Gently shape into patties, each 2$^1/_2$ to 3 inches across and not more than 3/4 inch thick. Cover with plastic and refrigerate for at least 1 hour and up to 8 hours.

Heat 1/2 inch of oil in a large skillet over medium-high heat until it begins to shimmer. Put the remaining egg in a shallow bowl and beat in 1 tablespoon water. Put the flour in another shallow bowl. Dredge each patty in flour, tap to get rid of the excess, and then dip in the egg. Slide a few patties, one by one, into the hot oil (you cook them in batches so they have room to brown, which they won't if you crowd them in the pan). Lower the heat to medium and cook, flipping once, until nicely browned on both sides and cooked in the center, about 6 minutes total. Drain on paper towels and keep warm while you cook the remaining patties.

Serve immediately, with the yogurt sauce. If you're not serving the patties right away, they can be kept warm in a low oven for 20 minutes.

YOGURT-CILANTRO SAUCE

This quick raita-type sauce for the meatballs is best made with whole-milk yogurt, but you can substitute half sour cream for half the yogurt if you care to.

MAKES ABOUT 1 CUP

1 cup plain yogurt
2 whole scallions, minced
1 small garlic clove, minced
1/4 cup loosely packed cilantro leaves, chopped
Fresh lime juice
Pinch of cayenne pepper
Coarse salt

Stir the yogurt, scallions, garlic, and cilantro together in a small bowl. Add a squeeze or two of lime, the cayenne, and salt to taste. This is best served right away (and it takes no time to make), but it will keep for a few hours in the refrigerator.

CORNED BEEF HASH

Hash is one of those recipes that can be gussied up and put on your finest china or kept simple and served cowboy-style right from the skillet. Depending on the ingredients, you might call it breakfast, lunch, or even a side for dinner. Since corned beef hash is a day-after dish made from last night's boiled dinner, a written recipe may seem to miss the point. (To find out more about hash and improvising your own, see page 236.) You can use a hunk of deli corned beef— but think how much better it would taste if you simmered your own. Rinse a 2-pound piece of corned beef or brisket, cover it with boiling water, and simmer very gently for about 2 hours. That will leave you enough for this recipe. We flip the hash three times to get that browned flavor all the way through the hash, not just on the bottom. And we do not consider poached eggs an optional ingredient.

3 tablespoons bacon drippings or vegetable oil
1 onion, chopped
1 pound cold boiled potatoes, peeled and cut into $1/2$-inch cubes
About 1 pound corned beef, cut into $1/2$-inch cubes
Freshly grated nutmeg
Coarse salt and freshly ground black pepper
$1/2$ cup heavy cream
6 large eggs, poached (see page 176)

Heat the drippings in a large heavy skillet, cast-iron if you have it, over medium-high heat. Add the onion and cook until it's softened and starting to brown, 3 to 4 minutes.

While the onion cooks, toss the potatoes and corned beef together in a big bowl and season with a grating or two of nutmeg, some salt (taste first—the beef can be salty), and plenty of pepper.

Dump the meat mix into the skillet and turn with a spatula to combine it with the onion. Press down hard with the back of your spatula to compress the hash. Right now, you may think the pan's too small, but don't worry; the hash will compress a lot as it cooks. Lower the heat to medium and leave the hash alone while it forms a bottom crust. Well, not completely alone, because you should press down on it a few times during the 8 to 10 minutes this will take. If the bottom seems to be browning too quickly, lower the heat a smidge.

Pour the cream over the hash and turn it with the spatula to break up the bottom crust and incorporate the cream. Flatten it again and let it cook, undisturbed save for the occasional pressing, for another 8 minutes.

Flip and turn one last time. By now the hash should be quite tender and easy to compress. Flatten it again and cook until there is a good, crisp crust on the bottom and all the cream has cooked away, about another 8 minutes.

Serve the hash from the skillet with a spatula, flipping each serving to its crusty side, and top each with a poached egg.

VARIATION
RED FLANNEL HASH

Besides contributing color—red flannel hash is rosy red—beets lend a sweetness that plays wonderfully off the saltiness of the corned beef.

Reduce the amount of potatoes to 3/4 pound and add 1/2 pound cold cooked beets that you've cut into 1/2-inch dice along with the potatoes.

IMPROVISING HASH

In its inception, hash was a humble hodgepodge made from leftover bits of cooked vegetables and meat (from the French word *hacher,* meaning "to chop"). Now all that's required to call something hash is that the ingredients be chopped and then cooked up in a heavy skillet to form a loose cake with a good ratio of crispy brown crust to moist and tender interior. (Think of hash-browned potatoes.)

We like to improvise, so here are some guidelines.

Start with roughly equal parts of diced cold boiled potatoes and diced leftover meat. Besides roast beef, chicken, ham, and lamb, you might want to try leftover salmon or trout. While the potatoes are the mainstay—their starch helps hold the hash together—you can supplement them with other leftover root vegetables, such as beets, rutabagas, turnips, or parsnips. For quantity, you'll need about 1 heaping cup combined vegetables and meat per serving. No less!

Toss the meat and vegetables together in a large bowl and season them before cooking. Hash likes to be highly seasoned, typically with a good blast of freshly ground black pepper. But there's no reason you shouldn't consider parsley, scallions, nutmeg, Worcestershire sauce, and other lively seasonings—like hot pepper sauce with roast beef hash.

We often moisten our hash with a bit of cream or milk, sometimes stock. This isn't absolutely necessary, but it does help the cake hold together better, and the protein in the liquid encourages browning. We confess to a weakness for cream, since it also makes the hash more tender. And if the meat is on the dry side, liquid isn't going to hurt—but don't go overboard. About 2 to 4 tablespoons per cup of hash will be more than adequate. You can either add it when you're tossing the ingredients with the seasonings or drizzle it into the skillet partway through cooking. The latter method gives you a good sizzle and immediate evaporation and caramelization when the liquid hits the hot skillet.

A well-seasoned cast-iron skillet is our pot of choice. We get the best crust from it and have the least trouble with sticking.

Begin with 2 to 3 tablespoons of fat over medium-high heat. We like bacon fat, but we'll use just about anything: butter, duck fat, vegetable oil. Sauté a chopped onion in the fat until the edges are starting to turn golden, then add the hash mixture and lower the heat a bit.

Now, be patient: patience is good for hash. Press down hard with the back of a flexible spatula and let the hash cook, undisturbed, long enough to form a good, crunchy bottom crust. Now use the spatula to turn the hash in pieces, stirring and distributing the crust. Press down hard again and let it form a new crust. You can do this a couple times more, but don't get carried away; you might be left without any tender center.

Serve the hash crust up. The crunch and flavor make it the perfect accompaniment to a runny poached egg.

POTATO, HAM, AND CHEESE CASSEROLE

Think of a cross between macaroni and cheese and a ham-and-Swiss sandwich and you'll start to picture this comforting casserole.

To make the rye bread crumbs, lightly toast 2 slices of seedless rye, let them cool, then grind to fine crumbs in a food processor. Yukons aren't the only potato possible; make this with any leftover boiled potato.

1/2 pound Black Forest or baked Virginia ham, cut into 1/4-inch cubes
2 teaspoons Dijon mustard
6 tablespoons (3/4 stick) unsalted butter
1 large onion, thinly sliced
Coarse salt and freshly ground white or black pepper
2 pounds cold boiled Yukon Gold potatoes, peeled and cut into 1/3-inch cubes
2 tablespoons all-purpose flour
2 cups milk
8 ounces good-quality Swiss cheese, such as Jarlsberg, shredded (2 cups)
2/3 cup dried rye bread crumbs

Heat the oven to 350 degrees. Butter a 2-quart casserole dish.

Put the ham in a big bowl and add the mustard. Stir to distribute the mustard evenly.

Melt 2 tablespoons of the butter in a heavy saucepan over medium heat. Add the onion, season with salt and pepper, and cook, stirring occasionally, until tender and golden, about 10 minutes. Add the onion to the ham and stir to combine. Add the potatoes and stir gently, so as not to break up too many of them.

Return the saucepan to the heat and add 2 more tablespoons of the butter. When the butter begins to foam, whisk in the flour and cook for a minute or two. Slowly add the milk, whisking to prevent lumps. Bring the milk to a simmer, stirring with a wooden spoon to prevent sticking. Let the sauce simmer until lightly thickened, 2 to 3 minutes.

Take the sauce from the heat, season with salt and pepper, and then slowly stir in the cheese, a handful at a time, until smooth. Pour the sauce over the ham and potato mixture and stir to combine. Transfer the mixture to the casserole dish.

Melt the remaining 2 tablespoons butter and toss the bread crumbs with it. Sprinkle the bread crumbs over the casserole and bake until the top is golden and the edges are bubbling, about 45 minutes. Let it sit for at least 5 minutes before serving.

DILLED COD WITH DUCHESS POTATOES

Thick fillets of cod are baked on a platter rimmed with a piped border of duchess potatoes—very country club. The edging of duchess potatoes shields the fillets from the oven heat so they cook a bit more slowly and stay tender and juicy. The dilled butter on top melts, mingles with the wine and fish juices, and makes a nice little sauce to spoon over the fish and potatoes.

Salmon or halibut fillets would be good here too. Whatever fillets you choose, be sure that they are skinless and 1 to 1½ inches thick so they cook in the same time as the potatoes. If you use thinner fillets, first bake the border of potatoes by themselves, then, after about 10 minutes, arrange the fillets in the center, top with the butter, and finish baking.

You'll need a large platter that can go from the oven to the table for this.

4 tablespoons (½ stick) unsalted butter, softened
1½ tablespoons chopped fresh dill
Duchess Potatoes (page 402)
1 large egg, beaten with 1 teaspoon water, for an egg wash
1 shallot, finely chopped
1½–2 pounds thick cod fillets
Coarse salt and freshly ground black pepper
1–2 tablespoons dry white wine, dry vermouth, or fresh lemon juice
Sprigs of curly parsley for garnish

Heat the oven to 400 degrees. Butter a large ovenproof serving platter.
Combine the butter and dill, whipping with a fork.
Fit a pastry bag with a large star tip and fill the bag with the duchess pota-

toes. Pipe a thick border, about 1 inch high, around the edge of the platter. Brush the potatoes with the egg wash—lightly, please, so you don't ruin your piping.

Scatter the shallot over the bottom of the platter. Arrange the fillets on top, tucking under any thin tail or belly pieces so that the fillets are an even thickness. The fillets should be lightly touching each other but not overlapping. Season the fish with salt and pepper. Dot the tops of the fillets generously with the dill butter. Splash on a tablespoon or so of the white wine.

Bake until the potatoes are just beginning to turn golden on the edges and the fish is cooked through, 20 to 25 minutes.

The *garni du jour* for this dish could only be sprigs of curly parsley. Serve from the platter.

BLUEFISH ON A BED OF POTATOES

I'm a longtime fan of bluefish, but I also know that if bluefish is going to be good, it had better be fresh. I'm certain you know what to look for: bright and shining eyes, vibrant gills, and an utter absence of any "fishy" smell. Get a whole fish and ask the fishmonger to fillet it. You can substitute other fish: Spanish mackerel, halibut, or haddock. I've even made this with scrod.

The potatoes start cooking first, softening and sopping up some of the juices from the tomatoes. Then they're ready for all the oils and juices from the fish. Peel the potatoes or not, as you like.

4 slices good white bread
2 pounds bluefish fillets with skin
Coarse salt and freshly ground black pepper
Olive oil
1½ pounds red-skinned or yellow-fleshed potatoes, scrubbed or peeled,
    cut into ⅛-inch-thick slices
1 onion, thinly sliced
2 ripe tomatoes, halved and thinly sliced
2 garlic cloves, thinly sliced
½ cup flat-leaf parsley leaves
½ teaspoon dried oregano or thyme
⅓ cup freshly grated Pecorino
2 tablespoons red wine vinegar

Heat the oven to 300 degrees.

Put the bread slices on one of the oven racks and leave them there for about 10 minutes, until golden. Let them cool on a rack. Increase the oven temperature to 350 degrees.

Take the fish out of the fridge and season it with salt and pepper.

Rub a large (3-quart) nice-looking casserole with a bit of olive oil. Spread out about a third of the potatoes in the dish and top with half the onion. Season with salt and pepper and drizzle with oil. Repeat, ending with a layer of potatoes. Top with the tomato slices and a sprinkling of salt. Pop the dish into the oven and bake for 45 minutes. By then, the potatoes should be just about done.

Finish the crumbs while the potatoes are cooking. Turn on the food processor and drop in the garlic slices. Once they're chopped, scrape the sides of the bowl, add the parsley, and hit the pulse button two or three times. Break up the bread and add that, with the dried herb of choice and the Pecorino. Turn the machine on again and let it go until you have fine and rather lovely green crumbs.

Lay the fish skin side down on the potatoes and tomatoes and pack all the crumbs on top of the fillets. You should still have some naked tomatoes and potatoes visible. Whisk together the vinegar and 3 tablespoons oil until creamy (or put in a jar and shake), then drizzle the vinaigrette over the crumbs. It'll look streaky; don't worry. Slip the dish back into the oven and bake for 30 minutes.

Bring the dish to the table in the casserole. That's why you used a nice-looking one. Serve hot.

SQUID WITH POTATOES

We turned to Marcella Hazan for inspiration for this truly great dish. The squid is meltingly tender and the potatoes are packed with flavor.

Plan on soup plates and plenty of bread to sop up the sauce.

3 pounds squid (or 2 pounds cleaned squid)
2 garlic cloves, chopped
$^1/_4$ cup olive oil
$^1/_4$ cup chopped flat-leaf parsley
$^1/_3$ cup dry vermouth
1 cup canned tomatoes, chopped, with their juice
$^1/_2$ teaspoon dried oregano, preferably Mediterranean
Crushed red pepper to taste
Coarse salt and freshly ground black pepper
1$^1/_2$ pounds red-skinned or white potatoes, peeled, halved, and cut into $^1/_2$-inch-thick slices
Extra-virgin olive oil for serving

TO CLEAN THE SQUID: Take hold of the tentacles and gently pull them from the body; the innards will follow. Cut off and discard the innards, and squeeze the center bit of the tentacles to expose the beak. Snip this off and toss it. Locate the quill, the long plasticlike spine, and pull it out; make sure it has not broken, leaving a piece in the body. Check the inside of the body with your index finger to find errant bits of innards, and then peel off the purplish skin. (No one said this was a fun job, but I don't believe fishmongers are ever as diligent in cleaning squid as one would hope, so I do it myself.) Rinse the squid well in cold water. Cut the bodies into 1-inch rings, the tentacles in half if they're very large, and dry thoroughly.

Put the garlic and olive oil in a large skillet, turn the heat to high, and cook until the garlic is golden. Add the parsley and cook for about 30 seconds. Add the squid a handful at a time (so you don't lower the heat of the pan) — and be alert while you do this: the squid will pop and spit, and the popping oil could result in a nasty burn. After 2 to 3 minutes, the squid will begin whitening and curling back at the edges, which is the signal for you to add the vermouth. Cook for 1 minute, then add the tomatoes, oregano, crushed red pepper, and salt and pepper to taste. Bring to a boil, then lower the heat and simmer for 45 minutes.

Stir in the potatoes and cook for about 40 more minutes, until the potatoes are tender. Taste for salt and pepper and serve. Pass a cruet of extra-virgin olive oil at the table for drizzling.

RED SNAPPER WITH A POTATO CRUST

Some ideas are too good to pass by. The notion of wrapping fish in thin scales of potato before cooking is one of them. The potatoes crisp as they cook, giving you a crunchy coating around a moist fish fillet. You'll need a mandoline to make paper-thin slices that will easily cling to the contour of the fillet. If snapper's not your thing, sea bass or halibut will do.

1 pound waxy potatoes, peeled
6 tablespoons (3/4 stick) unsalted butter, melted
1¼ pounds red snapper fillets, skin removed (cut into 4 pieces)
Coarse salt and freshly ground black pepper

Slice the potatoes into paper-thin slices on a mandoline and put them into a large bowl. Pour in the melted butter and toss to coat all the slices.

Season the fillets with salt and pepper. Arrange the potato slices on the surface of the fillets in an overlapping pattern to loosely imitate fish scales; press them down so they stick. Turn the fillets and cover the other side with potatoes. You may have leftover potatoes, depending on the shape and size of the fillets. Put the potato-wrapped fillets on a large plate and refrigerate until the butter solidifies, 20 to 30 minutes.

Heat the oven to 375 degrees.

Heat a large, preferably nonstick, ovenproof skillet over medium-high heat. Put the fillets into the skillet and cook until the bottom potato crust is nicely browned, about 4 minutes. Flip and then slide the entire skillet into the oven to finish cooking, another 8 to 10 minutes. Serve immediately.

PASTA, POTATOES, AND PANCETTA

SERVES 4

You want to overcook the pasta here until it's as soft as the potatoes. For cooks like us, who taste as they go, this simple dish will be a revelation. Just before it's done, there's a great leap of flavor when everything suddenly comes together.

Be sure to use best-quality canned tomatoes and pasta. We like it with linguine, but it can be made with pretty much any dried pasta. This weeknight supper dish started out in Mark Bittman's *How to Cook Everything.* He says it's Neapolitan.

1 tablespoon olive oil
1/4 pound pancetta, cut into 1/3-inch dice
2 garlic cloves, minced
1 teaspoon crushed red pepper
1 1/2 pounds all-purpose potatoes, scrubbed and cut into 1/2-inch pieces
Coarse salt and freshly ground black pepper
1/2 pound linguine, broken into 3-to-4-inch pieces (see note above)
1 (28-ounce) can whole tomatoes, with their juice

Put the oil and pancetta in a heavy 4-to-6-quart pot over medium heat. Cook until the fat has rendered and the pancetta is just starting to brown. Stir in the garlic and crushed red pepper and cook for a minute more. Add the potatoes and cook, stirring occasionally, until they begin to brown in spots, 5 to 7 minutes. Season with salt and pepper.

Add the pasta and tomatoes and stir to combine. Fill the tomato can halfway with warm water and pour it into the pot. Stir again. The liquid should just cover the pasta and potatoes. If not, add a bit more warm water. Cover partway and simmer, stirring from time to time, for 30 minutes. If things appear too dry during this time, add a bit more warm water. Remove the cover, stop adding water, and continue to simmer and stir occasionally until both the pasta and potatoes are very tender and the sauce is quite thick, 10 to 15 minutes longer. Taste for salt and pepper.

Serve in pasta bowls.

GNOCCHI WITH PASSATA

A couple of ground rules here. First, you need a ricer to make gnocchi. Second, the potatoes have to be peeled and riced immediately after you cook them. Keep a light hand and follow the rules, and you'll be rewarded with light gnocchi—just the way they should be.

There are countless ways of serving these little dumplings. Make the passata, use your favorite sauce, or see the variation.

1½ pounds russet potatoes, scrubbed
Coarse salt
1–1¼ cups all-purpose flour
1 tablespoon olive oil
1 garlic clove, minced
Crushed red pepper
2 cups passata (page 160)
Freshly grated Parmesan or Pecorino for serving

Put the potatoes in a saucepan, cover with cold water by at least an inch, add a good pinch of salt, and bring to a boil. Cover partway, reduce the heat to medium, and cook until the potatoes are tender. Drain on a rack set in the sink.

Peel the potatoes immediately—you can hold them in a kitchen towel to protect your hands—and put the potatoes back on the rack as you peel them. Once you've peeled them all, rice the potatoes into a large bowl or onto a baking sheet. Spread them out gently to expose as much surface as possible and take a deep breath. You can leave them to cool now, anywhere from 15 minutes to an hour.

Sprinkle the potatoes with 1 cup of the flour and a pinch of salt. Toss with your hands to distribute the flour, then start to gather the dough into a mass. Knead it briefly—just to make it come together smoothly. Lightly flour a board, pinch off a bit of dough, and roll it into a rope. If it crumbles, you need more flour. Add up to $1/4$ cup more, going through the same procedure: sprinkle, toss, gather, and knead.

Dump the dough onto your floured surface and flatten it into a rectangle about $1/2$ inch thick. Flour a knife and cut the rectangle into $1/2$-inch-wide strips. Roll each strip into a rope. Keep tossing flour onto the work surface as you need it. Cut the ropes into pieces just shy of an inch long.

You give gnocchi their final shaping by rolling them down the tines of a fork. Flour the work surface and hold the fork in one hand, tines resting on the work surface. Use your thumb (or index finger, if that feels more natural) to roll the dumpling down the length of the tines. You should end up with a deep indentation on one side and grooves along the back. Set the gnocchi on a floured tray for up to an hour before you cook them.

Heat the oil in a skillet over medium heat until it shimmers. Add the garlic and cook just until it becomes fragrant, a minute or two. Add a pinch of crushed red pepper and the tomato sauce. Simmer for 10 minutes.

Meanwhile, bring a large pot of water to a boil. Salt the water very well and add about one-third of the gnocchi. Bring back to a simmer and cook until all the gnocchi are floating. The simmer is important here: if the water is bubbling with vigor, it will force the gnocchi up to the top and you won't be able to tell if they're really floating. Take the gnocchi out with a large skimmer or slotted spoon and drain well. It's a big help to have several thicknesses of paper towels or kitchen towels on hand; blot the back of the skimmer holding the gnocchi, to wick out the water. Put the gnocchi in a warm serving dish. Spoon some of the tomato sauce over the top. Repeat with the remaining gnocchi, saucing as you go.

Serve any extra sauce on the side, and pass the cheese.

VARIATION

A classic way of presenting gnocchi is with pesto and green beans. Bring a pot of water to a boil. Drop in 1 pound string beans that have been topped and tailed, add some salt, and cook until the beans are tender, 7 to 8 minutes. Drain, rinse with cold water, and drain again very well. Add them to a serving dish with the gnocchi and sauce them with Pesto (page 251).

PESTO

Saucing gnocchi isn't the only use for this great pesto. I love beating it into mashed potatoes (see page 283), and you can also cut some potatoes and zucchini into big chunks, coat them well with the pesto, and roast them.

You can easily double the recipe and keep the extra, covered with a film of olive oil, in a well-sealed container in the refrigerator for a few days. This does freeze, but hold back the cheese; stir it in after the pesto has defrosted.

2 packed cups fresh basil leaves
3 garlic cloves, sliced
3/4 cup pine nuts
1 cup olive oil
3/4 cup freshly grated Parmesan
Coarse salt

Put the basil in a plastic bag and bruise the leaves with a rolling pin.

Turn the food processor on and drop the garlic slices in a few at a time. They'll fly around and end up in small bits on the sides of the bowl. Scrape the sides, add the basil and pine nuts, and hit the pulse button a few times to chop them up. Then turn the machine on and pour in the oil in an even stream. When you have a thick, smooth puree, turn off the processor and scrape the pesto into a bowl. Stir in the Parmesan and salt to taste.

EGGPLANT GNOCCHI

When my friend Susan came back from a trip to Milan raving about the eggplant gnocchi she had, I knew I had to develop a recipe. These dumplings, combined with a raw tomato sauce, sing of summer. The eggplant gives the gnocchi a rich, hearty flavor.

1 large eggplant (about 1½ pounds)
Coarse salt
1¼ pounds russet potatoes, scrubbed
1 large egg
1–1½ cups all-purpose flour
Salsa Cruda (page 254)

Heat the oven to 350 degrees.

Cut the eggplant in half the long way. Make crosshatch cuts through the flesh without going through the skin and rub the surface and cuts well with salt.

Make a tray of heavy-duty aluminum foil large enough for the eggplant and put it in the oven. Put the eggplant on the tray skin side down. Set the potatoes on the oven rack and set the timer for 30 minutes.

When your timer goes off, prick the potatoes all over with a fork or the tip of a sharp knife and put them back on the rack. Bake the potatoes and eggplant for another 30 minutes or so. Squeeze the potatoes to make sure they're done; you should leave an indentation.

Cut the potatoes in half right away, scoop out the flesh with a spoon, and rice it into a large bowl. Spread out the potato in the bowl and let it cool completely. Let the eggplant cool on its tray.

When the eggplant is cool, pull off the skin. Bits of flesh will want to come along with the skin; don't let them. Put the eggplant onto a clean kitchen towel and twist and squeeze it mercilessly over the sink to rid it of as much moisture as possible. Chop up the eggplant rather fine and add it to the potatoes.

Crack the egg into the eggplant and potatoes, add a big pinch of salt, and mix this all up. Then add 1 cup of the flour and work it in with your hands. Add as much of the remaining flour as you need to make manageable (pretty manageable) dough. It will be sticky, and it should be sticky.

Flour a board and scrape the dough out onto it. Knead the dough a few times to smooth it out; don't get obsessive. Pat the dough out a bit less than $1/2$ inch thick, then cut into $1/2$-inch-wide strips. Roll the strips with your hands to turn them into ropes, then cut the ropes into $1/2$-inch pieces. You don't need to use a ruler for any of this; it doesn't make that much difference. Just make little dumplings the size you want to eat. You can cook these right away or put them on a well-floured baking sheet and leave them out uncovered for a few hours. Never refrigerate them.

Bring a large pot of water to a boil, then salt it very well. Drop in some of the gnocchi (the amount depends on the size of the pot; don't crowd them) by handfuls and leave them alone for a minute. Then stir gently with a wooden spoon to separate them and unstick any from the bottom. Once the gnocchi have risen to the top, cook for $1^{1}/_2$ to 2 minutes, until done to your liking. Taste one to be sure.

Scoop the gnocchi out with a skimmer or slotted spoon, rest the skimmer on a kitchen towel to drain, and double the towel over to blot the dumplings dry. Be gentle. Drop the gnocchi into a serving bowl and add some of the salsa cruda. Repeat until you've cooked all the gnocchi, and serve immediately.

POTATO AND GOAT CHEESE RAVIOLI
WITH SALSA CRUDA

SERVES 4 TO 6

Potatoes—roughly mashed with a fork and flavored with goat cheese—stand in here for the more common ricotta filling in ravioli. The result is richer pasta. The filling is intended as a flavor, not the star. Play with the kind of potato you use here. Just about anything but a russet will work.

Please don't bother making the Salsa Cruda if you don't have summer tomatoes from your garden or a farm stand. Instead, sauce these with a simple tomato sauce (passata; see page 160). You might want to sweat a small minced onion in a knob of butter until it's limp, then add the sauce and cook for about 20 minutes.

FOR THE FILLING
$^{1}/_{2}$ pound potatoes (see note above), peeled and cut into chunks
Coarse salt
1 tablespoon heavy cream or milk
2 ounces ($^{1}/_{4}$ cup) fresh goat cheese
1 tablespoon chopped flat-leaf parsley
1 small garlic clove, minced very fine
Freshly ground black pepper

FOR THE PASTA
$2^{2}/_{3}$ cups all-purpose flour, plus more for kneading and rolling
Coarse salt
4 large eggs
1 tablespoon olive oil

Cornmeal for dusting

4 ripe summer tomatoes, seeded and chopped (see page 30)

2 garlic cloves, minced

1 chile pepper, minced

1/4 cup chopped mixed flat-leaf parsley and fresh basil (or use just one
of the herbs)

1/4 cup extra-virgin olive oil

Coarse salt and freshly ground black pepper to taste

FOR THE FILLING: Put the potatoes in a saucepan, cover with cold water by at least an inch, add a good pinch of salt, and bring to a boil. Cover partway, reduce the heat to medium, and cook until the potatoes are tender. Drain well, and return the potatoes to the pot. Put them back on the heat and shake the pan for a minute or so to dry the potatoes.

Mash the potatoes with a fork, then add the cream and whip with your fork until the potatoes are smooth and light. Beat in the cheese, parsley, garlic, and salt and pepper to taste. Put this out of the way somewhere, covered with plastic, while you make the pasta.

FOR THE PASTA: Pile the flour onto a work surface and mix in about 1 teaspoon salt (you can also do this in a wide shallow bowl). Make a well in the center of the flour and crack in the eggs. Spoon the oil onto the eggs and beat the eggs with a fork. Then use the fork to pull the flour into the eggs, little by little, trying not to break the flour "wall" and having the eggs run over the counter, just until you have a firm but still somewhat sticky dough that you can't work with a fork anymore. You won't use all the flour.

Move the dough to a well-floured surface—leave the extra flour and any small bits of egg and dough behind; they never really work into the dough, and you'd end up with tough bits in your pasta. Flour your hands well and knead the dough until it's satiny. Have a pile of flour at hand so you can add more as you need it. The finished dough should not be at all sticky. Wrap it in plastic and let it relax for about 20 minutes.

Now you're ready for the final kneading of the pasta. Cut off one-quarter of the pasta, flour it, and flatten it into a rectangle. (Leave the rest covered.) Put it through the pasta machine at the widest setting. Fold it in thirds, flatten it, and put it through the widest setting again. Repeat this two or three more times, flouring if the dough is sticky and changing the direction of your folds. You want to end up with a rectangle that's just slightly narrower than the rollers and with corners as squared off as possible.

Now roll the pasta. Turn the setting of the pasta machine down a notch and put the sheet through once. Continue feeding the sheet through the machine, moving the notch down a setting each time, until you have reached the next-to-last setting, flouring the pasta sheet as needed. Set the pasta sheet on a floured counter and repeat with the rest of the dough, working with one-quarter at a time.

You have two options for filling the pasta: you can make small ravioli or you can make larger ravioloni.

For the smaller pillows, spoon about ¹/₂ teaspoon of filling for each ravioli in a row along each of the 4 sheets of pasta, about an inch from the edge closest to you and about 1¹/₂ inches apart. Brush the edge closest to you and the spaces in between the filling with water and fold the top half of the sheet over the filling. Line up the edges and carefully work out any air pockets. Press along the sides and edges to seal. Cut down between the filling, check all the ravioli for tight seals, and transfer them to a tray dusted with cornmeal. Cover with a kitchen towel until you are ready to boil them.

For the ravioloni, use about 1 teaspoon of filling for each, making a row down the center of just 2 of the pasta sheets and placing the mounds of filling about 2 inches apart. Brush both edges and the spaces between the filling with water and cover each with a sheet of pasta. Work out the air pockets and press to seal. Cut down between the filling, check the seals, and transfer to trays dusted with cornmeal. Cover with a kitchen towel until you're ready to boil them.

FOR THE SALSA CRUDA: Combine the ingredients and leave the sauce on the counter until you're ready to use it; do not refrigerate it.

Bring a large pot of water to a boil. Add about 1 tablespoon salt and then drop in the pasta squares one by one. Cook until the pasta is tender, 2 to 3 minutes after the water returns to a gentle boil. Remove the ravioli with a spider or a slotted spoon to a kitchen towel to dry them, then put them in a wide shallow bowl. Spoon on the salsa and serve right away.

Potatoes Roasted in Salt, topped with
sour cream and salmon roe *page 34*

Roasted Sweet Potato Dip with Tamarind and Lime *page 46*

Samosas Filled with Potatoes and Peas *page 72*, served with Cilantro-Mint Chutney *page 75*

LEFT: Roasted Corn
Chowder *page 119*
BELOW: Kale, Potato,
Bean, and Linguiça Soup
page 110

Vietnamese Sweet Potato Shrimp Cakes *page 366*

Pissaladière-Stuffed Baked Red Potatoes *page 386*

Nancy Barr's Potato Cake *page 412*

LEFT: Saratoga Chips *page 314*
RIGHT: Small local russets and a
few old hand mashers
BELOW: Mash with Fresh Olivada
page 286

Potato Salad with Sweet Pickles and Buttermilk Dressing *page 146*

ABOVE: Fresh Tuna Salad with
Potatoes and Herbs *page 166*
LEFT: Rose Finn Apple
potatoes, a rosy-skinned
fingerling with yellow flesh

Lobster and Potato Salad with Tarragon *page 136*

Spicy Greens with Roasted Potatoes, String Beans, and Heirloom Tomatoes *page 174*

Pommes Anna, in the traditional
heavy copper pan (above) and
unmolded (right) *page 418*

Shoestring Fries *page 309*

Glazed Radishes and Red Bliss Potatoes *page 467*

Château Potatoes *page 324*

RIGHT: Yellow-fleshed Carola potatoes and Reddales,
a waxy, red-skinned variety
BELOW: Gratin Dauphinoise *page 442*

Leek and Potato Tart *page 262*

Spanish Potato Omelet *page 60*

Dilled Cod with Duchess Potatoes *page 240*

Gnocchi with Pesto *page 249*

Potatoes Roasted in Goose Fat   *page 393*

Shepherd's Pie *page 208*

RIGHT: Russian bananas, an heirloom potato
BELOW: Lyonnais Sausage and Warm Potato Salad with Lentils
page 222

ABOVE: Yukon Gold potatoes
LEFT: Potato-Cheddar Bread
with Chives *page 510*

Buttermilk Sweet Potato Biscuits *page 526*

Moravian Sugar Cake *page 538*

Caramel Sweet Potato Pie *page 560*

Sweet Potato Semifreddo *page 568*

Farmhouse Chocolate Cake *page 556*

SWEET POTATO RAVIOLI WITH CHIVE BUTTER

SERVES 4 TO 6

The idea for this filling comes from New York City chef Mario Batali, who one morning at the Union Square Greenmarket shared a list of ingredients and the caution that there should not be too much filling or too much sauce. The filling is light, satisfying, and flexible. You can roast or boil the potatoes, use fresh goat cheese instead of the ricotta, grate in a bit of nutmeg if you want, and substitute sage leaves for the chives in the butter sauce.

FOR THE FILLING
1½ cups cooked peeled sweet potato
⅓ cup freshly grated Parmesan
¼ cup ricotta
1 tablespoon minced flat-leaf parsley
Coarse salt and freshly ground black pepper

FOR THE PASTA
2⅔ cups all-purpose flour, plus additional for kneading and rolling
Coarse salt
4 large eggs
1 tablespoon olive oil

Cornmeal for dusting

FOR THE CHIVE BUTTER
6 tablespoons (¾ stick) cold unsalted butter
⅓ cup chive batons (chives cut into 1-inch lengths)

FOR THE FILLING: Whip the sweets with a fork or a small whisk until they're smooth. Beat in the cheeses, parsley, and salt and pepper to taste. Put this out of the way somewhere, covered with plastic, while you make the pasta.

FOR THE PASTA: Pile the flour on a work surface and mix in about 1 teaspoon salt (you can also do this in a wide shallow bowl). Make a well in the center of the flour and crack in the eggs. Spoon the oil onto the eggs and beat the eggs with a fork. Then use the fork to pull the flour into the eggs, little by little, trying not to break the flour "wall" and having the eggs run over the counter, until you have a firm but still somewhat sticky dough that you can't work with a fork anymore. You won't use all the flour.

Move the dough to a well-floured surface—leave the extra flour and any small bits of egg and dough behind; they never really work into the dough, and you'd end up with tough bits in your pasta. Flour your hands well and knead the dough until it's satiny. Have a pile of flour at hand so you can add more as you need it. The finished dough should not be at all sticky. Wrap it in plastic and let it relax for about 20 minutes.

Now knead the pasta. Cut off one-quarter of the pasta, flour it, and flatten it into a rectangle. (Keep the rest covered.) Put it through the pasta machine at the widest setting. Fold it in thirds, flatten it, and put it through the widest setting again. Repeat this two or three more times, flouring if the dough is sticky and changing the direction of your folds. You want to end up with a rectangle that's just slightly narrower than the rollers and with corners as squared off as possible.

Now roll the pasta. Turn the setting of the pasta machine down a notch and put the sheet through once. Continue until you have reached the next to last setting, flouring the pasta sheet as needed. Set the pasta sheet on a floured counter and repeat with the rest of the dough, working with one-quarter at a time.

You have two options for filling the pasta: small ravioli or large ravioloni.

For the smaller pillows, place about 1/2 teaspoon of filling in a row along each of the 4 sheets of pasta, about an inch from the edge closest to you and about 1 1/2 inches apart. Brush the edge closest to you and the spaces in between the filling with water and fold the top half of the sheet over the filling. Line up the edges and carefully work out any air pockets. Press along the sides and edges to seal. Cut down between the filling, check all the ravioli for tight seals, and transfer them to a tray dusted with cornmeal. Cover with a kitchen towel until you are ready to boil them.

For the ravioloni, use about 1 teaspoon of filling for each, making a row down the center of just 2 of the pasta sheets and placing the mounds of filling about 2 inches apart. Brush both edges and the spaces between the filling with water and cover each with a sheet of pasta. Work out the air pockets and press to seal. Cut down between the filling, check the seals, and transfer to trays dusted with cornmeal. Cover with a kitchen towel until you're ready to boil them.

FOR THE CHIVE BUTTER: Cut the butter into pieces into a skillet over medium heat. Once the foaming calms down, throw in the chives and cook for 30 seconds or so. Keep warm until the pasta is ready—next to the pasta pot is a good place.

Bring a large pot of water to a boil. Add about 1 tablespoon salt and then drop in the pasta squares one by one. Cook until the pasta is tender, 2 to 3 minutes after the water returns to a gentle boil. Remove the ravioli with a spider or slotted spoon to a kitchen towel to dry them, then put them in a wide shallow bowl. Pour the butter over them and serve right away.

CHEDDAR AND BACON SOUFFLÉ

Mashed potatoes, rather than the classic béchamel sauce, form the base of this soufflé. The result is a bit more substantial and rustic than a classic cheese soufflé, and cheesier too. Use a good sharp aged cheddar.

This makes a fine supper or a hefty first course.

1½ pounds russet potatoes, peeled and cut into large chunks
Coarse salt
2 tablespoons unsalted butter
¾ cup half-and-half or milk, heated
2 teaspoons Dijon mustard
½ teaspoon sweet paprika
Freshly ground pepper
5 large eggs, separated
8 ounces best-quality cheddar, shredded (about 2 cups)
¼ cup dried bread crumbs
½ pound sliced bacon
2 large egg whites
¼ teaspoon cream of tartar

Put the potatoes in a large saucepan, cover with cold water by at least an inch, add a good pinch of salt, and bring to a boil. Reduce the heat to medium, cover partway, and cook until the potatoes are very tender, 20 to 25 minutes. Drain the potatoes and return them to the pot. Set over medium heat for a minute or two, shaking and stirring so the potatoes don't stick, until the potatoes are floury and have made a film on the bottom of the pan. Remove from the heat.

Mash the potatoes with a hand masher, adding the butter as you go. Use a wooden spoon to beat the half-and-half into the potatoes, ¼ cup at a time. Season with the mustard, paprika, and salt and pepper. The potatoes should be highly seasoned. Beat in the egg yolks one at a time. Transfer the potatoes to a large bowl. Stir in the cheese and set aside to cool slightly.

Heat the oven to 375 degrees. Butter a 2-quart soufflé dish generously, and dust the inside with the bread crumbs, turning and shaking the dish to coat all sides and to shake out the excess.

Cook the bacon over medium-low heat until crisp. Drain, then crumble or chop into small pieces. Stir the bacon into the potatoes.

Combine all the egg whites (7 of them) in an impeccably clean mixing bowl. Beat until foamy and add the cream of tartar. Continue to beat until the whites are glossy and form soft peaks. Do not overbeat, or the soufflé won't rise as well as you'd like it to.

Using a large rubber spatula, stir one-third of the egg whites into the potato mixture. Then fold in the remaining whites gently but thoroughly. Fill the soufflé dish and bake on the lower rack of the oven until well risen, slightly firm, and golden brown on top, about 45 minutes. If you like a drier center—we prefer ours a bit moist—continue to bake for another 5 to 10 minutes. Serve immediately.

LEEK AND POTATO TART

We make a meal of this free-form tart with just a salad on the side
and sliced oranges for dessert. If you want, you can transform this
into a vegetarian dish by cutting out the bacon; add water by the
tablespoon if the leeks start to dry out when you're wilting them.

FOR THE PASTRY
1½ cups all-purpose flour
Coarse salt
12 tablespoons (1½ sticks) cold unsalted butter, cut into bits
1 large egg yolk

FOR THE FILLING
2 tablespoons unsalted butter
2 or 3 slices bacon, chopped
3½ cups sliced leeks (white and light green parts of 3–4 leeks)
Coarse salt and freshly ground black pepper
¾ pound cold boiled all-purpose potatoes, peeled and cut into ½-inch chunks
1 cup heavy cream
Freshly grated nutmeg
2 ounces Emmentaler or Gruyère cheese, shredded (about ½ cup)

FOR THE PASTRY: Put the flour in a bowl and add a good pinch of salt. Stir
with a fork. Add the butter, toss it in the flour, and then cut it into the flour
with a pastry cutter or your fingers. You want something that looks like very
coarse oatmeal, with some larger bits of butter. Drop in the yolk and work with
your fingers to distribute it evenly. Add 1 tablespoon ice water, toss the pastry
with a fork, and continue adding ice water and tossing and stirring with the
fork until the pastry comes together. You may need as much as 4 tablespoons
water. Gather the pastry into a ball, then form it into a disk on a lightly floured
countertop. Wrap it in plastic and refrigerate for 30 minutes.

Heat the oven to 350 degrees.

FOR THE FILLING: Heat the butter in a large skillet over medium heat. Add the bacon and cook until the fat has rendered and the bacon is beginning to brown. Raise the heat to medium-high, add the leeks, season with salt and pepper, and cook until the leeks are wilted and tender, about 7 minutes. Add the potatoes and cook for 3 to 5 minutes, until the potatoes just begin to brown.

Pour in 1/4 cup of the cream and cook, stirring and scraping the bottom of the pan, until the cream is mostly absorbed. Continue adding cream by 1/4-cup increments until it's all been mostly absorbed and the mixture is thick but still juicy. Remove it from the heat, grate in some nutmeg, and taste for salt and pepper.

Roll the pastry out to a 17-inch circle on a lightly floured counter. Transfer it to a parchment-lined baking sheet. Spread it with the leek mixture, leaving a border of about 2 1/2 inches all around. Strew the cheese over the top, and fold the border back over the filling.

Bake the tart for about 40 minutes, until it's bubbling and well browned. You can serve this hot or at room temperature.

MASHED

POTATOES

POTATO PRINCIPLES
MASHING POTATOES

If you want to be sure that you will have smooth, lump-free mashed potatoes, use a ricer. Nothing will beat the texture you end up with when you use one, but you can come pretty close with a hand masher. It just takes some practice and a strong arm. And no matter what you use to mash the potatoes, you will need a sturdy wooden spoon or a Japanese rice paddle (available at any cooking store for about $2.00) to beat the potatoes after they're mashed.

The masher I use most often has as its base a disk with square holes punched out. It works pretty well, as does the old-fashioned kind that looks like radiator coils. Others—the type with a square wire base with several other heavy wires set across it, for example—just don't do the job. The most venerable of all are the wooden pestles. Collect them, admire them, and dust them, but don't use them for anything but smashed potatoes. By the time you get the potatoes smooth for a mash with one of these, they will have turned into glue.

Cook the potatoes in plenty of water with a good pinch of salt until they are truly tender. The water shouldn't boil furiously—aim for solid, steady bubbles. You don't want the potatoes falling apart (which will happen if you overcook them or boil them too hard). Neither do you want them still firm in the center (fine for a plain boiled potato or many of the other recipes in the book), because you'll taste and feel those harder bits in the mash.

Drain the potatoes well and return them to the pot immediately without giving them time to cool. Stick them back over the heat and let them dry for about a minute. Shake the pan and stir the potatoes with a wooden spoon; don't let them stick. They'll break up some, and you'll see the transformation from slightly watery and gray to white and floury. It's a wonder. You'll see a similar transformation with yellow-fleshed potatoes; they won't turn white, but the yellow will become brighter and the potatoes more floury. Both russets and yellow will leave a film on the bottom of the pot when they're ready. Now turn the heat back to very low.

If you are using a ricer, dump the potatoes into a bowl and rice them back into the pot. Then proceed with whatever recipe you are following.

For just-about-lumpless potatoes with a hand masher, start mashing at the 12 o'clock position. Press down firmly and steadily, then move to 1 o'clock, 2 o'clock, and so on. If you've missed any pieces in the center, give them a firm mash. What you have will be fluffy, and you'll see some lumps. Work around in a circle again, this time a bit more vigorously and giving the masher a twist as you press down. The potatoes will start gathering into a mass. Work the masher even more vigorously now, making more of a circular whipping motion: down to the bottom of the pan, back toward you, and up. Once the potatoes have completely come together, the lumps should be gone, and the potatoes are ready for butter and cream or whatever else the recipe calls for.

About the ingredients you add to mashed potatoes: the butter should be soft—not runny and slumpy, but soft and still holding its shape. Sour cream, cream cheese, and goat cheese should all be at room temperature. And the liquids—milk or cream or potato water—should be hot. Yes, that usually means another dirty pan, but it makes a difference. Rinsing the saucepan with water before heating the cream or milk will make cleanup easier. If you have a microwave, use it to heat the cream or milk.

Add the liquid by small additions, usually no more than $1/4$ cup at a time. Stir with your wooden spoon or rice paddle until the liquid has been absorbed, then beat like the dickens to fluff the potatoes before you add more liquid.

Now, about the food mill and mash. You'll find lots of recipes in magazines and other books that suggest you put potatoes through a food mill when you're making mash. Molly and I both find that when we use this piece of equipment for mashing russets, the mill easily overworks them and we end up with gluey potatoes. We use the food mill for soups where there's plenty of added liquid to loosen things up, but we don't recommend it for plain mashed potatoes. As with soups, though, a food mill can come in handy for removing fibers when vegetables and potatoes are combined in a mash.

My mother uses a hand-held mixer to make mashed potatoes. They're not bad, but to me they're whipped, not mashed. If you want to use a hand mixer for any of these recipes except the classic French Mashed Potato Puree, go ahead. Just make sure they are *completely* free of lumps before you add any butter or liquid.

BASIC MASHED POTATOES

If you want a simple mashed potato, start here. You could make these with milk in place of the half-and-half.

You really should eat these right when you make them, but in a pinch, you can keep them warm for a short while over a pot of simmering water.

1½–1¾ pounds russet potatoes, peeled and cut into chunks
Coarse salt
4 tablespoons (½ stick) unsalted butter, softened
¾–1 cup half-and-half, heated
Freshly ground white pepper

Put the potatoes in a large saucepan, cover with cold water by at least an inch, add a good pinch of salt, and bring to a boil. Cover partway, reduce the heat to medium, and cook until the potatoes are tender. Drain the potatoes, return them to the pot, and put them back over the heat to dry. Shake the pan and stir until the potatoes are floury and have made a film on the bottom of the pan. Turn the heat to very low.

Put the potatoes through a ricer and return them to the pan, or mash them until perfectly smooth with a hand masher. Beat the butter into the potatoes with a sturdy wooden spoon. Add the half-and-half in small additions, about ¼ cup at a time, stirring first, then beating vigorously each time once the cream has been absorbed. You may not need all of it. It depends on how thirsty the potatoes are and how loose you like your mash. Season with salt and white pepper. Serve warm.

TRUFFLED MASHED POTATOES

Potatoes are the perfect backdrop to the heady, earthy flavor of truffles.

Stir 2 teaspoons truffle oil into the potatoes after you've beaten in the cream. Taste and correct the seasoning. Drizzle the potatoes with a bit more truffle oil just before serving. If you can get your hands on a fresh truffle, cut back on (or skip altogether) the truffle oil and finish with a few shavings of truffle.

MASHED POTATO PUREE

Ever wonder how those French restaurant chefs get their mashed potatoes so light and silky? Well, butter, for one thing. But if you really want to mimic their results, you'll need one of those large round drum sieves called a tamis. It takes a little time to push the puree through the sieve, but the results are ethereal. This recipe comes from restaurateur Georges Blanc. He suggests using a food mill, but we get much better results with a ricer.

2 pounds russet potatoes, peeled and cut into chunks
Coarse salt
12 tablespoons (1 1/2 sticks) unsalted butter, softened
1/2–3/4 cup heavy cream, heated, more if needed
Freshly grated nutmeg

Put the potatoes in a large saucepan, cover with cold water by at least an inch, add a good pinch of salt, and bring to a boil. Cover partway, reduce the heat to medium, and cook until the potatoes are tender. Drain the potatoes, return them to the pan, and put them back over the heat to dry. Shake the pan and stir until the potatoes are floury and have made a film on the bottom of the pan.

Put the potatoes through a ricer and return them to the pan over very low heat. Cut the butter into a few pieces, and beat the butter into the potatoes. Pour in 1/4 cup of the cream, stir until it is absorbed, and then beat the potatoes vigorously with a wooden spoon until light and fluffy. Repeat with a second addition of cream and, if needed to make a light puree, a third addition.

If you're going for the ne plus ultra potato puree, now's the time to push it through a drum sieve. What you do is place the tamis over a bowl, dump in the puree, and work it through with a rubber scraper. Afterward, heat the puree over very gentle heat or, better yet, in a double boiler.

Season the potatoes with nutmeg and salt and add more cream if the puree seems too stiff. Serve warm.

CURRIED MASHED POTATOES

Serve this deliciously spiced golden mash with robust stewed meats or poultry. If you feel like getting fancy, garnish it with chopped cilantro or the green of a scallion. And have a bit more coconut milk on hand in case you find you need it. Just warm the coconut milk; it separates if you boil it.

$1^1/_2$–$1^3/_4$ pounds russet potatoes, peeled and cut into chunks
Coarse salt
2 tablespoons unsalted butter
1 onion, chopped
1 tablespoon Madras curry powder (medium-hot)
1 garlic clove, minced
1 teaspoon grated fresh ginger
$^1/_2$ cup cream (heavy or light, your choice)
About $^1/_2$ cup coconut milk, warmed (see note above)
Pinch of cayenne pepper

Put the potatoes in a large saucepan, cover with cold water by at least an inch, add a good pinch of salt, and bring to a boil. Cover partway, reduce the heat to medium, and cook until the potatoes are tender.

Meanwhile, heat the butter in a skillet over medium heat. Add the onion and cook, stirring occasionally, until golden, about 10 minutes. Add the curry powder, garlic, and ginger and cook, stirring, until fragrant, about 1 minute. Pour in the cream and simmer until reduced by about half and quite thick, about 5 minutes. Remove from the heat.

As soon as the potatoes are tender, drain, return them to the pan, and put them back over the heat to dry. Shake the pan and stir until the potatoes are floury and have made a film on the bottom of the pan.

Mash the potatoes until perfectly smooth with a hand masher, or put them through a ricer and return them to the pan over very low heat. Stir in the curried onion mixture until well mixed. Then stir in the warmed coconut milk. If the puree seems too thick, thin it with a bit more coconut milk. Season with the cayenne and salt. Serve hot.

GOAT CHEESE MASHED POTATOES

Use the freshest goat cheese you can find, both for flavor and for the creamy texture. Russets are our potatoes of choice, but try Yellow Finns or Yukons for a mash that looks, and even tastes, more buttery.

$1^{1}/_{2}$–$1^{3}/_{4}$ pounds russet potatoes, peeled and cut into chunks
Coarse salt
4 tablespoons ($^{1}/_{2}$ stick) unsalted butter, softened
4 ounces fresh goat cheese, at room temperature
$^{3}/_{4}$ cup heavy cream, heated
3 tablespoons chopped fresh chives
Freshly ground black pepper

Put the potatoes in a large saucepan, cover with cold water by at least an inch, add a good pinch of salt, and bring to a boil. Cover partway, reduce the heat to medium, and cook until the potatoes are tender. Drain the potatoes, return them to the pan, and put them back over the heat to dry them. Shake the pan and stir until the potatoes are floury and have made a film on the bottom of the pan. Turn the heat to very low.

Put the potatoes through a ricer and return them to the pan, or mash them until perfectly smooth with a hand masher. Cut the butter into pieces and beat into the potatoes with a wooden spoon. Cut the goat cheese into bits and beat that in. Pour in $^{1}/_{4}$ cup of the cream, stir until it's absorbed, and then beat the potatoes vigorously with a wooden spoon. Repeat, making two more additions of cream. Stir in the chives, season to taste with salt and pepper, and serve right away, so they're good and hot.

MINTED MASHED POTATOES

We like the combination of potatoes and mint. Here the flavor of the mint is carried by cream, and it's an elegant mash.

If you can find black mint or peppermint, do use it, but spearmint will work fine; and choose a starchy potato.

1½–1¾ pounds starchy or all-purpose potatoes (russets, Superior, Kennebec), peeled and cut into chunks
1 garlic clove, peeled
Coarse salt
1 cup heavy cream
4 or 5 sprigs mint, plus 1 tablespoon chopped fresh mint
2–4 tablespoons unsalted butter, softened
Freshly ground black pepper

Put the potatoes and garlic in a large saucepan, cover with cold water by at least an inch, add a good pinch of salt, and bring to a boil. Reduce the heat to medium, cover partway, and cook until the potatoes are very tender. Drain the potatoes and garlic and return them to the pan. Set over medium heat and dry the potatoes for a minute or two, shaking the pan and stirring so the potatoes don't stick. You want them floury and you should see a film on the bottom of the pot.

While the potatoes are cooking, rinse out a small saucepan with cold water (which will make the pan easier to clean later), add the cream and mint sprigs, and bring to a simmer over medium heat. Turn off the heat and let the mint infuse the cream while the potatoes cook.

Put the potatoes through a ricer and return them to the pan, over very low heat, or mash them until perfectly smooth with a hand masher. Beat in the butter. Pull the mint sprigs out of the cream and discard them. Beat the cream into the potatoes in ¼-cup additions, beating vigorously each time once the cream has been absorbed. Season with salt and pepper and beat in the chopped mint. Serve right away.

TANGY MASHED POTATOES

Sometimes you want mashed potatoes to have some zing to them; for instance, when you're serving a stew with a sweet flavor, such as French classic beef and carrot stew.

Make sure you take the sour cream out of the refrigerator and put it next to the stove when you start boiling the potatoes, so the chill will be off it when you beat it in.

2 pounds russet potatoes, peeled and cut into chunks
Coarse salt
5 tablespoons unsalted butter, softened
2 tablespoons cider vinegar
1 cup sour cream, at room temperature
Freshly ground black pepper

Put the potatoes in a large saucepan, cover with cold water by at least an inch, add a big pinch of salt, and bring to a boil. Cover partway, reduce the heat to medium, and cook until the potatoes are quite tender. Drain, dump the potatoes back into the pan, and dry them over heat, shaking the pan and stirring, until they are floury and have made a film on the bottom of the pan.

Put the potatoes through a ricer and return them to the pan, over very low heat, or mash them until perfectly smooth with a hand masher. Cut the butter into pieces and beat in with a wooden spoon. Add the vinegar and $1/4$ cup of the sour cream. Once you have it amalgamated, beat it vigorously with a wooden spoon. Repeat, adding the sour cream $1/4$ cup at a time and beating vigorously once each addition is absorbed. Season to taste with salt and pepper and serve right away.

BUTTERMILK MASHED POTATOES

You know that buttermilk is low-fat, don't you? So here's a low-fat, country-supper mash, with the skins left on and mashed roughly with a hand masher. Try this with any thin-skinned yellow-fleshed potato—particularly heirloom varieties.

1½–1¾ pounds Yukon Gold or other yellow-fleshed potatoes, scrubbed and
   cut into chunks
Coarse salt
2 tablespoons unsalted butter, softened
¾–1 cup buttermilk, heated
Freshly ground black pepper

Put the potatoes in a large saucepan, cover with cold water by at least an inch, add a good pinch of salt, and bring to a boil. Cover partway, reduce the heat to medium, and cook until the potatoes are truly tender. Drain the potatoes, return them to the pot, and put them back over the heat to dry. Shake the pan and stir until the potatoes are floury and have made a film on the bottom of the pan. Turn the heat to very low.

Roughly mash the potatoes with a hand masher—you've left the skins on, so don't obsess. Stir the butter into the potatoes with a sturdy wooden spoon. Add the buttermilk in small additions, about ¼ cup at a time, stirring first, then beating vigorously once the buttermilk has been amalgamated. You may not use all the buttermilk; it depends on how thirsty the potatoes are and how loose you want the mash. Season with salt and plenty of black pepper. Serve hot.

MARTHA STEWART'S MASHED POTATOES

This is vintage Martha. Rich, luxurious, and creamy mashed potatoes. They are indeed, as Martha says, "infinitely edible."

The potatoes here are yellow-fleshed, and their color adds to the impression that these are the richest potatoes you've ever eaten. Russets are thirstier; you'll need to add more cream if you use them for this dish.

Take the cream cheese out of the refrigerator well in advance; it needs to be squishy soft. If not, it thickens the potatoes too much and they're hell to beat.

2½ pounds yellow-fleshed potatoes, peeled and cut into chunks
Coarse salt
8 tablespoons (1 stick) unsalted butter, softened
8 ounces cream cheese, at room temperature
¼ cup heavy cream, warmed
Freshly ground black pepper

Put the potatoes in a large saucepan, cover with cold water by at least an inch, add a good pinch of salt, and bring to a boil. Cover partway, reduce the heat to medium, and cook until the potatoes are tender. Drain the potatoes, return them to the pot, and put them back over the heat to dry them. Shake the pan and stir until the potatoes are floury and have made a film on the bottom of the pan.

Put the potatoes through a ricer and return them to the pan, over very low heat, or mash them until perfectly smooth with a hand masher. Beat in the butter, about one-third at a time, with a wooden spoon. Cut the cream cheese into bits and beat that in one-third at a time. Pour in the cream, stir until it's absorbed, and then beat the potatoes vigorously with a wooden spoon. Season to taste with salt and pepper and serve right away, so they're good and hot.

ROAST GARLIC MASH

This rustic mash is a good showcase for heirloom potatoes like Ruby Crescents. But if you can't find those, choose a yellow-fleshed potato with a thin skin. And if you want to be extravagant, cook the potatoes in chicken stock instead of water.

1 head garlic
Coarse salt and freshly ground black pepper
3 tablespoons plus 1 teaspoon olive oil
1 or 2 sprigs thyme
2 pounds Ruby Crescent or other medium-starchy potatoes, scrubbed

Heat the oven to 350 degrees.

Cut the top off the garlic head to expose all the cloves and put it in a small baking dish (an individual gratin dish is great). Sprinkle the garlic with salt and pepper, drizzle with 1 teaspoon of the oil and 1 tablespoon water, add the thyme, and cover tightly with aluminum foil. Roast for about 45 minutes, until the garlic is meltingly tender. Uncover the dish and let the garlic cool some.

Meanwhile, put the potatoes in a large saucepan, cover with cold water by at least an inch, add a good pinch of salt, and bring to a boil. Cover partway, reduce the heat to medium, and cook until the potatoes are very tender. Drain in a colander set over a bowl so you reserve the potato water. Return the potatoes to the pan, set over the heat, and dry, shaking the pan and stirring, until the potatoes are floury.

Mash the potatoes roughly with a hand masher over very low heat. Spoon in the remaining 3 tablespoons oil and beat with a wooden spoon. Squeeze the garlic from the skins and beat it into the potatoes. Then beat in potato water by 1/4-cup additions until you reach the consistency you like. Season with salt and pepper and serve.

MASHED POTATOES SOUBISE

We like soubise, that refined dish of rice and onions, so we decided to revise it with potatoes. Serve this with veal chops—it'll remind you of veal Orloff. If you wanted to be really fussy, you could press the onion sauce through a sieve before adding it to the potatoes, but we love the rough, creamy texture.

1½–1¾ pounds russet potatoes, peeled and cut into chunks
Coarse salt
2 tablespoons unsalted butter, softened
Onion Sauce (page 502), heated
Freshly grated nutmeg
Freshly ground white pepper

Put the potatoes in a large saucepan, cover with cold water by at least an inch, add a good pinch of salt, and bring to a boil. Cover partway, reduce the heat to medium, and cook until the potatoes are tender. Drain the potatoes, return them to the pan, and put them back over the heat to dry. Shake the pan and stir until the potatoes are floury and have made a film on the bottom of the pan.

Put the potatoes through a ricer and return them to the pot over very low heat, or mash them until perfectly smooth with a hand masher. Beat the butter into the potatoes. Stir in the onion sauce in several additions, stirring to combine each time. Season with nutmeg, salt, and white pepper. Serve warm.

BUTTERNUT MASH

Don't be fussy when you mash the squash into the potatoes; you want the combination of colors and tastes that you get from undermixing. This is terrific as the bed for a pork stew.

1 small (about 1½ pounds) butternut squash
2 pounds russet or yellow-fleshed potatoes, peeled and cut into chunks
Coarse salt
4 tablespoons (½ stick) unsalted butter, softened
½ cup sour cream, at room temperature
2 teaspoons sherry vinegar
Freshly grated nutmeg
Freshly ground white pepper

Heat the oven to 400 degrees.

Halve the squash lengthwise, scoop out and discard the seeds, and place it cut side down on a baking sheet lined with parchment or foil. Bake until the skin is browned and wrinkled and the flesh is very soft, about 50 minutes.

Put the potatoes in a large saucepan, cover with cold water by at least an inch, add a good pinch of salt, and bring to a boil. Cover partway, reduce the heat to medium, and cook until the potatoes are tender. Drain well and return the potatoes to the pot. Dry them over heat, shaking the pan and stirring, until the potatoes are floury and have made a film on the bottom of the pan. Turn the heat to very low.

Put the potatoes through a ricer and return them to the pan, or mash them with a hand masher until lump-free. Beat in the butter, then the sour cream, vinegar, a grating or two of nutmeg, and a few grinds of white pepper. Beat vigorously with a wooden spoon until fluffy.

Peel the skin from the squash and cut the flesh into chunks. Add it to the potatoes and whisk a few times to combine, but be sure to leave visible lumps of squash. Taste for seasoning and serve hot.

MASHED POTATOES WITH SUN-DRIED TOMATOES

SERVES 4 TO 6

This dish is bright red and vibrant with the tastes and smells of summer. You need plain sun-dried tomatoes here, not the kind that have been reconstituted, covered in oil, and priced astronomically.

1 ounce sun-dried tomatoes
1½–1¾ pounds russet potatoes, peeled and cut into chunks
Coarse salt
¼ cup olive oil
2 tablespoons chopped mixed flat-leaf parsley and fresh basil
　　(or use just one of the herbs)
Freshly ground black pepper

Put the tomatoes in a small bowl and cover with hot water (½ to ⅔ cup). Leave the tomatoes to soften while you cook the potatoes.

Put the potatoes in a large saucepan, cover with cold water by at least an inch, add a good pinch of salt, and bring to a boil. Cover partway, reduce the heat to medium, and cook until the potatoes are tender.

A few minutes before the potatoes are done, put the tomatoes and soaking water into a blender and whirl them until you have a fairly smooth puree. It will be pretty thick and not completely smooth—which is fine, since you want some flecks of tomato.

Drain the potatoes, reserving some of the cooking water, and return them to the pan. Put them back over the heat and dry them, shaking the pan and stirring, until they are floury and have made a film on the bottom of the pan.

Reduce the heat to very low and mash the potatoes with a hand masher, or put them through a ricer and return them to the pan. Beat in the oil with a wooden spoon, then scrape the tomato puree out of the blender and beat that in. Add some of the cooking water to loosen the mash (about ½ cup, added little by little), then beat in the herbs, season with salt and pepper, and serve hot.

MASHED POTATOES WITH PESTO

Think of these as a companion to grilled chicken, roasted peppers, and a romaine salad.

There's no milk or cream in these; it muddles the flavor of the pesto. So be sure to save the potato water.

1½–1¾ pounds russet potatoes, peeled and cut into chunks
Coarse salt
1 tablespoon olive oil
3 tablespoons pine nuts
½ cup Pesto (page 251)
Freshly ground black pepper

Put the potatoes in a large saucepan, cover with cold water by at least an inch, add a good pinch of salt, and bring to a boil. Cover partway, reduce the heat to medium, and cook until the potatoes are tender.

While the potatoes are cooking, heat the oil in a small heavy skillet over medium-high heat until it shimmers. Add the pine nuts and cook, stirring frequently, until the nuts have browned. Watch carefully; these little things can burn quickly. Scrape the nuts into a bowl (they'll continue to cook if you leave them in the skillet).

Drain the potatoes, reserving the potato water, and return them to the pan. Put them back over the heat to dry them. Shake the pan and stir until the potatoes are floury and have made a film on the bottom of the pan. Turn the heat to very low.

Put the potatoes through a ricer and return them to the pan, or mash them until perfectly smooth with a hand masher. Stir in the pesto. Add the potato water in small additions, about ¼ cup at a time, stirring first, then beating vigorously after the water has been absorbed each time; you will need about 1 cup total. Stir in the toasted pine nuts, season with salt and pepper, and serve right away.

CELERIAC MASH

SERVES 4 TO 6

This process—cooking potatoes and a vegetable in light stock, then mashing with just a little butter and the cooking water—is especially well suited to yellow-fleshed potatoes. It must be that the color of the potato tricks us into thinking they are loaded with butter.

You can make this as rustic or as refined as you want, depending on how you choose to mash.

1 pound yellow-fleshed potatoes, peeled and cut into chunks
1 knob (about ¾ pound) celeriac (celery root), peeled and cut into chunks
2 cups Chicken Stock (page 85)
1 garlic clove, peeled
1 bay leaf
Several sprigs thyme
Coarse salt
3–4 tablespoons unsalted butter, softened
Freshly ground black pepper

Put the potatoes, celeriac, stock, garlic, bay leaf, and thyme in a saucepan. Add enough cold water to cover by at least an inch and a good pinch of salt. Bring to a boil, then cover partway, reduce the heat to medium, and cook at a brisk simmer until tender. Drain in a colander set over a bowl to reserve the cooking water. Discard the bay leaf and thyme. Return the potatoes and celeriac to the pan and place over medium-high heat for a minute or two, tossing, to dry the potatoes. Turn the heat to very low.

Mash with a hand masher, or put through a food mill and return to the pan. Beat in the butter with a wooden spoon, then beat in cooking water, about ⅓ cup at a time, until the mash is the consistency you want. Add some pepper, taste for salt, and serve hot.

CAULIFLOWER MASH

No need to be obsessive about the mashing; you want recognizable bits of cauliflower and potato. This is a quick, comforting mash, lighter than some of the others because you loosen it with cooking water rather than cream.

1 pound yellow-fleshed potatoes, peeled and cut into chunks
1 medium (about 1½ pounds) cauliflower, cut into florets
6 cardamom pods, tied in cheesecloth and crushed
Coarse salt
6 tablespoons (¾ stick) unsalted butter, softened
1 teaspoon sugar
¼ teaspoon ground cardamom
2 tablespoons chopped flat-leaf parsley
Freshly ground black pepper

Put the potatoes, cauliflower, and cardamom packet in a large saucepan, cover with cold water by at least an inch, add a good pinch of salt, and bring to a boil. Cover partway, reduce the heat to medium, and cook until the potatoes are tender (the cauliflower will still have some tooth to it, which is just what you want).

Drain well, reserving some of the cooking water, and discard the cardamom pods. Return the potatoes and cauliflower to the pot over very low heat. Mash coarsely with a hand masher. Beat in 4 tablespoons of the butter, along with the sugar, ground cardamom, and parsley. Add enough of the cooking water to get the consistency where you want it. Season with salt and pepper and pile into a serving dish.

Make a well in the center and drop in the remaining 2 tablespoons butter. Serve hot.

MASH WITH
FRESH OLIVADA

Olives and potatoes are a fine combination, and mashed potatoes
with homemade olivada truly sing.

1½–1¾ pounds russet potatoes, peeled and cut into chunks
1 cup Chicken Stock (page 85, optional)
Coarse salt
2 tablespoons olive oil
½ cup Fresh Olivada (facing page)

Put the potatoes and stock, if you're using it, into a saucepan and add enough
cold water to cover the potatoes by at least an inch. (Yes, you can use all water,
but if you want an extra edge of flavor, use the stock.) Add a good pinch of salt
and bring to a boil. Cover partway, reduce the heat to medium, and cook until
the potatoes are very tender. Drain, reserving the potato water. Dump the
potatoes back into the pan and return them to the heat. Shake the pan and stir
the potatoes with a wooden spoon for about a minute to dry the potatoes until
they're floury and have made a film on the bottom of the pan. Turn the heat to
very low.

   Mash the potatoes with a hand masher. You can be as obsessive about this
as you like, but we like this one a little lumpy. Beat in the olive oil, then add 1
cup of the potato water, ⅓ cup at a time, beating the potatoes vigorously after
each addition of water. The potatoes may be very thirsty, or you may like a
thinner mash, so add more potato water if you want. Stir in the olivada and
serve hot.

FRESH OLIVADA

This keeps for a while, and it has innumerable uses, so the recipe makes a lot. It's an excellent sauce for a long pasta like linguine. Or spread it on bread, or on salt-roasted potatoes.

Use whatever olives you like best (barring anything that comes in a can), but strive for a mix of green and black.

1 pound mixed olives, pitted and coarsely chopped
1 tablespoon chopped fresh herbs (thyme and rosemary are a nice combination)
1 tablespoon chopped flat-leaf parsley
2 garlic cloves, minced
Grated zest of 1 orange
Grated zest of 1 lemon
Pinch of crushed red pepper
2 anchovy fillets, minced
1/4 cup extra-virgin olive oil
Freshly ground black pepper

Combine all the ingredients. Let sit for at least 1/2 hour before serving, and let the olivada come to room temperature if you've refrigerated it. It will keep, tightly covered in the refrigerator, for 4 to 5 days.

HEAVEN AND EARTH

SERVES 6 TO 8

Heaven and earth; apples and potatoes. This is a great mash. Cookbook author Nika Hazelton says it comes from the Rhineland. We say serve it with roast pork or chops or even a chicken. Or nestle a fat grilled sausage in it for Bangers and Mash.

It's a great dish for kids too. My nephew David told me about his own version of Heaven and Earth: "I took the mashed potatoes and then I took some applesauce that my mom made, and I mixed them."

2¼–2½ pounds russet potatoes, peeled and chunked
1 garlic clove, peeled
2 or 3 sprigs thyme
1 bay leaf
One 3-inch strip lemon zest
Coarse salt
3 Granny Smith apples (about 1½ pounds), peeled, cored, and chopped
5 tablespoons unsalted butter, softened
Freshly ground black pepper

Put the potatoes and garlic in a saucepan and cover with cold water by at least an inch. Tie the thyme, bay leaf, and lemon zest into a little bundle with kitchen string and drop it into the pan. Add a pinch of salt and bring to a boil. Reduce the heat to medium, cover partway, and simmer for 10 minutes. Add the apples and continue cooking until the potatoes and apples are tender, another 15 minutes or so.

Drain well, reserving some of the cooking water. Discard the herb bundle and return the potatoes and apples to the pan. Set over medium heat and dry the potatoes and apples for a minute or two, shaking and stirring so they don't stick.

Turn the heat to very low and mash the potatoes and apples with a hand masher. Beat in the butter, a few tablespoons at a time, with a wooden spoon. If the mash seems too dry, beat in some of the reserved cooking water until you get the consistency you like best. Often the apples are so juicy that you don't need to add any of the water. Season with salt and pepper and serve right away.

FRENCH MASHED POTATOES WITH CHEESE (ALIGOT)

SERVES 6

Part cheese fondue, part mashed potatoes, this dish from the French Auvergne is gorgeous, rich, ivory-colored, elastic. Buttery Cantal cheese is really what gives the potatoes their flavor and texture, and a true *aligot* is made at the source with fresh, unripened Cantal curds. If need be, you can make a passable *aligot* with English farmhouse cheddar. Some versions include a clove or two of garlic, but we prefer the simple taste of potatoes and cheese.

This is a kitchen dish; serve it immediately right from the pot.

2 pounds russet potatoes, peeled and cut into large chunks
Coarse salt
2 tablespoons unsalted butter, softened
1/2 cup heavy cream, warmed
Freshly ground white pepper
12 ounces Cantal cheese, shredded

Put the potatoes in a large heavy saucepan, cover with cold water by at least an inch, add a pinch of salt, and bring to a boil. Cover partway, reduce the heat to medium, and simmer until the potatoes are very tender.

Drain the potatoes. Put them through a ricer and return them to the saucepan. Set over medium-low heat and stir with a wooden spoon for a minute or two to evaporate some of the moisture. Look for a thin film on the bottom of the pot indicating that the potatoes are dry enough. Turn the heat to very low. Beat in the butter. Once the butter has been absorbed, stir in half of the cream. Beat vigorously until light, then repeat with the remaining cream—stir, then beat. Season with salt and white pepper.

Add the cheese a handful at a time, stirring after each addition but not waiting for the cheese to melt. Once all the cheese has been added, beat the potatoes energetically until the puree is ultrasmooth and elastic, a few minutes longer. The *aligot* should form long ribbons when you lift the spoon up from the pot. Taste for salt and pepper and serve instantly.

HOT MASHED
POTATO "SALAD"

This time we're flavoring mashed potatoes with ingredients from a church-supper salad. It's not a salad in the classic sense, but it sure is good with ribs or barbecued chicken.

1^1/$_2$ pounds russet potatoes, peeled and cut into chunks
Coarse salt
6 slices bacon
^{1}/$_3$ cup mayonnaise
^{1}/$_2$ teaspoon celery seeds
1 tablespoon white wine vinegar
Freshly ground black pepper
3 whole scallions, chopped
Paprika

Put the potatoes in a large saucepan, cover with cold water by at least an inch, add a good pinch of salt, and bring to a boil. Cover partway, reduce the heat to medium, and cook until the potatoes are tender. Drain, then put the potatoes back in the pan. Return them to the heat and dry them out for a minute, stirring and shaking the pan so the potatoes don't stick. Look for a film on the bottom of the pan.

While the potatoes are cooking, cut the bacon into matchsticks and cook in a skillet over medium-low heat until crispy. Drain the bacon on paper towels and spoon out ^{1}/$_4$ cup of the fat to add to the dressing (store any leftover fat in the refrigerator for when you need it).

Whisk the mayonnaise, celery seeds, and vinegar together with the reserved bacon fat and salt and pepper to taste.

Mash the hot potatoes with a hand masher over very low heat, making them as smooth or as lumpy as you want. Stir in the dressing, bacon, and scallions, dish them up, and sprinkle with paprika. Serve hot.

FENNEL AND OLIVE OIL MASHED POTATOES

So good. These are equally wonderful alongside lamb chops, roast chicken, or grilled salmon. Molly likes to add some chopped olives just before serving.

1¼ pounds russet potatoes, peeled and cut into 1-inch chunks
1 fennel bulb, trimmed, cored, and thinly sliced (about 2 cups)
2 garlic cloves, halved lengthwise
Coarse salt
⅓ cup olive oil
Splash of Pernod or Ricard (optional)
½ cup chopped Kalamata or niçoise olives (optional)
Freshly ground black pepper

Put the potatoes, fennel, and garlic in a saucepan, cover with cold water by at least an inch, add a pinch of salt, and bring to a boil. Reduce the heat to medium, cover partway, and cook until the vegetables are very tender, about 25 minutes. Drain well, reserving some of the cooking water, and return the vegetables to the pan. Set over medium heat and dry the vegetables for a minute or two, shaking and stirring the pan so they don't stick.

Turn the heat to very low and mash the vegetables with a hand masher. (Alternatively, for an ultrasmooth, fancier version, work the potatoes, fennel, and garlic through a food mill.) Beat in the oil with a wooden spoon. Add the Pernod, if you want that extra hit of anise flavor. Beat in potato water, a few tablespoons at a time, until you get the consistency you like best (we usually use about ⅓ cup). If you like, stir in the chopped olives. Season with salt and pepper and serve right away.

POTATO PRINCIPLES
MASHING SWEET POTATOES

Mashed sweets are much more forgiving than mashed potatoes for one important reason—they don't have the loads of starch that will turn to glue if overworked or abused. At the same time, mashed sweets will never have the fluffy, cloudlike texture of perfectly mashed russets. Instead, mashed sweets are custardy, dense, and creamy. And they are certainly less thirsty when it comes to soaking up butter and cream. Sweets for mashing can be boiled, steamed, or baked. Of these three methods, boiling is probably the easiest. The only caveat is that it's best to boil them with the skins on. Peeled sweet potatoes will become waterlogged as they boil and will lose some of their flavor. While peeling hot potatoes is a bit of a hassle, it's worth it to prevent your puree from being watered down. If the whole sweet potatoes are too large to fit in your pot, just cut them in half.

Steaming works well too. In this case, peel the sweets first, cut them into evenly sized chunks or thick rounds, and steam until tender. Because they don't have direct contact with the water, the flesh doesn't sop up water as it would if boiled.

Baking whole sweet potatoes for a mash is the method we prefer. Mashed sweets made this way have a slightly more concentrated sweetness, a softer texture, and a deeper hue. Just prick the skins in several places, plop the whole potatoes on a sheet of heavy-duty foil, and bake at 450 degrees until quite tender.

Probably the most convenient aspect of making mashed sweet potatoes is that you don't absolutely need to mash them while they are still hot. It's okay to let them cool a bit, or even entirely, then peel, mash, and reheat them to serve.

To mash sweet potatoes, typically we simply use a stiff whisk to crush the tender cooked potatoes, and then whisk in the other ingredients. To get very smooth-textured mashed sweets for something like a baked casserole, we may use the food mill or ricer—this gets rid of the thin fibers that otherwise give sweet potatoes some texture.

Sweets have a more intense flavor on their own and so don't adapt to quite as many variations as workhorse russets. Having said that, mashed sweets do have their place. With their vibrant orange color and deep, sweet flavor, they belong on many holiday tables and make a great side to meaty roasts and spicy stews.

BASIC MASHED
SWEET POTATOES

Plain is good.

2–2½ pounds sweet potatoes, scrubbed
2–4 tablespoons unsalted butter, softened
Coarse salt and freshly ground black pepper

Cook the sweet potatoes until tender (see page 294). Drain well if you boiled them. Hold the potatoes in a towel and peel them. Drop the peeled potatoes back into the pot or into a bowl.

Smash the flesh with a heavy wire whisk, then whisk until smooth. Whisk in the butter, season well with salt and pepper, and serve warm.

MASHED SWEETS
AND WHITES

Sometimes the flavor of sweet potatoes is too sweet for the rest of the dinner, but you still want a hint of sugar. So mix sweets and whites, and you temper the sweetness; you also get a mash that's much fluffier and creamier-tasting than plain mashed sweets.

1½ pounds russet potatoes, scrubbed
1 pound sweet potatoes, scrubbed
8 tablespoons (1 stick) unsalted butter, softened
¼ cup chopped fresh chives
Coarse salt and freshly ground black pepper

Heat the oven to 400 degrees.

Prick the potatoes all over with the tip of a small knife and put them into the oven. The russets go right on the rack; the sweets will need a piece of heavy-duty aluminum foil underneath them. Bake for 1 hour.

Cut the russets in half and scoop out the flesh; you'll need to hold them in a kitchen towel so you don't burn your hand. Put the flesh through a ricer or mash well with a hand masher in a mixing bowl. Peel the sweet potatoes and drop them into the bowl with the russets. Whip with a sturdy whisk to mash the sweets and combine them with the russets. Cut up 6 tablespoons of the butter and whisk this in, with the chives. Season well with salt and pepper—these want lots of pepper—and pile in a serving bowl. Make a well in the center, drop in the remaining 2 tablespoons butter, and serve hot.

MASHED SWEET POTATOES
WITH PEPPER AND FRESH THYME

Black pepper and aromatic thyme play nicely with the sweet of the potatoes. The easiest way to crack pepper is to put the peppercorns on a counter and press down on them in a rocking motion with a small heavy skillet.

2–2½ pounds sweet potatoes, scrubbed
2–4 tablespoons unsalted butter, softened
¼ cup cream, heated
1 teaspoon chopped fresh thyme
½ teaspoon freshly cracked black pepper (see note above)
⅛ teaspoon ground allspice
Coarse salt

Cook the sweet potatoes until tender (see page 294). Drain well if they were boiled. Hold the sweets in a towel and peel them, dropping them back into the pot or into a bowl as they're done.

Smash the flesh with a heavy wire whisk, then whisk it until smooth. Whisk in the butter and cream. Add the thyme, pepper, and allspice. Season with salt. Serve warm.

MASHED SWEET POTATOES
WITH CANDIED GINGER

The candied ginger adds a good touch of heat to the sweets. If you want them even sweeter, you can add a tablespoon or two of orange blossom honey. If you don't want to use demon rum, substitute orange juice.

2–2¹/₂ pounds sweet potatoes, scrubbed
2 tablespoons unsalted butter, softened
2 tablespoons dark rum
1¹/₂ teaspoons grated orange zest
¹/₈ teaspoon ground mace
Coarse salt and freshly ground white pepper
2 tablespoons finely chopped candied ginger

Cook the sweet potatoes until tender (see page 294). Drain well if you boiled them. Peel the sweets, holding them in a towel to protect your hands, and drop them back into the pot or into a mixing bowl.

Smash the flesh with a heavy wire whisk, then whisk until smooth. Whisk in the butter, rum, orange zest, and mace. Season with salt and pepper. Serve warm, sprinkling the candied ginger on top.

MASHED SWEET POTATOES WITH BALSAMIC

A splash of dark, syrupy balsamic vinegar adds a nice savory edge to sweet potatoes. We like the flavor of baked sweet potatoes best for this recipe.

This mash is particularly nice with a few tablespoons of crumbled bacon or minced prosciutto scattered on top. The recipe from New York's Union Square Café was chosen by Jean Anderson as one of the most popular recipes of the twentieth century in her *American Century Cookbook.*

2–2¹/₂ pounds sweet potatoes, scrubbed
2 tablespoons unsalted butter, softened
¹/₃ cup light cream or milk, warmed
1–2 teaspoons balsamic vinegar
Freshly grated nutmeg
Coarse salt and freshly ground black pepper

Heat the oven to 450 degrees.

Prick the potatoes with a skewer in several spots and place them on a sheet of heavy foil. Bake until tender. Let cool slightly.

Peel the sweet potatoes, holding them in a towel to protect your hands. Drop them into a bowl. Smash the flesh with a heavy wire whisk, then whisk until smooth. Whisk in the butter and cream. Season with the vinegar, a few gratings of nutmeg, and salt and pepper to taste. Serve warm.

MASHED SWEET POTATOES WITH DRIED APPLES

The small chunks of dried apple and a pinch of cayenne make this recipe one of our favorites.

2–2½ pounds sweet potatoes, scrubbed
⅔ cup chopped dried apples (about 2 ounces)
½ cup apple cider
4 tablespoons (½ stick) unsalted butter, softened
1 tablespoon fresh lemon juice
Good pinch of cayenne pepper
Coarse salt

Cook the sweet potatoes until tender (see page 294). Drain well if they were boiled.

Meanwhile, put the apples and cider in a small saucepan. Simmer over medium-low heat until the apples are reconstituted and most of the liquid has been absorbed, so the pan is almost dry, 10 to 15 minutes. Remove from the heat.

Peel the sweet potatoes, holding them in a towel to protect your hands. Drop them back into the pot or into a bowl. Smash the flesh with a heavy wire whisk, then whisk until smooth. Whisk in the butter. Stir in the apples and the lemon juice. Season with cayenne and salt. Serve warm.

FRIED

POTATOES

POTATO PRINCIPLES
PERFECT FRIES 1, 2, 3, 4, 5

They may be the epitome of fast food, but there's nothing fast about fries when you make them yourself. If you want them right, the potatoes need a long soak and a cooling rest in the refrigerator after the first cooking.

You'll need at least 3 inches of oil in the pot, and those 3 inches can't fill the pot more than half full. Potatoes have an unfortunate tendency to invite oil to bubble up and boil over. This can cause a huge mess, and it's extremely dangerous. So get out a big pot for frying. It's convenient, because you'll be able to fry larger batches of potatoes at a time, and it's a safeguard against the oil temperature dropping too quickly or drastically when you fry.

Fries need stirring as they cook for even browning and to prevent sticking. We like big metal skimmers or spiders for this job, but when you plunge a metal skimmer into boiling oil, it lowers the temperature. We heat up the skimmer in the hot oil, which helps on that front.

Why, you ask, all this worry about temperatures dropping? Here's the thing: if your oil isn't the right temperature, the potatoes start sopping it up like the little sponges they are. You won't get great fries; indigestion's more likely.

Russets are our potato of choice for fries that are dry and fluffy inside a crisp crust. We tested and tested to see if we couldn't streamline this process. Sorry. The best fries need all five steps.

1. Soak the potatoes in plenty of cold water for 2 to 3 hours. Freshen the water up with ice cubes if the bowl isn't in the refrigerator. The soak rinses away some of the surface starch so that the fries brown better. It

also helps make the fries crisp. Plus, russets will turn evil gray if you just leave them sitting, not bathing.

2. Dry the potatoes thoroughly, completely, meticulously. Boiling oil splatters dangerously when you add water to it.

3. Prefry the fries. Heat your oil to 310 to 325 degrees and fry to cook the potatoes but not brown them. This step, called "blanching" by cognoscenti, is your insurance that your fries will be fluffy, and cooked through—not burned before you get there. (If you're making shoestring fries or chips, though, you can skip this step; the potatoes will be cut thin enough to cook with just one fry.)

4. Drain the fries on paper towels, then put them on trays in a single layer and send them off to the refrigerator for at least 2 hours' chilling. Believe us, this makes them lighter and crisper.

5. Heat the oil to 375 degrees and fry.

CLASSIC FRENCH FRIES

SERVES 4 TO 6

This is as much a technique as it is a recipe. Two pounds of russets will give you enough fries for 4 to 6 people, but you can just cut up as many fries as you feel like eating. We do. Remember: this isn't a last-minute side dish.

While we don't say no to ketchup, we also like dipping our fries in mayonnaise.

2 pounds russet potatoes, peeled
Oil for frying (peanut or a neutral vegetable oil)
Coarse salt

Cut the potatoes lengthwise into 1/4-inch sticks. A mandoline is the tool you want to be using here, but if you don't have one, here's a good system: trim off a slice so the potato will lie flat on the cutting surface. Cut the potato into 1/4-inch-thick slices, then make manageable stacks of the slices and cut again, this time into sticks. Drop the potatoes into a big bowl of cold water as you cut them. Leave the potatoes to soak for at least 2 hours. If you've got room, pop the bowl into the refrigerator; if not, and you've got the bowl out on the counter, add ice cubes to keep it cold.

Pour at least 3 inches of oil into a large pot; do not fill the pot more than half full. Heat the oil to 325 degrees. While the oil heats, drain the potatoes, lay them out on clean towels, and blot them completely dry with paper towels. Heat up a skimmer or slotted spoon for the stirring and retrieval of the fries (just put it in with the oil).

Grab a handful of potatoes and drop them into the oil. Not too many, so you don't lower the temperature. Cook for 3 to 4 minutes, stirring once in a while for even frying. The spuds will be beginning to go limp and will show just the slightest hint of gold. Lift them out with your handy heated skimmer and drain them on paper towels.

Once you've prefried all the fries, spread them on trays and refrigerate for 2 hours.

Come dinnertime, heat the oil to 375 degrees and heat up that skimmer. Drop in the fries, again by handfuls and again not crowding them, and fry, stirring for even browning, until they are perfectly golden and crisp, 3 to 4 minutes. Drain on paper towels, sprinkle with salt, and serve hot.

VARIATIONS
STEAK FRIES

These sturdy hand-cut fries sit so nicely next to a juicy, thick steak. They'll never be as crisp as classic fries, but we love their creamier, potato-ier flavor. Leave the peels on for these, but scrub the spuds well.

Follow the method above, cutting the potatoes by hand into ¹/₂-inch sticks. The prefrying will take longer, 5 to 7 minutes. The second fry should be about the same, 3 to 4 minutes.

HERBED FRENCH FRIES

Follow the method above, but while the potatoes chill, prepare 1 cup mixed herb leaves (a combination of parsley, thyme, basil, and oregano is nice). Wash and dry the leaves thoroughly. After you've fried the last handful of potatoes, drop the herbs into the oil. Attention: they will spatter wildly, so stand back. Scoop out the herbs with the skimmer as soon as they crisp, which will take a mere 30 to 45 seconds. Scatter the herbs over the fries and serve.

BASIC MAYONNAISE

Ketchup and fries is a combination that's hard to beat, but there are times when we like doing as the Belgians do and dipping our fries in mayo.

This is a very sturdy, basic mayonnaise. You can easily extend it by adding an extra ½ cup oil without risking its breaking. To double the recipe, use only 3 yolks to 2 cups oil. For a slightly more piquant version, add ½ to 1 teaspoon Dijon mustard to the yolks at the start.

2 large egg yolks
1 teaspoon fresh lemon juice or white wine vinegar
1 cup vegetable oil, preferably corn oil
Salt and freshly ground white pepper

TO MAKE THE MAYONNAISE IN A FOOD PROCESSOR: Combine the egg yolks and lemon juice in the processor. Hit the "on" button and, once the yolks are frothy, start pouring in the oil in a slow, thin stream. Continue until all the oil has been incorporated and you have a good thick mayonnaise.

TO MAKE THE MAYONNAISE BY HAND: Combine the egg yolks and lemon juice in a mixing bowl and whisk until frothy. Then slowly begin to incorporate the oil, one drop at a time, until you have added about one-third of it. Once you see that the mayonnaise is thickening, start adding the oil in a thin, steady stream. Whisk continually and stop adding the oil immediately if at any point it appears to pool on the surface of the sauce. Vigorous whisking should restore the emulsion, and then you can continue drizzling in the remaining oil.

Season the mayonnaise with salt and white pepper. Use immediately, or refrigerate in a covered container for a day or two.

SHOESTRING FRIES

You really do need a mandoline to make shoestring fries. They are cut into long, thin strands—called *pommes paille*, or straw potatoes, by the French—so they cook up all crispy-crunchy with very little fluffy inside. In texture and taste, they are more like chips than fries. A strong advantage to shoestring potatoes is that they don't need to be cooked twice—they are so thin that they cook through and brown up all at once. Serve a high tangle of shoestring potatoes alongside roast chicken or grilled steak.

2 pounds russet potatoes, peeled
Oil for frying (we like peanut oil or a neutral vegetable oil)
Coarse salt

Use a mandoline to slice the potatoes into ¹/8-inch shoestrings. Drop the potatoes into a big bowl of cold water as you cut them. Leave the potatoes to soak for at least 2 hours. If you've got room, pop the bowl into the refrigerator; if not, and you've got the bowl out on the counter, add ice cubes to keep it cold.

Pour at least 3 inches of oil into a deep pot, making sure not to fill the pot more than half full. Heat the oil to 375 degrees, and heat your skimmer along with it.

Drain the potatoes and dry thoroughly. Laying them out on clean towels and patting dry with paper towels works best. Even the smallest drops of water left on the potatoes will make the hot oil spatter.

Drop the potatoes by large handfuls into the oil. Don't overcrowd the pot; cook the fries in batches. Cook, stirring a few times, until the fries are nicely browned and crisp, about 4 minutes. Lift them out with the skimmer, drain on fresh paper towels, sprinkle with your favorite coarse salt, and serve immediately.

SWEET POTATO FRIES

SERVES 4 TO 6

Because they have more sugar and less starch than russet potatoes, sweet potato fries will never equal the crisp-on-the-outside and tender-fluffy-on-the-inside character of classic French fries. Sweets do, however, make great fries. Expect them to be almost candylike inside and deeply caramelized outside. Beyond sprinkling them with sea salt, you may try a touch of cayenne, or make a dipping sauce by stirring a few spoonfuls of Curried Red Pepper Relish (page 181) into a bowl of mayonnaise.

Sweet potato fries are a lot quicker than classics—none of that long soaking and chilling. And you precook in water, not oil.

2 pounds sweet potatoes, peeled
Vegetable oil for frying
Coarse salt

Because sweet potatoes are so dense, they are difficult to slice on a mandoline. We have better luck with a very sharp large chef's knife. Cut the sweet potatoes into 1/4-inch sticks. Alternatively, cut them into long 1/2-inch wedges.

Put the sweet potatoes in a saucepan, cover with cold water by at least an inch, and bring to a boil. Reduce the heat to medium and simmer until crisp-tender, about 3 minutes for sticks, 5 for wedges. Drain and dry thoroughly on towels.

Heat at least 3 inches of oil in a deep pot to 360 to 365 degrees, and heat a skimmer or slotted spoon with it. Drop the sweet potatoes by large handfuls into the oil. Don't add too many at once, or you'll lower the temperature of the oil. Cook, stirring a few times, until the sweet potatoes are deeply golden, about 4 minutes. Lift the fries out of the oil with the spider or slotted spoon and drain on paper towels. Sprinkle with salt and serve immediately. If you must, you can keep the first batches of fries warm in a low oven while you cook the remaining sweet potatoes, but they are best eaten immediately.

OLIVE OIL–FRIED POTATOES

We happily eat these down plain, but they're terrific with a bowl of gutsy Aïoli (page 400) or Lemon Mayonnaise (page 134).

1¹/₂ pounds Yukon Gold or other yellow-fleshed potatoes, peeled
   and cut into ¹/₂-inch wedges
Olive oil for frying
Coarse salt

Put the potatoes in a saucepan, cover with cold water by at least an inch, and bring to a boil. Reduce the heat to medium and simmer until the potatoes are just barely tender, 2 to 3 minutes. Drain and spread out on a towel to dry. Once they're dry, transfer them to a tray and refrigerate for 1 to 2 hours.

Fill a large pot or deep fryer with at least 3 inches of oil. Heat to 360 degrees, and heat your skimmer or slotted spoon along with it.

Drop the potatoes by handfuls into the oil. Don't add too many potatoes at once, or you'll lower the temperature of the oil and the fries will be greasy. Cook until the fries are golden and crisp, stirring a few times for even frying, about 5 minutes. Lift the fries out of the oil with the skimmer or slotted spoon and let them drain on paper towels. Sprinkle with coarse salt and serve immediately. If you must, you can keep the first batches warm in a low oven while you cook the remaining fries, but no longer.

VARIATION
OLIVE OIL FRIES WITH PARSLEY AND GARLIC

They serve baskets upon baskets of something like this at Rose Pistola restaurant in San Francisco's North Beach neighborhood.

Chop 1 garlic clove together with a few tablespoons of flat-leaf parsley until finely minced. Sprinkle this mix over the hot fries, along with the salt.

POMMES SOUFFLÉES
(HEARTBREAK DISGUISED AS A POTATO)

Just about every source we examined doled out a recipe for these golden, air-filled potato pillows with simple "keys for success" (you cut them, fry them, and bingo! they puff). Don't be beguiled. These are more than tricky.

In Venice, Molly watched as the head chef of the Cipriani tried, one at a time, to get chips of potato to puff in hot oil. Finally, *one* did. A French chef friend we consulted asked, after he stopped laughing, "Why do you want to try to make those? *Pommes soufflées* are more difficult than a proper omelet." We weren't deterred. We tried every sort of pot, temperature combination, and potato variety. We soaked, we didn't soak. We sliced with a mandoline, we sliced by hand, we sliced thin, we sliced thick. And in the end, no matter what we did, the results were unpredictable, though we did get so we could make a decent batch of these legendary potatoes. If they don't happen to puff up for you, just call them chips and serve them anyway. The two pots are mandatory, and that means a lot of oil, so be prepared.

Peel a few russet or Yukon Gold potatoes. Fresher, in-season potatoes seem to work better than older storage potatoes. If you find a water marking, or vein, in your potato, give up on it immediately and try another. To get regularly shaped rectangular slices, begin by trimming the potato into a rectangular cube that is about 1½ inches by 2½ inches (and as long as the size of the potato will allow). Round the corners so that when you slice, each slice will have slightly rounded corners. This almost elliptical shape is important to allow the slice to puff out fully in the middle. Now, with either a mandoline or very sharp, steady knife, cut the potato into slices that are just shy of $^1/_8$ inch. If you need to slice the potatoes ahead of time, you can drop them in a bowl of cold water and leave them for an hour or two.

Fill two deep heavy pots with at least 3 inches of oil. Heat one pot to 260 to 280 degrees and the second to 380 to 390 degrees.

Drop a few potatoes into the lower-temperature oil—don't overcrowd the pot, because you need to be able to watch carefully as the potatoes cook. It helps if you gently swirl the oil in the pot to keep the potatoes moving as they fry. Fry until you see the first signs of small blisters on the surface, about 4 minutes. A few slices may actually puff up during this first cooking. This is a promising sign, but no guarantee. Remove the potatoes from the oil with a spider or slotted spoon and immediately drop them into the hotter oil. Watch (fingers crossed) as they magically explode to the surface in little air-filled pillows. Turn each puff a few times to brown both sides and fry until well browned, about 1 minute. Drain, sprinkle with salt, and serve immediately. *Pommes soufflées* don't wait.

SARATOGA CHIPS

SERVES 4 TO 6

The name Saratoga Chips is used here to identify what most folks simply refer to as potato chips. Up until the mid-nineteenth century, potato chips were all a good deal thicker than what we know today, and Saratoga—after the New York resort where they originated—became the name that identified the crisp, almost translucent chip that has become a favorite snack food.

With a bit of planning, homemade potato chips are actually pretty quick to make and a world above the packaged stuff. They stay crisp for about an hour or two after frying, depending on how humid it is. Try them sprinkled with really good salt or (Molly's favorite) salt and cider vinegar.

2 pounds russet potatoes, peeled
Vegetable oil for frying
Coarse salt

Use a mandoline to slice the potatoes into 1/16-inch-thick rounds. It's important that they are thin and even—otherwise, they won't crisp up nicely when you fry them. Drop the slices into a very large bowl of cold water and soak for 30 to 45 minutes. The slices will curl up, the way you expect a chip to look. Once they have, and they're almost brittle, you're ready to fry. (No hurry, though, just keep the water cold—add ice—if you've done this in advance.)

Heat 2 inches of oil in a deep pot to 375 to 380 degrees. Drain the potatoes and dry them thoroughly. Laying them out on clean towels and patting dry works best. Any drops of water left on the potatoes will make the hot oil spatter.

Drop the potatoes by large handfuls into the oil. Avoid adding too many potatoes at once, or you'll lower the temperature of the oil too much and the chips will be greasy. Cook, stirring a few times to keep them from clumping up, until the chips are crisp and nicely browned, 3 to 4 minutes. Lift the chips out of the oil with a spider or slotted spoon and drain on paper towels. Sprinkle with salt while still hot and serve within the hour.

VARIATIONS

SALT AND VINEGAR CHIPS

After frying and draining the chips, transfer them to a large mixing bowl, sprinkle on sea salt, and drizzle in cider or white wine vinegar to taste. Toss to mix. Serve right away; the vinegar can turn the chips soggy in spots.

GREMOLATA CHIPS

You know, there's no reason you can't steal this garlic-lemon-parsley paste (gremolata) to toss with fries.

Mince 2 cloves of garlic until they're almost a paste, and mix well with 1/2 cup chopped flat-leaf parsley and the grated zest of a lemon. After frying and draining the chips, dump them into a large mixing bowl, sprinkle in the gremolata, and toss. The moisture from the gremolata will soften the chips, so serve immediately.

WAFFLE CHIPS
(POMMES GAUFRETTE)

SERVES 4 TO 6

Who can resist these? Besides being charming to look at and nibble on, waffle chips have the added advantage of staying crisp for several hours. But I'm sorry, you need a mandoline to cut them.

See Saratoga Chips (page 314) for ideas about how to play with flavoring.

2 pounds russet potatoes, peeled
Vegetable oil for frying
Coarse salt

Take out your French mandoline, set it up with the fluted blade, and make a few test slices first to be sure you have the thickness right. You'll be cutting rounds, because you're making chips, and you test until you find where you can get the thinnest waffle. To get the waffle effect, rotate the potato 90 degrees after each slice. Put the slices into a big bowl, cover with cold water, and leave them to soak and curl and turn brittle for 30 to 45 minutes. If you want to leave them longer, fine; just keep them cool.

Heat at least 2 inches of oil in a deep pot to 375 to 380 degrees. Drain the potatoes and dry thoroughly. Laying them out on clean towels and patting dry is best. Any drops of water left on the potatoes will make the hot oil spatter.

Drop the potatoes by large handfuls into the oil. Try not to add too many potatoes at the same time, or you'll lower the temperature of the oil too much and the chips will stick together. Fry, stirring a few times to keep them from clumping up, until the chips are crisp and nicely browned, 3 to 4 minutes. Lift the chips out of the oil with a spider or slotted spoon and drain on paper towels. Sprinkle with salt while still hot and serve.

SWEET POTATO CHIPS

SERVES 4 TO 6

The sugar in sweets means these chips brown up in an instant. It also gives them that addictive combination of sweet, salt, and crisp.

2 pounds sweet potatoes, peeled
Vegetable oil for frying
Coarse salt

Use a mandoline to slice the potatoes into $1/16$-inch-thick rounds. It's important that they are thin and even—otherwise, they won't crisp up nicely when you fry them and the really thin bits will burn. Drop the slices into a large bowl of cold water and soak for 30 to 45 minutes. Once the slices have curled and they're almost brittle, you're ready to fry. (No hurry, though, just keep the water cold if you've done this in advance.)

Heat 2 inches of oil in a deep pot to 375 to 380 degrees. Drain the potatoes and dry them thoroughly. Laying them out on clean towels and patting dry works best. Any drops of water left on the potatoes will make the hot oil spatter.

Drop the potatoes by large handfuls into the oil. Avoid adding too many potatoes at once, or you'll lower the temperature of the oil too much and the chips will be greasy. Cook, stirring a few times to keep them from clumping up, until the chips are crisp and nicely browned, 3 to 4 minutes. Lift the chips out of the oil with a spider or slotted spoon and drain on paper towels. Sprinkle with salt while still hot and serve within the hour.

VARIATION
SPICED SWEET POTATO CHIPS

Toast 1 tablespoon cumin seeds and 2 teaspoons coriander seeds until fragrant and beginning to brown. Then grind the seeds to a coarse powder and add a good pinch of cayenne to the mix. As soon as the chips are done, sprinkle them with salt and the spice mix and serve.

POTATO PUFFS
(POMMES DAUPHINE)

SERVES 6

This is an ambitious undertaking, but it's worth it. Homemade *pommes dauphine* are much tastier and crunchier than the Tater Tots they inspired. Besides, we find them fun to make.

Baking the potatoes leaves them drier and fluffier, but no one's going to tell you that you can't boil them if you want. The routine is the same: drain on a rack, peel right away, and leave the peeled potatoes on the rack to dry. Baking's easier.

3 medium russet potatoes (about 2 pounds), scrubbed
4 tablespoons (½ stick) unsalted butter, cut into pieces
½ cup Chicken Stock (page 85) or water
Coarse salt and freshly ground white pepper
Freshly grated nutmeg
½ cup all-purpose flour
2–3 large eggs
Vegetable oil for frying

Heat the oven to 400 degrees.

Bake the potatoes until tender when pressed with your fingertips, about 1 hour. Remember to prick them after 30 minutes. Keep the potatoes warm while you prepare the *pâte à choux*.

Put the butter in a small saucepan with the stock. Season with salt (at least ½ teaspoon), pepper to taste, and a grating or two of nutmeg. Bring to a boil over medium-high heat. When the butter is melted and the liquid bubbling, dump in the flour all at once and stir vigorously with your wooden spoon. It will be sloppy, so be careful not to make a mess, but it will quickly form a ball. Keep beating, and the ball will tighten, then become glossy, and you will see a film on the bottom of the pot—now you're there. At most, this will take 2 minutes. Take the pan off the heat right away.

Leave the paste to cool for a few minutes. Then crack 1 of the eggs into it. Stir it to amalgamate the egg into the paste (it's messy, but the egg *will* go into the paste), then beat it with vigor. Repeat with another egg. Depending on how well you dried the paste on the stove, you may need only 2 eggs. Check the consistency by lifting a spoonful of dough from the pan. The dough should slowly fall from the spoon back into the pot. If it sticks to the spoon, crack the third egg into a small bowl and beat it with a fork to mix the white and yolk, then stir it in a bit at a time until the dough is soft enough to fall from the spoon.

Cut the baked potatoes in half and scoop the pulp into a food mill or ricer. Mill the potatoes directly into the dough, and stir to combine. Season with salt and white pepper. You can fry the puffs now, and they'll be fabulous, or cover the dough with plastic and refrigerate it for, well, 2 hours—but no more.

Heat 2½ inches of oil in a deep pot to 360 to 365 degrees. Drop the dough by the teaspoon into the oil and cook until golden, 4 to 6 minutes. (Or, if you have a pastry bag and you're dexterous, fit the bag with a plain tip, fill it with the dough, and cut off 1-inch lengths as you squeeze.) Transfer the cooked *dauphine* to paper towels to drain and sprinkle lightly with salt before serving. The potato puffs can be kept warm in a low oven for 20 minutes before serving.

VARIATION

The most classic—and maybe the fussiest—cook will roll fingers (little ones) of the dough and dip them first in beaten egg and then bread crumbs before frying. These should then be neatly stacked on a starched linen napkin to serve.

POTATO PRINCIPLES
EXCEPTIONAL SAUTÉED POTATOES

To get nicely browned slices or cubes of potatoes, you'll want to start with a waxy or medium-starch all-purpose potato for two reasons: First, the lower starch means more sugar, so the potatoes will be more apt to brown nicely when sautéed. Second, sautéing involves a fair amount of shaking and tossing, and the firmer texture of a waxy potato will hold up better, leaving you with whole pieces rather than mush.

Sliced or diced raw potatoes have a tendency to stick to one another, making it tricky to get them to cook evenly. One approach is to cook only one sparse layer at a time. While this works for small amounts and for diced potatoes, which take up less room than sliced, it's impractical if you want to serve more than two people. In addition, since low-starch potatoes (especially when they're at all new) have a high moisture content, they give off a fair amount of water as they cook. That makes it difficult to get them nicely browned and crisp.

A solution that we prefer is to cover the sauté pan as soon as the potatoes show the first signs of browning (you may also want to lower the heat). This slows the cooking and allows the potatoes to steam slightly so they cook through. When the potatoes are just about tender, remove the lid, increase the heat and cook, shaking and flipping, until they are crisp and brown.

A third, surefire technique for sautéed potatoes (one we use for home fries and hash browns) is to start with cold boiled potatoes. Boiling the potatoes ahead of time makes them less likely to steam and more eager to brown. Simply slice or dice the cold potatoes as you heat up the fat for sautéing. Whether or not you peel the potatoes before sautéing is a personal choice; for sliced potatoes, the skin can help hold the rounds together, and it adds crunch. When sautéing parboiled potatoes, you can get away with filling the pan with more than one layer of potatoes as long as you stand nearby to flip and turn them as they brown.

POTATOES FRIED
IN GOOSE FAT

Look back to the recipe for goose (page 202) and see how I plead for you to save the fat. The flavor is incredible; the aroma heavenly. Make these potatoes, a simple steak, and a salad with a good mustardy vinaigrette, and you can pretend you're in France. If you don't have goose fat, you can substitute duck fat, but both are more and more available from butchers and better markets.

Peel the potatoes if you want. I don't.

$^1/_4$ cup goose fat
$1^1/_2$ pounds Yukon Gold potatoes, scrubbed and cut into $^1/_2$-inch dice
Coarse salt and freshly ground black pepper

Melt the fat in a large skillet over medium heat. When the fat starts to shimmer, add the potatoes. Cook for a few minutes, stirring once in a while, until the potatoes begin to brown. Season with a pinch of salt and a lot of pepper, cover, and cook for about 10 minutes, until the potatoes are just about tender. You'll need to shake the pan a few times during this cooking. Remove the cover, increase the heat to high, and cook another minute or two to crisp them.

Remove the potatoes with a slotted spoon and drain them well on paper towels. Put them in a bowl, season well with salt, and serve as hot as you can.

"MELTING" POTATOES
(POMMES DE TERRE FONDANTES)

These are a cousin to Château Potatoes (page 324) but with two differences: the potatoes are cut into larger pieces, and they are covered during cooking, leaving them incredibly tender, creamy on the inside (melting), and crispy golden on the outside.

You can shape medium-sized potatoes into ovals for this, or just use any whole smallish (about 3 ounces) oblong potatoes.

2–2¹/₂ pounds white potatoes (or 1¹/₂ pounds smallish potatoes)
12 tablespoons (1¹/₂ sticks) unsalted butter, clarified (see page 28)
Coarse salt

If you're going the classic French route, turn the potatoes into large ovals, about 3¹/₂ inches long by 1¹/₂ inches at their thickest point (see page 488). Otherwise, peel the smallish potatoes.

Heat the clarified butter in a large skillet over medium-low heat. (This technique will work only if the potatoes are in a single layer.) Add the potatoes, turning with tongs to coat with the butter. Cover tightly and cook gently, turning with tongs frequently throughout cooking so they brown evenly. If the potatoes appear to be browning too quickly, lower the heat. Cook until the potatoes are tender enough to be pierced easily with the tip of a sharp knife, about 25 minutes.

Remove the lid and increase the heat to medium-high. Cook, shaking and turning the potatoes, until they are nicely browned, 5 to 10 minutes more. Season with salt and serve hot.

You can cook these potatoes several hours ahead, leave them at room temperature, and then reheat in a 350-degree oven for 15 to 20 minutes. Finicky French chefs would be horrified, but we like the drier crust of the reheated *fondantes*.

CHÂTEAU POTATOES
(POMMES DE TERRE CHÂTEAU)

SERVES 4

This recipe, plus variations, is really more an explication of technique than anything. Château Potatoes are raw potatoes shaped into perfect ovals, or "turned," so they look pretty, and then they're sautéed in butter. The amount of potatoes you'll need to serve 4 depends on how efficient you are at turning them. To make more or less, simply change the amount of potatoes (you'll need more butter if you double the potatoes). I've kept the recipe to 4 servings, because that's about my limit.

Peel the potatoes and turn them into small ovals, about 1¾ inches by ¾ inch (see page 488). You can turn the potatoes in the early afternoon and keep them in a bowl of cold water. When you're ready for dinner, drain the potatoes and dry them on paper towels.

12 tablespoons (1½ sticks) unsalted butter, clarified (see page 28)
2 pounds yellow-fleshed or white potatoes, turned into ovals (see note above)
Coarse salt and freshly ground black pepper
2 tablespoons chopped flat-leaf parsley (optional)

Pour the clarified butter into a skillet just large enough to accommodate the potatoes in a single layer. (If your skillet is too small, you'll need to cook the potatoes in batches. If it is too large, you'll need more clarified butter.) Heat the butter over high heat until quite hot but not smoking. Add the potatoes and cook until you see the first hints of a light crust, about 2 minutes. Reduce the heat to medium and continue to cook until the potatoes are golden and very tender, 9 to 12 minutes more. Roll the potatoes in the butter as they cook to brown them all over. Pull the potatoes out of the butter with a slotted spoon and blot them dry on paper towels.

Immediately toss them in a bowl with salt, pepper, and parsley, if desired. Serve, or keep warm in a low oven for up to 15 minutes.

NOTE: Strain the clarified butter and save it in the refrigerator to use again.

VARIATIONS

NOISETTE POTATOES
(POMMES DE TERRE NOISETTE)

Same thing, just a different shape. While Château Potatoes are turned, Noisettes are simply cut into little balls—about ¾ inch across, the shape of a hazelnut—with the smaller end of a standard melon baller. They cook a bit more quickly.

PARISIAN POTATOES
(POMMES DE TERRE PARISIEN)

This variation's here for those of us with advanced pantries who occasionally want tangy potatoes. The meat glaze you need is available from specialty butchers and some gourmet shops.

Make these in the shape of either Château or Noisette Potatoes. Once they're cooked, toss the hot potatoes with 2 to 3 teaspoons of warmed meat glaze, to taste, before adding the parsley.

NEW POTATOES
COOKED IN BUTTER

This is the shortcut version of *Pommes de Terre Fondantes* (page 323). No peeling, no turning. But you do need new potatoes, and that means you have to go to a greenmarket and buy from a farmer who is pulling potatoes every week in season. This works with all the heirloom varieties. If you have round potatoes, you might want to peel a belly band off them around their middles. The exposed flesh browns beautifully.

1¹/₂ pounds new potatoes, scrubbed
4 tablespoons (¹/₂ stick) unsalted butter
Coarse salt

Put the potatoes, butter, and a pinch of salt in a heavy skillet large enough to hold the potatoes in one layer. Turn the heat to medium-low. Once the butter has melted, toss the potatoes in it, cover the skillet, and cook for 20 minutes, or until the potatoes are tender. Shake the pan when you think of it so the potatoes cook and brown evenly.

Turn the potatoes in the butter, sprinkle with more coarse salt, and serve very hot.

VARIATION

Add a few sprigs of mint, thyme, lemon thyme, or a bay leaf to the butter as you melt it. Discard the herbs once the potatoes are cooked.

HOME FRIES

This is it: the real thing.

3 tablespoons bacon drippings or vegetable oil
1 red onion, sliced
1¹/₂ pounds cold boiled white potatoes, peeled and cut into ³/₄-inch chunks
Coarse salt and freshly ground black pepper

Heat the drippings in a large skillet, preferably cast iron, over medium-high heat. Add the onion and cook, stirring a few times, until it just begins to wilt, 3 to 4 minutes.

Add the potatoes and season with salt and plenty of black pepper. Cook, stirring and scraping the bottom frequently—use a metal spatula for this— until the potatoes have plenty of good crust and the onions are almost burned, 16 to 18 minutes. Serve hot.

HASH BROWN POTATOES

Breakfast fare, lunch fare, these hash browns cry out for an egg, poached or sunny-side up, just so the yolk can run through them. I like them crusty on top and creamy in the middle. You need cold leftover waxy potatoes to begin with, so plan the day before. And a well-seasoned cast-iron pan is a must.

1½ pounds cold boiled red-skinned potatoes (something waxy), peeled
    and cut into ¼-inch dice
¼ cup chopped flat-leaf parsley
1 tablespoon chopped fresh chives
Coarse salt and freshly ground black pepper
2 tablespoons unsalted butter, cut into pieces
¼ cup heavy cream

Toss the potatoes with the parsley, chives, and salt and pepper to taste (be assertive and make them pretty peppery).

Heat a well-seasoned 9-inch cast-iron skillet over medium-high heat. When it's good and hot, drop in the butter. Once the foaming subsides, add the potatoes and press them down hard with the back of a flexible spatula. Listen for the sizzle; when you hear it, you'll know that you're pressing hard enough. Let the potatoes cook until they start to brown, pressing down once or twice, about 5 minutes. Then pour in the cream and turn the potatoes with the spatula so some of the browned bits get distributed. Press down again. There really won't be a sizzle this time, and the cream will make them a bit sticky. Cook, pressing down every minute or so and shaking the pan to keep them moving and cooking evenly, until you have a rich brown crust on the bottom and the top has pretty much dried. This will take about 7 minutes from when you add the cream.

If you've done it right, you can turn the hash browns out upside down onto a platter. But you can always serve them straight from the skillet with a big spoon. Just make sure to dump them crust up on the plates. Serve these hot.

BRUSSELS SPROUT HASH

You can eat this as a side dish or as the start of dinner or as a meal in itself, topped with a poached egg or two. We like yellow-fleshed potatoes for this, but just about any leftover boiled potatoes except russets will do. Leave the skins on.

2 slices bacon, chopped
3 tablespoons olive oil
1 onion, chopped
1 pound cold boiled potatoes, cut into ½-inch chunks
1 pound Brussels sprouts, trimmed (halve them if they're big)
Coarse salt and freshly ground black pepper

Put the bacon and oil in a heavy skillet over medium heat. Cook until the bacon has rendered its fat and is starting to brown. Add the onion and cook until it's translucent, 3 to 4 minutes.

Add the potatoes and Brussels sprouts, season with salt and plenty of pepper, and add ¼ cup water. Cook until the sprouts are tender and have started to lose their bright green color, 20 to 25 minutes. Scrape the bottom of the pan and turn the hash with a spatula as it cooks, and if the hash is drying out too quickly, add a tablespoon or two of water. Taste for salt and pepper and serve hot.

O'BRIEN POTATOES

These are hash browns with a bit of green thrown in. Plan in advance, because the potatoes need to be cold for the best results. You won't get the crust that you will with hash browns (what crust you get seems always to stay in the skillet), but the finished cake is pretty, with flecks of brown and green and a garnish of bright red pimiento.

Bacon fat gives this the right flavor, but you can substitute goose or duck fat or even vegetable oil if you care to.

3 tablespoons bacon drippings
1 small onion, finely chopped
1 green bell pepper, cored, seeded, and cut into 1/4-inch dice
1 1/2 pounds cold boiled potatoes (white or red-skinned), peeled
    and cut into 1/4-inch dice
1/4 cup chopped flat-leaf parsley
Coarse salt and freshly ground black pepper
1/4 cup heavy cream
2 tablespoons chopped pimiento

Heat the drippings in a heavy 9-inch skillet (a well-seasoned cast-iron pan is ideal) over medium-high heat. Once it shimmers, add the onion and bell pepper and cook just until they are starting to soften, 3 to 4 minutes.

Toss the potatoes with the parsley, some salt, and a nice dose of pepper and add them to the skillet. Use a flexible spatula to flip them around and get them coated with fat, then cook until the potatoes are heated through, 5 to 6 minutes. Flip them with the spatula a few times while they heat.

Drizzle in the cream, flip the potatoes a few times to distribute the cream evenly, and then flatten them into an even cake with the back of the spatula. Let them settle a minute, then shake the pan to make sure the cake isn't sticking. When you shake the skillet, the cake will pull apart; push the edges in from the sides of the skillet with your spatula and flatten the cake again. Keep repeating this process—shake the skillet, push in the sides, and flatten the cake—for 5 minutes. By this time, you will have compacted the cake into an 8- or 9-inch round and it will spin in the pan when you shake it. It's done.

Put a plate over the skillet and invert the potatoes onto it, taking care not to burn yourself. Make a heap of the pimiento in the center of the potatoes and serve very hot.

SOUTH INDIAN POTATO HASH WITH DRY-ROASTED MUNG BEANS

SERVES 6

Let this vibrant hash be the star of the dinner plate, and serve it with plain chops or a simple fish dish.

Sizzling oil (*baghar*) is indispensable in much of the cooking of South Asia. Spices are fried in very hot oil to release their flavors and aromas, and the oil (with the spices) is then used to perfume the dish right before serving, before the fragrance has a chance to fade. This extraordinary dish is from cooking teacher Samia Ahad.

2 pounds russet potatoes, scrubbed
Coarse salt
1/3 cup split dried mung beans (see note)
1/4 cup vegetable oil
1 large onion, chopped
1 garlic clove, smashed and minced
One 1/2-inch piece fresh ginger, peeled, sliced, smashed, and minced
1 teaspoon brown mustard seeds
3 dried red chile peppers (see note)
2 stems (about 20 leaves) fresh curry leaves (see note)
3 tablespoons fresh lime juice

FOR THE BAGHAR (SIZZLING OIL)
2 tablespoons vegetable oil
1 teaspoon brown mustard seeds
1 stem (about 10 leaves) fresh curry leaves
3 dried red chile peppers

Put the potatoes in a large saucepan, cover with cold water by at least an inch, add a good pinch of salt, and bring to a boil. Cover partway, reduce to a simmer, and cook until the potatoes are just tender. Drain on a rack set in the sink and leave to cool.

Meanwhile, cover the mung beans with cool water and let them soak for 30 minutes.

Once the beans have soaked, heat the oil in a large heavy skillet over medium-high heat until it shimmers. Add the onion and cook until soft and beginning to brown. Stir in the garlic and ginger, then add the mustard seeds, chiles, and curry leaves. Cook until the seeds crackle and jump in the pan, about 2 minutes. The spices will become very fragrant.

Drain the mung beans and add them to the skillet. Reduce the heat to medium-low and cook, stirring once in a while, until the oil separates from the beans. This should take about 10 minutes.

Meanwhile, peel the potatoes and cut them into 1-inch cubes. Add them to the skillet, season with salt, and pour in ¼ cup cool water. Stir well, reduce the heat to low, cover, and cook for 20 minutes, stirring once in a while. Stir in the lime juice and spoon the hash into a serving dish.

WHEN YOU ARE READY TO SERVE, MAKE THE BAGHAR: Heat the oil in a small heavy skillet over medium-high heat until almost smoking. Add the mustard seeds, curry leaves, and chiles and cook, swirling the spices in the skillet, until the seeds pop and the leaves start to brown. Immediately pour the sizzling oil over the hash and run it to the table so all can revel in its fragrance.

NOTE: Mung beans, dried red chiles, and curry leaves are available by mail-order and on-line from Kalustyan's, 123 Lexington Avenue, New York, NY 10016; (212) 685-3451; fax (212) 683-8458; www.kalustyans.com.

POTATO, LEEK, AND BACON PANFRY

SERVES 4

Here's another great idea from Tom Colicchio, chef-owner of Craft restaurant and Gramercy Tavern in New York City. Not quite hash, not quite home fries: what it is, is delicious. If you can find them, try German Butterballs in this dish.

1/4 pound thick-cut bacon
2 tablespoons unsalted butter
4 heaping cups sliced leeks (white and light green parts of about 4 leeks)
Coarse salt and freshly ground white pepper
2 tablespoons vegetable oil
1 pound yellow-fleshed potatoes, scrubbed and sliced 1/16 inch thick
1 tablespoon chopped fresh thyme

Cut the bacon into matchsticks. Put it in a large skillet with 1 tablespoon of the butter and cook over medium heat until the bacon has rendered its fat but has not browned. Add the leeks, season with salt and white pepper, and cook until the leeks have begun to soften, about 5 minutes. Stir often while the leeks are cooking, and transfer the leeks and bacon to a bowl when they're done.

Spoon the oil into the skillet and heat it until it shimmers. Add the potatoes, the remaining 1 tablespoon butter, and salt and pepper to taste and cook until the potatoes are tender, 20 to 25 minutes. They will stick some and become translucent; stir with a metal spoon or spatula. Add the thyme, the leeks and bacon, and 1/4 cup water and cook, stirring frequently, until the leeks and potatoes are very tender and the flavors have melded, about another 5 minutes. Serve hot.

BREADED SWEET POTATOES

This dish from the Caribbean, which I adapted from a recipe in *Jean Anderson Cooks,* is a great change when you want the taste of sweets with some crunch. The salt and pepper at the end is essential—you want to taste it and feel it on your tongue the way you do on fries—and so are the homemade crumbs.

1–1¼ pounds sweet potatoes, scrubbed
Coarse salt
8 slices good-quality white bread
2 tablespoons minced fresh chives, plus additional for serving
Freshly ground black pepper
2 large eggs
2 tablespoons richly flavored honey
8 tablespoons (1 stick) unsalted butter

Put the sweet potatoes in a large pan, cover with a generous amount of cold water, and add a good pinch of salt. Bring to a boil, cover partway, reduce the heat, and simmer until they are just tender when you test them with a needle or skewer. Don't overcook them, or they'll turn to mush. Drain them on a rack set in the sink and leave them there to cool.

Peel the potatoes, wrap them individually in plastic—tightly, so they keep their shape—and chill them for at least an hour.

Meanwhile, heat the oven to 300 degrees.

Toast the bread on the oven rack until dry and light gold, 13 to 15 minutes. Let the bread cool on a rack, then process it into crumbs in a food processor. Season the crumbs with the chives and salt and pepper and set them out in a soup dish.

Crack the eggs into another soup dish and whip them with a fork. Spoon in the honey and whip that in.

Cut the sweets into ⅓-inch-thick slices. Dip them in the eggs, then in the crumbs, patting the crumbs on, and put the slices on racks to dry for a minute or so.

Heat a few tablespoons of the butter in a skillet over medium heat. Once the foaming subsides, add the sweets, in batches—don't crowd the pan—and fry until golden, about 2 minutes on each side. Keep the finished slices in a warm oven if you want while you cook the remaining potatoes, adding more butter as needed.

Sprinkle with salt and pepper and chives and serve hot.

POTATO PANCAKES

MAKES 3 TO 4 DOZEN; SERVES 10 TO 12

Whether you call these latkes or pancakes, they go perfectly with sour cream or homemade applesauce. They're crisp and dense—just right with an oniony brisket.

4 pounds russet potatoes
2 large onions
4 large eggs
2 teaspoons chopped fresh thyme
Coarse salt and freshly ground black pepper
Peanut or corn oil for frying

Peel the potatoes and grate them. We usually use the food processor for this. Just don't push down on the potato with the plunger on the feed tube. Let the potato work its own way down, and you'll end up with long shreds. Peel and grate the onions. Again, food processor or box grater as you prefer; just be sure to use the shredder disk on the processor, not the steel blade. Put the potatoes and onions in the center of a clean kitchen towel, catch up all the edges, and twist and squeeze aggressively to extract as much liquid as possible.

Put the potatoes and onions in a large bowl and stir in the eggs, thyme, and salt and pepper to taste. Do not stir again.

Place a couple of wire racks on a baking sheet, slide them into the oven, and heat the oven to 250 degrees.

Heat 1/4 inch of oil in a large heavy skillet until very hot, almost smoking. Drop the batter in by big pinches (a scant 1/4 cup if you're the measuring type) and flatten them with a spatula. Don't crowd them. Cook until very brown, flip, flatten them slightly with the spatula, and again cook until very brown. This takes about 2 minutes per side. Lift them out onto the wire racks in the oven to keep warm while you fry the rest of the pancakes.

No matter how thoroughly you squeeze the potatoes and onion at the start, this batter will weep. Nothing to be done about it but to avoid the puddles, and don't stir the batter after the initial mixing. Keep your eye on the oil and replenish it as needed, and be sure it's very hot before you add each batch. Serve hot.

SWEET AND WHITE POTATO PANCAKES

MAKES ABOUT 3 DOZEN; SERVES 6 TO 8

This is something I came up with one October in Nantucket, when I raided my friend Laura Simon's root cellar for some of the truly great potatoes she grows. They were delicious for dinner, but maybe even better for breakfast the next morning, when I reheated them in a toaster oven and my pal Susan and I ate them with poached eggs.

The flour in the batter makes these pancakes a bit cakier.

1 pound sweet potatoes
1 pound russet potatoes
1 large onion
3 large eggs
2 tablespoons all-purpose flour
1½ teaspoons ground coriander
Coarse salt and freshly ground black pepper
Corn or peanut oil for frying

Peel the potatoes and grate them. I usually use the food processor for this and it works fine. Just don't push down on the potato with the plunger on the feed tube. Let it work its own way down, so you end up with long shreds. Peel and grate the onion. Again, use a food processor or box grater as you prefer; just be sure to use the shredder disk on the processor, not the steel blade. Put the potatoes and onion in the center of a clean kitchen towel, catch up all the edges, and twist and squeeze with vigor to extract as much liquid as possible.

Put the potatoes and onion in a large bowl and stir in the eggs, flour, coriander, and salt and pepper to taste.

Place a couple of wire racks on a baking sheet, slide the setup into the oven, and heat the oven to 250 degrees.

Heat ¼ inch of oil in a large heavy skillet until very hot, almost smoking. Drop the batter in by big pinches (a scant ¼ cup if you like to measure) and flatten them with a spatula. Don't crowd them. Cook until very brown, flip, flatten them slightly with the spatula, and again cook until very brown. This takes about 2 minutes per side. Lift them out onto the wire racks in the oven to keep warm while you fry the rest of the pancakes.

This batter will weep, but you should stir it as you go along. Serve the pancakes hot.

DRAINING FRIED FOOD

For dishes like croquettes and potato pancakes, we often recommend that you drain them on racks set on a tray or baking sheet. This works better than draining on paper towels because whatever you've just fried isn't sitting on oily paper and steaming. Air can circulate, excess oil drips off, and you end up with a crisper dish. This setup has the added advantage of being ready to go into a warm oven (something you probably wouldn't want to do with a paper towel–lined tray).

THREE-ROOT PANCAKES

Adjust the amount of caraway according to your taste. We usually add just 1 teaspoon, which gives the pancakes a nice hint, not a clobber. We like these best with a thick, juicy pork chop and a dollop of sour cream.

1 big sweet potato (about 3/4 pound), peeled
3/4 pound parsnips, peeled
1 1/2 pounds russet potatoes, peeled
6 large eggs, separated
1–2 teaspoons caraway seeds, lightly crushed
Coarse salt and freshly ground black pepper
2–3 tablespoons vegetable oil
2–3 tablespoons unsalted butter

Grate the sweet potato and parsnips and toss them into a large bowl. Grate the russets, using the shredder disk of a food processor or a box grater, and place in the center of a clean kitchen towel. Squeeze to eliminate as much water as possible, then add the potatoes to the bowl. Stir in the egg yolks, caraway, and salt and pepper.

Put the egg whites in a very clean bowl, add a pinch of salt, and whisk them to a soft foam—not quite soft peaks, but without any liquid white left. Stir the whites gently into the batter

Heat the oven to 250 degrees.

Heat 1 tablespoon of the oil and 1 tablespoon of the butter in a large skillet over medium heat until hot. Drop the pancake mixture by 1/4-cups into the hot pan, making several at once but without crowding; as soon as each pancake hits the pan, flatten and shape it with the back of a spoon into a neat round cake. Fry, flipping once, until nicely browned and cooked through, about 5 minutes on the first side and 3 minutes on the second. Drain on paper towels and keep warm on a plate in the oven while you cook the rest (these cakes are a bit too fragile to rest on racks).

Add more oil and butter to the pan as needed between batches, and stir up the remaining mixture occasionally to incorporate any liquid that has accumulated at the bottom of the bowl. Serve the pancakes hot.

ZUCCHINI AND POTATO CAKES

Try these for a Sunday-morning breakfast alongside scrambled eggs, or have them later in the day with broiled scallops. Note that they should be drained on paper towels, not racks.

$1^1/_2$ pounds zucchini, ends trimmed
$3/_4$ pound Maine or all-purpose potatoes, peeled
2 large eggs
$1/_2$ cup fresh bread crumbs
$1/_4$ cup freshly grated Pecorino
1 garlic clove, minced
$1/_4$ teaspoon crushed red pepper
Coarse salt and freshly ground black pepper
Olive oil for frying

Grate the zucchini in a food processor or box grater as you prefer. Put the zucchini in the center of a clean kitchen towel. Pull up the edges and squeeze to eliminate as much water as possible—really squeeze it, zucchini are *wet*—and put the zucchini in a large bowl. Grate the potatoes and repeat the process of wringing out as much water as possible; add the potatoes to the bowl.

Add the eggs, bread crumbs, Pecorino, garlic, crushed red pepper, salt to taste, and lots of black pepper and stir to combine.

Heat the oven to 250 degrees.

Pour enough olive oil into a large skillet to generously coat the bottom and heat over medium heat until hot. Shape several small pancakes (about $2^1/_2$ inches across and $1/_2$ inch thick) and slide them into the hot oil. Cook, flipping once, until golden and cooked through, about 5 minutes on the first side and 3 minutes on the second. Transfer to paper towels to drain and keep warm on a plate in the oven while you cook the rest.

Add a bit more oil to the pan between batches if necessary and stir up the zucchini-potato mixture once or twice to incorporate any liquid that accumulates at the bottom of the bowl. Serve hot.

VARIATION

Zucchini and Potato Cakes are best when first cooked, but if you have leftovers and some tomato sauce and mozzarella in the refrigerator, you can make these. Spread some sauce in a small casserole, add the cakes and more sauce, then cover with shredded cheese. Bake at 350 degrees until browned and bubbling.

POTATO-CARROT PANCAKES

Sometimes I make these bite-sized, to pass with drinks. Other times I make them larger for dinner, as here. Crème fraîche and little bits of fresh dill make a nice garnish.

1 pound all-purpose potatoes, peeled
1 pound carrots, grated
2 tablespoons all-purpose flour
2 large egg whites
1 1/2 tablespoons chopped fresh dill
1 teaspoon grated fresh ginger
Coarse salt and freshly ground white pepper
Vegetable oil for frying

Grate the potatoes, using the shredder disk of a food processor or a box grater, and place in the center of a clean kitchen towel. Squeeze hard to eliminate as much water as possible, and toss the potatoes and carrots together in a large bowl. Stir in the flour, egg whites, dill, and ginger. Season with salt and pepper.

Place a couple of racks on a baking sheet, slide the setup into the oven, and heat the oven to 250 degrees.

Pour 1/4 inch of oil into a large skillet and heat over medium-high heat until very hot. Drop the potato-carrot mixture by tablespoonfuls into the hot oil, cooking several pancakes at once but without crowding the pan; as soon as they hit the hot oil, spread the pancakes with the back of a fork to form flat, lacy rounds. There should be holes in the pancakes that allow the hot oil to bubble up in spots; if not, they are too thick and won't cook through. Cook, flipping once, until the cakes are browned and crisp, about 2 minutes on the first side and 1 1/2 minutes on the second side. Transfer the pancakes to the racks in the oven to keep warm while you fry the balance.

Stir the potato-carrot mixture from time to time to reincorporate any liquid that weeps out. Serve the pancakes hot.

SWISS POTATO PANCAKE
(ROESTI)

SERVES 4 TO 6

This big potato pancake is creamy inside, crusty and brown outside. A large (12-inch) pan gives you a thinner pancake with more of the crispy crust; a smaller (10-inch) pan gives you more of the creamy center.

2–2¹/₂ pounds white potatoes, peeled
Coarse salt and freshly ground black pepper
4 tablespoons (¹/₂ stick) unsalted butter

Grate the potatoes, using the shredding disk of a food processor or the large holes of a box grater. Transfer to a large bowl and toss with salt and pepper to taste.

Heat 3 tablespoons of the butter in a 10- or 12-inch cast-iron skillet over medium-high heat. When the butter is very hot—it will stop foaming—dump in the potatoes. Press hard on the potatoes with a flexible metal spatula to form a large pancake, and cook, continuing to flatten every so often, for 5 minutes. Lower the heat to medium-low, cover tightly, and cook for 5 more minutes.

Uncover and continue to cook, pressing on the top and gently lifting the sides to make sure that the roesti is browning and not sticking, for 6 to 8 more minutes, until the bottom is nicely browned and the top begins to look rather dry. This process of lid-off, lid-on, lid-off is what makes the roesti creamy and cooked through on the inside yet crispy and dry on the outside. Loosen the roesti with your spatula, lift and tilt the pan, and slide the potato cake onto a large flat plate. Scrape up any stuck bits of potato so the pan is clean.

Return the pan to medium heat and add the remaining 1 tablespoon butter. To brown the other side, flip the roesti and slide it back into the pan, browned side up. Cook, loosening the cake with the spatula and shaking the pan to make sure that there's no sticking, for about 5 more minutes.

Cut into wedges and serve warm.

YUKON GOLD AND ASIAGO CAKES WITH GREEN OLIVES

MAKES 12 TO 15 CAKES; SERVES 6

Parboiling the potatoes gives these little cakes a denser, creamier inside than cakes made from raw potatoes. Also, because the potatoes are precooked, the cakes can be made ahead and held in the refrigerator for several hours without weeping or discoloring before panfrying.

1½ pounds Yukon Gold or other yellow-fleshed potatoes
Coarse salt
2 tablespoons olive oil, plus more for frying
1 small onion, finely chopped
Freshly ground black pepper
1 garlic clove, minced
⅓ cup chopped green olives
⅓ cup freshly grated Asiago
1 large egg, lightly beaten
3 tablespoons all-purpose flour, plus more for dredging

Put the potatoes in a saucepan, cover with cold water by at least an inch, add a good pinch of salt, and bring to a boil. Reduce the heat to medium and simmer for 5 minutes. Drain on a rack in the sink and leave them to cool some.

Meanwhile, heat the 2 tablespoons olive oil in a skillet over medium heat until it slides across the pan. Add the onion, season with salt and pepper, and cook until soft and just golden, about 8 minutes. Add the garlic and cook for a minute more. Remove from the heat.

Peel the potatoes and grate them into a large mixing bowl. A box grater's your only choice for this. Add the cooked onion and garlic, along with the olives and Asiago. Toss to combine. Season with salt and pepper. Add the egg and the 3 tablespoons flour and stir with a wooden spoon until evenly mixed.

You can make this ahead, and cover and refrigerate it for several hours. Or shape the cakes ahead, but be aware that they will need to be dredged again in flour before frying.

Shape the potato dough into small, plump cakes, each about 2½ inches across and ¾ inch thick. You can dip your hands in a little flour as you work to prevent the dough from sticking too much. Dredge the cakes in flour, patting lightly to shake off the excess.

Place a couple of racks on a baking sheet, slide the setup into the oven, and heat the oven to 250 degrees.

Pour enough olive oil into a large skillet to coat the bottom generously and heat over medium heat until hot. Cook the cakes in batches, flipping once, until they are golden and cooked through, about 10 minutes total. (The first side always takes longer.) Transfer the cakes to the racks set in the oven to keep warm while you fry the remaining cakes.

Serve hot.

POTATOES WITH JUNIPER BERRIES
(POMMES DE TERRE À L'ARDENNAISE)

This dish, from British food writer Elizabeth David, is a favorite of cooking expert Diana Kennedy and has become one of my favorites, too—particularly when I make it with Yukons. Elizabeth David suggests that once cooked, the potatoes be turned out onto a platter, there to become a bed for whatever meat you're serving. Diana Kennedy adds lots of minced garlic to them.

1½ pounds waxy or yellow-fleshed potatoes
10 juniper berries, crushed or chopped
Coarse salt and freshly ground black pepper
4 tablespoons (½ stick) unsalted butter
1 tablespoon olive oil

Peel the potatoes and shred them on a box grater. Put them in a colander and rinse them well to rid them of the starch they will be exuding. Lift them out onto a kitchen towel, catch up the ends of the towel, and squeeze the potatoes dry.

Dump the potatoes into a bowl. Add the juniper berries and season well with salt and pepper. Toss with your hands, or stir if you're being tidy.

Heat the butter and oil in a heavy 9-inch skillet over medium heat and, when the foaming subsides, add the potatoes. Pan size and heat are important; too big a pan or too high heat, and the cake will dry out and, with it, the perfume of the juniper. Flatten the potatoes with the back of a spatula and let them cook gently for about 5 minutes. Turn the potatoes with the spatula—you do it in pieces, don't worry. Flatten the potatoes again and start to push in at the edges to make a cake. Let this cook another 5 minutes, then repeat: turn in pieces, flatten, and form back into a cake. By this time, you should be able to shake the pan and have the cake slide in it. Cook for another 5 minutes, shaking a few times and compressing the mass back into a cake if it splits (it will until it's cooked, so don't worry). The potatoes are done when they are quite tender and hold together in a cake with a light crust on the bottom.

Invert onto a flat plate and serve.

FRENCH POTATO CROQUETTES

(SUBRIC)

MAKES ABOUT 18; SERVES 4 TO 6

Subric are little French croquettes bound with an egg-enriched béchamel and fried without breading. For this version, diced potatoes go inside, along with a bit of cheese and grated onion, to make tender and creamy cakes with a crispy, butter-fried outside. Serve them alone for a light supper or in place of Yorkshire pudding alongside something big and beefy.

1 pound white potatoes, peeled
Coarse salt
2 tablespoons unsalted butter
1 small onion, grated
2 tablespoons all-purpose flour
1 cup milk
2 large egg yolks
1/2 cup shredded Gruyère or Swiss cheese (about 2 ounces)
Freshly grated nutmeg
Pinch of cayenne pepper
Freshly ground white pepper
1 large egg, lightly beaten with 1 tablespoon milk
2 tablespoons chopped flat-leaf parsley
4 tablespoons clarified butter, as needed (see page 28)

Put the potatoes in a saucepan, cover with cold water by at least an inch, add a good pinch of salt, and bring to a boil. Reduce the heat to medium, cover partway, and cook until the potatoes are very tender. Drain the potatoes on a rack set in the sink and leave them there to cool.

Melt the butter in a small saucepan over medium heat. When the foaming calms down, add the onion. Cook, stirring once or twice, until soft and fragrant, about 3 minutes. Whisk in the flour. Cook for a minute or two, then whisk in the milk. Bring to a gentle simmer, whisking occasionally. Let the sauce simmer for a few minutes, until smooth and slightly thickened. Remove from the heat and immediately whisk in the egg yolks.

Switch to a wooden spoon and stir in the cheese—the sauce should be hot enough to melt the cheese. Season with a grating or two of nutmeg, the cayenne, and salt and white pepper.

Cut the cooled potatoes into small dice, about $1/3$ inch. Scrape the sauce into a mixing bowl and add the potatoes, the beaten egg, and the parsley. Stir to combine.

Heat the oven to 250 degrees.

Heat 2 tablespoons of the clarified butter in a large skillet (nonstick works well here) over medium heat. When the butter is quite hot, drop the batter by rounded tablespoons into the pan. Fry, flipping once, until nicely browned and cooked through, 3 to 4 minutes per side. Drain on paper towels and keep warm on a plate in the oven while you cook the rest. Add more butter to the pan as needed between batches.

Serve the croquettes hot.

POTATO CROQUETTES

MAKES 12 TO 16 LARGE CROQUETTES OR 32 SMALL ONES

You can serve these right from the skillet or fry in advance and keep them warm while you finish the rest of the dinner. You can make them large and serve as a side dish, or you can make them small, to be passed at cocktail time. You can make them with potatoes cooked fresh or use leftover baked potatoes.

Assorted herbs are best here: mint, basil, thyme, parsley, chervil. Use a combination or just your favorite.

1½ pounds yellow-fleshed or russet potatoes, scrubbed
Coarse salt
1 shallot, minced
2 tablespoons chopped fresh herbs (see note above)
2 large eggs
Freshly ground black pepper
1 cup dried bread crumbs
4 tablespoons (½ stick) unsalted butter

Put the potatoes in a large saucepan, cover with cold water by at least an inch, add a big pinch of salt, and bring to a boil. Reduce the heat to medium, cover partway, and cook until the potatoes are tender. Drain on a rack set in the sink and let cool.

Peel the potatoes and put them through a ricer into a mixing bowl. Add the shallot, herbs, 1 of the eggs, and salt and pepper to taste. Mix well, then cover with plastic and refrigerate for at least 30 minutes.

Beat the remaining egg with 2 tablespoons water in a shallow bowl, and put the crumbs in another bowl. Start melting the butter in a skillet over medium heat. Form the seasoned potatoes into croquettes—oblong patties, big or small, depending on how you plan to serve them—and dip first in the egg, then in the crumbs.

Fry the croquettes until they are heated through and nicely browned on all sides. Drain them on a rack set over a baking sheet, and keep them warm in a 250-degree oven if you're not serving them immediately.

VARIATIONS

Fry a couple of pieces of bacon and crumble them into the potatoes. Or mince a few slices of ham and add that. You can also cut a small bell pepper into tiny dice, sauté it in a bit of oil, and stir that in. With each, remember to choose herbs that will complement the flavor of what you add (I think mint with the ham is a great combination).

CHICKEN CROQUETTES

These are repurposed leftovers, but you'd never know it. Made small and breaded, they are great nibbles to serve with cocktails. Larger ones make a fine lunch dish.

If you don't have leftover potatoes on hand, boil some up and let them cool completely.

FOR THE ROUX
1 cup milk
2 shallots, peeled
1 tablespoon unsalted butter
1 tablespoon all-purpose flour
Coarse salt

1 pound yellow-fleshed potatoes, boiled
1 pound roast chicken (skin and bones removed)
1/2 cup freshly grated Parmesan
2 or 3 slices prosciutto, minced (optional)
3 tablespoons finely chopped flat-leaf parsley
Freshly ground white pepper
8 tablespoons (1 stick) unsalted butter
2 lemons, cut into wedges, for serving

FOR THE ROUX: Rinse out a small saucepan with cold water (which will make cleanup easier later) and add the milk and shallots. Bring to a simmer over medium heat. Turn off the heat and let the shallots infuse the milk for 10 minutes or so.

Melt the 1 tablespoon butter in a small saucepan over medium-low heat. Stir in the flour and cook this roux for at least 5 minutes, stirring constantly. Discard the shallots and pour the milk into the roux all at once. You might want to switch to a whisk at this point, but either way, stir well until it's smooth and beginning to thicken. Season with salt and let the béchamel come to a boil;

simmer it for 3 to 5 minutes after that. You want a thick, well-cooked sauce. Remove from the heat.

Peel the potatoes and rice them into a mixing bowl. Cut the chicken into chunks and put it in the bowl of a food processor. Hit the pulse button a few times to mince the chicken. Take it easy with this step: you want fine pieces of chicken, but you don't want paste. Add the chicken to the potatoes, along with the grated cheese, prosciutto (if using), parsley, and pepper. Stir in the béchamel.

Form the mixture into 12 balls, then flatten them into disks. The classic croquette shape is more of an oval, with lovely tapered ends, and if you want to impress yourself, go for it.

Melt 4 tablespoons of the butter in a skillet over medium-high heat. When the butter stops sputtering, add half of the croquettes. Now just leave them be. The cheese will melt, then brown to form a crust; but if you keep moving the croquettes around before the crust forms, you'll end up with a mess. After about 7 minutes, carefully turn the croquettes. Reduce the heat to medium and cook until the second side is browned, 6 to 7 minutes. Move the croquettes to a serving plate and repeat with the remaining butter and croquettes.

Serve with the lemon wedges.

VARIATION

The more traditional way to finish these is to give them an egg wash, then coat with bread crumbs before browning. They are also a bit easier to handle, and it gives you a sturdier crust if you want to make little ones to serve as finger food.

Beat an egg with 2 tablespoons water and spread 1 cup fine dried bread crumbs on a plate. Dip the croquettes in the egg, let any excess drip off, and then roll them in the crumbs. They will take 3 to 5 minutes to brown on each side.

CUBAN POTATO CROQUETTES WITH BEEF PICADILLO (PAPAS RELLEÑAS DE PICADILLO)

MAKES 12 CROQUETTES

These fried potato packets are the Cuban version of *Charp* (page 362), with a filling of picadillo. *Papas Relleñas* are bigger, and you make them round, but the technique is the same. Serve them with a bright slaw or tropical salad as a small supper or as part of a larger meal.

2 pounds russet potatoes, scrubbed
Coarse salt
1 large egg, lightly beaten
1/4 cup all-purpose flour
3 tablespoons chopped flat-leaf parsley
Freshly ground black pepper
1/2 cup dried bread crumbs
Vegetable oil for frying
1/2 recipe Picadillo (page 358)

Put the potatoes in a large saucepan, cover with cold water by at least an inch, add a good pinch of salt, and bring to a boil. Reduce the heat to medium, cover partway, and cook until the potatoes are very tender. Drain the potatoes on a rack set in the sink and let cool slightly.

As soon as the potatoes are cool enough to handle, peel and rice them into a large bowl. Spread them out and leave to cool.

Add the egg, flour, and parsley to the riced potatoes and mix well with your hands or a wooden spoon. Season with salt and pepper. Dump the potatoes out onto a lightly floured board and knead into a smooth and cohesive dough. Divide it into 12 even portions.

One by one, shape each portion into a ball and flatten it in the palm of your hand to form a thin round about 4 inches across. Put a tablespoon of the Picadillo in the center of the round and pinch the edges together to seal. Smooth the packet into a round ball, check for cracks in the exterior, and set it on a tray. Roll the croquettes in the bread crumbs to coat.

Heat 3/4 inch of oil in a heavy saucepan to about 350 degrees. Slide the croquettes into the oil—in batches, so as not to crowd the pan. Fry, flipping once, until deeply browned and crisp, 6 to 8 minutes. Drain on a cooling rack set over a baking sheet. Serve immediately, or keep warm in a 250-degree oven for up to 20 minutes. All fried food is best eaten right away, but if you must, you can hold them at room temperature for a few hours and reheat.

PICADILLO

Here's your filling for the *Papas Rellenas* (page 356): tender beef with high notes of olives, raisins, and capers. But think about making this all for itself. It's a great dinner with a big pile of Saratoga Chips (page 314).

1¹/₂ pounds ground beef (chuck has the best flavor)
1 small onion, finely chopped
¹/₂ green bell pepper, finely chopped
1 garlic clove, minced
¹/₄ cup chopped pimiento-stuffed green olives
3 tablespoons raisins, chopped
2 tablespoons drained capers
1 heaping tablespoon tomato paste
1 teaspoon dried oregano, preferably Mexican
¹/₂ teaspoon ground cumin
¹/₄ teaspoon ground allspice
Freshly ground black pepper
2 tablespoons olive oil
Splash of sherry vinegar
Coarse salt

Crumble the ground beef into a mixing bowl and add the onion, bell pepper, garlic, olives, raisins, capers, tomato paste, oregano, cumin, allspice, and a few turns of the pepper grinder. Gently mix together with your hands. Cover with plastic and leave at room temperature for 30 minutes.

Heat the olive oil in a large skillet over medium heat. Add the meat mixture, the vinegar, and a pinch of salt. Cook, without browning, breaking up the meat with a wooden spoon frequently. During the first 10 minutes, the mixture will throw off a lot of liquid. Lower the heat a bit if the meat begins to brown at all, and continue to cook until most of the liquid has evaporated, about 30 minutes. The picadillo should be juicy, but not soupy.

CORN AND POTATO PANCAKES

Corn and potato cakes are tender and delicate, and they don't hold well once they are fried. But the batter will keep, so plan on making it an hour or so ahead and leaving it on the counter, covered, then frying the pancakes at the last minute. These are good with roast chicken.

1 cup milk
1 1/2 cups corn kernels (it's fine to use frozen for this)
Pinch of sugar
1 1/4 pounds russet potatoes, baked
2 tablespoons all-purpose flour
2 large eggs, lightly beaten
1/4 cup heavy cream
1 whole scallion, minced
Coarse salt and freshly ground black pepper
Corn oil for frying

Heat the oven to 250 degrees.

Bring the milk to a simmer in a small saucepan. Add the corn (if you're using frozen, rinse it under warm water first) and the sugar. Bring back to a simmer and cook very gently for 5 minutes.

Meanwhile, peel the potatoes and rice them into a mixing bowl. Add the flour, eggs, cream, scallion, and salt and pepper to taste and mix well.

Drain the corn (send the milk down the drain) and add it to the batter.

Heat 1 to 2 tablespoons oil in a skillet over medium-high heat until it shimmers. Add the batter by heaping tablespoons and fry until golden brown, 2 to 3 minutes. Flip the pancakes, fry until golden on the second side, and drain them on a baking sheet lined with paper towels.

Keep the first batches warm in the oven only for as long as it takes to cook the rest of the pancakes, then serve right away.

INDIAN POTATO CUTLETS

This is another recipe from Samia Ahad, my Indian food guru. I'd call them croquettes (since my training is French), but the right term here is indeed the English word "cutlets," since they resemble little chops. They pack some very nice heat, and the lemon juice adds an appealing, perky taste.

If you want, use this as a filling for samosas (see page 72), or skip the frying and serve this up as a mash.

1½ pounds russet potatoes, scrubbed
Coarse salt
1 small onion, chopped
¼ cup chopped cilantro leaves
3 green chiles, minced (see note, page 333)
2 tablespoons fresh lemon juice
1 tablespoon vegetable oil, plus additional for frying
1 teaspoon black mustard seeds
10 curry leaves (see note, page 333)
3 garlic cloves, very thinly sliced

Put the potatoes in a saucepan and cover with cold water by at least an inch. Add a good pinch of salt and bring to a boil. Cover partway, reduce the heat to medium, and cook until the potatoes are tender. Drain on a rack set in the sink and leave them there to cool. (Or, if you're serving this as mashed potatoes—see note above—peel and rice the potatoes right away.)

Peel the potatoes and put them through a ricer into a mixing bowl. Add the onion, cilantro, chiles, lemon juice, and salt to taste and mix well.

Heat the 1 tablespoon vegetable oil in a small heavy skillet over medium-high heat until it shimmers. Add the mustard seeds and cook, stirring, until they begin to pop. Then add the curry leaves and garlic and cook for 20 to 30 seconds, just until you start to smell the garlic—you do not want to brown the garlic. Add this right away to the potatoes and mix well.

Form the potato mixture into 12 patties.

Heat a thin film of oil in a large skillet over medium heat until it shimmers. Add half of the cutlets and cook until browned, about 3 minutes. Turn them over carefully—they are very fragile—and brown the other side, which will take about 2 minutes. Repeat with the rest of the cutlets, adding a bit more oil if you need it, but be stingy—if you use too much oil, the cutlets will fall apart. Serve warm.

PERSIAN POTATO CROQUETTES WITH SPICED MEAT FILLING

(CHARP)

MAKES 16 CROQUETTES

For these croquettes, you make a mashed potato dough, fold it around a spiced ground meat filling (*kibbeh*), then fry. Serve three or four per person with a salad, or stuff them into a pita. These can also be made cocktail-size. They take a little more work that way, but they're great pop-in-your-mouth treats to serve with drinks. If you're making pita sandwiches or passing these with drinks, have a bowl of Yogurt-Cilantro Sauce (page 233) on hand.

2 pounds russet potatoes, scrubbed
Coarse salt

FOR THE MEAT FILLING
2 tablespoons olive oil
1 onion, finely chopped
3 tablespoons pine nuts
$^{1}/_{2}$ teaspoon ground coriander
$^{1}/_{4}$ teaspoon ground ginger
$^{1}/_{4}$ teaspoon ground allspice
Freshly grated nutmeg
$^{1}/_{3}$ pound ground lamb or beef
Coarse salt and freshly ground black pepper

$^{1}/_{4}$ cup all-purpose flour
1 large egg, lightly beaten
Coarse salt and freshly ground black pepper
$^{1}/_{2}$ cup dried bread crumbs
Vegetable oil for frying

Put the potatoes in a saucepan, cover with cold water by at least an inch, add a good pinch of salt, and bring to a boil. Reduce the heat to medium, cover partway, and cook until the potatoes are very tender. Drain the potatoes on a rack set in the sink and let cool briefly.

As soon as the potatoes are cool enough to handle, peel and rice them into a large bowl. Spread them out and leave to cool.

MEANWHILE, FOR THE MEAT FILLING: Heat the olive oil and onion in a skillet over medium heat and cook until the onion is translucent, about 7 minutes. Stir in the nuts and all the spices (a grating or two of nutmeg is all you need), and cook until the mixture is very fragrant and the nuts are beginning to toast, about 4 minutes. Crumble in the ground meat and season with salt and pepper. Cook, breaking up the meat with a wooden spoon, until the meat is cooked through, another 4 to 5 minutes. Remove from the heat.

Add the flour and egg to the riced potatoes and mix well with your hands or a wooden spoon. Season with salt and pepper. Dump the potatoes out onto a lightly floured board and knead into a smooth and cohesive dough. Divide it into 16 even portions.

One by one, shape each portion into a ball and flatten it in the palm of your hand to form a thin round about 3 inches across. Put about a tablespoon of the meat filling in the center of the round and pinch the edges together to seal. Smooth the *charp* into a football shape, check to make sure no filling is peeking out, and put it on a tray. Roll the *charp* in the bread crumbs to coat.

Heat ½ inch of oil in a heavy saucepan to about 375 degrees. Slide the *charp* into the oil in batches—if you crowd the pan, they won't brown well. Fry, flipping once, until deeply browned and crisp, 3 to 5 minutes. Drain on a cooling rack set over a baking sheet. Serve immediately, or keep warm in a 250-degree oven for up to 20 minutes. These can also be held at room temperature for a few hours and reheated—but they really are at their best right after frying.

TUNISIAN FRIED EGG AND POTATO TURNOVERS
(BRIK)

Picture this: impossibly flaky pastry, so crisp, encasing seasoned mashed potatoes. Hidden within, an egg. What a lunch! Molly adapted this from a recipe by our friend cooking teacher Joanne Weir. Just like the very best fried eggs, these are cooked so that the whites are set but the yolks are still runny. Moroccan cooks always have preserved lemon on hand (there's a great recipe for a quick version in *Paula Wolfert's World of Food*), but you can make substitutions.

3/4 cup mashed potatoes
2 whole scallions, chopped
1 tablespoon chopped flat-leaf parsley
1 tablespoon minced preserved lemon peel (or use
   1/2 teaspoon fresh lemon juice and 1/4 teaspoon grated zest)
Coarse salt and freshly ground black pepper
5 large eggs
4 sheets phyllo dough
6 tablespoons olive oil
Peanut or vegetable oil for frying

Season the mashed potatoes with the scallions, parsley, and lemon. Add some salt and pepper and mix well.

Lightly beat 1 of the eggs in a small dish. You'll use this egg wash to seal the phyllo triangles.

Brush a sheet of phyllo lightly with olive oil. Fold the sheet into quarters — so you have a 6-by-8-inch rectangle. Fold over 2 inches of the long side to form a perfect 6-inch square. Spoon a quarter of the potatoes onto one corner of the square. Spread the potatoes out into a triangle, covering half of the phyllo square, leaving about a $1/3$-inch border at the edges, then make a well in the center of the potatoes for the egg. Brush the phyllo with egg wash. Break an egg into the potato well. Fold the phyllo over to form a triangular turnover and press the edges to seal. Repeat with the remaining ingredients, to make 4 turnovers.

Heat $1/4$ inch of oil in a heavy skillet over medium heat until hot but not smoking. Add any olive oil left over from brushing the phyllo. Fry the turnovers, in batches if necessary, until well browned on both sides, 2 to 3 minutes per side. Drain briefly on a cooling rack set over a baking sheet and serve hot.

VIETNAMESE SWEET POTATO SHRIMP CAKES

MAKES ABOUT 2 DOZEN

Wrap one of these spidery bird's-nest fritters in a cool, tender lettuce leaf and be transported. Don't worry if the fritters are irregular, with lots of little crispy bits that break off. When we serve these, the platter comes back picked clean.

The dipping sauce gets its heat from the rings of habanero pepper floating on its surface. Make sure no unsuspecting guest tries to eat one of these rings, though: they're powerful.

FOR THE DIPPING SAUCE
$^1/_3$ cup fish sauce (nuoc mam; see note)
$^1/_3$ cup fresh lime juice
2 tablespoons sugar
I small habanero chile, cut into thin rings (or 2 serranos, minced)

Peanut oil for frying

FOR THE FRITTERS
$^3/_4$ pound sweet potato, peeled and grated
$^1/_2$ pound medium shrimp, peeled, deveined, and cut into $^1/_2$-inch bits
3 whole scallions, chopped
I garlic clove, crushed
I tablespoon grated fresh ginger
I teaspoon coarse salt or to taste
$^1/_2$ cup cornstarch
3 large egg whites

I head Boston or Bibb lettuce, leaves separated and any thick ribs removed
Cilantro and mint leaves

FOR THE DIPPING SAUCE: Pour the fish sauce and lime juice into a small bowl. Dissolve the sugar in ¼ cup warm water and add it to the sauce. Stir in the chile and let the sauce sit for 20 minutes before you serve it.

Fill a heavy pot or deep fryer with at least 3 inches of oil—but make sure that this fills the pot no more than halfway—and heat it to 350 degrees. Place a couple of racks on a baking sheet, slide it into the oven, and heat the oven to 250 degrees.

FOR THE FRITTERS: Toss the sweet potato, shrimp, scallions, garlic, ginger, and salt together in a mixing bowl. Sift in the cornstarch and toss again until evenly combined.

Put the egg whites in a separate bowl with 2 tablespoons warm water and whisk until you have a soft foam—not yet soft peaks, but there shouldn't be any liquid white. Stir the egg whites into the sweet potato batter.

Use a large flat spoon to scoop up a very generous tablespoon of the fritter batter and slide it into the hot oil. Add a few more spoonfuls to the pot, but don't crowd. Fry, turning a few times, until browned and crisp, 3 to 5 minutes. Transfer to the racks in the oven to keep warm while you fry the remainder.

Serve the warm fritters with a plate of lettuce leaves, cilantro, and mint for wrapping and a bowl of the sauce for dipping.

NOTE: Fish sauce (nuoc mam) can be found in Asian markets or in the Asian foods section of supermarkets.

ROLLED POTATO PANCAKES
STUFFED WITH ONIONS AND BUTTERED BREAD CRUMBS

MAKES 10

These Hungarian goodies are something between a dumpling and a filled crepe. They're traditionally made with lard, but we love them with sweet-tasting butter and fried in bacon drippings just before serving. Serve one per person alongside a roast or stew, or make a supper out of two.

Don't bother with these if you're not up for making fresh bread crumbs.

2^1/$_2$ pounds russet potatoes, scrubbed
Coarse salt
9 tablespoons (1 stick plus 1 tablespoon) unsalted butter
1 onion, finely chopped
^{2}/$_3$ cup fresh bread crumbs
Freshly ground black pepper
1 large egg, lightly beaten
1^1/$_2$ cups all-purpose flour
Bacon drippings or butter for frying

Put the potatoes in a saucepan, cover with cold water by at least an inch, add a good pinch of salt, and bring to a boil. Reduce the heat to medium, cover partway, and cook until the potatoes are very tender. Drain the potatoes on a rack set in the sink and let them cool some.

As soon as the potatoes are cool enough to handle, peel and rice them into a large bowl. Add 1 tablespoon of the butter and salt to taste. Set aside to cool.

Melt the remaining butter—yes, 8 tablespoons—in a heavy skillet over low heat. Add the onion and cook gently, without browning, stirring from time to time, until very soft and fragrant, 15 to 20 minutes. Stir in the bread crumbs, increase the heat to medium, and cook until the crumbs begin to brown, another 3 to 4 minutes. Season with a pinch of salt and about ¹/₂ teaspoon pepper. Remove the filling from the heat.

Dump the cooled potatoes onto a marble or wooden work surface. Make a well in the center and pour the egg and flour into it. Using your hands, incorporate the egg and flour into the potatoes until evenly mixed. Scrape the work surface clean with a dough scraper and knead the dough tenderly for a few minutes, until it is smooth and soft.

Dust the work surface very lightly with flour and roll out the potato dough to a 15-by-10-inch rectangle about ¹/₃ inch thick. Try to keep the edges as square as possible, but don't fuss to make them perfect. Cut the rectangle into ten 5-inch squares. Spoon about 2 tablespoons of the filling onto each square. Spread the filling over the squares, leaving a ¹/₄-inch border on three sides and a ¹/₂-inch border on the fourth.

Roll the squares up around the filling as you would a small jelly roll — rolling toward the side with the largest border. Squeeze the ends of the roll to seal and press gently along the seam so that there are no openings. Set the rolls on a lightly floured tray once they're done.

Bring a large wide pot of water to a boil. Salt it lightly, reduce the heat to a simmer, and slide 3 or 4 rolls at a time, so as not to overcrowd the pot, into the water. Don't let the water boil again, or you risk breaking up the delicate rolled pancakes. Simmer until the pancakes float to the top, about 4 minutes. Use two spatulas or a wide skimmer to lift the rolls gently from the water — be careful to support the length of each roll, or it may break — and transfer the pancakes to a lightly oiled tray. Set aside while you cook the remainder. The pancakes can be made ahead up to this point and held for several hours before frying.

Heat 2 to 3 tablespoons bacon drippings in a skillet (and why shouldn't it be the one you cooked the onion in?) over medium-high heat. Fry the pancakes, flipping once, until nicely browned and crisp, about 5 minutes. Serve immediately, or keep the first batch warm in a 250-degree oven while you fry the rest.

MUSHROOM-AND-SPINACH-STUFFED POTATO GALETTE

SERVES 6

Galettes are crunchy, hot cakes, a clever means to use up odd bits of leftovers. Once you've got the hang of making a stuffed galette, you might try your hand at other combinations. Any filling ingredients should be cooked (with the exception of tender-leafed vegetables such as baby spinach or fresh sorrel), and the filling should never overwhelm the potatoes. When we're feeling especially brave, we may add ⅓ cup or so of shredded cheese, but be forewarned, this can lead to trouble and make the galette stick to the pan. We're grateful to chef Randall Price for this recipe.

6 tablespoons (¾ stick) unsalted butter
½ pound mushrooms (a combination of button and chanterelle is nice), trimmed, and sliced
Coarse salt and freshly ground black pepper
1 shallot, minced
2 pounds white or all-purpose potatoes, peeled
2 cups loosely packed tender spinach leaves, any tough stems removed

Melt 2 tablespoons of the butter in a skillet over medium-high heat. Add the mushrooms, season with salt and pepper, and sauté, shaking and stirring often, until browned and very dry, about 10 minutes. Add the shallot and cook for another minute. Take from the heat and set aside.

Grate the potatoes with the fine julienne blade of a mandoline or the large holes of a box grater. Toss the shreds with salt and pepper to taste.

Heat 3 tablespoons of the butter in a 10-inch cast-iron or heavy nonstick skillet over medium-high heat. When the butter is very hot—it will stop foaming—dump in half of the potatoes. Flatten them a bit with your hand and cover with the sautéed mushrooms. Top with the spinach leaves. Cover with the remaining potatoes and press hard on top with a flexible metal spatula to form a large pancake. Cook, continuing to compress with the spatula, until the cake is browned on the bottom and holding together, about 10 minutes. If it appears to be browning too quickly, lower the heat a smidge—if you cook the galette at too high a heat, the potatoes inside won't cook through. During the last few minutes, use the spatula to loosen the galette and peek underneath to make sure that it's not sticking.

You have two options for flipping the galette: either lift and tilt the pan, and slide the galette onto a large flat plate, or set a large round plate over the skillet, and quickly flip the whole ensemble. Whichever method you choose, loosen any stuck bits of potato in the pan before continuing.

Add the remaining 1 tablespoon butter to the pan. Flip the galette and slide it back into the pan, browned side up, to cook on the other side. Cook, loosening the cake with the spatula and shaking back and forth to make sure that there's no sticking, for 8 to 10 more minutes, until browned on the bottom.

Cut into wedges and serve warm.

BAKED &

ROASTED POTATOES

POTATO PRINCIPLES
MASSAGE YOUR POTATO

When you eat a baked potato, what you end up doing more often than not is mashing it with your fork as you eat to break up the large chunks. For a fluffy potato, try Molly's method.

As you take a baked potato out of the oven, hold it in a folded towel or two clean pot holders and massage it. Roll firmly but gently—just like a good massage—between your hands to break up the flesh without cracking the skin. Then place the potato on the plate, cut a cross in the skin, and pinch, pushing the flesh up and out.

BAKED POTATOES

The classic baked potato is a crispy-skinned long russet. Nice, but it's hardly the only option. Bill Leritz, owner of Fox Hill Farm in Upstate New York, bakes the delicious heirloom potatoes that he grows. His Estimas — yellow-fleshed potatoes about the size of a golf ball — make great baked potatoes. So do German Butterballs and Carolas, as do the local russets I've been finding in my farmers' market, little ones, just three inches long. Leritz is up-front about the way he cooks them. "Aw," he told me, "I just put them in the oven. If you have a good potato, why get fancy?" He's right. This method will provide good baked potatoes with crispy skins.

What are the things you shouldn't do? Don't wrap the potatoes in foil, don't rub the skins with oil or prick them until they're cooked halfway, don't crowd the potatoes or put them on a baking sheet — and never bake a potato in the microwave.

Potatoes
Butter
Sour cream
Coarse salt and freshly ground black pepper

Heat the oven to 350 or 400 degrees.

Scrub the potatoes and dry them well. Place the potatoes in the center of the oven, directly on the rack, and bake them until they are tender. You test this by squeezing: if you leave an indentation, the potato is done. Large russets will take 60 to 70 minutes; smaller Butterballs may be done in 30 minutes. Now, this is important: halfway through the baking time, prick the skins all over with a fork to let the steam escape. Just reach in and grab each potato with a pot holder. If you're a diligent type, you can turn the potato over when you put it back on the rack.

Massage the finished potatoes and put them on a platter. Serve with plenty of butter and sour cream and salt and pepper on the table.

POTATO PRINCIPLES
TWICE-BAKED POTATOES

As much as we love the simplicity and honest goodness of a plain baked potato, there are times when we can't resist fiddling. This is where twice-baked potatoes come in. By baking russets a bit in advance, scooping out the insides, and adding all sorts of things before stuffing the filling back into the jacket, we make something altogether more than the sum of its parts. There are a lot of advantages to twice-baked potatoes, not the least being that they can be assembled a day or two in advance and pulled out of the refrigerator for a quick weeknight supper or a winter weekend brunch. You can make these potatoes as simple or fancy as you like, and kids love them.

Select russets that are all about the same size. We like 3/4-pound ones because they're large enough to hold a good amount of mashed potato filling, but not too large for an ordinary appetite to manage. After baking, slice off the top lengthwise to form a sort of boat. For smaller portions, to serve as a side dish, or if the potatoes are enormous, you may want to slice them in half lengthwise and make two servings from each potato.

While the potatoes are still warm, scoop out the flesh. Use a tablespoon to do this, and be careful to leave enough flesh so that the jacket doesn't collapse. Mash the flesh with a hand masher, a ricer, or even just a fork. And now, here's where the fun comes in: enrich and season the potatoes as you would mashed potatoes.

We generally add warm milk or cream (no more than 4 teaspoons per potato), a bit of softened butter, maybe some sour cream or yogurt, and cheese. You want a consistency that is just a bit stiffer than most mashed potatoes. If you make it too soft, the filling will tend to overflow when you rebake the potatoes.

Once you have your basic mash, you can add any range of flavorings: crumbled bacon, chopped ham, fresh crabmeat, smoked fish, stewed mushrooms, sautéed fennel, caramelized onions, steamed vegetables, pesto, olives, capers, horseradish, herbs, spices. Scan through the chapter on mashed potatoes for ideas.

Spoon the filling into the potato skins without compacting it too much. Mound it up and top with bits of butter or grated cheese. Bake the potatoes in a moderate oven until they are heated through and browned on top.

TWICE-BAKED POTATOES
WITH SCALLION AND BACON

SERVES 4

We often make these potatoes for nights alone in front of a video. As you'll see from the variations that follow, the technique adapts itself to a range of flavors. Let inspiration be your guide when creating your own versions, but play it smart: avoid the kitchen-sink approach and stick with just one or two assertive ingredients.

4 russets (each about 3/4 pound), scrubbed
2 tablespoons unsalted butter
1/3 cup heavy cream, warmed
6 slices bacon, fried until crisp, and crumbled
3 whole scallions, chopped
Coarse salt and freshly ground black pepper
1/4 cup shredded Swiss cheese (about 1 ounce)

Heat the oven to 350 degrees.

Place the potatoes on the center rack and bake until tender, 60 to 70 minutes. About halfway through the baking, prick the skins in a few spots with a fork to allow steam to escape.

Move the potatoes to a cutting board and increase the oven temperature to 375 degrees. Holding each potato with a towel or pot holder to avoid scorching your hands, slice the top quarter lengthwise off the potato. You'll be making a sort of potato "boat" to refill with the filling. Scoop out the flesh with a tablespoon into a mixing bowl. Leave enough meat in the potatoes so that the skins stand up on their own. Don't forget to scoop the flesh from the lids too. (You can then discard the lids or slather them with butter and broil them up for a good little snack.)

Mash the potatoes with a fork and add the butter. Work in the cream until fluffy and smooth. Stir in the bacon and scallions and season with salt and pepper.

Season the skins with salt and pepper. Spoon the filling into the skins, mounding it nicely on top, and put the filled potatoes on a baking sheet. You may need to give them a little squish so that they sit upright without toppling over. Sprinkle the cheese over the tops. You can make the potatoes ahead up until this point and refrigerate them for several hours or even overnight.

Slide the potatoes into the oven and bake until the filling is hot throughout and the tops are getting browned, 20 to 25 minutes. (If you've refrigerated the stuffed potatoes, expect them to take almost twice as long to heat through.) Serve hot.

TWICE-BAKED POTATOES
WITH GOAT CHEESE AND PARSLEY

SERVES 4

We like to use a mild and creamy fresh goat cheese. Save the stronger, sharper aged kind for a recipe with lots of other assertive ingredients.

4 russet potatoes (each about ¾ pound), scrubbed
3 tablespoons unsalted butter
⅓ cup heavy cream, warmed
4 ounces fresh goat cheese, at room temperature
2 tablespoons chopped flat-leaf parsley
Coarse salt and freshly ground black pepper

Follow the method for Twice-Baked Potatoes with Scallion and Bacon (page 378).

Beat 2 tablespoons of the butter into the mash. Work in the cream until fluffy and smooth, then beat in the goat cheese, parsley, and salt and pepper. Pinch off bits of the remaining 1 tablespoon butter to dot the potatoes before you bake them.

TWICE-BAKED POTATOES
WITH CHEDDAR AND BROCCOLI

SERVES 4

Cheddar and broccoli is the classic combination, but you might try cauliflower and aged Gouda or Swiss cheese.

4 russet potatoes (each about 3/4 pound), scrubbed
1 1/2 cups small broccoli florets
3 tablespoons unsalted butter
1/3 cup milk, warmed
2 ounces cheddar, finely chopped (about 1/2 cup)
Dash of hot red pepper sauce
Coarse salt and freshly ground black pepper

Follow the method for Twice-Baked Potatoes with Scallion and Bacon (page 378).

While the potatoes are baking, bring a medium pot of salted water to a boil and drop in the broccoli. Cook until just tender, 3 to 4 minutes; drain and rinse with cold water. Drain again. Chop roughly and put the broccoli in a strainer so any excess water can continue to drain.

Once you've mashed the potatoes using 2 tablespoons of the butter and the milk, stir in the broccoli and cheddar and season with the hot pepper sauce and salt and pepper. Pinch off bits from the remaining 1 tablespoon butter and dot the potatoes after you've filled them.

POTATO PRINCIPLES
THE MICROWAVED POTATO

I don't have a microwave in my New York kitchen, but my good friends Tom and Marian have one in their Virginia house, and I use it when I'm there. It comes in handy when I need to heat milk or cream for mashed potatoes or when we're eating leftover gratin for lunch and we want it hot. Although I'll make mashed sweets early in the afternoon and pop them in the microwave right before dinner, I don't use this piece of equipment for cooking.

Nonetheless, I was ready to take the plunge and find out the best way to bake a potato in it. Where else to begin but with Barbara Kafka's *Microwave Gourmet*? Imagine my relief when I read that she dismisses out of hand the notion that you can make a real baked potato in the microwave. If Mrs. Kafka says to bake it in the oven, so do I.

Here's a tip that I got from food writer Melissa Clark, though. Her husband makes mashed potatoes for himself six nights out of seven. He pricks the potato and cooks it in the microwave, warming the milk in there too. Then he scoops out the flesh, mashes it, works in a tablespoon or two of butter, and whips in the milk. It's a clever solution when you're making mashed potatoes for just one or two and you're not worried about the skin being limp and insipid.

TWICE-BAKED POTATOES WITH CHILI

This is the kind of thing you want to have on hand when there's a football game on television. It's guy food. You want bowls for serving this, because the chili is spooned over the potatoes after they're stuffed and baked.

4 russet potatoes (each about ¾ pound), scrubbed
2 tablespoons unsalted butter
¼ cup sour cream
Coarse salt and freshly ground black pepper

FOR SERVING
1½ cups Chili (page 384)
⅓ cup Monterey Jack or cheddar, shredded
1 small white onion, finely chopped
Sour cream (optional)

Follow the method for Twice-Baked Potatoes with Scallion and Bacon (page 378).

Beat the butter, ¼ cup sour cream, and salt and pepper into the mash, and stuff it into the potato skins.

Bake the stuffed potatoes until the filling is hot throughout and the tops are getting brown, 20 to 25 minutes.

About 15 minutes before the potatoes are ready, heat up your chili.

Transfer the potatoes to soup bowls, and spoon the chili over the top. Sprinkle on the cheese and a bit of chopped onion. If you really want to go whole hog here, add a good dollop of sour cream. Serve immediately.

CHILI

You probably have your own favorite recipe for chili, but here's a good basic one. There's nothing fancy here, no sleight of hand and no beans, but a little heat that sneaks up on you—so it makes perfect sense to combine it with a twice-baked potato. This makes so much more than you will need for chili-potato night, but chili takes a long time to cook, so why make less? It freezes beautifully.

3¹/₂ pounds chuck roast
2 tablespoons vegetable oil, or more if necessary
3 slices bacon, cut into matchsticks
Coarse salt and freshly ground black pepper
1 large onion, chopped
4 teaspoons chili powder (use your favorite)
¹/₂ teaspoon cayenne pepper
¹/₂ teaspoon dried oregano, preferably Mexican
1 (28-ounce) can crushed tomatoes, with their juice
1 tablespoon cider vinegar
1 teaspoon sugar

Trim the fat and gristle from the chuck, then cut the meat into ¹/₃-inch cubes. I know, it takes forever, so do it with a partner. I find it immensely satisfying, though, to look at the bowl of hand-cut meat when I'm through, and there's no beating the texture of the finished chili.

Heat a large saucepan over medium-high heat and add the vegetable oil and bacon. Cook until the bacon has rendered its fat and is just starting to brown. Remove the bacon with a slotted spoon and leave it in a bowl or on a paper towel. Add a handful or two of the beef, enough to barely cover the bottom of the pan, season it with salt and pepper, and brown it on all sides. (If you put in too much meat, it will steam instead of brown—so don't.) Once the meat is browned, take it out with a slotted spoon, leaving as much fat as possible in the pan and drop it in a bowl, then add more meat to the pan. Season each batch of meat as you brown it, and if you run out of fat in the pan, add a tablespoon or two more oil and get it good and hot before you put in more meat.

Once all the meat's browned, check the fat in the pan; you want about 1 tablespoon. Add the onion and cook, stirring a few times, until it's softened, about 4 minutes. Add the chili powder and cayenne, crumble in the oregano, and cook for 2 to 3 minutes.

Dump in the beef and any meat juices in the bowl and add the bacon, tomatoes, vinegar, sugar, and 2 cups cool water. Bring this to a boil, then reduce to a simmer and cook for 1 hour 45 minutes. Keep a close eye toward the end of the cooking. This is a pretty thick chili (which you want if you're going to serve it over potatoes), so stir it diligently to make sure it doesn't stick and burn. If you must, add a tablespoon or two of water. Serve hot.

PISSALADIÈRE-STUFFED BAKED RED POTATOES

SERVES 4

Anchovy and onion are the distinctive flavors in *pissaladière*—that crusty tart you find all through Provence—flavors that marry well with potatoes. Molly often makes one of these for herself for lunch when she's home alone in her Vermont kitchen. She uses whatever piquant little bits and pieces she has on hand and adjusts the amounts accordingly.

3 tablespoons olive oil
1 small onion, finely chopped
1/2 fennel bulb, trimmed and finely chopped (about 1/2 cup)
3 small garlic cloves, minced
Coarse salt and freshly ground black pepper
3 or 4 anchovies, chopped
A few sun-dried tomatoes, soaked in hot water to soften and
    finely chopped (about 2 heaping tablespoons)
2 tablespoons chopped flat-leaf parsley
1 tablespoon capers, drained, rinsed and chopped
4 good-sized red-skinned potatoes (about 1/2 pound each)

Heat the oven to 375 degrees.

Heat about half of the oil in a skillet over medium heat and add the onion. Cook until it is beginning to soften, 4 to 5 minutes. Add the fennel and garlic, season with salt and pepper, and cook until they're just starting to brown, another 5 minutes. It should smell really nice by now too. Remove from the heat and stir in the anchovies, sun-dried tomatoes, parsley, and capers. Taste for salt and pepper.

Slice a thin sliver off the bottom of each potato to form a flat seat—you want them to stand without rolling. Then slice the top quarter off each pota-to. Discard the slices from the top and bottom of the potato, or you'll end up with too much filling. Use a melon baller to scoop out the insides of the potatoes, leaving a 1/2-inch-thick wall all around. Pile the scooped-out insides on a cutting board and finely chop. (If you like, and don't mind washing another thing, chop the potatoes in a food processor by pushing the pulse button.) Stir the potatoes into the skillet with the other ingredients.

Rub the potato shells inside and out with some of the remaining olive oil and sprinkle the insides with salt and pepper. Spoon the filling into the potatoes, pressing down to compress it as you go and mounding it up on top. Arrange the filled potatoes in a baking dish. Drizzle a bit of oil over each potato. Brush the dull side of a piece of foil with oil and use it to cover the dish tightly—the oil will keep the foil from sticking to the potatoes. Bake for 45 minutes.

Remove the foil and spoon any juices in the pan over the potatoes to baste. Increase the temperature to 400 degrees and continue to bake, uncovered, until the potatoes are lightly browned on top, another 10 to 15 minutes. Serve hot.

POTATO PRINCIPLES
ROASTING POTATOES

The best potatoes for roasting are low-starch, waxy, and all-purpose types. The most common supermarket varieties that lend themselves well to roasting are red, Yukon Gold, Yellow Finn, and California white (sometimes called long white). Specialty potatoes, such as creamer potatoes, fingerlings (Russian Banana, French Fingerling, Ruby Crescent, and the like), True Blue (or other purple potatoes), and other heirloom varieties, are also excellent for roasting.

Figure on ¼ to ⅓ pound per person, depending on how many other things you're serving.

Since many low-starch potatoes have a thin skin, they don't need to be peeled before roasting. Just scrub them with a vegetable brush and then dry thoroughly—leaving the skins wet will interfere with browning. If they're thick-skinned, peel them. (To judge how thick the skin is, give it a flick with your fingernail. You'll be able to tell right away.)

Round bite-sized creamer potatoes or oblong fingerlings can be roasted whole, while larger potatoes need to be cut up into chunks or wedges: anything smaller than ¾ inch will cook too quickly and dry out, and anything over 2 inches won't have enough cut surfaces to get all nicely crisped and brown.

In side-by-side tests of potatoes boiled before roasting and roasted without parboiling, we found only very slight differences between the two methods. You get a richer, crispier crust when the potatoes are roasted raw. The insides are just a bit creamier and moister than when the potatoes are parboiled. Parboiled potatoes tend not to stick to the roasting pan as much as raw potatoes during roasting. That means you won't need to hover as close to the oven during roasting to stir and turn the potatoes. It also means that you can get away with using less oil or other fat to coat the potatoes.

When we want to sneak potatoes alongside a roast for the last 30 to 40 minutes of roasting to absorb all the juices and savor of the roast, we parboil. Another slight advantage of parboiling is that you can get the potatoes ready for roasting—diced, parboiled, and seasoned—and let them sit out for a few hours without having them discolor.

To parboil potatoes, cover them with cold water, add a good pinch of salt, and bring to a simmer. Simmer for 3 to 5 minutes—no longer—drain, and then add a drizzle of oil and season them, or put them directly in to roast. If they're left to cool without being seasoned and oiled, they'll form a tough seal that will be impervious to further seasoning.

Choose a heavy pan that will accommodate the potatoes in a single layer without leaving too much space in between. You might use a medium-sized roasting pan, a sturdy brownie pan, a large gratin dish, or a rimmed baking sheet—the rim is important so that the potatoes don't roll off when you turn them during roasting.

Toss the potatoes in a little fat for flavor and to encourage browning. Olive oil, butter, and goose or duck fat are all good choices. The potatoes should be lightly coated but not swimming in fat, which would cause them to fry. The fat will also help the seasonings adhere to the surface of the potatoes.

Roast the potatoes in a moderately hot oven—350 to 400 degrees. If the recipe calls for 375 degrees, and you've got something else in the oven at 400, just roast the potatoes for a shorter time. Check for doneness by piercing a few potatoes with a skewer or needle—it should sink easily into the tender flesh; the outsides should be nicely browned and crisp in places. After roasting, you can hold the potatoes in a low oven for half an hour or so before serving.

BASIC ROASTED POTATOES

This is the simplest of recipes. It can be made with any low- or medium-starch potatoes (see page 388). We prefer rosemary, but no one's going to quibble if you want to use thyme. No one will mind if you make this your own either: see the variations for a road map.

Roasted potatoes do cook down. If you have a lot of other side dishes, this amount of potatoes will serve six—just. But it's easy enough to double.

Bigger bits of pepper are nice here. To crack peppercorns with the base of a small heavy skillet, put the peppercorns on the counter and press down with the skillet, rocking it.

1½ pounds red-skinned potatoes, left whole if small, halved, quartered, or
   cut into 1½-inch chunks if large
3 tablespoons olive oil, melted butter, or duck or goose fat
1 heaping tablespoon chopped fresh rosemary
Coarse salt and coarsely cracked black pepper

Heat the oven to 375 degrees.
   Dump the potatoes into a roasting pan, large gratin dish, or rimmed baking sheet large enough to accommodate them in a single layer. Drizzle with the oil and season with the rosemary, salt, and pepper.
   Roast, tossing with a spatula a few times so they brown up evenly, until the potatoes are tender throughout and the skins are somewhat shriveled and crisp, about 1 hour. Serve hot.

HERB-ROASTED POTATOES

Use olive oil for the fat and 2 tablespoons of any combination of chopped hardy herbs, such as fresh rosemary, thyme, savory, marjoram, and sage. Roast as directed.

As soon as the potatoes are done, toss with 3 tablespoons of any combination of chopped tender fresh herbs, such as parsley, chives, and/or chervil, and the juice of 1 lemon.

ROASTED POTATOES WITH SHALLOTS AND GARLIC

Add 6 peeled shallots and 6 to 10 peeled garlic cloves to the potatoes and roast as directed. Make sure that the pan isn't too big, or you'll risk burning the shallots and garlic. If the shallots and garlic are done (browned and very tender) before the potatoes, remove them while the potatoes finish roasting, adding them back to the pan during the last few minutes to reheat.

MUSTARD-ROASTED POTATOES

This is as easy as it sounds. The mustard crust is rich and tangy, making the dish a fine accompaniment to chops or chicken.

Same goes here as for any roasted potato—you can make substitutions. But red-skinned potatoes are so easy to find in the grocery.

2 pounds red-skinned potatoes, scrubbed and cut into large chunks
6 tablespoons Dijon mustard
1 garlic clove, minced
1 tablespoon chopped fresh rosemary
2 tablespoons olive oil
1 tablespoon dry vermouth
Coarse salt and freshly ground black pepper

Heat the oven to 350 degrees.

Toss all the ingredients together on a large baking sheet (or toss them in a bowl and transfer them to a baking sheet, if you want to dirty another dish).

Bake for about an hour, tossing the potatoes with a spatula a few times, until the crust is a deep brown. Serve hot.

POTATOES ROASTED
IN GOOSE FAT

This is château fare at its best. I met chef Randall Price, an old friend of Molly's, on a visit to Château du Fey in Burgundy. There's always a container of goose fat in Randall's refrigerator, and when you use it to cook potatoes, its flavor is more succulent than you can imagine. Duck fat is the only possible substitute.

We like this best with new potatoes, and if they are very small, we leave them whole. You can also make this with heirlooms, Yukon Golds, or red-skinned, peeled or not—your choice.

1/4 cup goose fat
1 1/2 pounds new potatoes, scrubbed and cut into 1 1/2-to-2-inch chunks (see note above)
5–6 garlic cloves, unpeeled
3 bay leaves (use fresh if you can)
3 sprigs rosemary
Coarsely cracked black pepper
Coarse salt

Heat the oven to 400 degrees.

Put the goose fat into a heavy roasting pan or large gratin dish—the dish needs to be large enough so the potatoes fit in one pretty loose layer—and heat the fat for 10 to 15 minutes in the oven.

Dump the potatoes, garlic, and herbs into the pan. Season with pepper. Carefully shake and stir to coat the potatoes with hot fat. Return the pan to the oven and immediately lower the heat to 375 degrees.

Roast the potatoes, shaking and stirring the pan every 10 minutes (especially during the first half-hour), until they are crisp and golden on the outside and tender inside, 45 to 50 minutes. Discard the garlic and herbs, season the potatoes with salt, and serve quite warm.

ROASTED POTATOES AND TURNIPS

We like the contrast of buttery yellow-fleshed potatoes against the sweet taste of roasted turnips. Both the potatoes and turnips are peeled and cut into pretty large chunks so they cook slowly, giving them time to absorb the stock and butter and turn sweet.

Adding a bit of stock at the start of roasting gives these potatoes a creamier, softer texture than if they were dry-roasted—more like potatoes that have been roasted alongside a hefty cut of meat. Celeriac, rutabaga, carrots, and parsnips can all be substituted for the turnips.

3 small bay leaves
2 sprigs thyme
1 pound yellow-fleshed potatoes, peeled and cut into 1½-inch chunks
1 pound turnips, peeled and quartered or cut into 1½-inch chunks
½ cup Chicken Stock (page 85); water also works, but the dish won't be as tasty
4 tablespoons (½ stick) unsalted butter, cut into pieces
Coarse salt and freshly ground black pepper

Heat the oven to 375 degrees.

Place the bay leaves and thyme in a large gratin dish or a medium roasting pan. Dump the potatoes and turnips on top. Pour in the stock and scatter the butter around. Season with salt and pepper.

Roast, tossing with a spatula a few times, until the vegetables are very tender and browned in spots, about an hour. Remove and discard the thyme and bay leaves and serve warm.

ROASTED POTATOES WITH BREAD CRUMBS

Raw potatoes and bread crumbs roasted together shouldn't make such a tasty and moist dish. But with this recipe, they do. Make these when you've got a leg of lamb, pork roast, or hunk of beef roasting in the oven. You'll need a pan large enough to accommodate the roast without crowding the potatoes; too small a pan, and the potatoes—and meat—will steam instead of roast.

1³/₄ pounds yellow-fleshed potatoes
1 large sweet onion (Vidalia, Walla Walla, or the like)
¹/₄ cup olive oil
¹/₄ cup dried bread crumbs
Coarse salt and freshly ground black pepper

Since you make these with a roast, the oven will already be on and probably set at 350 degrees, which is what you want.

About an hour before you want to serve dinner, peel the potatoes and cut them into large chunks. Peel the onion and cut it into thick wedges. Toss the potatoes and onion in a mixing bowl with the oil, crumbs, and salt and pepper to taste. Add this mix to the roasting pan with your roast and stir it in whatever fat and drippings are in the pan.

Bake for an hour, stirring and flipping with a spatula a few times. If you've timed this right, the roast will be done about 10 minutes before the potatoes. Remove the meat to let it rest, and slide the potatoes back into the oven. This way, the potatoes will still be piping hot when the meat's carved.

POTATOES WITH CRISPY GREENS

SERVES 4 TO 6

Yes, the greens do crisp in the oven, and the potatoes get deliriously crusty. This is an ideal companion for Easy Chicken "Confit" (facing page), but there's no reason it can't exist happily on a plate with steak or chops. Peel the potatoes, or don't.

You need a large pan with low sides, like a jelly roll pan. If you don't have one, use the bottom of your broiler pan.

1 pound winter greens (such as a mix of Swiss chard, mustard greens, red mustard, and kale), trimmed and well washed
1½ pounds white or yellow-fleshed potatoes, scrubbed
2 garlic cloves, minced
Coarse salt and freshly ground black pepper
½ cup olive oil

Heat the oven to 400 degrees.

Separate the stems from the greens and chop them. Pile up the leaves and cut them into ½-inch strips. Cut the potatoes in half lengthwise, then into slices about ½ inch thick.

Dump the greens, potatoes, and garlic onto a large baking sheet. Season well with salt and pepper, then drizzle the oil all over them. Mix this up well with your hands and slide the pan into the oven. Roast for about an hour, tossing occasionally with a spatula, until the potatoes are crusty and the greens are crisp but not burned. Serve hot.

EASY CHICKEN "CONFIT"

This chicken ends up meltingly tender and with a crackling skin—a texture that mimics duck legs that have been preserved in fat. But it's so much simpler to make than confit, and it's easy enough to make in advance; you just leave the final browning for right before dinner. The quantities are for 4 to 6, but adjust up or down with abandon. The recipe comes from my friend Tom Pearson.

Do not even think of trying this with boneless, skinless thighs; it won't work.

12 chicken thighs
Coarse salt and freshly ground black pepper

Wash and dry the chicken and sprinkle on both sides with salt and pepper. Set the thighs skin side down in a baking dish that will hold them snugly in one layer. Cover with foil and refrigerate for at least an hour.

Heat the oven to 325 degrees.

Bake the chicken—still covered with foil—for 1 hour. Turn the pieces skin side up, replace the foil, and bake for another hour. You can set the chicken aside at this point. Leave it on the counter for an hour or two until you're ready to finish it, or let it cool, then refrigerate it.

To finish the chicken, turn the heat up to 400 degrees and put a cast-iron skillet into the oven to heat for 10 minutes.

Add the chicken skin side up to the pan and roast for 15 to 20 minutes, until the skin is browned and crackly.

POTATOES ROASTED WITH SUMMER VEGETABLES

SERVES 4 TO 6

You need a large shallow casserole for this recipe. A 12-inch terra-cotta one is ideal. There's no reason to dirty a bowl; just toss everything together in the baking dish.

1½ pounds all-purpose potatoes, scrubbed and cut into 1-inch chunks
2 small bell peppers (red, yellow, orange, or purple), cored, seeded, and
    cut into chunks
1 red onion, coarsely chopped
1 summer squash, cut into 1-inch chunks
2 large tomatoes, seeded and chopped (see page 30)
1 serrano chile, minced
¼ cup olive oil
Several sprigs thyme
Coarse salt and freshly ground black pepper

Heat the oven to 400 degrees.

Toss all the ingredients together in a large (12-inch) shallow casserole, then spread them out evenly.

Bake for 1 to 1¼ hours, basting once in a while, until the potatoes are fully cooked. The potatoes that stick up from the surface will get crusty and brown; the ones below the surface, where the tomatoes will make a little sauce, will be meltingly tender.

This is equally good piping hot and at room temperature.

OVEN FRIES

Molly got this recipe from a wafer-thin friend who cuts the fat from her recipes anytime she can. We were skeptical but soon converted. Soaking the fries in advance washes away some of the starch so that they brown up nicely in the oven without the help of a lot of oil or fat. They turn out a sort of cross between roasted potatoes and steak fries, browned and crisp on the outside and light and fluffy inside. Do we miss the point, though, when we serve them with a big bowl of Aïoli (page 400) for dipping?

2–2½ pounds russet potatoes, scrubbed
Pan spray or olive oil
Coarse salt and freshly ground black pepper

Cut the potatoes lengthwise into ½-inch-thick wedges. Drop them into a large bowl of cold water and soak for 45 to 60 minutes.

Heat the oven to 450 degrees.

Drain the potatoes and dry them thoroughly on towels. Spray two baking sheets with pan spray or, if using olive oil, brush lightly with the oil.

Rinse and dry the bowl you used for soaking the potatoes and return them to it. Spray the potatoes with pan spray or drizzle with just a bit of olive oil, enough to lightly coat the fries, and season with salt and pepper. Toss to coat.

Arrange the fries flat, with a small space between each, on the baking sheets. Bake until browned on the bottom, 20 to 25 minutes. Flip and continue to cook until browned on the other side, another 20 minutes or so. Serve warm.

AÏOLI

We like this garlicky mayonnaise of Provence as a dip for Oven Fries (page 399) and Olive Oil–Fried Potatoes (page 311), and it's also wonderful as a sandwich spread.

The best way to make aïoli is in a large mortar and pestle. Failing that, use a wooden bowl and a flat wooden spoon. Although you may be accustomed to making mayonnaise-type sauces with a metal whisk or in the food processor, don't even consider it here: When you beat extra-virgin olive oil with a metal whisk or with the blade of a blender, it turns bitter and quite unpleasant.

3 or 4 garlic cloves, peeled
Coarse salt
1 large egg yolk
¾ cup extra-virgin olive oil
1 tablespoon fresh lemon juice (or water)

Put the garlic and a large pinch of salt into a mortar and crush it to a paste or place the garlic on a cutting board, sprinkle on the salt, and use the blade and side of a large chef's knife to make it into a paste, chopping, scraping with the side of your knife, and chopping again. Scrape the paste into a wooden bowl.

Add the egg yolk to the garlic and, using a flat wooden spoon, work the two together until well combined. Slowly begin to drizzle in the oil, continuing to stir with the spoon all the time. After you have added a few tablespoons of olive oil and the mixture is well combined, stir in the lemon juice. Return to drizzling in the olive oil and stirring. As you go, you should find that the mixture becomes thicker and that you are able to add the olive oil in a steadier stream. If, at any time, the oil appears to be pooling on the surface and not incorporating into the sauce, stop adding oil and stir vigorously until the sauce comes back together. Taste for salt and lemon.

Serve immediately, or refrigerate for up to 1 day.

HASSLEBACKS

For this Swedish side dish, whole potatoes are sliced almost through to the base so that they fan out as they cook. Bay leaves are typically stuck between the slices to season the potatoes, and a few bread crumbs are sprinkled on to brown up at the end. We sometimes use thyme or fresh sage in place of the bay, and a little finely grated Parmesan is nice mixed in with the bread crumbs.

4 medium waxy potatoes (6–8 ounces each), peeled
12 small or 6 large bay leaves
3 tablespoons unsalted butter, melted
Coarse salt and freshly ground black pepper
2 tablespoons fine dried bread crumbs

Heat the oven to 375 degrees.

Set 1 potato on the cutting board and, with a large knife, starting at one end of the potato, make a series of vertical slices about 1/8 inch apart and down to within about 1/2 inch of the bottom. To avoid accidentally cutting all the way through the potato, we place the handle of a wooden spoon along the far side of the potato. When the tip of the knife hits the handle, we know to stop. After you have made slices all the way across the potato, it might remind you of a venetian blind. Continue with the remaining potatoes.

If you have small bay leaves, slide a few into the cuts. Break larger leaves in half before putting them in the potatoes. Set the potatoes in a buttered baking dish and drizzle half of the butter over them. Season with salt and pepper and cover the dish with foil.

Bake until the potatoes are tender, about 45 minutes. Remove the foil, drizzle the remaining butter on top, and sprinkle each potato with some bread crumbs.

Heat the broiler and slide the potatoes under the broiler to brown up, 3 to 5 minutes. Serve warm.

DUCHESS POTATOES

SERVES 4 TO 6 (MAKES ABOUT 3 CUPS POTATO PUREE)

With their fragile crust and fluffy interior, duchess potatoes add a touch of class to any plate—with the advantage of being able to be prepared hours in advance. They became something of a cliché in "Continental" restaurants, almost as trite as the garnish of curly parsley. But they're too good to forget.

2 pounds russet potatoes, peeled and cut into chunks
Coarse salt
6 tablespoons (¾ stick) unsalted butter, softened
1 large egg, lightly beaten
2 large egg yolks
Freshly ground white pepper
Pinch of freshly grated nutmeg
1 large egg, beaten, for an egg wash (optional)

Put the potatoes in a large saucepan, cover with cold water by at least an inch, add a good pinch of salt, and bring to a boil. Cover partway, reduce the heat to medium, and cook until the potatoes are tender. Drain the potatoes, return them to the pot, and put them back over the heat to dry. Shake the pan and stir until the potatoes are floury and have made a film on the bottom of the pan.

Put the potatoes through a ricer and return them to the pot. Stir in the butter. Beat in the whole egg and the 2 yolks. Season with salt, white pepper, and nutmeg.

Fit a pastry bag with a large star tip and fill it with the potatoes. Pipe the potatoes into shapes (rosettes, stars, or whatever inspires you) onto a greased baking sheet or around a greased ovenproof platter as a decorative border for serving fish or meat. Alternatively, shape the potatoes with your hands into smallish oblong egg shapes or flat round cakes and set them on a greased baking sheet. The potatoes can be made ahead up to this point, covered with buttered plastic wrap, and refrigerated for several hours before baking and serving.

To finish the potatoes, heat the oven to 400 degrees.

Brush the tops of the potatoes with a bit of beaten egg if you'd like a glossier appearance. Bake them until golden and slightly puffy, 20 to 30 minutes depending on their shape and size. Serve hot.

VARIATIONS
FRIED DUCHESS CROQUETTES

Make the potatoes as directed above. Flour a work surface and roll the potatoes into fingers about 2 inches long and 1 inch thick. Leave them on a sheet of waxed paper until just before serving; refrigerate if you're leaving them for more than 30 minutes.

Heat 2 inches of vegetable oil in a deep heavy saucepan to 370 degrees. Beat an egg with a pinch of salt in a small bowl, and place 1 cup fresh bread crumbs in a shallow bowl. Dip the potato croquettes into the beaten egg, then roll in the bread crumbs.

Fry in batches until very golden and crisp, 3 to 5 minutes. Drain on paper towels and sprinkle with salt. Serve piping hot, or keep in a warm oven for 15 minutes.

CHEDDAR DUCHESS

Make the potatoes as directed above. Grate 4 ounces sharp cheddar (you should have about 1 cup), and stir it into the potatoes. Shape the mixture into round 3-to-4-inch cakes (the French call them galettes) and set them on a buttered baking sheet.

Heat the oven to 400 degrees.

Cut 2 ounces of cheddar into thin slices and cover each galette with a slice of cheese. Bake until golden and lightly puffed, about 20 minutes.

FLUETTERS

Each time I make these little baked dumplings, guests say, "I love these things!" Fluetters are an Alsatian cousin of duchess potatoes, with a hint of garlic and parsley. I found the recipe in Alice B. Toklas's *Aromas and Flavors.* Miss Toklas says to serve them with choucroute, Molly puts them out with beef stew, and I like them with roast turkey. This is a great thing to make with kids. My nephew David Rossler is a pro at painting the fluetters with butter.

Make them ahead; butter them right before you bake them.

2 pounds russet potatoes, scrubbed
Coarse salt
2 large eggs
2 tablespoons chopped flat-leaf parsley
1 small garlic clove, minced
Freshly ground black pepper
4 tablespoons (½ stick) unsalted butter, melted

Put the potatoes in a large saucepan, cover with cold water by at least an inch, add a good pinch of salt, and bring to a boil. Reduce the heat to medium, cover partway, and cook until the potatoes are very tender. Drain the potatoes on a rack set in the sink.

As soon as the potatoes are cool enough to handle, peel them and rice them into a large bowl. Spread them out with a wooden spoon so that they cool and do not steam.

When the potatoes are cool, stir in the eggs, parsley, garlic, and salt and pepper.

Use your hands to shape quarter-cupfuls of the potatoes into balls or egg-shaped dumplings. The fluetters can be made ahead and covered and refrigerated for several hours.

Heat the oven to 350 degrees. Butter a baking sheet or large baking dish.

Set the fluetters at least $1/2$ inch apart on the baking sheet or in the dish. Paint the tops and sides of the fluetters generously with about half of the melted butter. Bake, brushing with the remaining butter partway through cooking, until heated through and lightly golden on top, 35 to 45 minutes. Serve warm.

PARTY POTATOES

Do you know these? They're what you make when you have a crowd coming and you want mashed potatoes that can sit on the buffet. You put the casserole together well in advance and bake it when you need it. And because you whip them up with an electric mixer, Party Potatoes are light and fluffy. They're also pretty rich and luscious.

3 pounds russet potatoes, peeled and chunked
Coarse salt
8 tablespoons (1 stick) unsalted butter, cut into $1/2$-inch pieces
8 ounces cream cheese, at room temperature
$1/2$ cup sour cream, at room temperature
$2/3$ cup milk, warmed
Freshly ground black pepper
Paprika

Put the potatoes in a large saucepan, cover with cold water by at least an inch, add a good pinch of salt, and bring to a boil. Reduce the heat to medium, cover partway, and cook until the potatoes are very tender. Drain and return them to the pot. Set over medium heat for a minute or two, shaking and stirring so the potatoes don't stick, until they are floury and have made a film on the bottom of the pot.

Remove the potatoes from the heat and break them up with a hand-held electric mixer on low speed. Gradually drop in 6 tablespoons of the butter and beat until it is absorbed. Refrigerate the remaining butter. Continue with the cream cheese and sour cream, beating well after each addition. Beat in the milk, adding a little at a time. You want the potatoes to be fluffy and light; if they seem to be getting too wet, don't add all the milk. Season with salt and pepper. (If you don't have an electric mixer, use a hand masher to start and then use a wooden spoon to beat in the butter, cheese, sour cream, and milk. Beat the milk into the potatoes one-third at a time, beating vigorously after each addition.)

Butter a 9-by-13-inch baking dish and spoon the potatoes into it. Smooth the top and then, with a spatula or fork tines, swirl or score the surface of the potatoes to leave little peaks that will brown up nicely during baking. Refrigerate, covered tightly with plastic wrap, for up to 2 days before baking.

Heat the oven to 350 degrees.

Dust the top of the potatoes with paprika. Cut the remaining 2 tablespoons butter into small pieces and scatter them over the surface. Bake until the potatoes are heated through and the top is lightly golden, about an hour. (Expect it to take only half the time if the potatoes haven't been refrigerated.) Serve hot.

COLCANNON

What distinguishes this classic Irish dish—sometimes made with green cabbage and leeks, and sometimes with kale and scallions—is how it is served: spooned into a casserole, with a well in the center that you fill with butter. You can skip this step if you like, or you can go overboard and add an extra 4 tablespoons butter to the potatoes just before you add the milk.

We like it made ahead and reheated so the top gets nice and crusty, but you can also just slide it under the broiler before serving.

2¹⁄₂–3 pounds russet potatoes, peeled and cut into large chunks
Coarse salt
1¹⁄₂ cups milk
3 whole scallions, chopped
1¹⁄₂ pounds kale, washed (discard the very tough stems)
Freshly ground black pepper
4 tablespoons (¹⁄₂ stick) unsalted butter, softened (see note above)

Put the potatoes in a large saucepan, cover with cold water by at least an inch, add a good pinch of salt, and bring to a boil. Reduce the heat to medium, cover partway, and cook until the potatoes are very tender.

While the potatoes are cooking, rinse a small saucepan in cold water (this will make the pan easier to clean later), and add the milk and scallions. Scald over medium heat. Remove from the heat.

Meanwhile, fill a large saucepan three-quarters full with water, add a pinch of salt, and bring to a boil. Plunge the kale into the water and cook until tender, about 10 minutes. Drain, rinse with cold water, and drain again. Gently squeeze the kale to get rid of the excess water and then roughly chop it.

As soon as the potatoes are tender, drain and return them to the pot. Set over medium heat for a minute or two, shaking and stirring so the potatoes don't stick, until they are floury and have made a film on the bottom of the pot.

Remove the potatoes from the heat and mash with a hand masher. Beat the milk and scallions into the potatoes with a wooden spoon, one-third at a time, beating vigorously after each addition. Stir in the kale and season with salt and pepper. Transfer the colcannon to a 2- or 3-quart casserole dish and make a small well in the center.

If you are serving the colcannon right away, heat the broiler and brown the top of the dish quickly. Just before serving, scoop the butter into the well and serve it up.

If you've made this in advance, heat the oven to 400 degrees and bake the colcannon until it is heated through and the top is beginning to brown, about 30 minutes. Spoon the softened butter into the center and serve piping hot, making sure everyone gets some butter.

BAKED EGGS IN A MASHED POTATO NEST
(OEUFS AU NID)

SERVES 2

Come lunchtime, nothing can be more soothing than a nest of hot mashed potatoes filled with baked eggs.

1¹/₂–1³/₄ pounds russet potatoes, peeled and cut into chunks
Coarse salt
4 tablespoons (¹/₂ stick) unsalted butter, softened
1 cup milk or cream, warmed
Freshly grated nutmeg
Freshly ground black pepper
4 large eggs
¹/₄ cup shredded Gruyère or cheddar (about 1 ounce)

Heat the oven to 400 degrees. Butter a medium oval gratin dish or a 1¹/₂-quart baking dish.

Put the potatoes in a large saucepan, cover with cold water by at least an inch, add a good pinch of salt, and bring to a boil. Reduce the heat to medium, cover partway, and cook until the potatoes are very tender. Drain the potatoes and return them to the pot. Set over medium heat to dry for a minute or two, shaking and stirring so the potatoes don't stick.

Remove the potatoes from the heat and mash with a hand masher. Beat in 2 tablespoons of the butter with a wooden spoon. Beat in the milk one-third at a time, beating vigorously after each addition. Season with nutmeg, salt, and pepper.

Spoon the mashed potatoes into the gratin dish and smooth them with the back of a spoon. Make 4 deep holes in the potatoes, each large enough to hold an egg. With the tines of a fork, shape the sides and edges of the holes so that they vaguely resemble nests. It's important that the nests are large enough to hold the eggs without spilling over. Expect to leave only the thinnest layer of mashed potato on the bottom of the nest, and don't worry if the bottom of the dish shows through — this will help the eggs cook more quickly.

Drop a bit of the remaining 2 tablespoons butter into each hole and then crack an egg into it. Season the eggs with salt and pepper, and then scatter the cheese over the top. Distribute any remaining bits of butter over the surface.

Bake until the cheese is melted and the egg whites are just set, about 15 minutes. The eggs will continue to cook after the dish comes from the oven. Divide between two warmed plates and serve immediately.

NANCY BARR'S POTATO CAKE
(GATTÓ DE PATATE)

SERVES 6 TO 8

When I first told my friend Nancy that I was working on this book, she immediately said I *must* try the potato cake in her book *We Called It Macaroni*. She was right. This is Italian-American home cooking at its best—richly flavored mashed potatoes with a well of mozzarella. Nancy serves it as a side dish on a buffet table. I've gotten raves putting it next to a simple roast chicken. And leftovers are amazing for lunch.

When you buy the prosciutto, ask to have it cut into thick slices.

4 ounces fresh mozzarella, cut into small dice
4 ounces smoked mozzarella, cut into small dice
3 tablespoons olive oil
Coarse salt and freshly ground black pepper
2 pounds russet potatoes, peeled and cut into chunks
8 tablespoons (1 stick) unsalted butter
1/2 cup homemade dried bread crumbs
4 ounces Pecorino, grated (about 1 cup)
1/4 pound sliced prosciutto (see note above), cut into small dice
2 large eggs
1/4 cup chopped flat-leaf parsley

Combine both mozzarellas in a bowl with the olive oil and salt and pepper to taste. Leave this on the counter while you prepare the rest of the dish.

Put the potatoes in a large pot, cover with cold water by at least an inch, add a good pinch of salt, and bring to a boil. Cover partway, reduce the heat to medium, and cook until the potatoes are tender.

While the potatoes are cooking, heat the oven to 375 degrees. Use 1 tablespoon of the butter to grease an 8-inch springform pan; coat with bread crumbs (you won't use all of them; save what's left for the top).

When the potatoes are tender, drain, then return them to the pan over high heat to dry them out, stirring and tossing, for about a minute. Rice the potatoes into a bowl and beat in 5 tablespoons of the butter. Add the Pecorino, prosciutto, eggs, parsley, and pepper to taste and mix very well.

Put a bit more than half of the potato mixture into the pan and work it up the sides to make a well. Fill the well with the cheeses and top with the remaining potatoes. Pat down gently, sprinkle with the remaining bread crumbs, and dot with the last 2 tablespoons butter.

Bake until golden brown, 45 to 50 minutes. Let cool for about 15 minutes before removing the sides of the pan, and serve warm, sliced into wedges.

CABBAGE AND
POTATO CAKE

With its flavoring of cabbage and pancetta, this potato cake has a
northern Italian heritage. It's certainly rustic-looking, but the flavor
is anything but. Serve it sliced into wedges alongside chicken or pork.

You can substitute bacon for the pancetta, but if it's very smoky,
blanch it first.

2–2¼ pounds white potatoes, scrubbed
Coarse salt
2 tablespoons olive oil
¼ pound pancetta, chopped
1 onion, thinly sliced
1½ pounds savoy cabbage, cored and thinly sliced
Freshly ground black pepper
1 lemon
Freshly grated nutmeg
4 tablespoons (½ stick) unsalted butter
½ cup freshly grated Parmesan or Pecorino
½ cup fresh bread crumbs

Put the potatoes in a large saucepan, cover with cold water by at least an inch,
add a good pinch of salt, and bring to a boil. Reduce the heat to medium, cover
partway, and cook until the potatoes are very tender. Drain the potatoes on a
rack set in the sink.

Heat the oil in a large skillet over medium-high heat. Add the pancetta and
cook until it begins to brown. Add the onion and cook for 2 minutes or so to
soften it, then add the cabbage a handful at a time, seasoning with salt and pepper and tossing after each addition. Cook, stirring often, until the cabbage is
browned and very tender. Add 3 tablespoons water and continue to cook,
scraping the bottom of the pan to dissolve the brown bits, until the mixture is

fairly dry again, about 4 minutes. Grate in the zest of the lemon, season with nutmeg to taste, and taste again for pepper. The cabbage should have a zing to it. If it needs it, squeeze in some lemon juice. Remove from the heat.

Peel the potatoes, put them in a bowl, and mash them roughly with the side of a big spoon. Beat in 2 tablespoons of the butter. Reserve a tablespoon or two of the grated cheese for the topping and beat the rest into the potatoes, with a lot of black pepper. Combine this mixture with the cabbage—there's no need to go overboard stirring here.

Heat the oven to 350 degrees. Butter a 10-inch springform pan with 1 tablespoon of the butter and coat it with the crumbs. Shake the pan to spread the loose crumbs evenly over the bottom. Wrap the outside of the pan with a piece of aluminum foil.

Scrape the potato mixture into the pan and pat it down so it's even. Sprinkle with the reserved cheese and dot with the last tablespoon of butter. You can leave this at room temperature for a few hours before baking.

Bake for about 40 minutes, until browned and pulling away from the sides. Let it cool on a rack for at least 20 minutes before releasing the sides. You can serve it from the springform base, but you can also use a long thin spatula to transfer it carefully from the base to a flat serving dish. This is best served warm and cut into wedges.

POTATO AND SWEET ONION FLAN

This dish is something like a crustless quiche, mellow and with subtle flavor. We like to serve it alongside a rib-eye steak or a nice big veal chop.

It's a good way to use up leftover boiled potatoes, but you can also start from scratch. If your prosciutto has a thick edge of fat, trim it off and add it to the butter when you're cooking the onions. We adapted this from Richard Olney's *Simple French Food*.

3 tablespoons unsalted butter
2 sweet onions (about 1 pound), such as Vidalia or Texas, thinly sliced
Coarse salt and freshly ground white pepper
2 ounces thinly sliced prosciutto or Westphalian ham, cut into fine julienne
1 pound cold boiled red-skinned potatoes, peeled
3 large eggs
1 1/2 cups heavy cream or half-and-half
Pinch of freshly grated nutmeg

Heat the oven to 350 degrees. Butter a small oval gratin dish or a 1 1/2-quart baking dish.

Melt the butter in a skillet over medium-low heat and add the onions. Season with salt and pepper and cook gently for 10 minutes, or until the onions begin to wilt. Reduce the heat to low and continue cooking until the onions are completely soft and lightly golden, another 20 minutes or so. Stir the prosciutto into the onions and remove from the heat.

Spread one half of the onion mixture in the bottom of the gratin dish.

Slice the boiled potatoes thin and arrange half of them on top of the onions. Season with salt and pepper. Cover with the remaining onions, then finish with the remaining potatoes. Season the top with salt and pepper.

Whisk together the eggs and cream. Season with nutmeg and pour the mixture over the potatoes.

Bake until the custard is lightly puffed, nicely browned around the edges, and just barely set in the center, about 40 minutes. Let the flan sit for about 5 minutes before serving.

POMMES ANNA

This is it: the queen of potato dishes. Rounds of potatoes are layered in neat concentric circles, doused in butter, and baked until a glorious brown. No doubt about it, Pommes Anna is gorgeous. Present it whole and cut it at the table, where it will grace any meal.

If you have an urge to expand your *batterie de cuisine,* by all means invest in a heavy copper Pommes Anna pan, which the French use. But Molly and I find that our trusty 10-inch cast-iron skillets work fine.

Any starchy or all-purpose potato is what you want here. We like russets or long whites, because their cylindrical shape is easier to handle on the mandoline and gives us neat, regular rounds for the prettiest presentation.

2 1/2 pounds russet, white, or yellow-fleshed potatoes, peeled
10 tablespoons (1 1/4 sticks) unsalted butter, melted
Coarse salt and freshly ground black pepper

Slice the potatoes into very thin rounds on a mandoline, dropping them into a large bowl of cold water as you go. Once all the potatoes are sliced, drain and spread them out onto towels to dry. Pat dry. The potatoes must be very dry for the best texture and to prevent sticking.

Ladle about 3 tablespoons of the butter into a 10-inch cast-iron skillet—or a classic Pommes Anna pan—and tilt to coat the sides. Starting in the center and working out clockwise in very neat, overlapping concentric circles, make a layer of potatoes. Drizzle on a bit more of the butter and season liberally with salt and pepper. Make another layer, this time reversing the direction of the potatoes—so you are working counterclockwise—drizzle on butter, and season with salt and pepper. Continue layering—reversing the direction each time and seasoning each layer. After 2 or 3 layers, you may want to press down on the potatoes with the palm of your hand to compress the cake and keep it even. In the end, you should have 4 to 6 layers. Once all the potatoes are in the pan, press down with the palm of your hand to compact.

Pour any remaining butter over the top. Butter a tight-fitting lid or a sheet of foil and cover the skillet. Bake for 35 minutes. Remove the lid and continue baking, uncovered, until the edges are crisp and brown and the potatoes are tender enough to be easily pierced with the tip of a knife, 20 to 25 minutes more.

Remove from the oven and set on a cooling rack for 5 minutes. To unmold, test with a flexible spatula to be sure that the cake is not stuck at all to the bottom of the pan. Then set a large round plate over the skillet, and quickly flip the whole ensemble. (Some cooks like to drain off any excess butter before flipping.) Cut into wedges with a very sharp knife and serve hot.

CHEZ LOUIS POTATO CAKE

Since the 1930s, hungry Parisians and visitors have paid homage to the famous potato cake at the legendary L'Ami Louis bistro. But there's a debate about it: are the potatoes precooked or not? Now literary agent Susan Lescher is an ardent admirer of both the restaurant and the dish, and she led me to this version by restaurateur David Liederman. This, she assures me, has the goods. This is an amazingly beautiful and completely delicious dish. It's a perfect rustic cake meant to be served with roast chicken.

The quantities may sound impressive for the number of servings, but try it. You probably won't be able to stop eating it either.

Read this through once or twice before you start, and be prepared to dirty a lot of pots. It's worth it. And one more thing: a 12-inch cast-iron skillet is key. It won't work in a smaller or lighter pan. But that's not saying you can't halve the quantities and bake the cake in a 9-inch cast-iron pan.

5 pounds russet potatoes, peeled
Coarse salt
Freshly ground black pepper
3/4 pound (3 sticks) unsalted butter
1 tablespoon finely chopped garlic
2 tablespoons chopped flat-leaf parsley

Place the potatoes in a large pot with cold water to cover them by at least an inch. Add a good pinch of salt, bring to a boil, and cook for 15 to 20 minutes. The potatoes should be slightly underdone, so you'll feel resistance when you test them with a skewer or larding needle. (They will finish cooking when you brown and bake them.)

While the potatoes are cooking, put a 12-inch cast-iron skillet into the oven and turn on the heat to 450 degrees.

Drain the potatoes and place them in a second large skillet over medium-high heat. Season liberally with salt and pepper, cut in 2 sticks of the butter, and start chopping the potatoes into uneven hunks (about 2 inches) with the side of a large metal spoon. Keep turning the pieces over in the butter so they brown evenly. This should take about 15 minutes.

Meanwhile, melt the remaining stick of butter in a small saucepan. When the potatoes have browned, take the iron skillet out of the oven, pour in the butter, and immediately add the potatoes. (The skillet needs to be smoking hot—and if you tried to melt the butter in it, it would burn.) Press down with the back of your metal spoon or a spatula to flatten the potatoes in the skillet. Cook it over medium-high heat for 3 minutes, then pop it in the oven and bake for 15 minutes.

Take the skillet from the oven and carefully pour off any butter (you can save this butter and recycle it if you want). Cover the skillet with a heavy flat baking sheet and invert it so the cake falls out onto the sheet. Put the cake back in the oven and bake for 15 minutes. Remove it from the oven and pour off any of the butter in the pan. Carefully slide the cake onto a flat serving dish.

The garnish is a circle of chopped garlic around the center of the cake, surrounded by a larger circle of parsley. But you might just want to combine the garlic and parsley and scatter it evenly over the top. Serve this hot, cut into wedges.

JANSSON'S TEMPTATION

SERVES 6

In her landmark *American Century Cookbook,* Jean Anderson tells us that in Sweden this dish is as popular as pizza is in America. That's not surprising: Jansson's Temptation is rich and creamy, and the brininess of the anchovies hints deliciously of the sea. And thanks to Jean, I, too, now use anchovy paste instead of minced anchovies in Jansson's Temptation. It does perfume the dish completely.

4 tablespoons (½ stick) unsalted butter
4 onions, thinly sliced
Coarse salt and freshly ground black pepper
3 pounds russet potatoes, peeled and cut as for shoestring potatoes (long strips, the
    length of the potato, and about ¼ inch by ¼ inch)
3–4 tablespoons anchovy paste
2 cups half-and-half

Heat the oven to 350 degrees. Butter a 3-quart casserole.

Melt the butter in a large skillet over medium heat. Add the onions, a little pinch of salt, and a grind or two of pepper and cook, stirring often, until the onions are limp and beginning to color; this will take 8 to 10 minutes. Remove from the heat.

Put one-third of the potatoes in the casserole, season lightly with pepper, and cover with half of the onions. Repeat the process: another third of the potatoes, pepper, and the remaining onions; then the rest of the potatoes and some pepper. Dissolve the anchovy paste in the half-and-half and pour it over the potatoes.

Bake until the potatoes are tender and bubbling, with a rich brown crust, 1½ to 2 hours. Serve this right away.

BACON AND POTATO CAKE

Since the flavor of the bacon really dominates here, this cake is worth making only if you have truly fine thin-sliced bacon. Go to the butcher and have it sliced fresh. The dish is served at The Monkey Bar in New York City, and we wonder if they adapted their cake from a similar recipe by French chef Alain Ducasse, as we adapted ours from theirs.

8 thin slices (about 5 ounces) best-quality bacon
2 pounds all-purpose potatoes, peeled and very thinly sliced
1 small onion, thinly sliced
Coarse salt and freshly ground black pepper
1 tablespoon unsalted butter

Heat the oven to 400 degrees. Butter a 10-inch cast-iron skillet.

Arrange the bacon slices in the bottom of the skillet so they resemble the spokes of a wheel. Leave the ends hanging over the sides—these will get folded over later to sandwich the potatoes inside.

Layer the potatoes in the pan, scattering the onion and seasoning with salt and plenty of pepper between the layers. When all the potatoes are in the pan, press down with the palm of your hand to compress the layers, then fold the ends of the bacon strips over the top. If the bacon ends overlap in the middle, shift them enough so that they fan out a bit. Don't worry too much about appearances—this will become the bottom of the cake when it is unmolded. Dot the spaces between the strips with the butter

Bake until the bacon is crisp and the potatoes are tender enough to be easily pierced with the tip of a knife, 45 to 50 minutes. Press down on the cake with a spatula a few times during cooking to compress the layers.

Remove from the oven and very carefully tip the skillet to pour off a bit of the bacon fat. Let the potato cake sit on a cooling rack for 5 minutes.

To unmold, set a large round plate over the skillet, and quickly flip the whole ensemble. Cut into wedges and serve hot.

TORTA WITH ANCHOVY, MOZZARELLA, AND TOMATO

Think of this savory Italian cake as an anchovy pizza in reverse. The top is crusty and crunchy, the inside creamy. It makes a great lunch or a fine first course.

½ cup soft bread crumbs
6 ounces fresh mozzarella, cut into small dice
4–6 anchovy fillets, chopped
1 teaspoon dried oregano, preferably Mediterranean
1 tablespoon olive oil
Pinch of crushed red pepper (optional)
Freshly ground black pepper
¾ cup canned tomatoes
1½ pounds all-purpose or red-skinned potatoes, peeled
Coarse salt

Heat the oven to 425 degrees. Butter a 10-inch springform pan generously and wrap the outside with aluminum foil (this dish leaks, so you'll make a mess in your oven if you skip this step). Coat the springform with the bread crumbs, using them all.

Combine the mozzarella, anchovies, oregano, about 2 teaspoons of the oil, the crushed red pepper, if you want, and a good hit of black pepper in a bowl. Stir.

Put the tomatoes in a bowl and crush them with your hands.

Make paper-thin slices of potato on a mandoline. You're ready to start layering.

Use one-quarter of the potatoes to make an even layer in the springform. Season with pepper and spread with a third of the tomatoes. Scatter a third of the cheese mixture over the tomatoes. Repeat the process: three more layers of potatoes, two more of the tomatoes and cheese. Season the top layer of potatoes with salt and pepper and drizzle with the remaining 1 teaspoon oil.

Bake until the torta is bubbling and very rich brown, about 45 minutes. Let it cool on a rack for about 10 minutes, then run a blade around the outside before releasing the sides of the springform. If you're careful, you can use a long thin spatula to release the torta from the springform bottom and slide it onto a plate, or you can make your life easy and not.

I think this is best just warm or at room temperature. Slice it into wedges with a very sharp knife.

TOMATO AND EGGPLANT TORTA

Oniony smashed potatoes are turned into a crust for this pie topped with eggplant and tomato. This is a great lunch or light dinner.

1 red onion, thinly sliced
1/4 cup olive oil
1 garlic clove, minced
1 1/4 pounds yellow-fleshed potatoes, scrubbed
Coarse salt and freshly ground black pepper
3 tablespoons dried bread crumbs (homemade, if possible)
1 small eggplant (about 1/2 pound)
2 ripe tomatoes, sliced about 1/3 inch thick
1/2 teaspoon dried oregano, preferably Mexican
2 tablespoons freshly grated Parmesan

Put the onion and 2 tablespoons of the oil in a skillet and turn the heat to medium. Cook until the onion is completely limp and starting to brown at the edges, about 8 minutes. Add the garlic and cook for another minute or two, until the garlic is very fragrant. Remove from the heat.

Meanwhile, put the potatoes in a saucepan, cover with cold water by at least an inch, add a good pinch of salt, and bring to a boil. Cover partway, reduce the heat to medium, and cook until the potatoes are tender. Drain well and return them to the pot.

Break up the potatoes with the side of a big metal spoon, then use the spoon to smash them. Stir in the onion mixture and salt and pepper to taste.

Oil a 10-inch pie plate and coat it with the bread crumbs. Spoon in the potatoes and pack them down into the plate and up the sides.

Heat the oven to 350 degrees.

Heat a ridged cast-iron stovetop grill pan over medium-high heat. Going the long way, cut 4 strips of skin from the eggplant, making a one-quarter turn each time, then cut the eggplant into 1/3-inch-thick rounds. Brush the rounds on both sides with about 1 tablespoon of the oil and sprinkle them with salt. Grill the eggplant rounds until nicely marked and cooked through, 3 to 4 minutes per side.

Make a ring of alternating slices of eggplant and tomato (just use the larger inside slices of tomato) on top of the potatoes. Chop any remaining slices and pile them in the middle. Crumble the oregano over the top, drizzle with the remaining 1 tablespoon oil, and sprinkle with the Parmesan.

Bake for 1 hour, or until very browned and crusty. Serve hot.

POTATO KUGEL

What a great language Yiddish is. Without it, we would have to call this dish potato pudding, which doesn't even come close to evoking how good it is. But listen to that hard "k" sound and the glottal "g" and you get a picture of a very crusty casserole with a creamy interior. In a way, it's like a giant latke, baked instead of fried.

Schmaltz (rendered chicken fat) is the fat of choice for this kugel. To make it, pull the fat from a chicken, cut it up, and put it in a small skillet or saucepan with a tablespoon of water. Cook it over low heat until the water has cooked away and any solid bits have begun to brown.

I've adapted this recipe from one in Joan Nathan's *Jewish Cooking in America.*

1/4 cup schmaltz (see note above) or vegetable oil
1 large onion, chopped
Coarse salt
4 or 5 whole scallions, chopped
2 pounds russet potatoes
4 large eggs
3–4 tablespoons chopped fresh dill
Freshly ground black pepper

Heat the oven to 400 degrees. Smear a large gratin dish or 3-quart casserole with half of the schmaltz.

Heat the remaining 2 tablespoons schmaltz in a heavy skillet over medium-high heat. Add the onion and a pinch of salt and cook until the onion softens. Add the scallions and cook, stirring often, until the onion is very well browned. Let this cool while you prep the potatoes.

Peel the potatoes and grate them in a food processor fitted with the shredding blade. (Yes, you can grate the potatoes on a box grater if you want.)

Beat the eggs and dill in a mixing bowl. Add the potatoes, onion mixture, and salt and pepper—be generous with the pepper. Get your hands into the bowl and mix it well.

Spread the potatoes out in the casserole, and bake in the upper third of the oven for 45 to 50 minutes, until a rich brown. Serve hot.

POTATO PRINCIPLES
ROASTING SWEET POTATOES

Over the course of writing this book, Molly and I have roasted a lot of sweet potatoes, trying them several different ways. What we ended up liking best is a high-temperature roast. Cooked this way, the potatoes start to caramelize under the skin, becoming even sweeter, and the flesh turns almost custardy soft.

Heat the oven to 450 degrees.

Scrub the potatoes and prick them all over with the tip of a knife or a larding needle. Make a baking tray from a double thickness of a piece of heavy-duty aluminum foil large enough to accommodate all the potatoes, and fold up the edges all around to make a lip about 3/4 inch high.

Put the foil on the oven rack, add the potatoes, and shut the door. Medium potatoes should be done in an hour. The juices that have seeped out will have started to burn, which is why you put the potatoes on foil. No scrubbing a baking sheet.

You can tart them up any way your heart desires, but we like them best just with butter, salt, and pepper. No matter what, always roast more than you plan on serving right away so you have them on hand to make biscuits, crackers, pie, or semifreddo.

SWEET POTATO CASSEROLE

Creamy, tender, smooth, and comforting, this is one of those dishes that tastes as if Grandma made it. It's easy enough to double this and prepare it well ahead, so it's rather nice for a holiday buffet.

We like to use the food mill for this casserole to eliminate any fibers and make it smooth. If you like your sweets really sweet, include the brown sugar.

2–2¹/₂ pounds sweet potatoes, scrubbed
Coarse salt
5 tablespoons unsalted butter, softened
2 tablespoons heavy cream
¹/₄ teaspoon ground allspice
¹/₄ teaspoon ground ginger
Freshly grated nutmeg
Freshly ground white pepper
2 tablespoons brown sugar (optional)
2 large eggs, lightly beaten

TO BOIL THE POTATOES: Place the sweet potatoes in a large saucepan with a copious amount of cold water and a pinch of salt and bring to a boil. Reduce the heat and simmer until the potatoes are just tender. Drain on a rack.

TO BAKE THE POTATOES: Heat the oven to 450 degrees. Prick the sweet potatoes with the tip of a knife and bake them on a foil tray until very tender, about 1 hour. Let cool slightly.

Heat the oven to 350 degrees. Butter a 2-quart casserole dish (an 8-inch square baking dish is fine).

As soon as the potatoes are cool enough to handle, peel and pass them through a food mill or mash with a whisk in a large bowl. Beat in 4 tablespoons of the butter and the cream. Season with the allspice, ginger, nutmeg, salt and pepper, and sugar, if using. Beat in the eggs.

Scrape the sweet potatoes into the casserole and dot the top with the remaining 1 tablespoon butter. The casserole can be made ahead up until this point, covered with plastic wrap, and refrigerated for a day before baking.

Bake the sweet potatoes until lightly puffed and beginning to brown, about 1 hour. (If you've refrigerated the casserole, the baking time will be a bit longer.) Serve hot.

VARIATION
ORANGE SWEET POTATO CASSEROLE WITH PECANS

Add 1 teaspoon grated orange zest and 1/4 cup orange juice to the potatoes in place of the cream. Eliminate the allspice and ginger, and add a splash of bourbon. Sprinkle the top with 1/4 cup pecan pieces and bake.

IS IT A YAM
OR A SWEET POTATO?

Chances are, if you're in the grocery store, the item sitting under the sign that says "yams" is a sweet potato. It's an American thing, this confusion, and vegetable authority Elizabeth Schneider has traced the misnomer back to the arrival of slaves, who might have introduced the word because the American sweet potato had a slight resemblance to the tuber they knew in Africa. But the resemblance ends there. Yams and sweet potatoes come from different families and have different flavors and different uses. The yam is nowhere as sugary as a sweet potato; cooked, it is more like a potato, without the custardy texture of a sweet. For the peoples of the world who eat it, it is most often a savory.

We choose not to perpetuate the error in labeling. If you're looking for candied "yams," you won't find them in this book, but you will find candied sweet potatoes. We think you'll be happy with the results.

BAKED CANDIED SWEET POTATOES

These sweet potatoes have the advantage that you can prepare them ahead and then just slide them into the oven an hour before dinner. If you want to double this recipe for a holiday crowd, layer the sweet potatoes in the casserole, adding some of the butter and sugar (or maple syrup) between layers. Then pour 1/4 cup apple cider or water over the top, cover tightly with foil, and bake until tender and syrupy, about an hour. The candied glaze won't be as caramelized, but the sweet potatoes will be delicious, and you won't have to stir at all as they bake.

2 pounds sweet potatoes, scrubbed
Coarse salt
3–4 tablespoons light brown sugar, to taste
Freshly ground white pepper
4 tablespoons (1/2 stick) unsalted butter

Put the sweet potatoes in a large saucepan with a large amount of cold water, add a small pinch of salt, and bring to a boil. (If the potatoes are too long to fit in the pan, cut them in half.) Reduce the heat to medium and simmer until the potatoes are just tender but not at all mushy. Drain on a rack set in the sink and let cool.

Heat the oven to 350 degrees. Butter a large casserole or a 9-by-13-inch baking dish.

When the potatoes are cool enough to handle, peel and cut them into 3/4-inch-thick slices or 1-inch chunks. Spread them in the casserole and sprinkle with the brown sugar. Grind in a little white pepper and dot the top with the butter. The sweet potatoes can be prepared ahead up until this point and kept refrigerated overnight.

Bake, stirring gently a few times, until the sweet potatoes are glazed and the sugar is caramelized and bubbly around the edges of the pan, about an hour. Serve warm, scooping out some of the syrup with each serving of potatoes.

VARIATIONS

MAPLE BAKED SWEET POTATOES

Replace the brown sugar with ¼ to ⅓ cup maple syrup.

CANDIED SWEET POTATOES WITH APPLES

Peel and core 1 pound tart apples and cut them into 1-inch chunks. Add the chopped apples to the sweet potatoes just before baking.

BAKED SWEET POTATOES WITH MARSHMALLOWS

You can add a marshmallow topping to the basic recipe or to any of the variations. Remove the sweet potatoes from the oven about 10 minutes before they are fully cooked, and scatter about 2 dozen regular-sized marshmallows (or 1½ cups miniature) over the surface. Return the casserole to the oven and finish cooking until the marshmallows are all melty and lightly browned, about 10 minutes. Serve hot.

RIVER ROAD BAKED SWEET POTATOES
WITH MARSHMALLOWS

SERVES 8 TO 10

Jean Anderson unearthed this embroidered version of the favorite casserole from the 1959 *River Road Recipes* by the Junior League of Baton Rouge. How many marshmallows you use—and whether they're big or mini—is up to you. You can replace the milk with 1 cup canned crushed pineapple. You can also spike the potatoes with some sherry or rum.

3–3^1/$_2$ pounds sweet potatoes
^{1}/$_2$ teaspoon ground cinnamon
Freshly grated nutmeg
1 tablespoon orange juice
1 cup milk
1 teaspoon vanilla extract
3 tablespoons sugar
4 tablespoons (^{1}/$_2$ stick) unsalted butter
Marshmallows (see note above)

Heat the oven to 450 degrees.

Prick the sweet potatoes with a fork and bake them on a foil tray until tender, about 1 hour. Lower the oven temperature to 350 degrees.

Butter a large gratin dish or 3-quart casserole. Peel the potatoes and mash them in a bowl with a fork. Stir in the cinnamon, a few gratings of nutmeg, and the orange juice.

Combine the milk, vanilla, sugar, and butter in a saucepan over medium heat and bring just to a boil. Stir this into the potatoes.

Spoon half of the potatoes into the baking dish. Cover with a layer of marshmallows, then repeat with the remaining potatoes and another layer of marshmallows. Bake until well browned, about 20 to 25 minutes. Serve hot.

SWEET POTATOES
WITH HORSERADISH

SERVES 4 TO 6

This recipe comes from John Martin Taylor—Hoppin' John to fans of his important books on lowcountry cooking and his grits and pickles, which he sells on his Web site. John described it as his favorite recipe in *The New Southern Cook,* and I had to find out why. It sounded almost too simple. But that simplicity is just what the dish has going for it. The horseradish mellows while it cooks with the cream and is exactly the right accent for the sweets.

1½–1¾ pounds sweet potatoes
3 tablespoons grated fresh horseradish (or substitute the stuff in a jar, but drain it)
1 cup heavy cream

Heat the oven to 400 degrees.

Peel the potatoes and cut them into ¼-inch-thick slices. Toss them in a bowl with the horseradish and cream to coat evenly, then transfer to a 9-by-12-inch casserole. Be sure to scrape in all the cream.

Cover the dish with foil and bake for 30 to 45 minutes. The potatoes will seem to have eaten the cream and will be tender. Carefully spoon them out into a serving dish (try not to break up the slices), scraping in any of the sauce in the casserole, and serve right away.

VARIATION

You can turn this into a soup if you like. Make the recipe as described above and, after baking, puree the sweet potatoes in the food processor or put them through a food mill fitted with the fine disk. Simmer with 2 cups beef stock for about 10 minutes. Drizzle the soup with heavy cream if you feel extravagant—either in a tureen or in individual bowls.

GINGERED SWEET POTATO PUDDING WITH MERINGUE

SERVES 6 TO 8

Think of this as a downtown version of sweets with marshmallow topping. Downtown as in South American, and adapted from a recipe by the late chef Felipe Rojas-Lombardi. Sautéed pears add a sweet note without making these candied. It's a gorgeous holiday side dish.

Be careful when you toast the almonds. If you brown them too much, they'll burn when you bake the casserole, so aim for beige.

1/2 cup sliced almonds, very lightly toasted (see note above)
3 pounds sweet potatoes, baked until very tender (see page 294)
3 tablespoons unsalted butter
2 ripe Comice or Bartlett pears, peeled, quartered, cored, and sliced
2 tablespoons light brown sugar
2 tablespoons brandy or cider
1 teaspoon ground ginger
1/4 teaspoon ground allspice
Freshly grated nutmeg
Coarse salt and freshly ground white pepper
3 large eggs, separated
1/2 teaspoon ground cinnamon
3 dashes hot sauce

Heat the oven to 350 degrees. Generously butter an 8-inch square baking dish or a round 3-quart casserole and sprinkle a heaping 1/4 cup of the almonds over the bottom and sides.

Peel the sweet potatoes and pass them through a food mill into a big mixing bowl.

Heat the butter in a large skillet over medium-high heat. When the butter stops foaming, add the pear slices and cook, stirring once or twice, until they are evenly coated with butter. Sprinkle on 1 tablespoon of the brown sugar and cook until the pears are starting to fall apart and the juices are beginning to caramelize, about 5 minutes. Transfer the sautéed pears to the food mill and puree them into the bowl with the potatoes.

Return the pan to the heat and pour in the brandy. Bring to a quick boil, scraping with a wooden spoon to dissolve the caramelized bits, and then stir the liquid into the mashed sweet potatoes. Season with the ginger, allspice, a few gratings of nutmeg, and salt and white pepper.

Whisk the egg yolks until they are light and frothy. Stir the yolks into the sweet potatoes and scrape the lot into the baking dish. Bake until heated through and beginning to bubble around the edges, 40 to 45 minutes.

During the last few minutes of baking, whisk the egg whites with the remaining 1 tablespoon brown sugar, the cinnamon, and a pinch of salt to soft peaks. Fold the hot sauce and 2 tablespoons of the almonds into the meringue.

Remove the casserole from the oven and spread the meringue evenly over the sweet potatoes. Sprinkle the remaining 2 tablespoons almonds on top of the meringue and return the dish to the oven. Bake until the meringue is golden brown, another 10 to 12 minutes, and serve.

GRATINS &

SCALLOPED POTATOES

GRATIN DAUPHINOISE

There is much said and written about the correct way to make the ultimate gratin. Some add eggs to help thicken; some abhor the addition of cheese; others insist on simmering the potato slices first in milk, draining them, and adding fresh cream for baking. We like our version—simple enough to make and marvelously rich. While we use a bit more cream than milk, you can just as well prepare this with any combination of the two, as long as you come up with 2½ cups—enough to just cover the potatoes. Never worry about making too much of this, because a cold slice of gratin is one of the best breakfasts we can imagine.

2 pounds Yukon Gold or russet potatoes, peeled and very thinly sliced
Coarse salt and freshly ground white pepper
1 cup milk
1½ cups heavy cream
3 ounces Gruyère cheese, shredded (about ¾ cup)

Heat the oven to 375 degrees. Place a sheet of heavy-duty aluminum foil on the rack under the one you'll be baking the gratin on. Gratins can make a serious mess when they spill over. Butter a large gratin dish or a 3-quart flameproof casserole dish.

Arrange the potatoes in the dish in overlapping layers, sprinkling with salt and pepper as you go.

Combine the milk and cream and pour it over the potatoes. Heat the dish over medium-high heat until the cream begins to simmer. Watch carefully so that it doesn't boil over and make a real mess.

Sprinkle the cheese on top and bake until the top is very brown and bubbly, about 40 minutes. Because of the cheese, the surface of this gratin will get quite a bit more browned than others in this chapter. Don't chicken out and remove it from the oven before the potatoes are completely tender and the edges of the gratin look as if the cream has broken.

Let the gratin sit for about 10 minutes before serving.

THE MAGIC MANDOLINE

In the mid-1980s, I was editing a cookbook by the Michelin three-star chef Georges Blanc and reached his recipe for vegetable "vermicelli." Martha Stewart happened to be in the office that day, and I showed her the recipe, saying that while it was a fun idea to cut zucchini into tiny shreds and cook them the way you would spaghetti, I also thought it wasn't fair, since you needed special equipment. Nonsense, said Martha, everyone should have a mandoline.

It wasn't until years later, when I was given a French mandoline as a gift, that I realized how right she was. This slicer has become an invaluable tool in my kitchen, and it's nowhere more helpful than when I make gratins. Once the potatoes are peeled and the slicer is set to less than 1/8 inch, it's a matter of moments before I have a heap of perfectly cut, perfectly thin rounds of potato. It's what I take out when I want almost transparent rounds for Saratoga chips, and having one is the only way to make *pommes gaufrette* and shoestring fries.

Sure you can pull out a sharp knife to slice potatoes for gratins, and, yes, the big French model is expensive. But there are other options beyond the Rolls-Royce. Check kitchen supply stores for slicers from Japan and elsewhere. Everyone should have one.

LEEK-POTATO GRATIN

Potatoes and leeks were meant to be together, and this pairing, with its accent of Gorgonzola, is a happy one indeed. It cries out to be served with rib-eye steaks.

Sweet Gorgonzola (*dolce*) is the blue cheese of choice here; the more aged type (*naturale*) is too sharp. And you can make this with yellow-fleshed potatoes if you care to.

1 garlic clove, halved
3 tablespoons unsalted butter, plus more for the dish
Generous 5 cups sliced leeks (white and light green parts of 5 or 6 leeks)
Coarse salt and freshly ground black or white pepper
Freshly grated nutmeg
1–1¼ pounds russet potatoes, peeled and sliced ¹⁄₁₆ inch thick
4 ounces Gorgonzola dolce (see note above)
1½ cups milk
½ cup heavy cream
2 tablespoons freshly grated Parmesan

Heat the oven to 350 degrees. Place a sheet of heavy-duty aluminum foil to go on the rack underneath the gratin. Rub a medium gratin dish or a 1½-quart flameproof casserole with the garlic. Let the garlic juice dry and then butter the dish well.

Melt the butter in a large skillet over medium-high heat. Add the leeks and season with salt and pepper. Cook, stirring often, until tender and rather dry, 10 to 12 minutes. Grate in some nutmeg and taste for salt and pepper. Remove from the heat.

Layer one-third of the potatoes in the gratin dish. Season with salt and pepper, spread with half of the leeks, and crumble half of the Gorgonzola over them. Repeat, and finish with the last third of the potatoes. Combine the milk and cream, pour into the dish, and bring to a simmer over medium-low heat. Watch that it doesn't boil over and make an unholy mess.

Dust the gratin with the Parmesan and bake for about 40 minutes, until well browned and bubbling. Stick a knife into the gratin to make sure the potatoes are tender. Let it sit for 10 minutes before serving.

POTATO-SHIITAKE GRATIN

SERVES 4 TO 6

I will be ever grateful to cooking expert Diana Kennedy for showing me this method for cooking mushrooms. It coaxes flavor even out of button mushrooms—not an easy task—but what it does with wild mushrooms!

Holding back some of the cream to add after a gratin has been baking for a while is a great trick when you want a very rich crust.

1 pound shiitake mushrooms (or a combination of wild and cultivated mushrooms, stems trimmed), stems removed, and very thinly sliced
2 garlic cloves, chopped
3 tablespoons unsalted butter
1 tablespoon olive oil
Juice of $1/2$ lemon
Coarse salt and freshly ground black pepper
$1^1/4$–$1^1/2$ pounds russet potatoes, peeled and cut into $1/16$-inch slices
$1^1/2$ cups milk
$3/4$ cup heavy cream

Heat the oven to 300 degrees.

Combine the mushrooms, garlic, 2 tablespoons of the butter, the olive oil, lemon juice, and salt and pepper to taste in a large baking dish—something big enough to accommodate the mushrooms in no more than two layers. Toss and bake for 45 minutes to 1 hour, stirring two or three times, until the mushrooms are starting to dry at the edges but are still juicy.

Take the mushrooms out and increase the oven temperature to 350 degrees. Place a sheet of heavy-duty aluminum foil on the rack below the one you'll be baking on.

Butter a flameproof gratin dish well and add one-third of the potatoes. Season with salt and pepper and cover with half of the mushrooms. Repeat with another layer of potatoes, then the remaining mushrooms, and finish with the last third of the potatoes.

Combine the milk with 1/2 cup of the heavy cream and pour over the potatoes. Bring to a simmer over medium heat—watch it carefully, so it doesn't boil over. Dot the top with the remaining 1 tablespoon butter.

Transfer the gratin to the oven. Bake for 25 minutes. Pour the remaining 1/4 cup cream over the top and return the gratin to the oven for another 15 minutes or so, until the gratin is bubbling and the top is richly browned. Let it rest for 10 minutes before serving.

FOUR-CHEESE GRATIN

This gratin is rich and gooey. Serve it with roasts or grilled meats. Or make a salad of bitter greens and call it supper.

1 garlic clove, halved
4 ounces fresh goat cheese
2 ounces mild blue cheese, such as Danish
1½ pounds russet potatoes, peeled and sliced very thin
Coarse salt and freshly ground white pepper
4 ounces Swiss cheese or fontina, shredded
Freshly grated nutmeg
2 cups half-and-half or light cream
½ cup freshly grated Parmesan

Heat the oven to 350 degrees. Place a sheet of heavy-duty aluminum foil on the rack below the one you'll be baking on. Rub the garlic all over the inside of a large flameproof gratin dish, a flameproof 2-quart baking dish, or a 10-inch cast-iron skillet, pressing hard to release the juices. Let the garlic juice dry, then butter the dish.

Combine the goat cheese and blue cheese in a small bowl and mash with a fork until well crumbled and evenly combined.

Arrange one-third of the potatoes in the gratin dish. Season with salt and pepper. Scatter half of the Swiss cheese over the top, then dot with half of the goat–blue cheese mix. Cover with another third of the potatoes, and season again with salt and pepper. Scatter the remaining Swiss and goat–blue cheese mix over the potatoes. Cover with a final layer of potatoes and season with salt and pepper.

Stir the nutmeg into the half-and-half, and pour it over the potatoes. Heat the potatoes over medium-high heat until the cream begins to simmer. Watch it like a hawk, so it doesn't boil over.

Sprinkle the Parmesan over the top and slide the gratin into the oven. Bake until the top is very brown and bubbling, about 1 hour. Let the gratin rest for 10 minutes before you serve it.

FENNEL-POTATO GRATIN

Like most gratins, this one reheats beautifully. You may want to try the restaurant trick of dishing up portions in individual gratin dishes and scattering with a bit more cheese before reheating. German Butterballs are wonderful in this dish.

1 garlic clove, halved
2 fennel bulbs, trimmed, cores removed, and thinly sliced (about 4 cups)
3 tablespoons unsalted butter
Coarse salt
1/4 cup dry white wine or dry vermouth
13/4–2 pounds yellow-fleshed potatoes, peeled and very thinly sliced
8 ounces Emmentaler or Gruyère, shredded
2 1/2 cups milk (substitute cream for some of the milk if you care to)
Freshly ground white pepper

Heat the oven to 325 degrees. Place a sheet of heavy-duty aluminum foil on the rack below the one you'll be baking on. Rub a large gratin dish or a 3-quart flameproof casserole with the garlic. Once the garlic juice is dry, butter the dish well.

Heat a large skillet over medium-high heat. Add the fennel, 2 tablespoons of the butter, and some salt and cook, stirring, for about 2 minutes. Add the wine, cover, and cook, stirring once in a while, until the fennel is tender, 15 to 20 minutes. If the pan is too dry, add a tablespoon or two of water. You want the fennel tender but not browned. Remove from the heat.

Toss the potatoes with about two-thirds of the cheese, the fennel, and salt and pepper in a large bowl. Spread into the casserole and pour in the milk. Scatter with the rest of the cheese and dot with the remaining 1 tablespoon butter.

Bake the gratin until well browned and bubbling, 1 hour and 20 to 30 minutes. Let this rest for 10 minutes before you serve it.

GRATIN FROM THE AUVERGNE

This is a lush, creamy gratin inspired by a Paula Wolfert recipe. The potatoes are first simmered in milk, then combined with buttery Cantal and the mild blue cheese of France's Auvergne region.

2½ pounds yellow-fleshed potatoes, peeled and sliced ¹/₁₆ inch thick
2 cups milk
1 cup heavy cream
Coarse salt
1 garlic clove, halved
4 ounces Bleu d'Auvergne or Roquefort, crumbled
3 ounces Cantal cheese, shredded
Pinch of cayenne pepper
Freshly grated nutmeg
Freshly ground white pepper
2 tablespoons unsalted butter

Heat the oven to 375 degrees. Place a sheet of heavy-duty aluminum foil on the rack below the one you'll be baking on.

Put the potatoes in a large saucepan with the milk, cream, and a pinch of salt. Bring to a boil—watch and make sure it doesn't boil over—then reduce to a simmer, cover partway, and cook until the potatoes are just tender and the liquid is quite thick, about 12 minutes.

Meanwhile, rub a large gratin dish or a 3-quart casserole with the garlic. When the garlic juices dry, butter the dish liberally.

Lift about a third of the potatoes out of the milk with a slotted spoon and layer them in the dish. Scatter half of the Bleu d'Auvergne and half of the Cantal over them. Cover with a second layer of potatoes, being stingy so you have plenty left for the top layer, and scatter with the rest of the cheese. Finish with a last layer of potatoes.

Season the milk-cream mixture with the cayenne, nutmeg, salt, and white pepper. Pour over the potatoes and shave the butter over the top.

Bake until the gratin is browned and most of the liquid has been absorbed, about 50 minutes. Let this sit for 10 minutes before you serve it.

POTATOES IN BEER

We're taking a slight break from the potatoes cooked in milk and cream theme, but to call this dish "slight" would be doing it incredible disservice. We found the recipe in Richard Olney's *Simple French Food,* and we are very glad we did. The beer gets all winy and sort of sweet as it cooks. The end result is remarkable.

1 large onion, sliced into thin rounds
1½ pounds Yukon Gold potatoes, peeled and thinly sliced
Coarse salt and freshly ground white pepper
1 (12-ounce) bottle lager beer
2 tablespoons unsalted butter, cut into thin slices
½ cup heavy cream

Heat the oven to 425 degrees. Butter a shallow 2-quart baking dish.

Arrange a few onion rings in the bottom of the dish, and then alternate layers of potatoes and onion, seasoning with salt and pepper as you go and ending with potatoes. Pour the beer over the top and dot the surface with the butter.

Put the dish into the oven. After 10 minutes, turn the heat down to 375 degrees. Bake for 40 minutes more, or until the potatoes are tender and the surface has begun to brown. Pour the cream over the surface and bake for an additional 10 minutes. Let rest for 15 to 20 minutes. It's best served warm, not hot.

NOTE: We've found that late-season (March through June) storage potatoes are often not thirsty enough for this dish. If the gratin is still very liquid after 40 minutes of baking, spoon out most of the beer before adding the cream.

GRATIN
FROM THE SAVOIE

SERVES 6 TO 8

The satisfying gratin from the Savoie distinguishes itself with eggs that form bits of tender custard as the dish cooks slowly and gently. You want a waxy potato this time, one that will hold its shape even while it drinks up all the stock you use in the dish.

Use a Beaufort cheese from the Savoie region if you can find it, or French Comté or even Gruyère. As with all gratins, leftovers heat well—they're good cold too.

2 garlic cloves, halved
2 large eggs
2 pounds red-skinned or white potatoes, peeled and very thinly sliced
2 tablespoons all-purpose flour
1 1/2 cups shredded Beaufort, Comté, or Gruyère (about 6 ounces)
Freshly grated nutmeg
Coarse salt and freshly ground white pepper
2 cups Chicken Stock (page 85) or vegetable stock
2 tablespoons unsalted butter

Heat the oven to 300 degrees. Rub the garlic all over the inside of a large gratin dish or 3-quart casserole, pressing hard to release the juices. Let the garlic juice dry, then generously butter the dish. Place a sheet of heavy-duty aluminum foil on the rack under the one you'll be baking on.

Lightly beat the eggs in a large mixing bowl. Add the potatoes and toss to combine. Sprinkle in the flour and 1 cup of the cheese, season with nutmeg, salt, and pepper, and toss again until evenly mixed. Transfer the potatoes to the gratin dish, flattening them into an even layer. Pour over the stock. Scatter the remaining 1/2 cup cheese over the top and dot the surface with the butter.

Bake until the top is very brown and all the liquid has been absorbed, about 1 hour. Let the gratin sit for about 10 minutes before serving.

DELMONICO POTATOES

The name Delmonico refers to two very different potato dishes: either boiled potatoes served simply with parsley and lemon or, more commonly, a substantial gratinlike dish such as this. In place of the stodgy white sauce that is sometimes used, we make this with straight cream and milk. And unlike other gratins, the potatoes are cubed and topped with cheesy bread crumbs.

2 pounds russet potatoes, peeled and cut into $^1/_3$-inch cubes
1$^1/_2$ cups milk
$^1/_2$ cup heavy cream
Freshly grated nutmeg
Coarse salt and freshly ground black pepper
$^1/_2$ cup fresh bread crumbs
3 tablespoons freshly grated Parmesan

Heat the oven to 375 degrees. Butter a 2$^1/_2$-to-3-quart shallow casserole or large oval gratin dish. Place a sheet of heavy-duty aluminum foil on the rack below the one you'll be baking on.

Combine the potatoes, milk, and cream in a large saucepan. Season with nutmeg, salt, and pepper and bring to a gentle simmer over medium heat. Let the potatoes simmer ever so gently for a minute or two, then remove from the heat. Transfer the potatoes and their liquid to the baking dish.

Stir the bread crumbs and cheese together and sprinkle this mix over the top of the potatoes. Let the dish sit for a few minutes so the crumbs can absorb some of the liquid.

Slide the potatoes into the oven and bake until they are tender and the top is bubbly and brown, about 1 hour. We like this served warm directly from the casserole.

AREQUIPEÑA POTATOES

This amazing dish comes from the late chef Felipe Rojas-Lombardi, and it's the Peruvian version of mac and cheese. Toss potatoes with cheese and cream, then bury a hot pepper in the center, fill it with oil, and bake.

2½ pounds yellow-fleshed potatoes, peeled and cut into small dice
8 ounces Muenster, cut into small dice
8 ounces fresh mozzarella, cut into small dice
¼ cup olive oil
Coarse salt
½ cup heavy cream (you can substitute milk)
1 fresh poblano chile (or an ancho)

Heat the oven to 350 degrees.

Dump the potatoes into a bowl and add the cheeses, 1 tablespoon of the oil, and salt to taste. Toss and stir to combine. Spread the potatoes and cheese out in a baking dish (9-by-13-inch works well for this) and pour in the cream.

Slice off about one-quarter from one side of the chile; you want to make a small bowl. Pull out the seeds and nestle the chile, cut side up, in the center of the potatoes. Spoon the remaining 3 tablespoons oil into the chile.

Bake the dish until the potatoes are tender and starting to brown nicely in spots, 1 to 1½ hours. Bring the casserole to the table, spoon the oil from inside the chile over the potatoes, and serve.

HUNGARIAN POTATO CASSEROLE
(RAKOTT KRUMPLI)

SERVES 4

I've adapted this from Susan Derecskey's *Hungarian Cookbook,* one of the definitive books on the cuisine. Make it in advance, then bake it right before dinner. The only potato that won't work here is the russet.

1 1/2 pounds potatoes, scrubbed
Coarse salt
1 small onion, minced
2 tablespoons vegetable oil (or lard or bacon drippings)
2 tablespoons dried bread crumbs
1/2 cup sour cream
3 large eggs, hard-cooked (see page 127)

Put the potatoes in a large saucepan, cover with cold water by at least an inch, add a good pinch of salt, and bring to a boil. Cover partway, reduce the heat to medium, and cook until the potatoes are tender. Drain them on a rack set in the sink and leave them there to cool.

Meanwhile, cook the onion in the oil over medium heat until translucent. Scrape the onion and oil into a small bowl and let cool.

Heat the oven to 300 degrees. Lightly oil a small gratin dish or a 9-inch pie plate. Coat the dish with the crumbs. Peel the potatoes and cut them into 1/4-inch slices. Add the sour cream to the onion, salt to taste, and whisk until smooth. Scrape the cream into the potatoes and fold, coating each slice.

Layer half of the potatoes in the gratin dish. Slice the eggs and make a layer on top of the potatoes. Cover evenly with the rest of the potatoes and press down firmly to compact the casserole. There's no graceful way to layer the potatoes or compact them in the dish without using your hands.

Bake for 30 minutes in the upper third of the oven. Then turn on the broiler for a few minutes until the casserole browns lightly. Serve this hot.

POTATO, CHEDDAR, AND CHIVE CASSEROLE

SERVES 6 TO 8

We love this recipe, which our friend Martha Holmberg shared with us. Very cheesy. Very '50s. Very tasty. You'll be happiest if you use the best sharp orange cheddar you can find.

1½–2 pounds russet potatoes, scrubbed
Coarse salt
4 tablespoons (½ stick) unsalted butter, melted
1 cup sour cream
1½ cups shredded cheddar (about 6 ounces)
¼ cup chopped fresh chives
Freshly ground black pepper

Put the potatoes in a saucepan, cover with cold water by at least an inch, add a good pinch of salt, and bring to a boil. Reduce the heat to medium, cover part-way, and cook until the potatoes are just barely tender (you need to be able to grate them without the potatoes turning to mush). Drain the potatoes on a rack set in the sink.

Heat the oven to 350 degrees. Butter a 2-quart casserole dish (an 8-inch square pan works pretty nicely for this).

As soon as the potatoes are cool enough to handle, peel and grate them on a box grater into a large bowl. Stir in the butter, sour cream, cheese, and chives. Season with salt and pepper. Scrape the mixture into the casserole dish, smoothing the top with a spatula.

Bake until the top is golden and bubbling around the edges, about 40 minutes. Serve warm.

SCALLOPED POTATOES

Yankee cooks scallop just about anything—parsnips, oysters, codfish, leftover turkey—but this is the classic.

A heavy lidded casserole or Dutch oven is best here—pull out the cast-iron if you have one—but you can also use a deep flameproof baking dish, with heavy-duty foil to cover.

2 pounds russet potatoes, peeled
1 onion, peeled
Coarse salt and freshly ground black pepper
3 cups milk
1 1/2 tablespoons unsalted butter, cut into small pieces

Heat the oven to 350 degrees. Butter a 3-quart casserole.

Use a mandoline or sharp knife to slice the potatoes and onion into 1/8-inch slices (be sure to slice the onion crosswise, so you can separate the slices into thin rings). Layer the potatoes in the casserole, tossing in a few onion rings between layers and seasoning with salt and pepper as you go. Pour the milk over the top and dot the surface with the butter.

Cover the casserole tightly and bake for 40 minutes. Remove the lid and continue to bake until the potatoes are very (incredibly, completely) tender and the top has begun to brown, about 30 minutes more. Let sit for about 10 minutes and serve warm, directly from the casserole.

SCALLOPED POTATOES AND RUTABAGA

SERVES 8

One fixture on my mother's Thanksgiving table is a bowl of mashed potatoes and a bowl of mashed rutabaga, which she always mixes together on her plate. This is for her.

1½ pounds rutabaga
1½ pounds Maine potatoes
¼ cup dried bread crumbs
⅓ cup freshly grated Pecorino
2 tablespoons all-purpose flour
2 teaspoons fresh thyme leaves
1 teaspoon ground ginger
1 teaspoon ground mustard
Coarse salt and freshly ground black pepper
3 cups half-and-half
2 tablespoons cold unsalted butter

Heat the oven to 350 degrees. Generously butter a 9-by-13-inch casserole. Place a sheet of heavy-duty aluminum foil on the rack below the one you'll be baking on.

Quarter the rutabaga, peel it, and cut it into very thin (¹/₁₆-inch) slices. Peel the potatoes and cut them into ¹/₁₆-inch slices. Combine the bread crumbs, Pecorino, flour, thyme, ginger, mustard, and salt and pepper to taste.

Layer half of the rutabaga slices in the casserole. Cover with half of the potatoes and then sprinkle with half of the cheese mix. Repeat the layers of rutabaga and potatoes. Pour in the half-and-half, then dust the top with the remaining cheese mix. Shave the butter over the top

Slip the casserole into the oven and bake until nicely browned and tender, about 1 hour 20 minutes. Let the casserole rest for 10 minutes or thereabouts before serving.

BRAISED POTATOES

"SEETHED" POTATOES

SERVES 4 TO 6

Take out a wide saucepan, add the potatoes and the butter or oil that you would be using to dress them, pour in water, and cook until the water's cooked away, and bingo, you're seething. It's an old technique and one you can experiment with. For this recipe, we use oil with garlic and bay leaf, but there's no reason you can't try butter and rosemary, for example.

As for the potatoes: keep them small and go for heirloom varieties. Russian Banana are particularly good cooked this way, but then so too are small French Fingerlings. You want potatoes small enough so that they can be cooked whole.

1½ pounds small potatoes, scrubbed (see note above)
2 garlic cloves, peeled
1 small bay leaf
3 tablespoons olive oil
Coarse salt and freshly ground black pepper

Put the potatoes, garlic, bay leaf, and oil in a wide saucepan or deep skillet; you want the potatoes in a single layer. Barely cover with water, add a pinch of salt, and bring to a boil. Cover partway, reduce the heat to medium-high, and cook for about 20 minutes. The potatoes should be tender and most of the water will have cooked away.

Uncover and cook, stirring or shaking the pan frequently, until all the water has evaporated and the oil is sizzling. The garlic will fall apart and end up coating the potatoes.

Remove the bay leaf, dish up the potatoes in a nice bowl, and season with salt and pepper. Serve these hot.

BRAISED LAUREL POTATOES

SERVES 4 TO 6

What a technique this is! As you will see here and in the following recipe, it adapts itself to very different flavors and is suitable for medium-starchy to waxy potatoes (try it with white potatoes, skin on). The finished dish is rather like risotto; the potatoes have a bit of bite to them, and they're surrounded by a creamy sauce. Delicious.

Use the best bay leaves you can find.

1½ cups Chicken Stock (page 85)
3 bay leaves
4 tablespoons (½ stick) unsalted butter
1½ pounds red-skinned potatoes, scrubbed and cut into ⅓-inch dice
Coarse salt and freshly ground white pepper
1 garlic clove, minced
½ cup chopped flat-leaf parsley

Combine the stock and bay leaves in a small saucepan. Bring to a boil, then reduce to the lowest possible heat. Cover partway and let infuse for 30 minutes. No bubbling, though. If it starts to simmer, turn off the heat.

Melt 3 tablespoons of the butter in a saucepan over medium-high heat. Add the potatoes and some salt and white pepper and cook for 10 minutes, scraping the bottom of the pan as the potatoes start to stick. Add the garlic and parsley and cook for 2 minutes more. Pour in the stock and bay leaves and bring to a boil, then reduce to a simmer and cook, covered, for 10 minutes, stirring once or twice. Uncover the pan, increase the heat to medium-high, and cook for a minute or two to reduce the sauce. What you want is something very moist, but not soupy, and the potatoes should be just tender.

Discard the bay leaves, stir in the remaining 1 tablespoon butter, and taste for salt and pepper. Serve this right away.

BRAISED MUSHROOM POTATOES

SERVES 4 TO 6

The flavoring here is dried mushrooms, making the dish a fine accompaniment to steak. Compare this with the recipe for Braised Laurel Potatoes (page 463), and learn them well. See if they don't inspire you to come up with your own variations on this technique.

1½ cups Chicken Stock (page 85)
1 ounce dried porcini mushrooms
4 tablespoons (½ stick) unsalted butter
1½ pounds yellow-fleshed potatoes, scrubbed and cut into ⅓-inch dice
Coarse salt and freshly ground black pepper
2 generous tablespoons minced shallots
½ teaspoon chopped fresh thyme
⅓ cup freshly grated Parmesan

Bring the stock to a boil and turn off the heat. Add the dried mushrooms and let them sit for 20 minutes or so, until completely reconstituted. Spoon the mushrooms out of the stock and chop them coarsely.

Melt 3 tablespoons of the butter in a saucepan over medium-high heat. Add the potatoes and some salt and pepper and cook for 10 minutes, scraping the bottom of the pan as the potatoes start to stick. Add the shallots and thyme and cook for 2 minutes more.

Add the mushrooms and pour in the stock (do this carefully, so you leave behind any grit from the mushrooms). Bring to a boil. Reduce to a simmer, cover, and cook for 10 minutes, stirring once or twice. Uncover the pan, bring the heat back to medium-high, and cook for a minute or two to reduce the sauce. You want it moist, but not soupy.

Stir in the remaining 1 tablespoon butter and the Parmesan, taste for salt and pepper, and serve right away.

PAPRIKA POTATOES

As complicated as its flavors are, this is a simple dish to make. Serve it with pork (chops or a roast), or even a chicken, and a cucumber salad. Have some bread or rolls on hand too, for sopping.

You want a potato that will keep its shape, so white and red-skinned are the obvious choices. But I've also made this with new Yellow Finns and been more than happy with the results.

3 tablespoons unsalted butter
1 onion, thinly sliced
Coarse salt
2 teaspoons paprika
1 1/2 pounds all-purpose potatoes, peeled and cut into 1-inch chunks
3/4 cup Chicken Stock (page 85)
1 plum tomato, chopped
2 bay leaves
1 green bell pepper, cored, seeded, and cut into 1/3-inch strips
1/4 cup sour cream, at room temperature

Melt the butter in a wide saucepan over medium heat. Add the onion, 1 table-spoon water, and a pinch of salt. Cover the pan and cook, stirring once or twice, until the onion is very soft and translucent, 6 to 7 minutes.

Stir in the paprika, then add the potatoes, stock, tomato, bay leaves, and salt to taste. Bring to a boil, then scatter the bell pepper over the top. Cover the pan and simmer for 10 minutes, until the potatoes are just tender. Take the lid off, increase the heat to medium-high, and cook for another few minutes to reduce the sauce slightly. Taste for salt and reduce the heat to low.

Spoon out about 1/4 cup of the sauce into a small bowl and stir it into the sour cream, beating until completely smooth. Scrape the cream into the pan and cook just until the cream is heated. (Boil it, and it breaks—so don't.) Remove the bay leaves and serve hot.

PRIMAVERA POTATOES

This is the taste of spring.

Get the newest potatoes, the freshest peas, the most flavorful lettuce (French Crisp, if you can find it, although Bibb or Boston will work quite nicely). Vary the herb to your taste; tarragon as the cooking herb and parsley as the garnish are a good combination.

1 head lettuce (see note above), cut into ribbons
1½ pounds new red-skinned potatoes, scrubbed and cut into ¾-inch chunks
1 pound peas in the pod, shelled (about 1 cup peas)
1 tablespoon plus 1½ teaspoons chopped fresh chervil
Coarse salt and freshly ground black pepper
4 tablespoons (½ stick) unsalted butter
¼ cup Chicken Stock (page 85)

Spread the lettuce in the bottom of a saucepan. Add the potatoes and peas. Sprinkle with 1½ teaspoons of the chervil and season with salt and pepper. Cut the butter into pieces and scatter them over the vegetables, then pour in the stock. Bring to a simmer, cover, and cook gently for 30 minutes, until the potatoes are very tender.

Spoon the vegetables out with a slotted spoon into a bowl. Bring the sauce to a boil and reduce it by half.

Pour the sauce over the vegetables, sprinkle with the remaining 1 tablespoon chervil, and serve hot.

GLAZED RADISHES AND RED BLISS POTATOES

Cooked radishes are often overlooked, but we love them so. Here the radishes bleed into the potatoes, leaving the whole dish a charming rosy pink. They also give the dish a refreshing bite, just the tiniest bit peppery. And you get to use that melon baller that's been sitting in the back of the utility drawer. If you can't find small radishes, use fewer and cut them in half. If you can find fresh-dug potatoes the size of radishes, use them and skip the shaping. You need one pound.

1 1/2 pounds Red Bliss potatoes, scrubbed
2 dozen small radishes, trimmed (see note above)
3 tablespoons unsalted butter
1/2 cup Chicken Stock (page 85)
Coarse salt and freshly ground white pepper
5–7 chives, cut into 1-inch pieces

Using a 1-inch melon baller, scoop little balls out of the potatoes and drop them into a bowl of cold water to prevent discoloring. Don't worry about getting perfectly round balls—it's near impossible to do—but try to leave a bit of red peel on one side of most balls to add to the rosy color of this dish. Discard the potato trimmings. If the radishes are a lot bigger than the potato balls, cut the radishes in half.

Drain the potatoes and combine them with the radishes in a large skillet over medium heat. Add the butter and stock and season with salt and white pepper. Bring to a simmer, stir to distribute the butter, and cover tightly. Simmer until the potatoes are tender when pierced with a skewer, about 20 minutes.

Remove the cover, increase the heat to high, and continue to cook, shaking the pan to prevent sticking, until the liquid has reduced to a glaze, 3 to 4 minutes. Serve immediately, sprinkled with the chives.

NEW POTATOES AND YOUNG TURNIPS

I usually make this with very small new potatoes and Japanese turnips that are about the same size as the potatoes. Of course, this means a lot of fussy peeling of the turnips. You can easily substitute larger potatoes and turnips, both cut into ½-inch chunks.

For the potatoes, choose red-skinned or yellow-fleshed; just make sure they're really new.

2 tablespoons unsalted butter
1 large bunch (about ¼ pound once you've trimmed the tops)
   Japanese turnips, peeled
1¼ pounds small new potatoes (see note above), scrubbed
Coarse salt
½ cup heavy cream
Freshly ground black pepper
2 tablespoons thin shreds fresh basil or chopped chervil

Melt the butter in a wide saucepan over medium-high heat. Add the turnips, potatoes, and a pinch of salt and cook, stirring, for about a minute. Barely cover the potatoes with water (you'll be adding less than 2 cups) and bring to a boil. Cook, stirring occasionally, until most of the water has boiled away or been sucked up. This will take about 15 minutes.

Pour in the cream and boil until it has thickened and reduced slightly, 2 to 3 minutes. Turn off the heat, add a good hit of pepper, and taste for salt. Then spoon it all into a serving dish, garnish with the basil shreds, and serve hot, with more pepper at the table.

POTATOES IN CREAM

Only the French could come up with something so sublime, so decadent: nothing but potatoes and cream, slow-cooked together. Use any medium-starch white boiling potato (all-purpose) and heavy cream that isn't ultrapasteurized if you can get it.

The potatoes should cook in the water for just 8 to 12 minutes (depending on their size and age). Watch them carefully; you should be able to just push a skewer in, but still feel resistance. If you overcook them at this stage, you'll end up with sludge.

1½ pounds small white potatoes, scrubbed
Coarse salt
Freshly grated nutmeg
Freshly ground white pepper
1½ cups heavy cream

Put the potatoes in a saucepan, cover with cold water by at least an inch, add a good pinch of salt, and bring to a boil. Reduce the heat to medium and cook until just barely tender, 8 to 12 minutes, depending on their size. Drain the potatoes on a rack set in the sink.

When the potatoes are just cool enough to handle, peel and slice into rounds about ⅓ inch thick. Arrange the potatoes in a 10-inch skillet. Season with a few gratings of nutmeg, some salt, and some white pepper and pour in the cream. The cream should just barely cover the potatoes.

Slowly bring to a simmer over medium-low heat. Don't stir the potatoes, or they may break apart. Instead, gently shake the pan from time to time to ensure that the potatoes aren't sticking. Continue to simmer softly until the cream becomes ivory-colored and quite thick, about 25 minutes. The cream should have reduced by about half in volume.

Remove from the heat, correct the seasoning, and let the potatoes sit for 5 minutes before serving.

SOUPY STEWED POTATOES

This is a recipe for those times when you have a handful of
mismatched potatoes left in the bin. Start with one medium russet
and add whatever yellow-fleshed and waxy varieties you can find.
The russet cooks down to soft-edged bits, offering its starch to
thicken the dish, while the waxier varieties maintain their shape,
adding texture and color to the soupy mix. Chives would be good in
place of, or in addition to, the parsley. Chervil too. This is from
Deborah Madison's *Vegetarian Cooking for Everyone.* As she says,
"Sometimes the plainest foods are the most satisfying."

1½ pounds mixed potatoes (see note above), peeled and cut into ½-inch cubes
3 tablespoons unsalted butter
6 whole scallions, chopped
1 cup milk
Coarse salt and freshly ground black pepper
2 tablespoons chopped flat-leaf parsley

Combine the potatoes, butter, scallions, and milk in a wide saucepan. Add
enough water so that the potatoes are just barely covered. Season with salt and
pepper and bring to a boil over medium heat. Lower the heat to a simmer,
cover, and cook until the potatoes are tender, 18 to 20 minutes. Check from
time to time to see that the liquid is not boiling too vigorously.

Remove the cover and increase the heat to medium-high. Boil gently, stirring a few times, to evaporate some of the liquid and thicken the stew, 5 to 8
minutes. Stir in the parsley and taste for salt and pepper. Serve warm.

SICILIAN POTATOES WITH SAFFRON AND HERBS
(PATATE ALLA ZAFFERANO)

Here's the best of Sicilian cooking: a simple dish with refined flavor. Sicilians always put onions and garlic into a cold pan when they start cooking. It's actually a lovely technique, which helps ensure that you don't scorch the aromatics. I learned the technique, and this recipe, from cooking teacher Anna Tasca Lanza.

Generous pinch of saffron threads
1 red onion, chopped
¼ cup olive oil
2 pounds yellow-fleshed potatoes, peeled and cut into 1-inch chunks
⅔ cup chopped flat-leaf parsley
1 teaspoon dried oregano, preferably Mediterranean
2 tablespoons freshly grated Pecorino
Coarse salt and freshly ground black pepper
2 lemons, cut into wedges

Crumble the saffron into 1 cup warm water and let it sit for about 10 minutes.

Put the onion and oil in a large skillet (one that will just about hold the potatoes in a single layer, and that has a cover). Turn the heat to medium and cook until the onion is soft and translucent and just starting to turn gold at the edges. Add the potatoes, the saffron water, and 2 more cups warm water. Bring to a boil, reduce the heat to low, cover, and simmer gently until the potatoes are very tender, about 20 minutes.

Uncover the pan, add the parsley, oregano, and Pecorino, and increase the heat to medium. Cook, stirring and breaking up the potatoes, until the cooking liquid has been absorbed. Season with salt and pepper, and serve on a flat dish surrounded with the lemon wedges, so you can get a nice fresh hit of lemon with each serving.

LYONNAISE POTATOES

Lyonnaise refers to the addition of onions to most any dish. The classic formula for these potatoes is one part potato to four parts onion.

This is especially nice with smaller potatoes, because small rounds are easier to sauté. With young, thin-skinned varieties, we like to leave the skin on. Yes, we like the texture, but more, we like that the skin helps hold the rounds together. Classically, though, the potatoes are peeled before slicing. Escoffier would add the chopped parsley at the end.

1½ pounds all-purpose or red-skinned potatoes, scrubbed
Coarse salt
4 tablespoons (½ stick) unsalted butter
2 onions, thinly sliced
Freshly ground black pepper
3 tablespoons vegetable oil, or as needed
2–3 tablespoons chopped flat-leaf parsley (optional)

Put the potatoes in a saucepan, cover with cold water by at least an inch, add a good pinch of salt, and bring to a boil. Reduce the heat to medium, cover partway, and cook until the potatoes are just tender enough to pierce with a skewer, 5 to 7 minutes, depending on their size. Drain the potatoes on a rack set in the sink.

While the potatoes cook, melt 3 tablespoons of the butter in a large skillet over medium-low heat. Add the onions, season with salt and pepper, and cook, stirring often, until very soft and blond, 12 to 15 minutes. Transfer the onions to a bowl, scraping the pan to remove any last bits. Save the skillet for sautéing the potatoes.

As soon as the potatoes are cool enough to handle, peel if desired and slice into ¼-inch-thick rounds. Set the skillet over medium-high heat and add the remaining 1 tablespoon butter and enough oil to generously coat the pan. When hot, add only as many potatoes as you can fit in two layers. Unless you have a very large skillet, plan to sauté the potatoes in at least two batches, adding a bit more oil in between; otherwise, they will turn to mush and never brown up. Sauté the potatoes, turning with a spatula, until nicely browned on both sides, 12 to 15 minutes.

Return all the potatoes and the onions to the pan. Toss to combine and cook for another minute. Taste for seasoning, add the parsley, if desired, and serve warm.

POTATOES IN WINE

Another simple side dish, this time from the south of France. Serve it with roasted or grilled meat. Use waxy potatoes; if you can find small—two-bite size—red-skinned potatoes, use them and leave them whole. You needn't peel them completely; just take off a belly band.

4 slices bacon
1 tablespoon unsalted butter
1/2 pound pearl onions, peeled
1 pound waxy potatoes, peeled and cut into chunks (see note above)
1 1/2 cups dry white wine
1 bay leaf
Coarse salt and freshly ground black pepper

Dice the bacon and brown it in a saucepan. Remove the bacon with a slotted spoon and set aside; pour off all but about 1 tablespoon of the fat.

Add the butter and onions to the pan and cook for several minutes, to give the onions some color. Add the potatoes, wine, bay leaf, and salt and pepper to taste and bring to a boil. Cook, uncovered, until the potatoes are very tender.

Remove the potatoes and onions with a slotted spoon and place in a serving dish. Cook the wine over high heat until reduced and slightly syrupy, 3 to 5 minutes. Remove the bay leaf, sprinkle the potatoes with the bacon, pour the sauce over, and serve.

POTATOES WITH CUMIN SEEDS AND RED CHILES

This recipe works with either Yukons or waxier red or white potatoes. While the waxy potatoes tend to hold their shape better, we prefer Yukons because they get a bit creamier and soak up more flavor. The pan is tightly covered during cooking, so the potatoes become saturated with the flavor of the spices. They're addictive. The recipe comes from our friend Samia Ahad.

Use whole dried Thai chiles. Don't chop them, or the seeds will make the whole dish too hot. If you can't find Thai, use dried cayenne peppers.

1/4 cup vegetable oil
1 tablespoon cumin seeds
6 small dried chiles (see note above)
6 garlic cloves, thinly sliced
1 1/2 pounds yellow-fleshed or all-purpose potatoes, peeled and sliced into 1/4-inch-thick rounds
Coarse salt

Heat the oil in a large, preferably nonstick, skillet over medium heat. Add the cumin seeds and chiles and cook until fragrant and the cumin seeds are lightly browned, 2 to 3 minutes. Add the garlic and cook for another 30 seconds.

Add the potatoes and salt to taste. Shake and stir to distribute the seasonings. Cover the skillet and immediately lower the heat to medium-low. Cook, flipping the potato slices gently with a spatula occasionally, until the potatoes are tender, about 30 minutes. If the potatoes begin to brown during cooking, lower the heat a bit. They should be quite tender and saturated with flavor.

Serve hot.

CURRIED GREEN BEANS AND POTATOES

You control the heat here by seeding (or not) the jalapeño (it's nice being in control, isn't it?). This is a fine spicy side dish, or serve it over rice as a main course—in which case, plan on its feeding only 4.

1 tablespoon mustard seeds
2 teaspoons cumin seeds
2 tablespoons vegetable oil
1 tablespoon garam masala (available in Indian markets)
1 small jalapeño or serrano, seeded if desired, minced
1 red onion, thinly sliced
1 teaspoon grated fresh ginger
1 garlic clove, minced
3/4 pound green beans, topped, tailed, and cut into 1-to-2-inch lengths
Coarse salt and freshly ground black pepper
1 pound small yellow-fleshed potatoes, scrubbed and cut into 1-inch pieces
1 cup plain yogurt
2 tablespoons chopped cilantro

Toast the mustard and cumin seeds in a large heavy saucepan over high heat, shaking frequently until they pop, about 2 minutes. Add the oil, garam masala, and jalapeño and cook for another few seconds. Lower the heat to medium and add the onion, ginger, and garlic. Cook, stirring occasionally, until the onion is tender, about 5 minutes.

Add the green beans and 1 1/2 cups water, and season with salt and pepper. Bring to a boil, cover partway, and lower the heat to a simmer. Cook until the beans are quite tender and the liquid has almost all evaporated, about 25 minutes.

Meanwhile, cook the potatoes in salted water until just tender. Drain.

Add the potatoes to the beans after the initial 25 minutes. Stir to combine and cook for another minute. Reduce the heat to medium-low and stir in the yogurt. Simmer until the liquid is somewhat reduced, another 10 minutes. Stir in the cilantro and taste for salt and pepper. Serve warm.

POTATO RATATOUILLE
WITH CUMIN AND CILANTRO

Adding potatoes to tomatoes and eggplant, as our friend Samia Ahad does in this twist on ratatouille, makes perfect sense. The little bit of sugar in the potato offsets any bitterness the eggplant may bring to the dish, and it balances the heat of the chiles. This stew has a nice deep heat, and the Yukon potatoes get all creamy and soak up the flavor of the spices.

If you can get them, use local ripe plum tomatoes. And if you can't find green chiles at an Indian or Asian market, substitute serranos or jalapeños. We like to leave the skin on the eggplant to add color to the dish.

$^1/_4$ cup vegetable oil

2 teaspoons cumin seeds

2 garlic cloves, minced

1 teaspoon grated fresh ginger

$^1/_2$ teaspoon ground turmeric

1 (28-ounce) can whole peeled tomatoes, with their juice, or $1^1/_2$ pounds
  ripe plum tomatoes, peeled (see page 30)

2 teaspoons sugar

Coarse salt

$1^1/_4$–$1^1/_2$ pounds yellow-fleshed potatoes, peeled and cut into $^1/_2$-inch cubes

4 small green chiles, minced (see note above)

1 eggplant (about 1 pound), unpeeled, cut into $^3/_4$-inch cubes

2 tablespoons fresh lemon juice

$^1/_4$ cup packed cilantro leaves, chopped

Heat the oil in a large saucepan over medium-high heat until it shimmers. Add the cumin seeds and fry until fragrant and beginning to darken, about 1 minute.

Stir in the garlic, ginger, and turmeric and cook for 30 seconds. Add the tomatoes with their juice and break them up a bit with a wooden spoon. Season with the sugar and salt and cook until heated through, about 3 minutes.

Stir in the potatoes and chiles. Reduce the heat to medium-low, cover, and simmer gently until the potatoes are just tender enough to yield to a skewer, about 15 minutes.

Add the eggplant, stir to combine, cover, and continue cooking, stirring occasionally, until all the vegetables are tender, 25 to 30 minutes longer.

Stir in the lemon juice and cilantro. Taste for salt and serve warm. This is a very forgiving dish and tastes just as good—some folks say better—reheated a few hours or even a day later.

BOILED POTATOES

STEAMED NEW POTATOES

SERVES 4 TO 6

The flavor of new potatoes—real freshly dug new potatoes—is much more delicate than that of potatoes that have been stored. And their texture is meltingly soft. They deserve to be gently treated, and an herby steaming is just such a gentle treatment.

I've given quantities here, but this is the kind of thing you should adapt to your own taste. Do look for the smallest, newest potatoes you can find.

1 cup dry vermouth
1 bay leaf
1½ pounds new potatoes, scrubbed
4 tablespoons (½ stick) unsalted butter, at room temperature
¼ cup chopped fresh herbs (use a mix of tender herbs like basil, mint, tarragon, chervil, and/or thyme)
Coarse sea salt

Combine the vermouth and bay leaf with 1 cup water in the bottom of a steamer. Cover, bring to a boil, reduce the heat to a simmer, and cook for 5 minutes.

Put the potatoes in the steamer insert, place it in the pot, cover, and steam until very tender. Check for doneness with a skewer.

Turn the potatoes out into a serving bowl, toss with the butter and herbs, sprinkle with sea salt, and serve right away.

VARIATION

If you can't find any truly new potatoes, use very small red-skinned ones. Just as you finish steaming them, melt the butter in a skillet over medium heat. Add the steamed potatoes and herbs to the skillet, and roll the potatoes around until they are well coated. Sprinkle with salt and serve.

COMPOSED BUTTERS

We use these mostly for boiled potatoes, but once you've made a few batches, you'll find lots of other uses: as a spread on good bread, melted onto a steak or a piece of fish hot off the grill, whisked into pan sauces just before serving, and so on.

Below are some of our favorites for potatoes, but we encourage you to come up with combinations of your own.

8 tablespoons (1 stick) unsalted butter, softened
Flavorings of choice (see below)

Smash the butter with a wooden spoon in a smallish bowl. The butter should be soft enough to work easily, but if it starts to look oily at all, return it to the refrigerator for a bit to firm up.

Add the ingredients from the choices listed on the following pages and work them into the butter with a wooden spoon. Taste for salt and pepper, but not all the butters need this seasoning.

Scoop the butter out onto a sheet of waxed paper or foil and use a spatula to shape the butter into a rough log, say, 4 to 5 inches long. Wrap the paper around the butter, shaping it into a uniform cylinder as you roll it. Twist the ends closed—it will look something like a long party-popper. Refrigerate until solid and well chilled, at least 2 hours.

These butters will keep in the refrigerator for several days and in the freezer for up to a month.

ANCHOVY BUTTER
6–8 anchovy fillets, drained and minced
1 teaspoon fresh lemon juice
Coarse salt and freshly ground white pepper

HERB BUTTER
3 tablespoons mixed herbs, including chives, parsley, chervil, and tarragon (use less
    tarragon proportionately than other herbs; any herb blossoms make a pretty addi-
    tion)
1 teaspoon fresh lemon juice
Coarse salt and freshly ground white pepper

DILL-LEMON BUTTER
2 tablespoons chopped fresh dill
1 small shallot, minced
1/2 teaspoon grated lemon zest
1/2 teaspoon fresh lemon juice
Coarse salt and freshly ground white pepper

ORANGE-MINT BUTTER
2 tablespoons chopped fresh mint
1 teaspoon grated orange zest
1 tablespoon fresh orange juice
Coarse salt and freshly ground white pepper

CAPER-ROSEMARY BUTTER
2 tablespoons capers, rinsed, drained, and chopped
1 tablespoon minced fresh rosemary
Coarse salt and freshly ground white pepper

CUMIN-LIME BUTTER

1 1/2 teaspoons ground cumin (freshly toasted and ground seeds are best)

1 teaspoon ground coriander

1/8 teaspoon cayenne pepper, or to taste

Juice of 1/2 lime

1 garlic clove, minced

1 teaspoon sweet paprika (optional)

Coarse salt

ROASTED GARLIC BUTTER

10–12 garlic cloves, unpeeled

1 teaspoon olive oil

Coarse salt and freshly ground black pepper

Heat the oven to 350 degrees. Place the garlic on a sheet of foil, drizzle with the oil, season with salt and pepper, and seal into a tight package. Roast until quite soft, about 30 minutes. Then cool, peel, and mash the garlic before combining it with the butter. Season again with salt and pepper.

SHALLOT, BLACK PEPPER, AND BALSAMIC BUTTER

2 tablespoons chopped shallots

1 tablespoon balsamic vinegar

Coarse salt

1 1/2 teaspoons cracked black pepper

Heat a small skillet over medium-high heat. Add about 2 teaspoons of the butter and the shallots and sauté until soft, about 4 minutes. Add the balsamic and cook until it's reduced and syrupy. Let the shallots cool completely before you add them to the remaining butter. Season with salt and the pepper.

NEW POTATOES
WITH BACON

SERVES 4 TO 6

You don't really need a recipe for this, but I want to make sure you know about it. This is a nice thing to do to a potato.

1½ pounds new potatoes, scrubbed
Coarse salt
4–6 slices best bacon, cut into matchsticks
2–3 tablespoons unsalted butter, at room temperature
Freshly ground black pepper
1 tablespoon chopped flat-leaf parsley (optional)

Scrape belly bands from the potatoes, put them in a pot with cold water to cover by at least an inch, add a good pinch of salt, and bring to a boil. Cover partway, reduce the heat to medium, and cook until the potatoes are tender. Drain well, return them to the pot, and cover with a kitchen towel. Leave them in a warm spot to steam for 5 minutes or so.

Meanwhile, cook the bacon in a skillet over medium heat until crisp. Remove it with a slotted spoon and drain it on paper towels.

To serve, toss the potatoes gently with the butter, bacon, and a few grindings of pepper, taste for salt, and garnish with parsley, if you want.

486   ONE POTATO, TWO POTATO

POMMES VAPEUR

What earns these simple steamed potatoes their French pedigree is that you shape or "turn" the potatoes into little footballs. The size depends on what you're serving them with. For example, those accompanying fillet of sole would be slender and dainty, while those alongside sausages or chops would be bigger and beefier. You'll need 2 to 2½ pounds of potatoes to make 4 servings because you lose a good deal in trimmings when you shape the potatoes. But think how much you'll gain in elegance.

2–2½ pounds red-skinned or white potatoes, peeled
2 teaspoons chopped flat-leaf parsley
Coarse salt

Use a sharp paring knife to "turn" the potatoes (see page 488) into quenelle or football shapes—about 2 inches long by 1 inch thick if you're serving them with fish, 2½ inches by 1½ inches if meat or poultry is on the menu. Drop them into a large bowl of cold water as you work; discard the trimmings, or use them right away for a quick soup or sauté. When all the potatoes are cut, drain them.

Steam the potatoes over boiling water until tender. Toss the potatoes with the parsley and season with salt. Serve warm. And no, they really *don't* need butter.

THE ART AND CRAFT OF *TOURNER*

Only the French would come up with a method of carving small chunks of vegetables to make each perfectly tidy and identical to the next. The practice of "turning" was popularized in the heyday of France's haute cuisine by Carême, one of the greatest chefs of all time. Today the idea may seem silly. Maybe it's wicked waste. But just maybe. There are times when we think these neatly carved spuds have their place.

The relatively soft flesh of a potato (compared with a carrot, say) makes it one of the least laborious vegetables to turn.

First step is to peel the potato. Then cut it into blocks or wedges a bit longer and fatter than you intend the end shape to be (3 inches long by about 2 inches wide is a good place to start). Hold one of the blocks of potato with the thumb and forefinger of one hand and choke up on a small paring knife in the other hand, getting the handle deep into the palm of your hand and your fingers up at the base of the blade. The first cut you want to make is a continuous arc curving from the exact center of the top of the block, coming down, widening out, and then curving back in to the center of the bottom of the block. After you make one cut, rotate the piece of potato slightly and make a subsequent identical cut. The idea is to work your way around the potato, trimming it into a neat elongated miniature football or zeppelin shape. It may help to imagine a long skewer running lengthwise through the exact center of the block of potato. Each of the arcing cuts should start and end at the exact spots where the skewer would enter and leave the potato.

Once you get the hang of trimming square blocks of potatoes into smooth oblong shapes, you should be able to make swift continuous movements—you get smoother, prettier results this way. Choppy stop-and-go whittling will make an amateurish turned potato. Classically, a turned vegetable will have seven matching sides, but unless you intend to enter a cooking competition, who's counting? The main objective is to get the pieces to be all more or less the same shape and size. You can take a look at the photograph of Château Potatoes for a good idea of how a nicely turned potato should look.

As you turn the potatoes, drop them into a bowl of cold water to keep them from browning. It's a good idea to pick one of your best pieces, though, and set it down on the counter as a model to work from. Otherwise, you may find that as you work, your pieces gradually distort from the original, getting skinnier, rounder, longer, or otherwise mis-shapen.

There's no denying that turning potatoes takes time and creates quite a bit of waste. If you like, the trimmings can go into a soup, mashed potatoes, or croquettes—or you may find it easiest just to add them to the compost heap. For cooks whose *batterie de cuisine* is never complete, there are hook-shaped knives intended for turning vegetables.

DILLED NEW POTATOES

SERVES 4 TO 6

Save this recipe for the summer, when heaps of fresh dill are easy to
find and there are plenty of tiny new potatoes around. If you've got
dill in the garden, use the flowers as well as the tender stems and
fronds. When simmered with the herbs, the potatoes (which should
be of the creamy and thin-skinned school, something like a French
Fingerling, Desiree, Red Gold, or Red Norland) become deeply
infused with the sweet anise flavor of dill, so much so that they don't
even need butter.

You might think about cooking potatoes this way to use in salad
too. It gives them an extra flavor dimension that carries through
even after they've been cooled.

1¹/₂ pounds small potatoes (see note above), scrubbed
2 cups loosely packed fresh dill (include tender stems)
Coarse salt
Unsalted butter (optional)
Fresh lemon juice (optional)

Leave the potatoes whole if they are very small; otherwise, cut them in half.

Put the dill into a large saucepan and dump the potatoes on top—this will
keep the dill from floating at the start. Fill the pan with cold water to cover the
potatoes by at least an inch and add a good pinch of salt. Bring to a boil, then
reduce to a moderate simmer. Cover partway and cook until the potatoes are
tender. Drain, and lift out the largest bits of dill. Don't worry if there are a few
pieces of dill left on the potatoes—they'll only add flavor. Serve plain or toss
with butter. A squeeze of lemon is not unwelcome either.

DRYING BOILED POTATOES

There's no getting around it: cook a potato in water, and it will come out slightly soggy. Here are two options for drying them out before you season and serve them.

If your potatoes have fairly sturdy skins (as do flavorful Estima and other yellow-fleshed potatoes) and you've left them whole and unpeeled, you can return them to the pot and put them back over the heat, shaking the pan and stirring gently for a minute or so until the potatoes dry. The disadvantage is that you run the risk of breaking the potatoes.

Your best bet is to drain the potatoes in a colander, return them to the pot—make sure there's no water left in it—and cover the pot with a kitchen towel. Let the potatoes sit in a warm corner of the stove for 5 minutes.

LEMON POTATOES

Lemon dressing is a nice sharp foil to the sweetness of new potatoes. Make this in advance of when you plan to serve it to give the potatoes a chance to cool in the dressing and absorb its goodness.

New red potatoes are best (French Fingerlings are also especially nice), but the recipe will work well with older waxy potatoes. If your potatoes are large, peel them and cut them into 2-inch chunks. Lemon thyme really makes the dish, but you can substitute regular thyme — just up the amount of zest.

1½ pounds small new Red Bliss potatoes, scrubbed
Coarse salt
Grated zest of 1 large lemon
3 tablespoons fresh lemon juice
½ teaspoon sugar
½ teaspoon chopped fresh lemon thyme (see note above)
Pinch of dried oregano, preferably Mexican
Freshly ground black pepper
5 tablespoons fruity olive oil

Scrape off a belly band around the waist of each potato. Put the potatoes in a saucepan, cover with cold water by at least an inch, add a good pinch of salt, and bring to a boil. Cover partway, reduce the heat to medium, and boil gently until the potatoes are tender. Drain, then return them to the pot and cover with a kitchen towel so they can steam dry while you make the dressing.

Combine the lemon zest, juice, sugar, thyme, oregano, and salt and pepper to taste in a small bowl. Give it a whisk. Pour in the oil in a thin stream, whisking all the while, until the dressing is lightly frothy and emulsified.

Put the potatoes in a wide serving dish (they should all be able to sit in the dressing), pour in the dressing, and stir to coat well. Cover the dish and let the potatoes sit for at least half an hour before serving, stirring once or twice.

These can be served warm or at room temperature.

GRATING THE EASY WAY

A few years ago, a tool called the rasp made the trip from the fine-woodworking shop to the kitchen. If you haven't been converted yet, go and buy one. With next to no effort, you get piles of light, fluffy grated zest or horseradish. Rasps—also known as microplanes—are available in most specialty kitchen stores and in a wide variety of on-line and mail-order sources, such as Amazon.com and Martha by Mail (1-800-950-7130).

SAFFRON POTATOES

Simple, and quite elegant. These belong on your fancy china, with anything from a roast to a stew. For even cooking, make sure the potatoes are all about the same size. If you have the time and want to show off your knife skills, by all means turn them (see page 48).

If you want the most intense color, use a yellow-fleshed potato. If you're a lily gilder, by all means serve the potatoes with butter.

Pinch of saffron threads
3 tablespoons unsalted butter
2 pounds smallish waxy or all-purpose potatoes, peeled
Coarse salt

Crumble the saffron into about a cup of warm water and let it dissolve.

Melt the butter in a wide saucepan (you want a lot of surface area so you can brown the potatoes) over medium heat. When the foaming subsides, add the potatoes and brown them on all sides, 10 to 15 minutes. Add the saffron water and salt, with enough additional water to just cover the potatoes. Cook, uncovered, until the potatoes are very tender and the water has evaporated. Turn the potatoes over with a wooden spoon as they cook.

Serve hot.

WIDOWED POTATOES
(PATATAS VIUDAS)

SERVES 4

According to Spanish cooking expert Penelope Casas, from whom I've adapted this recipe, "widowed" refers to the idea of the potatoes being the only main ingredient in the dish. This began as a meal, but Casas converted it into a side dish. I like it sitting next to veal cutlets, with a squirt of lemon on both the veal and the potatoes.

1½ pounds white potatoes, peeled and cut into ¾-inch cubes
Coarse salt
2 tablespoons olive oil
1 small onion, finely chopped
2 garlic cloves, minced
2 tablespoons chopped flat-leaf parsley
1 bay leaf
2 tablespoons dry vermouth or dry white wine
½ teaspoon paprika (sweet or hot, it's your choice)

Put the potatoes in a saucepan, cover with cold water by at least an inch, add a good pinch of salt, and bring to a boil. Reduce the heat to medium, cover partway, and simmer until the potatoes are just tender.

Meanwhile, heat the oil in a large skillet over medium heat until it shimmers. Add the onion, garlic, parsley, and bay leaf and sauté until heated through, about 2 minutes. Season with salt. Add the vermouth, cover, and reduce the heat to medium-low. Continue cooking until the onion is soft, about 10 minutes. Stir in the paprika and leave the skillet in a warm corner of the stove.

Drain the potatoes, saving ⅓ cup of the cooking water. Return the skillet with the onion to medium heat. Dump the potatoes and reserved cooking water into the skillet and stir to combine. Cook, stirring a few times, until some of the liquid is absorbed and the seasonings lightly coat the potatoes, about 2 minutes. Remove the bay leaf and serve warm or hot.

SUGAR-BROWNED POTATOES

SERVES 4

I found this in Nika Hazelton's invaluable *The Unabridged Vegetable Cookbook*. She says the origin's Danish.

It's actually a rather nice change from plain buttered potatoes, and the salty caramel coating makes these a fine match for a ham or duck or a crusty roast of pork.

12 small red-skinned or white potatoes, peeled
Coarse salt
2 tablespoons unsalted butter
3 tablespoons sugar

Put the potatoes in a large saucepan, cover with cold water by at least an inch, add a good pinch of salt, and bring to a boil. Cover partway, reduce the heat to medium, and cook until the potatoes are tender. Drain carefully—you don't want to break the potatoes—on a rack set in the sink.

Melt the butter in a skillet large enough to hold the potatoes in a tight single layer. Add the sugar and about 1 teaspoon salt and cook over medium heat, stirring vigilantly, until the sugar melts and turns a pleasant medium-amber color. Reduce the heat to low and add the potatoes. Cook, turning the potatoes constantly and gently, until they are well coated and most of the caramel has been absorbed.

These look rather nice on a small platter, rather than in a bowl. If you want them to look even prettier, garnish them with some fresh herb leaves. Serve hot.

CANDIED SWEET POTATOES

Yes, you can candy sweets on top of the stove after you've boiled them and they'll be sweet and tender, just as they should be. Back the sugar down to 2 to 3 tablespoons if you like, but then they won't really be candied. The salt and pepper isn't traditional, but we like it.

2 pounds sweet potatoes
Coarse salt
4 tablespoons (1/2 stick) unsalted butter
1/4 cup packed light brown sugar
Freshly ground white pepper

Put the sweet potatoes in a saucepan with a large amount of water, add a small pinch of salt, and bring to a boil. (If the potatoes are too long to fit in the pot, cut them in half.) Reduce the heat to medium and simmer until the potatoes are just tender and not at all mushy, 15 to 25 minutes, depending on their size. Drain and let the sweet potatoes cool on a rack in the sink.

When the potatoes are cool enough to handle, peel and cut them into 3/4-inch slices or 1-inch chunks.

Melt the butter in a large wide saucepan over medium heat. Stir in the brown sugar and 1/4 cup water and heat until the sugar is dissolved.

Put the sweet potatoes into the sugar-butter mix, season lightly with salt and white pepper, and stir gently to coat. Reduce the heat to medium-low and cover the pan. Cook, gently shaking and stirring occasionally, until the potatoes are glazed and tender, 10 to 15 minutes.

Serve warm.

WALNUT AND CUMIN SAUCE

The thick and spicy sort of walnut pesto is easily and quickly made while you boil up some potatoes. And if that, indeed, is when you make it, spoon in potato water to thin the sauce. Otherwise, plain tap water will do just fine.

2 small garlic cloves, smashed
2 tablespoons chopped walnuts
2 tablespoons chopped flat-leaf parsley
2 tablespoons minced pimiento
¹/₂ teaspoon cumin seeds
Coarse salt
¹/₄ cup extra-virgin olive oil

Combine the garlic, walnuts, parsley, pimiento, and cumin seeds in a small food processor or a large mortar. Add a good pinch of salt and process to a rough puree, or use a pestle to mash in the mortar. Add up to 2 tablespoons of the potato water as you work to achieve a pastelike consistency.

Drizzle in the olive oil with the motor running, or while stirring with the pestle. Taste for seasoning.

The sauce can be made ahead and kept covered in the refrigerator for a day. Let it return to room temperature before serving.

Spoon the sauce over warm boiled potatoes, tossing to coat, or pass it at the table.

MUSHROOM SAUCE

The pairing of mushroom sauce and boiled potatoes is Swedish. But try the sauce on a steak, on toast, or just on its own. You can make it as simple or as exotic as you like by varying the types of mushrooms you use.

2 pounds mushrooms (cremini and button), thinly sliced
3 tablespoons unsalted butter
1 tablespoon olive oil
1 small white onion, minced
1 lemon
Coarse salt and freshly ground black pepper
1/2 cup sour cream
Chopped fresh dill, plus 1 sprig, for garnish

Heat the oven to 300 degrees.

Put the mushrooms in a baking dish large enough to hold them in just about two layers. Dot with the butter, drizzle with the oil, and scatter in the onion. Squeeze the juice from half the lemon over the mushrooms and season with salt and pepper.

Bake for 45 minutes, stirring several times, until the mushrooms are well cooked and the juices have thickened.

Spoon about a third of the mushrooms into a food processor and add 1/4 cup water—or potato water, if you have it handy. Puree until fairly smooth; it will be thick. Scrape the puree and the rest of the mushrooms, with any juices in the pan, into a mixing bowl, add the sour cream, and mix well. Squeeze in lemon juice to taste and check for salt and pepper.

Serve garnished with chopped fresh dill and a big sprig of dill. You want this in a bowl to pass at the table rather than tossed with the potatoes; it's nicer-looking that way.

ROMESCO SAUCE

In its original incarnation, this Spanish sauce was intended to accompany grilled meats or fish, but it's also good with boiled potatoes. Think of it, too, as a dip or spread for Potatoes Roasted in Salt (page 34).

If you don't have a gas stove, you can char the pepper and tomatoes in a hot cast-iron skillet.

1 red bell pepper
2 plum tomatoes
2 tablespoons olive oil
2 large garlic cloves, coarsely chopped
1 slice good white bread, crusts discarded and cut into small cubes
3 tablespoons walnut halves
¼ cup dry red wine
2 tablespoons red wine vinegar
½ teaspoon paprika
Coarse salt and freshly ground black pepper

Roast the pepper over an open flame on the stove, turning often, until charred all over. Put it in a bag (plastic or paper) or wrap it in foil, and let it steam for at least 15 minutes. Spear the tomatoes on a fork and hold them over the flame, turning until the skin has charred and blistered all over.

Rub the skin off the pepper, pull out the stem and seeds, cut off the ribs, and coarsely chop the pepper. Move it to a bowl (don't forget to scrape up and add any of the pepper juices from your cutting board). Coarsely chop the tomatoes—no need to peel them—and add them to the peppers. Capture these juices too.

Heat the oil in a skillet over medium-high heat until it shimmers. Add the garlic and fry until lightly browned. Remove the garlic with a slotted spoon and drop it in the food processor. Add the bread cubes to the oil and fry until golden. Remove the bread with a slotted spoon and add to the garlic. Fry the walnuts for 2 minutes, then remove, slotted spoon again, and add to the garlic.

Pour the peppers and tomatoes into the skillet and fry for 2 minutes. Pour in the wine and vinegar and bring to a boil. Scrape this into the food processor and let cool for a few minutes, then puree the sauce until smooth.

Transfer to a bowl and stir in the paprika and salt and pepper to taste. This will keep for a day or two in the refrigerator, but bring it to room temperature before serving.

Spoon some of the sauce over boiled potatoes and stir to coat, or pass it at the table.

ONION SAUCE

This is wonderfully sweet, with a little bite at the back from the cayenne. It's based on an old Victorian recipe. We like this spooned not just over boiled potatoes but over breaded chops too. And it's great in mashed potatoes (see page 280).

3 large onions, thinly sliced
1 tablespoon unsalted butter
Coarse salt
1 cup heavy cream
Pinch of cayenne pepper

Combine the onions with the butter and a good pinch of salt in a covered saucepan and sweat over medium-low heat until limp. This may take about 15 minutes.

Pour in the cream and bring to a simmer. Cover partway and simmer for 30 minutes. Let the onions cool for about 5 minutes, then puree in batches in a blender or food processor. You want this utterly smooth.

Clean the pan you've been using and pour the sauce back in. Add cayenne to taste—it really wants just a pinch, though—and cook over medium to medium-low heat until thick and reduced by half. Count on this process taking about 40 minutes. Keep an eye on it, and stir frequently so it doesn't scorch.

Serve this warm, either spooned over boiled potatoes or in a bowl on the table—or both.

ALPEN MACARONI

No doubt about it, this is nursery food. Molly got the recipe from a friend of a friend, who said he makes it whenever he needs something filling and comforting—usually late at night.

When it has just come off the stove, it wants to be served in a soup bowl and eaten with a spoon. Leave it for a bit, and it sets up like mac and cheese. If you want it really cheesy, use the stronger Gruyère and use the full amount. For a milder dish, use Emmentaler and use the smaller amount.

$1^{1}/_{2}$ pounds red-skinned or white potatoes, peeled and cut into $^{1}/_{3}$-inch dice
$3^{1}/_{2}$–4 cups Chicken Stock (page 85), or more as needed
Coarse salt and freshly ground black pepper
6 ounces elbow macaroni
2 tablespoons unsalted butter
4–6 ounces Emmentaler or Gruyère, shredded (1–$1^{1}/_{2}$ cups), to taste

Put the potatoes into a large saucepan. Add enough stock, about 2 cups, to just cover. Season with salt and pepper and bring to a simmer over medium heat. Simmer until the potatoes are almost tender, 10 to 15 minutes, adding more stock if necessary as it evaporates.

Add the macaroni and 1 more cup stock, or to cover, and return to a simmer. Continue to simmer until both the potatoes and macaroni are tender. During cooking, add $^{1}/_{2}$ to 1 cup more stock as needed so that the potatoes and macaroni are just covered.

Turn the heat to high and simmer vigorously for 2 to 3 minutes to evaporate some of the stock. The consistency will be something between a thick soup and a loose risotto. Add the butter and stir until melted. Reduce the heat to medium-low and stir in the cheese, in two additions. Season to taste with salt and pepper. Serve the macaroni immediately, or let it sit for about 10 minutes to thicken up some.

GERMAN POTATO DUMPLINGS
(KARTOFFEL KLOESSE)

MAKES ABOUT 24 DUMPLINGS

To make these light dumplings, you have to hurry and peel the potatoes immediately after cooking, then wait until they are thoroughly cool before mixing in the flour. You also have to stay alert and watch how much flour you add. Too much, and you end up with sinkers. Anne Martin, the mother of my high-school friend Dennis, first taught me to make these. She used to hide the croutons in the center of the dumplings, but I think it's nicer to fold the croutons into the dough, and that way, you're sure of finding one in every mouthful.

These really belong on the dinner table with sauerbraten and lots of spicy gravy. But I'm giving you an optional topping if you want to serve them with stew or something else juicy.

1³/₄–2 pounds russet potatoes, scrubbed
Coarse salt
4 slices good white bread, slightly stale
8 tablespoons (1 stick) unsalted butter, at room temperature
2 large eggs
¹/₄ cup farina (not instant, not quick)
Freshly grated nutmeg
About 1 cup all-purpose flour

FOR THE TOPPING (OPTIONAL)
4 tablespoons (¹/₂ stick) unsalted butter
1 cup homemade dried bread crumbs (see page 336)

Put the potatoes in a large saucepan, cover with cold water by at least an inch, add a good pinch of salt, and bring to a boil. Cover partway, reduce the heat to medium, and cook until the potatoes are tender. Drain on a rack set in the sink.

Peel the potatoes right away, holding them in a kitchen towel and putting them back on the rack as they're peeled. Once they're all peeled, put them through a ricer into a very wide bowl or onto a baking sheet. Spread them out and leave them to cool completely. (Completely means at least 2 hours.)

Trim the crusts from the bread and cut the slices into $1/4$-inch dice. Melt 4 tablespoons of the butter in a large skillet over medium heat and, when the foaming stops, add the bread. Stir well to coat all the cubes with butter and cook, stirring once in a while, until the croutons are nicely and evenly golden brown. Shake them out into a bowl and let them cool completely.

Use your hands to work the remaining 4 tablespoons butter into the potatoes—squeeze, as if you were making meat loaf. Crack in the eggs, add the farina, a few gratings of nutmeg, and salt, and mix. Add about $1/2$ cup flour and mix it in with your hands. What you want in the end is a fairly stiff, but still slightly sticky, dough. Add more flour to get there, but no more than another $1/2$ cup. How much will depend on the weather, the potatoes, and the kitchen god. Add the croutons and mix to distribute them.

Form into balls about 2 inches across and place them on a tray lined with waxed paper. You can refrigerate them, uncovered, for up to two hours.

Bring a kettle of water to a boil. (The bigger the pot, and the more water, the happier you'll be with the results.) Salt it well and drop in about half of the dumplings one by one. Try not to drop them on top of one another, and add just enough to make a single layer. Leave them be for a minute or so, then poke them gently with a wooden spoon so they don't stick to one another or to the bottom. Once the dumplings rise to the top, set the timer for 8 minutes and monitor the heat to keep the water at a steady simmer. No rolling boil. Taste a dumpling; it should be cooked all the way through, without any gumminess in the center. Remove with a slotted spoon, and place in a serving bowl, bring the water back to a full boil, and repeat with the rest of the dumplings.

FOR THE OPTIONAL TOPPING: Melt the butter in a skillet over medium heat. When it stops foaming, add the bread crumbs and cook, stirring, until the crumbs are browned. Sprinkle the crumbs over the dumplings. Serve right away.

BREADS
& ROLLS

POTATO YEAST

MAKES ABOUT 2¹/₄ CUPS

This potato yeast is a snap to make, and it's got terrific flavor—a little bit sweet and the tiniest bit sour.

Refrigerated, potato yeast will keep for about 2 weeks, but always make sure it's still living before using it: Take out what you need, let it come to room temperature, and add a pinch of sugar and a tablespoon or two of flour. If it's active, it will start bubbling in about 10 minutes.

About ³/₄ pound russet potatoes, peeled and cut into large chunks
2 tablespoons all-purpose flour
2 teaspoons molasses
1 tablespoon sugar
1 teaspoon coarse salt
1 teaspoon active dry yeast

Put the potatoes into a small saucepan with 4 cups cold water. Bring to a boil, cover partway, reduce the heat to medium, and cook until the potatoes are just about falling apart. Drain, reserving the water.

Push the potatoes through a strainer or put them through a ricer into a bowl. Add the potato water and let cool to lukewarm.

Add the flour, molasses, sugar, salt, and yeast and whisk until smooth. Cover and let sit in a warm place for 3 to 6 hours. Depending on how old your potatoes are and how much liquid they absorbed, the yeast may be quite thick. Bubbles may come quick or slow, and it will be an eerie-looking thing; if you don't see bubbles, put your ear down and listen for them. The longer you let it sit, the deeper the flavor will be.

You can use the yeast now or transfer it to a plastic container with a lid and refrigerate it. Let it come to room temperature before you proceed with any recipe. Feeding this yeast to keep it alive doesn't work; it's easier to just toss out what you don't use.

POTATO BREAD

Here's a sandwich loaf: good, simple white bread but with so much more flavor than you'd expect. It toasts beautifully, and it makes great French toast, and even better bread-and-butter pudding.

1 cup milk, plus more for glazing
4 tablespoons (½ stick) unsalted butter
2 tablespoons sugar
2½ teaspoons coarse salt
1 cup Potato Yeast (page 508), at room temperature
5–5½ cups all-purpose flour

Pour the milk into a saucepan, add the butter, sugar, and salt, and warm it over low heat, stirring, until the butter melts and the sugar dissolves. Let it cool to lukewarm.

Put the potato yeast in a large bowl, add the milk mixture, and stir in 2 cups of the flour. Beat it with a wooden spoon until it's smooth. You've made a sponge. Cover it with plastic wrap or a damp towel and let it sit in a warm place until it's light and bubbly, about 1 hour.

Stir the sponge well, then work in the remaining 3 to 3½ cups flour, to make a dough that has a nice, firm feel to it. Scrape it out onto a floured work surface and knead it until very smooth, 8 to 10 minutes.

Divide the dough in half and roll each half out to a rectangle about 9 by 15 inches. Roll each one up loosely, starting at a narrow end, and place seam side down in a buttered 8½-by-4½-inch loaf pan. Cover the pans with damp towels and let rise in a warm place until doubled, which will take about an hour. If the towels dry out during this time, remoisten them.

About 20 minutes before the end of the rising time, heat the oven to 375 degrees.

When the oven is hot, brush the loaves with milk, and carefully cut a few slashes in the tops with a very sharp knife. Bake until golden brown, about 45 minutes. Turn out of the pans and allow to cool completely on wire racks.

Store cut loaves tightly wrapped in plastic.

POTATO-CHEDDAR BREAD WITH CHIVES

MAKES 1 LARGE LOAF

This big braid is packed with potato flavor. Toast it up for ham sandwiches—what's better than cheese bread that's toasted?—or roast beef with pickles. Or pile it with crab salad, top with more grated cheddar, and broil.

This would certainly work with block cheddar from the dairy cooler, but please try to find a great cheddar like an Irish farmhouse or aged Vermont.

1/3–1/2 pound russet potato, peeled and cut into chunks
Coarse salt
2 tablespoons unsalted butter
1 cup Potato Yeast (page 508), at room temperature
4–4 1/2 cups all-purpose flour
8 ounces best-quality cheddar, shredded
1/3 cup minced fresh chives
1 large egg, beaten with 1 tablespoon milk, for an egg wash

Put the potato in a saucepan, cover with cold water by at least an inch, add a pinch of salt, and bring to a boil. Cover partway, reduce the heat to medium, and cook until the potato is just about falling apart. Drain, reserving 1 cup of the potato water.

Drop the butter into the cup of warm potato water, stir to melt the butter, and let cool to room temperature. Push the potato through the strainer into a large mixing bowl—or rice it.

Add the potato yeast, 1 cup of the flour, and the potato water to the potato and beat until smooth. Cover and let this sponge sit in a warm place for about an hour, until doubled and bubbling.

Stir in 3 cups of the flour and 2 teaspoons salt and stir well. Add another 1/2 cup flour if you need it to make a fairly stiff and not very sticky dough. Scrape the dough onto a floured work surface and knead it until very smooth. You can do these first two steps (the sponge and the dough) in a standing mixer. Just give the dough a few turns by hand to finish it.

Let the dough rest for about 5 minutes, then roll or pat it out into a large rectangle. Strew the cheese and chives over the dough, roll it up, and knead a few times in an attempt to distribute the cheese. The dough will tear, the cheese will fall out, and you will think you're doing something wrong. You're not. Patch up the dough as best you can, put it in a well-oiled bowl, turn it over, and cover it with a damp cloth. Let it sit in a warm corner until it has doubled, again about an hour.

Again scrape the dough onto a floured surface and knead it several times. Now you'll be able to work the cheese evenly through the dough in just a few turns. Divide the dough into thirds and roll each third into a rope about 2 feet long. Lay the ropes on a heavy baking sheet, with one set of ends at the far edge of the sheet. Pinch these ends together and braid the ropes loosely. (You know how to do this: outside left over middle, outside right over middle, outside left over middle, until you're done. Just remember that each time you cross an outside over a middle, that outside becomes the new middle.) Pinch the bottom ends together and tuck the top and bottom underneath the braid to neaten its appearance. Cover with a damp cloth and move it back into that warm corner to double, 45 minutes to 1 hour.

About 20 minutes before the end of the rising time, heat the oven to 375 degrees.

When the oven's hot and the dough is risen, brush the loaf with the egg wash and slip it into the center of the oven. Bake until golden brown and crusty, about 40 minutes. Cool it completely on a rack before cutting.

Store the cut loaf tightly wrapped in plastic.

SWEET POTATO–CORNMEAL SANDWICH LOAF

MAKES 2 SMALL LOAVES

Deep gold on the outside, this bread has a warm orange crumb. Slice it up for morning toast, chicken sandwiches (with romaine), or BLTs with a difference.

1 cup milk

1/4 cup sugar

1 1/2 teaspoons coarse salt

8 tablespoons (1 stick) unsalted butter, in pieces

2 packets active dry yeast

1 1/2 cups mashed sweet potatoes

5–5 1/2 cups all-purpose flour

1 cup cornmeal

1 large egg, beaten with 1 tablespoon milk, for an egg wash

Bring the milk, sugar, and salt to a boil in a small pot, stirring to dissolve the sugar. Add the butter and let cool to room temperature.

Dissolve the yeast in 1/4 cup warm water.

Put the sweet potatoes in your bread bowl and whip them vigorously with a fork. Add the liquids (milk and dissolved yeast) and stir, then add 5 cups of the flour and the cornmeal. Beat well, adding up to an additional 1/2 cup of flour if you need it to make a fairly stiff dough, then dump it out onto a floured surface and knead until smooth and glossy. (Yes, you can do all this in a standing mixer fitted with a dough hook, but you'll still have to knead it for a minute or so to finish it.)

Put the dough in a well-oiled bowl, cover it with a damp towel, and leave it in a warm place until doubled, 1 1/2 to 2 hours.

Punch it down, pull it out onto a lightly floured surface, and divide it in half. Roll each piece out into a rectangle about 8 inches wide and 12 inches long. Start at a narrow side, roll up each piece of dough lightly and put seam side down in a small (about 8-by-4-inch) loaf pan. Cover the pans with a damp cloth and leave the loaves in a warm place to rise until doubled, about 1 hour.

About 20 minutes before the end of the rising time, heat the oven to 400 degrees.

When the oven is hot, bake the loaves for 20 minutes, then brush the tops with the egg wash. Continue baking until done, about another 20 minutes. The loaves will sound hollow when tapped. Cool completely on racks.

Store cut loaves tightly wrapped in plastic.

YELLOW FINN FOCACCIA WITH THYME

MAKES ONE 11-BY-17-INCH FOCACCIA

This simple focaccia is thinner than most. Cut it into squares and put them out with drinks or pile them into a bread basket on the dinner table.

This needs fresh thyme—no substitutes, please—and good tasty potatoes. Use a good olive oil too.

1 packet active dry yeast
7 tablespoons extra-virgin olive oil
1/4 cup cornmeal, plus more for dusting
About 1 tablespoon coarse salt
3 1/2–3 3/4 cups all-purpose flour
2/3 pound Yellow Finn or other yellow-fleshed potatoes
1 tablespoon chopped fresh thyme
Coarse sea salt

Sprinkle the yeast into the bowl of a standing mixer and dissolve it in 1/4 cup warm water. Leave it be until creamy.

Add 1 1/4 cups room-temperature water to the bowl along with 1/4 cup of the oil. With the dough hook turning at low speed, add the cornmeal and 2 1/2 teaspoons of the coarse salt. Add 3 1/2 cups of the flour and, once the dough begins to come together, increase the speed to medium. Continue to knead for 7 minutes, stopping and pushing the dough down off the hook a few times. The dough should be smooth but still somewhat sticky. If it is too wet, add a few tablespoons more flour and continue kneading.

Scrape the dough out onto a lightly floured counter and shape it into a ball. Clean and oil the bowl and return the dough to it. Cover with plastic and let rise in a warm spot until about doubled, 1 to 1 1/2 hours.

Oil an 11-by-17-inch rimmed baking sheet and dust the surface with cornmeal. Turn the dough out onto a lightly floured work surface and stretch or roll it to fit the baking sheet. (It may be easier to get an even focaccia with the rolling pin, but I prefer to do it all by hand.) Transfer the dough to the baking sheet and press it to fit all the way into the corners. Stretch and shift the dough until it's even. Cover with plastic and return the dough to that warm spot to rise for another 45 to 50 minutes.

Heat the oven to 425 degrees. (If you have a pizza stone, place it on the lower rack to heat for at least 30 minutes.)

Peel the potatoes and slice them very thin. Toss with 1 tablespoon of the oil, the thyme, and a pinch of coarse salt.

Brush the surface of the focaccia generously with the remaining 2 tablespoons olive oil. Scatter the potatoes evenly on top and then, using your fingertips, make shallow indentations or dimples over the entire surface of the focaccia. Sprinkle with the sea salt and let the dough sit for 15 minutes.

Slide the focaccia onto a lower rack in the oven, putting the baking sheet directly onto the pizza stone if you're using it. Immediately lower the heat to 375 degrees and bake until just the edges are golden, about 30 minutes. Don't overbake the focaccia, or it will become too crisp.

Slide the focaccia off the baking sheet onto a cooling rack. Cut into squares and serve warm, or within a few hours of baking.

FOCACCIA FROM PUGLIA

Tender, tall, and airy. Brushing the oil and tomato paste (use the sun-dried paste if you've got it in your cupboard) over the top of the dough leaves a gorgeous rosy blush. This great focaccia, which we've adapted from a recipe by the incomparable Italian cooking expert Carol Field, is ideal for splitting in half for sandwiches.

The dough is fairly sticky and is easiest to make in a standing mixer.

1 pound white or all-purpose potatoes, peeled and cut into chunks
1 packet active dry yeast
2$^{1}/_{2}$ teaspoons coarse salt
4–4$^{3}/_{4}$ cups all-purpose flour
2 tablespoons extra-virgin olive oil
1 teaspoon tomato paste
1 teaspoon dried oregano, preferably Mediterranean
Coarse sea salt for sprinkling

Put the potatoes in a saucepan, cover with cold water by at least an inch, and bring to a boil. Reduce the heat to medium, cover partway, and cook until the potatoes are very tender. Drain the potatoes, reserving 1 cup of the cooking water.

Return the potatoes to the pan. Set over medium heat for a minute or two, shaking and stirring so the potatoes don't stick. Mash with a hand masher and beat in $^{1}/_{3}$ cup of the reserved potato cooking water. Set aside to cool.

When the potatoes have cooled to lukewarm temperature, sprinkle the yeast into the bowl of a standing mixer and dissolve it in $^{1}/_{4}$ cup warm water. Let it sit until creamy.

Add the cooled potatoes, the remaining $^{2}/_{3}$ cup cooking water, and the salt. Mix, using the paddle attachment, until well combined.

Change to the dough hook and add the flour, 1 cup at a time, kneading on low speed. Once the dough begins to come together, increase the speed to medium. Continue to knead for 7 minutes, stopping and pushing the dough down off the hook a few times. The dough should be elastic, and it will be rather sticky.

Scrape the dough onto a lightly floured work surface and shape it into a ball. Clean and oil the bowl and return the dough to it. Cover with plastic and let rise in a warm spot until about doubled, 1 to 1½ hours.

Oil two 9- or 10-inch round pans (cake pans or springform pans both work well). Turn the dough out onto a lightly floured work surface and divide it in half. Shape each half into a round and transfer the rounds to the cake pans. Oil your fingertips and gently stretch and push the dough to reach the edges of the pans. Let rest for 15 minutes.

Stretch the dough again to the edges of the pans and make dimples all over the surface with your fingertips. Cover with plastic and return the dough to that warm spot to rise for another 45 to 50 minutes. About 20 minutes before the end of rising, heat the oven to 425 degrees.

Whisk the olive oil and tomato paste until smooth. Brush the surface of the focacce with the tomato-oil mixture. Sprinkle the tops with the oregano and a bit of coarse sea salt. Let the dough sit until fully risen.

Slide the focacce onto a lower rack in the oven. Immediately lower the heat to 375 degrees and bake until golden and the edges pull away from the sides, 30 to 35 minutes. Let the focacce sit on a cooling rack for at least 10 minutes.

Cut into wedges and serve warm, or within a few hours of baking.

POTATO ROSEMARY PIZZA

We like our pizza without too many toppings. If you want to load it up, add ¼ pound of Italian sausage, sliced and fried in a bit of olive oil.

Use any tasty, not-too-starchy potato here, and bring out your best olive oil. You'll notice we use a smaller-than-usual amount of yeast in this method. The dough takes longer to rise this way, but we like the texture and flavor that results.

1 teaspoon active dry yeast
1¾–2 cups all-purpose flour
2 tablespoons cornmeal, plus more for dusting
1 teaspoon coarse salt, plus more for seasoning
3 tablespoons olive oil, plus more for brushing the crust
½ pound waxy potatoes, peeled and cut into ⅓-inch dice
1 small red onion, very thinly sliced
2 garlic cloves, minced
2 teaspoons chopped fresh rosemary
Freshly ground black pepper
4 ounces fontina, shredded (about 1 cup)

Dissolve the yeast in ¾ cup lukewarm water in a large mixing bowl or the bowl of a standing mixer. Stir in 1 cup of the flour and beat with a wooden spoon until smooth. Add the cornmeal, salt, and 1 tablespoon of the oil. Continue adding flour, ¼ cup at a time, until the dough becomes too stiff to stir. Knead the dough by hand or with the dough hook on low speed until it becomes smooth and elastic, 8 to 10 minutes, adding more flour if needed for a dough that is soft but not too sticky.

Place the dough in a lightly oiled bowl. Cover with plastic or a dampened towel and let it sit in a warm place until doubled, 2 to 2½ hours.

When the dough is nearly risen, put the potatoes in a small saucepan, cover them with cold water by at least an inch, add a good pinch of salt, and bring to a boil. Cook for 3 minutes, then drain. Transfer the potatoes to a mixing bowl and stir in the remaining 2 tablespoons olive oil, the onion, garlic, rosemary, and a good bit of salt and pepper.

Punch down the dough and let it rest for 15 minutes.

Heat the oven to 475 degrees. If you have a pizza stone, put it in the oven to heat for at least 30 minutes.

Pull the dough out onto a lightly floured surface and roll it into a 10-by-15-inch rectangle. Transfer the dough to a cornmeal-dusted peel or rimless baking sheet, and scatter the potato mixture evenly over the surface. Brush the edges with olive oil for a crisper crust. Let rise for another 15 to 20 minutes.

Cover the pizza with the cheese. Slide the pizza onto the stone, if using, or onto a baking sheet, and bake until the bottom crust is brown, about 12 minutes. Cut into squares and serve right away.

MASHED POTATO PIZZA

MAKES ONE 10-BY-15-INCH PIZZA

Yes, yes, mashed potatoes on a pizza. Go on, try it.

FOR THE DOUGH
1 teaspoon active dry yeast
1³/₄–2 cups all-purpose flour
2 tablespoons cornmeal, plus more for dusting
1 teaspoon coarse salt, plus more for seasoning
1 tablespoon extra-virgin olive oil, plus more for brushing the crust

FOR THE POTATOES
³/₄ pound russet potatoes, peeled and cut into chunks
1 small garlic clove, peeled
Coarse salt
2 tablespoons extra-virgin olive oil
2 ounces crumbly blue cheese (Maytag Blue would be fine)
Freshly ground black pepper
2 tablespoons freshly grated Parmesan
2 whole scallions, trimmed

FOR THE DOUGH: Dissolve the yeast in ³/₄ cup lukewarm water in a large mixing bowl or the bowl of a standing mixer. Stir in 1 cup of the flour and beat with a wooden spoon until smooth. Add the cornmeal, salt, and 1 tablespoon of the oil. Continue adding flour, ¹/₄ cup at a time, until the dough becomes too stiff to stir. Knead the dough by hand or with the dough hook on low speed until it becomes smooth and elastic, 8 to 10 minutes, adding more flour if needed for a dough that is soft but not too sticky.

FOR THE TOPPING: Place the dough in a lightly oiled bowl. Cover with plastic or a dampened towel and let it sit in a warm place until doubled, 2 to 2¹/₂ hours.

When the dough is nearly risen, put the potatoes and garlic in a small saucepan, cover them with cold water by at least an inch, add a good pinch of salt, and bring to a boil. Reduce the heat to medium, cover partway, and cook until the potatoes are tender. Drain them, reserving the potato water, and dump the potatoes back into the pan. The garlic will have turned to mush, so just leave it with the potatoes. Put the potatoes back on the heat and dry them, shaking the pan and stirring, until they are floury and have left a film on the bottom of the pan.

Mash them with a hand masher until very smooth, then beat in 1 tablespoon of the olive oil. Add about 3/4 cup of the potato water, little by little, beating well after each addition, to make a very loose puree. Crumble in the blue cheese and season with salt and pepper. Keep this warm (easiest to do if you cover it and put it over simmering water).

FOR THE RISING AND BAKING: Punch down the dough and let it rest for 15 minutes.

Heat the oven to 475 degrees. If you have a pizza stone, put it in the oven to heat for at least 30 minutes.

Pull the dough out onto a lightly floured surface and roll it into a 10-by-15-inch rectangle. Transfer the dough to a cornmeal-dusted peel or rimless baking sheet and spread the potatoes evenly over the surface. Brush the edges with olive oil for a crisper crust. Let rise for another 15 to 20 minutes.

Sprinkle the pizza with the Parmesan. Slide the pizza onto the stone, if using, or onto a baking sheet, and bake until the bottom crust is brown, about 12 minutes.

While the pizza cooks, cut the scallions into 2-inch lengths, then into thin julienne strips.

Scatter the scallions over the pizza when you take it out of the oven and drizzle with the remaining 1 tablespoon olive oil. Cut into squares and serve immediately.

YEASTY POTATO DINNER ROLLS

I don't think you can get any more American than this: tender, buttery, soft dinner rolls. This recipe makes lots, but they keep well in plastic bags, and leftovers are great for sandwiches and hamburgers.

3/4 pound russet potatoes, peeled and cut into large chunks
1 packet active dry yeast
1/4 cup sugar
5 1/2 cups all-purpose flour
4 large eggs
1/2 pound (2 sticks) unsalted butter, melted
1 1/2 teaspoons coarse salt
Milk for glazing
Coarse sea salt for sprinkling (optional)

Put the potatoes in a saucepan, cover with cold water by at least an inch, and bring to a boil over high heat. Cover partway, reduce the heat to medium, and cook until the potatoes are very tender, just about falling apart. Drain, reserving the water. Push the potatoes through a strainer or put through a ricer.

When the potato water has cooled to lukewarm, measure 1/2 cup, dissolve the yeast in it, and let it sit until bubbly.

Combine the potato, yeast mixture, sugar, 1 cup of the flour, and an additional 1/2 cup potato water in the bowl of a standing mixer or in a large bowl. Stir until smooth, cover with plastic wrap, and leave this sponge in a warm place until bubbling and doubled, about 30 minutes.

Add the eggs, butter, the remaining 4 1/2 cups flour, and the salt to the sponge and beat with a dough hook for about 5 minutes to make a soft, sticky, and very smooth dough. (You can also do this by hand, with a strong arm and a sturdy wooden spoon.) Cover with plastic wrap and leave it in a warm place until doubled, 2 to 2 1/2 hours.

Flour your work surface and your hands, punch down the dough, and pull it out of the bowl. Pat it out to about 3/4 inch thick. Cut out rolls with a 3-inch round cutter and place them, well spaced, on two parchment-lined baking sheets. Cover loosely with plastic and let rise until doubled, about 1 hour.

About 20 minutes before the end of the rising time, heat the oven to 425 degrees.

Brush the rolls with milk and sprinkle them with sea salt if you care to (I rather like them salted). When the oven is hot, bake the rolls until golden brown, 10 to 13 minutes, reversing the baking sheets after about 5 minutes so the rolls will brown evenly. Serve them hot.

The rolls will keep in plastic bags at room temperature for about 3 days.

ANGEL BISCUITS

Please make these. They have great flavor, a beautiful color, a tender crumb. And you can prepare the dough the day before (or even further ahead), then pull it out of the refrigerator and cut the biscuits while the oven heats, bake them, and end up with perfection.

Why? I think it's the belt-and-suspenders approach: not just yeast but baking powder and baking soda thrown in to boot. These came from the South, where they're also known as Bride's Biscuits. (Did they think the bride needed all that leavening to come up with a biscuit as light as Mama's?)

2¼ cups all-purpose flour
2 teaspoons baking powder
1 teaspoon baking soda
2 tablespoons sugar
½ teaspoon coarse salt
½ cup vegetable shortening, chilled
½ cup plain yogurt
¼ cup milk
½ cup Potato Yeast (page 508), at room temperature

Sift the flour, baking powder, baking soda, sugar, and salt into a bowl, then whisk a few times to combine them well. Add the shortening and work it in with your fingers until the mixture looks like coarse cornmeal (use a pastry cutter if you don't like to use your fingers).

Whisk the yogurt, milk, and yeast together, then pour the wets into the dry and stir with a fork until almost combined. Dump the dough out onto a lightly floured board and knead for just 30 seconds to a minute to pull it all together. You're making biscuits, not bread here: keep a light hand.

At this point, you can continue or put the dough in a plastic container, snap on the lid, and refrigerate it for up to 5 days. Either way, the baking process is the same.

Turn the oven to 400 degrees. Pat the dough out to $^1\!/_2$ inch thick, cut out biscuits with a $2^1\!/_2$-inch cutter, and put them on a baking sheet. You can gather the scraps together and cut out more biscuits. Cover with a damp cloth.

When the oven's fully heated, pop in the biscuits and bake for 15 minutes, or until they've risen well and are truly golden. Serve them hot.

BUTTERMILK SWEET POTATO BISCUITS

MAKES ABOUT 16

We sometimes adapt this biscuit dough to make a crust for a potpie or a cobbler, but there's no beating it as a plain old biscuit. Light and crusty, with a glowing orange interior, it cries out for a pat of soft butter that will melt and dribble down your chin.

2 cups all-purpose flour
2 teaspoons baking soda
1 teaspoon baking powder
Coarse salt
6 tablespoons (3/4 stick) unsalted butter, well chilled
1 cup cold baked sweet potato, peeled
1/2–1 cup buttermilk, as needed

Heat the oven to 400 degrees

Stir the flour, baking soda, baking powder, and 1/2 teaspoon salt with a fork in a mixing bowl. Drop in the butter and toss it in the flour, then cut it into pieces. Work the butter into the flour until it resembles oatmeal.

Whip the sweet potato with a fork until it's very smooth, then add it to the bowl. Work it in lightly but thoroughly with your fingers. Add 1/2 cup of the buttermilk and stir. Add just enough additional buttermilk to make a smooth and only slightly sticky dough.

Dump the dough onto a floured surface and knead it two or three times. Flatten it out to 1/2 inch thick—you can dirty a rolling pin for this if you want, but your hands will do the job just fine—and cut out biscuits with a 2 1/2-inch cutter. Put the biscuits on a baking sheet. Gather the scraps together, pat it down, and cut out more biscuits.

Brush the biscuits with buttermilk and bake for about 15 minutes, until well risen and appealingly browned. Serve hot.

SWEET POTATO
CORN MUFFINS

MAKES 12

Crusty on the outside, moist inside, these muffins are yet another compelling reason for you to roast extra sweet potatoes. I've adapted this from a recipe by southerner John Martin Taylor.

4 tablespoons (1/2 stick) unsalted butter, melted
2/3 cup cold baked sweet potato, peeled
1/2 cup corn kernels (fresh are best, but you can use frozen)
2 teaspoons minced jalapeño pepper
1 cup plain yogurt
1 cup milk
1 large egg
1 3/4 cups yellow cornmeal
1 teaspoon baking powder
1 teaspoon baking soda
1 teaspoon coarse salt

Brush 12 muffin cups with a bit of the butter. Set the muffin pan on a shelf in the middle of the oven and turn the oven on to 425 degrees.

While the oven is heating, whip the sweet potato with a fork until it's light and smooth. Add the corn, jalapeño, yogurt, milk, and egg and beat until fairly smooth. Stir in the cornmeal. Sift the baking powder, baking soda, and salt onto a little piece of waxed paper.

Once the oven's hot, stir the remaining butter and the sifted leavening into the batter.

Open the oven, pull out the rack, and quickly divide the batter among the muffin cups. Bake for 15 to 18 minutes, until the tops are golden and the muffins cooked through. They're good hot, and they're fine the next day. They keep well in plastic bags.

SWEET POTATO CRACKERS

This idea of turning a biscuit dough into crackers came from the late Southern cookbook author Bill Neal, and boy, is it a good one. They're a bit spicy, a bit sweet. Serve them with cocktails or cool lemonade.

If you've made these well in advance, you can reheat them in a 350-degree oven for 10 to 15 minutes, which will crisp them some— but we like them best within a few hours of baking.

1¼ cups all-purpose flour
2 teaspoons baking powder
1 teaspoon coarse salt
¼ teaspoon cayenne pepper
4 tablespoons (½ stick) unsalted butter, well chilled
1 cup cold baked sweet potato, peeled
About 2 tablespoons white (hulled) sesame seeds
Coarse sea or kosher salt for sprinkling

Heat the oven to 350 degrees.

Whisk the flour, baking powder, salt, and cayenne together in a mixing bowl. Cut in the butter and work it with your fingers until the mixture resembles oatmeal.

Whip the sweet potato with a fork until it is very light and smooth. Add to the dough and work it with your hands until roughly combined.

Dump the dough onto a lightly floured work surface and knead it a few times to make it smooth. Roll the dough out into a rectangle about ⅛ inch thick. The thinner you roll the dough, the crisper the crackers will be. Sprinkle the dough with about 1 tablespoon of the sesame seeds and salt to taste and roll it lightly with the rolling pin to embed the seeds in the surface. Flip the dough over, sprinkle with about 1 tablespoon more sesame seeds and salt to taste, and roll again. Cut out small crackers, about 1 by 2 inches, and place them on baking sheets.

Bake for 10 to 12 minutes, until the bottoms are nicely browned. Flip the crackers over, switch the position of the baking sheets, and bake for another 4 to 5 minutes, until crisp.

Transfer the crackers to wire racks to cool.

IRISH POTATO BREAD
(BOXTY)

MAKES 1 SMALL ROUND LOAF

What a sweet little Irish dinner bread this is. You shape the dough into a rough round on a baking sheet, not unlike soda bread, bake it until golden, and then serve it cut into wedges—ideally, slathered with plenty of sweet butter. The mix of cooked and raw potatoes makes a bread that is wonderfully tender and moist with a good bit of crunch along the edges and the bottom. If you like, add some chopped chives or maybe a few teaspoons of caraway seeds to the dough as a variation.

Serve this with stews or roasts.

3/4 pound russet potatoes, peeled
1 cup cold mashed potatoes
1 large egg
1/2 cup milk or cream, plus more for glazing
3 tablespoons unsalted butter, melted and cooled
1 cup all-purpose flour
1 tablespoon baking powder
1 scant teaspoon coarse salt

Heat the oven to 375 degrees. Grease a baking sheet.

Grate the raw potatoes, using the large holes of a box grater. Place the grated potato in the center of a clean kitchen towel, gather up the edges, and squeeze to eliminate as much water as possible. Dump the potato into a large bowl and stir in the mashed potato.

Beat the egg, milk, and butter together with a fork or whisk. Stir this into the potatoes. Stir the flour, baking powder, and salt together in a small bowl. Add the dry ingredients to the potato mixture and stir to combine. You want to make a dough that will hang together.

Flour your hands, transfer the dough to the center of the baking sheet, and pat it lightly to flatten it into a 7-inch round. Ideally you want to shape it so that it is ever so slightly raised in the center. Score a large X into the surface with a sharp knife and brush the top with milk or cream.

Bake until golden, about 30 minutes. Cut into wedges and serve. Boxty is excellent hot from the oven but can also be baked several hours in advance.

NORWEGIAN POTATO PANCAKES (LEFSE)

MAKES 8 TO 10

These thin, crepelike pancakes are both tender and a bit chewy. Because they are cooked quickly in a dry skillet, they get nice and crisp in spots as well. We make them about 8 inches across so they fit in a regular skillet and are easier to handle, but a true *lefse* cook will make them much bigger.

Molly's favorite way to eat these is hot off the griddle, smeared with butter and jam or honey. On the savory side, they are also great wrapped around thin, thin slices of smoked fish or meat.

Like crepes, *lefse* are forgiving and can keep for a day or two in the refrigerator. Simply reheat them again in the skillet you used to make them.

3/4 pound russet potatoes, peeled and cut into large chunks
2 tablespoons unsalted butter, softened
3 tablespoons cream or milk
1/2 teaspoon coarse salt
1/2 teaspoon sugar
3/4 cup all-purpose flour

Put the potatoes in a saucepan, cover with cold water by at least an inch, and bring to a boil. Reduce the heat to medium and cook until very tender. Drain the potatoes and return them to the pot. Set over medium heat for a minute or two to dry, shaking and stirring so the potatoes don't stick. Remove from the heat.

Push the potatoes through a ricer or a strainer into a bowl. Add the butter and cream and stir vigorously with a wooden spoon until smooth. Season with the salt and sugar.

Add the flour and gently work the dough with your hands to incorporate.

Do not knead the dough, but rather just turn it gently in the bowl until the dough is smooth and soft. Cover with plastic wrap and refrigerate for 4 hours, or overnight.

Turn the dough out onto a lightly floured work surface. Cut the dough in half and then cut each half into quarters or fifths. (You might want to try to roll out one pancake first to decide the size you like.) Taking one piece at a time, pat the dough into a round disk. Then use a rolling pin to gently roll the dough into a very thin pancake, about 8 inches across. You are not rolling out pie dough here—*lefse* dough is very tender and will squish and fall apart under too much pressure. Use a light hand and rotate the pancake frequently, dusting underneath with more flour and dusting the rolling pin as needed to prevent sticking. Once you get the hang of rolling out the *lefse*, you can roll one while cooking another, but at first, we find it's best to just do one thing at a time.

Heat a 9- or 10-inch cast-iron skillet over medium heat (you can use a heavy nonstick pan if you haven't got cast iron). Transfer the *lefse* to the skillet and cook until the pancake gets toasty brown in spots, about 1 minute. Flip and cook the other side for another minute. The *lefse* will puff up in spots as it cooks—these bubbles will later deflate. *Lefse* should remain tender and pliable; don't let them overcook. Transfer them to a platter or baking sheet. You may keep them warm in a low oven while you continue to roll out the remaining *lefse* and cook them. If you plan on keeping the *lefse* for a day or two, stack the cooled pancakes on a plate, separated with sheets of waxed paper. Wrap the stack in plastic and refrigerate. Reheat briefly in the same skillet before serving.

CHOCOLATE WALNUT BREAD

Here's a nice unexpected use for potato yeast. Spread slices of the bread thick with sweet butter or whipped cream cheese for an afternoon pick-me-up. Or toast slices, cut them into fingers, and serve them alongside poached fruit and ice cream.

2 ounces unsweetened chocolate, chopped
1/3 cup sugar
1 1/2 teaspoons coarse salt
1/2 teaspoon baking soda
1 cup milk
1 cup Potato Yeast (page 508), at room temperature
2 teaspoons vanilla extract
3 1/2–4 cups all-purpose flour
1 cup chopped walnuts

Combine the chocolate, sugar, salt, and baking soda in a bowl. Bring the milk to a simmer and pour it over the chocolate. Set aside to melt and cool, stirring occasionally.

Combine the potato yeast, vanilla, and 2 cups of the flour in a large bowl. Add the chocolate mixture and beat vigorously with a wooden spoon until very smooth. Cover with plastic wrap or a dampened towel and set it to rise in a warm place until doubled, 1 1/2 to 2 hours.

Work in 1 1/2 cups of the remaining flour—add up to an additional 1/2 cup if you need it to make a firm dough that isn't sticky—then turn the dough out onto a floured surface and knead until smooth and elastic. (This is a much easier task if you use a standing mixer and a dough hook. Use the smaller amount of flour and knead with the hook for 5 minutes.)

Knead the walnuts into the dough. Put the dough into an oiled bowl, cover again with plastic, and set it to rise in a warm place until doubled, about 1 hour.

Punch down the dough and scrape it onto a lightly floured counter. Roll it into a 9-by-12-inch rectangle, then roll it up loosely, starting at one of the narrow ends. Put it seam side down in a 9-by-5-inch loaf pan, cover loosely with plastic or a dampened towel, and leave it to rise until doubled, about 40 minutes.

About 20 minutes before the end of the rising time, heat the oven to 350 degrees.

When the oven is hot, make a few slits in the top of the loaf with a very sharp knife, and bake it for 40 minutes. Cool it completely on a rack before you slice it.

Store the cut loaf tightly wrapped in plastic.

STREUSEL POTATO CAKE
(KARTOFFEL KUCHEN)

There are a lot of things called potato cake in this book, but this one's a real cake, of the coffee cake school. It's based on an old Pennsylvania Dutch recipe.

1 pound russet or all-purpose potatoes, peeled and cut into chunks
8 tablespoons (1 stick) unsalted butter, cut into pieces
1 packet active dry yeast
3/4 cup sugar
2 large eggs
6 1/2 cups all-purpose flour
1/4 teaspoon freshly grated nutmeg
1/2 teaspoon coarse salt

FOR THE STREUSEL
1 cup all-purpose flour
3/4 cup packed light brown sugar
1/2 teaspoon ground cinnamon
8 tablespoons (1 stick) unsalted butter, at room temperature
1/2 cup chopped walnuts or pecans

Put the potatoes in a large saucepan, cover with cold water by at least an inch, and bring to a boil. Cover partway, reduce the heat to medium, and cook until the potatoes are very tender, just about falling apart. Drain, reserving the potato water.

Push the potatoes through a strainer or put them through a ricer. Combine the butter in a bowl with 1 1/2 cups of the potato water and leave it to melt and cool to lukewarm. Measure another 1/4 cup of potato water, let it cool to lukewarm, and then dissolve the yeast in it. Let this sit until it's bubbling.

Put the potatoes, potato water and butter, the yeast, sugar, eggs, and 2 cups of the flour in the bowl of a standing mixer (or a large bowl) and beat it until it's smooth. Cover the sponge with plastic and leave it in a warm place until it's bubbling happily, about 1 hour.

Stir the remaining 4½ cups flour, the nutmeg, and salt into the sponge. Beat with the dough hook (or a sturdy wooden spoon) for 5 minutes, until very smooth. Cover again and leave it to rise until doubled, about 1 hour.

Punch the dough down and turn it out onto a lightly floured surface. Divide it in half and shape it into two rounds. Place in two 10-inch round cake pans, cover with plastic, and leave in a warm spot to rise until doubled. This rise usually takes about 45 minutes.

About 20 minutes before the end of the rising time, heat the oven to 400 degrees and make the streusel.

FOR THE STREUSEL: Stir the flour, brown sugar, and cinnamon together in a bowl and add the butter. Work the butter in with your fingers. The mixture will become softened and a bit sticky and the color will deepen. Work in the nuts.

Strew the streusel over the cakes, taking a handful at a time and squeezing it before breaking it into large and small crumbs. Once both cakes are covered with streusel, dimple the cakes, pushing down with your fingers. You'll bury some of the crumbs and leave others on top.

Bake the cakes until golden, 20 to 25 minutes. Let them cool on a rack. Not completely cool, mind—this is so good warm. You can freeze the second cake if you care to.

MORAVIAN SUGAR CAKE

MAKES ONE 12-BY-18-INCH OR 9-BY-12-INCH CAKE

The tender, buttery potato dough for this cake is pocked with little craters filled with brown sugar and butter. The topping will seep through and make a crust under parts of the cake, and there's nothing better for breakfast, tea, snack time—whenever you need a sugar high. This doesn't keep for very long, but it's so good that it is usually gone well before it has time to get stale.

You do need a standing mixer fitted with a bread hook to make this—or a sturdy wooden spoon and a strong arm.

$^1/_3$–$^1/_2$ pound russet potato, peeled and cut into chunks
1 packet active dry yeast
5 tablespoons sugar
$2^1/_2$ cups all-purpose flour
6 tablespoons ($^3/_4$ stick) unsalted butter, melted and cooled,
   plus 2 tablespoons for the pan
2 large eggs
$^1/_2$ teaspoon coarse salt

FOR THE TOPPING
1 cup packed dark brown sugar
6 tablespoons ($^3/_4$ stick) unsalted butter
Freshly grated nutmeg

Put the potato in a small saucepan, cover with cold water by at least an inch, and bring to a boil. Cover partway, reduce to a low boil, and cook until the potato is tender. Drain, reserving the cooking water.

Measure out $^1/_2$ cup of the cooking water (discard the rest) and let it cool to lukewarm. Stir in the yeast and 1 tablespoon of the sugar and set aside to proof. It should be bubbling away in 10 to 15 minutes.

Meanwhile, rice the potato or push it through a strainer into the bowl of a standing mixer fitted with the dough hook (or a large bowl). Add 1 cup of the flour, the melted butter, eggs, yeast mixture, and the remaining 1/4 cup sugar. Mix until smooth, then beat for about 2 minutes. Mix in the salt and the flour, then beat with the hook at medium-high speed until the dough is very smooth (you can also do this with a wooden spoon). The dough will be really sticky and moist. Cover with plastic and set aside in a warm place to rise until doubled, about 1 hour.

Use the 2 tablespoons butter to grease a 12-by-18-inch baking (jelly-roll) pan generously (see note).

When the dough has risen, turn it out into the pan and push it out as far as you can. You won't be able to get it to fill the pan, but don't worry about it. Cover with plastic and let rise in a warm place for about 30 minutes.

Now gently work the dough out all the way to the edges of the pan, cover it again, and let it rise until doubled, 30 to 50 minutes.

FOR THE TOPPING: Combine the sugar, butter, and nutmeg to taste in a small saucepan. Bring to a boil over medium heat, stirring. Remove from the heat.

Heat the oven to 375 degrees. Put a large piece of heavy-duty foil on the shelf under the one you'll be using to bake the cake.

Once the dough is risen in the pan, poke it all over with your fingers and pour on the topping, paying particular attention to filling the holes. If it's a humid day, the dough may be very sticky and you won't be able to leave holes with your fingers; not to worry. Spread on the topping, then poke the cake all over with the handle of a wooden spoon.

Bake until the cake is golden brown and bubbling, about 15 minutes. Let it cool slightly and serve it warm.

If tightly wrapped, the cake will keep for a day or two, but think about warming it up some before serving it.

NOTE: If you don't have a jelly-roll pan, you can use a deep 9-by-12-inch (brownie) pan. You'll be able to spread the dough out in the pan right away, and it will take a bit longer to bake, about 18 minutes total.

STICKY BUNS

My biggest complaint with homemade sticky buns is that they always seem dry, no matter how much goop you put in them. Well, not these. Potato makes the dough moist and flavorful.

1/2 pound russet potato, peeled and cut into chunks
1 packet active dry yeast
3 cups all-purpose flour
1/4 cup sugar
2 large eggs
4 tablespoons (1/2 stick) unsalted butter, melted
Coarse salt

FOR THE GOOP
4 tablespoons (1/2 stick) unsalted butter
1 cup packed dark brown sugar
1/4 cup honey
1 heaping cup pecan halves

FOR THE FILLING
1/4 cup sugar
1/2 cup raisins
1 teaspoon ground cinnamon
Grated zest of 1 lemon

4 tablespoons (1/2 stick) unsalted butter, melted

Put the potato in a saucepan, cover with cold water by at least an inch, and bring to a boil. Reduce the heat to medium, cover partway, and cook until the potato is very tender, almost falling apart. Drain, reserving the water.

Push the potato through a strainer or put it through a ricer. Let the potato water cool to lukewarm.

Dissolve the yeast in ¹/₂ cup of the potato water (discard the rest of the water). Let it sit until bubbling, about 10 minutes. Then add it to the bowl of a standing mixer or a large mixing bowl, with the potato, 1 cup of the flour, and the sugar. Stir until smooth, cover with plastic, and let rise in a warm place until doubled, 35 to 45 minutes.

Add the eggs, butter, the remaining 2 cups flour, and a big pinch of salt to the sponge and beat with the dough hook or a wooden spoon until smooth and shiny, about 5 minutes. This will take a good 10 minutes of kneading by hand. Cover with plastic and again let rise in a warm spot until doubled, about 1 hour 15 minutes.

MEANWHILE, MAKE THE GOOP: Combine the butter, brown sugar, and honey in a saucepan and cook over medium-low heat until the butter has melted. Pour into a buttered 9-by-13-inch baking (brownie) dish and tip the dish back and forth to spread the goop out. Scatter with the pecans.

Punch the dough down and turn it out onto a floured surface. Pat and stretch the dough into a 9-by-18-inch rectangle.

FOR THE FILLING: Toss the sugar, raisins, cinnamon, and lemon zest together.

Brush the dough with the melted butter, and strew the filling over the dough, leaving about a ³/₄-inch border along the far long side. Roll the dough up from the long side without a border and pinch the seam to seal it. Cut into 12 pieces and place, cut side up, in the pan on top of the goop. Cover with plastic and let rise until doubled, about 1 hour.

About 20 minutes before the end of the rising time, heat the oven to 350 degrees.

When the oven is hot, bake the buns until the tops are golden brown and the goop is bubbling, about 30 minutes. Let cool for a few minutes, then run a knife along the edges of the pan. Cover with a baking sheet, invert, and lift off the pan—without burning yourself. Let the buns cool a bit before serving.

Leftovers will keep for a day or two tightly wrapped in plastic.

SWEET POTATO
SWEET ROLLS

MAKES ABOUT 16

The soft, rich, tender dough gets its appealing orange color from
sweet potatoes. Make these rolls for afternoon tea, or serve them the
morning after Thanksgiving, when you've got a houseful of guests.
Put the dough together the night before, using up your leftover
sweets, and let rise in the fridge overnight. If you don't have leftover
sweets, bake a pound for an hour.

1 packet active dry yeast
1 cup baked sweet potato, peeled
2 large egg yolks
6 tablespoons (3/4 stick) unsalted butter, melted and cooled
1/4 cup sugar
1 teaspoon coarse salt
3–3 1/2 cups all-purpose flour

FOR THE FILLING
5 tablespoons unsalted butter, at room temperature
1/4 cup packed light brown sugar
2 tablespoons sugar
1 teaspoon ground cinnamon
Freshly grated nutmeg
1/3 cup raisins, soaked in 3 tablespoons warm water or rum to soften, then drained

1 large egg, beaten with 1 tablespoon water, for an egg wash

Combine the yeast and 1/4 cup lukewarm water in the bowl of a standing mixer
or in a large mixing bowl. Stir to dissolve. If the potatoes have been refrigerated, warm them gently before continuing.

Add the sweet potato, egg yolks, butter, sugar, and salt to the yeast mixture

542   ONE POTATO, TWO POTATO

and stir with a wooden spoon to combine. Stir in 2 cups of the flour, adding it 1 cup at a time. When the dough gets too stiff to stir, begin to knead it with the dough hook, or by hand on a lightly floured board. Add 1 more cup flour, 1/2 cup at a time, and continue to knead, adding a bit more flour if necessary, until the dough is smooth and elastic, 5 to 8 minutes; the dough should remain slightly sticky. If you are using an electric mixer, stop the mixer occasionally to push the dough down off the dough hook.

Put the dough into a lightly buttered bowl, cover with plastic wrap, and let rise in a warm spot until doubled in size, 1 1/2 to 2 hours.

Punch down the dough and let it rest for about 15 minutes.

MEANWHILE, MAKE THE FILLING: Combine the butter, sugars, cinnamon, and nutmeg in a small bowl and mix with a wooden spoon until smooth.

Butter two 9-inch round cake pans. Roll out the dough on a lightly floured surface into an 18-by-12-inch rectangle, about 1/4 inch thick. Spread the filling mixture with a rubber scraper evenly over the surface, leaving a 1/2-inch border on all sides, and sprinkle the raisins over the top. Brush one of the longer sides with egg wash and roll up from the other long side like a jelly roll. (Reserve the remaining egg wash.) Cut the roll into pieces about 1 inch thick, discarding the end pieces, and arrange the rolls cut side up about 1/2 inch apart in the pans.

Cover with plastic wrap and let rise in the pans for 25 minutes. Or pop them into the refrigerator overnight and bake them in the morning. Simply let the rolls sit at room temperature for the time it takes the oven to heat.

Heat the oven to 375 degrees.

When the oven is hot, brush the tops of the rolls lightly with the reserved egg wash and bake until lightly browned and the sugar is beginning to bubble, 25 to 30 minutes. Serve warm, or let cool and wrap in plastic to keep for a day.

MAPLE WALNUT CREAM SCONES

So here you are: teatime scones. I have to thank Ina Garten for pointers on making scones. The ones she developed for Barefoot Contessa, her specialty food shop in the Hamptons, are legendary. Adding potatoes to the dough keeps them moist, and the butter— yes, I know it's a lot—ensures that these will be the flakiest scones you ever ate.

$^1\!/_2$ pound russet potato, peeled and cut into chunks
4 cups all-purpose flour
1 tablespoon baking powder
1 tablespoon baking soda
2 teaspoons coarse salt
$^3\!/_4$ pound (3 sticks) very cold unsalted butter, cut into bits
1 cup chopped walnuts
$^1\!/_2$ cup heavy cream
$^1\!/_2$ cup pure maple syrup
3 large eggs
1 large egg, beaten with 2 tablespoons milk, for an egg wash

FOR THE GLAZE
$1^1\!/_2$ cups confectioners' sugar, sifted
$^1\!/_2$ cup pure maple syrup
Coarse salt

$^1\!/_3$ cup finely chopped walnuts

Put the potato in a saucepan, cover with cold water by an inch, bring to a boil, and cook until very tender. Drain, then push the potato through a strainer or ricer into a bowl. Let it cool.

Heat the oven to 400 degrees.

Combine the flour, baking powder, baking soda, and salt in the bowl of a standing mixer fitted with the paddle (you can do this by hand in a large bowl or with a pastry cutter if you wish). Mix for a few seconds. Toss the butter bits with the flour, then mix on low speed to cut in the butter. Don't go overboard with the mixing here; for flaky scones, you want big, almost pea-sized pieces of butter. Mix in the walnuts.

Add the cream, syrup, and 3 eggs to the potato and whisk until smooth. Add this all at once to the bowl and mix until the dough is just combined. You'll be left with some dry ingredients in the bottom of the bowl. Don't worry about it.

Dump the contents of the bowl onto a floured work surface, flour your hands, and knead the dough just enough to bring it together. Shape it into a square and then flatten it out with your hands or a floured rolling pin to a 12-inch square. Pat the edges to neaten them, then cut the dough into 9 equal pieces. Cut each of these smaller squares on the diagonal and place them on parchment-lined baking sheets.

Paint the tops of the scones with the egg wash and bake for 20 to 25 minutes, until nicely risen and well browned. You'll need to switch the top and bottom sheets halfway through to make sure they bake evenly.

FOR THE GLAZE: While the scones bake, stir the sugar and syrup together with a pinch of salt until smooth.

Let the scones cool for just a minute or two, then gently spread them with about 2 teaspoons each of the glaze. Sprinkle with the finely chopped walnuts and let cool completely—if you can wait—before serving.

OAT-POTATO WAFFLES

MAKES FOUR OR FIVE 7-INCH WAFFLES

These waffles have a bit more tooth than the garden-variety kind. The oats add good crunch and an almost nutty flavor, while the mashed potato in the batter keeps the inside moist and creamy—so much so that these waffles don't really need butter on top. We love spooning warm, chunky applesauce on them, but they are equally appreciated drenched with maple syrup. If you are making these with last night's leftover mashed potatoes, simply measure out 3/4 cup. This recipe can easily be doubled, but use only 1 tablespoon baking powder if you do.

1/2 pound russet potato, peeled and cut into chunks (or 3/4 cup cooled mashed potatoes)
1 1/4 cups all-purpose flour
1/2 cup old-fashioned rolled oats (*not* quick)
1 tablespoon sugar
2 teaspoons baking powder
1/2 teaspoon coarse salt
2 large eggs
4 tablespoons (1/2 stick) unsalted butter, melted and cooled
1 cup milk plus about 2 tablespoons, or as needed
1/4–1/2 teaspoon vanilla extract
Chunky Applesauce (page 548) or pure maple syrup

If using raw potato, put the potato in a saucepan, cover with cold water by at least an inch, and bring to a boil. Reduce the heat to medium and cook until very tender. Drain and return the potato to the pot. Set over medium heat for a minute or two, shaking and stirring so the potato doesn't stick. Remove from the heat.

Push the potato through a strainer or ricer into a bowl. Let cool.

Heat a waffle iron.

Combine the flour, oats, sugar, baking powder, and salt in a big mixing bowl and whisk to combine.

Add the eggs to the potato and whisk until light and smooth. Whisk in the butter, 1 cup of the milk, and vanilla to taste.

Pour the wet ingredients into the dry and stir together just to combine; do not overwork the batter. The batter will be quite thick and airy, but if it appears too stiff to fall easily from a ladle, stir in a bit more milk.

Cook the waffles in your waffle iron as directed by the manufacturer. Serve immediately with applesauce or syrup. The first batches of waffles can be held in a warm oven while you finish cooking the rest.

CHUNKY APPLESAUCE

This is as good on waffles and potato pancakes as it is alongside roast pork.

2 tablespoons unsalted butter
2 large tart apples (about 1 pound) peeled, cored, and chopped
1/2 cup apple cider, plus more if needed
Freshly grated nutmeg
1 tablespoon light brown sugar

Heat the butter in a skillet over medium-high heat. Add the apples and cook, stirring, for a few minutes, until the apples are sizzling and well coated with butter. Pour in the cider, add a grating or two of nutmeg, and bring to a simmer. Cover, lower the heat to medium-low, and let simmer until the apples are tender and just barely keeping a shape, about 15 minutes.

Stir in the sugar with a wooden spoon, smashing some of the apple chunks and leaving some whole. If the applesauce is too dry, add 1 to 2 more tablespoons cider. Heat to dissolve the sugar. Taste for sweetness and serve warm. The applesauce can be made a day ahead, refrigerated, and reheated before serving.

APPLE–SWEET POTATO PANCAKES

Here's a handy use for leftover sweets and a great way to make friends. Have these pancakes for breakfast, or serve them for supper with pea soup—as my Swedish great-great-aunt would.

1 tart apple, peeled, cored, and shredded on a box grater
1/2 cup baked sweet potato
2 tablespoons unsalted butter, melted
2 tablespoons molasses
1 large egg
1 1/3 cups milk
1 cup all-purpose flour
1 1/2 teaspoons baking soda
Coarse salt
Softened unsalted butter and maple syrup for serving

Combine the apple, sweet potato, butter, molasses, egg, and milk in a bowl and stir briskly with a fork. Sift the flour and baking soda with a big pinch of salt and add to the wet ingredients. Stir until just combined. These are pancakes, so you want lumps in the batter.

Heat a griddle over medium heat until very hot. Brush it lightly with butter and drop large spoonfuls (about 1/4 cup) onto the griddle. Let the pancakes cook until the entire surface is bubbling and the edges are starting to dry. Flip and cook until the pancakes are well risen. If you're not eating these immediately, you can keep them warm for a few minutes in a warm oven.

Serve with butter and maple syrup.

DESSERTS

SWEET POTATO CHOCOLATE CAKE
WITH BROILED TOPPING

MAKES ONE 9-BY-13-INCH CAKE

Sweet, moist, and brownielike, this cake gets its elusive flavor from sweet potato and has the bonus of crunch on top. Bake a large sweet potato especially for the cake, or use leftovers.

FOR THE CAKE
Cocoa powder for dusting
2 ounces unsweetened chocolate, chopped
1 tablespoon honey
8 tablespoons (1 stick) unsalted butter, at room temperature
1 cup packed light brown sugar
Grated zest of 1 orange
3/4 cup baked sweet potato, at room temperature
2 large eggs
2 cups all-purpose flour
1 teaspoon baking soda
1/2 teaspoon coarse salt
1 cup sour cream
1 tablespoon Grand Marnier or other orange liqueur

FOR THE TOPPING
1 cup pecan halves
3/4 cup sweetened flaked coconut
1/2 cup packed light brown sugar
2/3 cup heavy cream
2 tablespoons unsalted butter, at room temperature
1 large egg yolk

FOR THE CAKE: Heat the oven to 350 degrees. Butter a 9-by-13-inch (brownie) pan and dust it generously with cocoa powder.

Put the chocolate and honey in a small bowl and pour in 1/3 cup boiling water. Let it sit for a few minutes, then stir until perfectly smooth.

Cut the butter into the bowl of a standing mixer, or a mixing bowl if you're using a hand mixer. Add the brown sugar and zest and beat with the paddle until very light. Add the sweet potato and beat again until well mixed, smooth, and light. Add 1 of the eggs and beat for 1 minute, then add the other egg and beat for another minute. This may sound like a lot of beating, but it makes a difference. Beat in the chocolate.

Sift the flour, baking soda, and salt onto a piece of waxed paper. Stir about a third of the flour into the batter, then add half the sour cream, stirring until just combined. Repeat with another third of the dry ingredients and the rest of the sour cream. Stir in the last of the dry, then add the Grand Marnier and beat until smooth. This is a thick batter.

Scrape the batter into the pan and smooth the top. Rap the pan lightly once or twice on your counter to burst any air bubbles, then bake the cake for about 30 minutes. A cake tester should come out pretty clean, with maybe a crumb or two. Leave the cake on a cooling rack for 10 minutes. Then turn on the broiler and make the topping.

FOR THE TOPPING: Put the pecans in the food processor and hit the pulse button a few times to chop them fine. Or just chop them with a knife. Put the pecans, coconut, brown sugar, heavy cream, and butter in a saucepan over medium heat. Bring to a simmer, stirring. Remove it from the heat, beat in the egg yolk, and spread the topping over the warm cake.

Put the cake under the broiler for about 1 minute. Keep the door open and keep moving the pan around to cook the topping evenly. It should start to brown and be bubbling furiously.

Let the cake cool completely on a rack. Serve it in squares, cut right from the pan.

SWEET POTATO CHIFFON CAKE

MAKES ONE 10-INCH CAKE

This cake is light and moist and deeply flavorful. Use the fruitiest olive oil you can find. And please, take the time to prep the sweet potato as directed. If you just shred it, the pieces will be too big and they will sink in the cake. And if you cut the potato into chunks and just process them, you will end up with a mess.

3/4 pound sweet potato, peeled
1 3/4 cups sugar
3/4 cup extra-virgin olive oil
4 large eggs, separated
2 1/4 cups cake flour
1 teaspoon baking powder
1 teaspoon baking soda
1/2 teaspoon coarse salt
1 teaspoon ground ginger
Grated zest of 1 lemon
1 teaspoon vanilla extract

Heat the oven to 350 degrees. Have ready an ungreased 10-inch tube pan.

Fit your food processor with the shredding disk and shred the sweet potato. Dump it out into a bowl, then put the metal blade into the processor. Add half the shreds and hit the pulse button 3 or 4 times to chop the shreds coarse. Don't get carried away and make mush. Scrape out the chopped potato and repeat with the rest of the shreds.

Combine 1 1/4 cups of the sugar and the oil in a large bowl with an electric mixer. Beat until well mixed, then add the egg yolks one at a time, beating on high speed for at least 30 seconds after each addition. With the mixer running, drizzle in 1/2 cup hot water, then beat until light and lemon-colored. This will take 3 to 4 minutes if you're using a standing mixer, longer if you've got a hand-held. Keep with it.

Sprinkle ¼ cup of the flour over the chopped potato and toss well. Sift the remaining 2 cups flour, the baking powder, soda, salt, and ginger onto a piece of waxed paper. Add the dry to the wet ingredients and mix well. Then add the potatoes, lemon zest, and vanilla and mix again.

Whip the egg whites in an impeccably clean bowl until they hold soft peaks. Add the remaining ½ cup sugar, a tablespoon or so at a time, and beat until the whites are glossy and hold stiff peaks.

Fold the whites into the batter—be thorough but very gentle—and pour the batter into the tube pan. Smooth out the top and bake for 50 minutes. Cut the oven temperature back to 325 degrees and bake for another 10 minutes or so. The cake is done when it's lightly browned and a cake tester comes out clean (or with just a crumb or two).

Invert the cake in its pan and allow it to cool completely upside down (it's got a delicate structure and this helps prevent it from sinking).

Run a thin blade around the outside of the cake and along the tube to release it from the pan, and turn it out onto a plate. This cake needs no further gilding.

FARMHOUSE CHOCOLATE CAKE

MAKES ONE 10-INCH TUBE CAKE

This is a rich, moist cake, the kind of cake that you'd find on a big scrubbed pine table. It cries out for a glass of cold milk.

Pepper's controversial. Some folks just can't imagine why you'd add it to a cake, but we think it gives a great zing. You can skip it if it scares you.

3/4 pound all-purpose potatoes, peeled and cut into chunks
Coarse salt
Cocoa powder for dusting
5 ounces unsweetened chocolate, chopped
2 tablespoons honey
1/2 cup boiling water
1 3/4 cups all-purpose flour
2 teaspoons baking soda
1/4–1/2 teaspoon freshly ground black pepper
8 tablespoons (1 stick) unsalted butter, at room temperature
1/4 cup vegetable shortening
2 cups sugar
5 large eggs, at room temperature
2 teaspoons vanilla extract
Confectioners' sugar for dusting (optional)

Put the potatoes in a saucepan, cover with cold water by at least an inch, add a pinch of salt, and bring to a boil. Cook until the potatoes are tender. Drain well, put the potatoes through a ricer, and measure out 1 cup.

Heat the oven to 350 degrees. Butter a 10-inch tube pan and dust it generously with cocoa.

Put the chocolate and honey in a small bowl. Pour in the boiling water and leave the chocolate to melt and cool, stirring occasionally until it's very smooth.

Sift the flour, baking soda, a pinch of salt, and the pepper together.

Cut the butter into chunks and put it in a large mixing bowl. Beat with an electric mixer until light. Add the vegetable shortening and beat until combined and light. Gradually pour in the sugar and beat until this mixture is very light and fluffy. Add the eggs one by one, beating for at least a minute after each addition. Beat in the chocolate, then the potatoes, then the vanilla. Scrape the sides of the bowl.

Add the dry ingredients to the batter alternately with 1/2 cup cold water, stirring just until combined and smooth.

Scrape the batter into the pan, shake the pan and rap it lightly on the counter to get rid of any air bubbles, and bake until the cake tests done (a skewer will come out clean), about 50 minutes. Cool in the pan on a rack for 10 minutes or so, then turn out the cake, flip it right side up, and leave it on a rack to cool completely.

If you want, dust the cake generously with confectioners' sugar right before serving.

POTATO-ALMOND CAKE

MAKES ONE 8-INCH LAYER CAKE

You find layer cakes like this in Italy and Spain. They have an old-fashioned feel to them—not too sweet, and with a beautiful crumb. It won't keep for a very long time, so plan on making this when company's coming. Use the larger amount of preserves if you want them to drizzle down the sides.

3/4 pound russet potatoes, peeled and cut into chunks
1/2 pound blanched almonds
1 3/4 cups sugar
6 large eggs, at room temperature
1/2 teaspoon vanilla extract
1/4 teaspoon almond extract
1 cup all-purpose flour
1/4 teaspoon coarse salt
1/3–1/2 cup best-quality preserves or jam (blackberry, raspberry, or cherry)
2 tablespoons white rum
Confectioners' sugar for dusting

Put the potatoes in a small saucepan, cover with cold water by at least an inch, and bring to a boil. Cover partway, reduce to a low boil, and cook until the potatoes are very tender. Drain and return them to the pot. Set over medium heat for a minute or two, shaking and stirring so the potatoes don't stick. Remove from the heat and set aside to cool.

Meanwhile, heat the oven to 350 degrees. Butter two deep 8-inch round cake pans and line the bottoms with parchment.

Put the almonds in the bowl of a food processor with 3/4 cup of the sugar and process until finely ground. Transfer to a bowl. Rice the potatoes into the bowl with the almonds and toss to combine.

Beat the eggs in a large bowl with an electric mixer for a minute or two to break them up, then beat in the remaining 1 cup sugar. Beat at high speed until very light and tripled in volume. This will take 3 to 7 minutes, depending on the temperature of your eggs and the vigor of your mixer. Beat in the extracts and stir in the flour and salt. With the mixer running on medium-low, add the potato-almond mixture by the handful. Mix for about a minute after the last addition.

Pour the batter into the pans and bake until the cakes test done—a toothpick will come out clean, with just a crumb or two—30 to 35 minutes. Cool for a few minutes on racks, then turn them out of the pans, remove the parchment, and allow the cakes to cool completely.

Combine the preserves or jam and rum in a small saucepan and bring to a boil, stirring, over medium heat. Remove from the heat.

Place one cake layer, upside down, on a cake dish and spread it with the preserves. Top with the second layer, top side up this time, and dust heavily with confectioners' sugar.

CARAMEL SWEET POTATO PIE

Butter and cream and sugar are all standards in a sweet potato pie filling, so why not make a caramel sauce out of them for an even richer-tasting pie? Serve with plain whipped cream to let the flavors of the potato and caramel shine through. The potatoes will roast in a 450-degree oven in about an hour; remember to prick them with a fork first.

FOR THE PASTRY
Pinch of coarse salt
1¼ cups all-purpose flour
4 tablespoons (½ stick) cold unsalted butter
¼ cup vegetable shortening, chilled

FOR THE FILLING
3 tablespoons unsalted butter
1 cup sugar
1 cup heavy cream, heated to a boil
2 sweet potatoes (about 1¼ pounds), baked
3 large eggs, lightly beaten
1 teaspoon vanilla extract
Pinch of coarse salt

Whipped cream for serving (optional)

FOR THE PASTRY: Stir the salt into the flour in a large bowl. Drop the butter into the flour, toss it, and then cut it into bits. Use your fingers to start working the butter into the flour. Drop the shortening into the flour, toss it, and cut that into bits. Continue working the fat into the flour until the mixture resembles very coarse oatmeal; you still want visible chunks of fat.

Add 2 tablespoons ice water and toss in with a fork. Continue adding ice water by the tablespoon until the pastry starts to come together; you will need at least 2 more tablespoons. Flour your hands and form the pastry into a flat disk, wrap in plastic and chill for 30 minutes.

FOR THE FILLING: Melt the butter in a deep heavy saucepan over medium-high heat. Add the sugar and cook, stirring often, until liquefied and a deep caramel color. Be careful not to burn it or let it turn too dark, or it will be bitter. Immediately put the pan in the sink and pour in the heated cream. It will boil up and spatter and look volcanic; be careful not to burn yourself. Return to medium heat and cook, stirring, until the caramel is very smooth. Let cool.

Position a rack in the lower third of the oven and heat the oven to 425 degrees.

Peel the potatoes and drop them into a bowl. Mash them roughly with a fork. Stir in the eggs and vanilla, then the caramel and salt.

Flour your work surface lightly and roll out the pastry to a 13-inch circle. Fit it into a 9- or 9½-inch pie pan and trim the excess to 1 inch. Fold the edge and make a high fluted rim. Pour in the filling.

Bake for 15 minutes. Reduce the oven temperature to 350 degrees and bake for another 15 to 20 minutes, until the edges of the filling have puffed and the center is still very slightly jiggly. Cool on a rack for at least an hour before serving.

If you like, add a big dollop of whipped cream to each slice.

POTATO DOUGHNUTS

One of my clearest memories of growing up was visiting a German baker on Sundays after church. My mother was a sucker for his jelly doughnuts, still warm and sticky with granulated sugar, a bit of raspberry jelly oozing out. But me, I wanted his potato doughnuts; they were like clouds.

You'll need a doughnut cutter for this. I got mine at a tag sale, but check reliable kitchenware stores.

3/4 pound russet potatoes, peeled and cut into chunks
Coarse salt
4 tablespoons (1/2 stick) unsalted butter
1 packet active dry yeast
1/4 cup sugar
1 large egg
3–3 1/2 cups all-purpose flour
Vegetable oil or vegetable shortening for frying
Confectioners' sugar or honey for serving (optional)

Put the potatoes in a saucepan, cover with cold water by at least an inch, add a pinch of salt, and bring to a boil. Cook until very tender. Drain, reserving the potato water. Measure out 3/4 cup of the water (discard the rest) and add the butter. Set aside until the butter melts.

Put the potatoes through a ricer or a strainer and measure out 3/4 cup.

Dissolve the yeast in 1/4 cup lukewarm water. Add a pinch of the sugar and leave it for 10 to 15 minutes, until it bubbles up.

Combine the potato water and butter, potato, yeast mixture, and the remaining sugar in a large bowl. Add some salt, the egg, and about 1 1/2 cups of the flour. Beat well with an electric mixer or wooden spoon until it's very smooth. Then add enough additional flour, up to about 2 cups more, to make a fairly stiff dough. Cover the bowl with plastic and leave it in a warm place to rise for about an hour, until doubled.

Turn the dough out onto a lightly floured surface. Punch it down, then pat or roll it to about 1/2 inch thick. Cut out doughnuts with a floured doughnut cutter and transfer them—and the holes—to a floured board. Cover with plastic and let rise for 30 to 45 minutes, until doubled.

Fill a wide pan with about 2 inches of oil and heat to 365 degrees. Fry the doughnuts 2 or 3 at a time—don't crowd them—until golden brown, about 1 minute per side. Drain well on paper towels.

These are delicious just as is, or you can dust them with confectioners' sugar while they are still slightly warm. You can also drizzle them with a very thin stream of honey. Eat these the day they're made.

BLACKBERRY COBBLER
WITH SWEET POTATO BISCUITS

The deep purple-black color of fresh blackberries under these pale orange biscuits is a pretty sight. The touch of black pepper is perfect with the perfume of the berries and the lemon zest. If blackberries aren't in season, you can make this with a mix of other summer fruits—blueberries, peaches, nectarines, and plums.

FOR THE TOPPING
2 tablespoons sliced almonds
1 tablespoon light brown sugar
Freshly grated nutmeg

FOR THE FRUIT
3 pints blackberries, picked over and washed
$1/4$ cup all-purpose flour
$1/3$ cup sugar
Grated zest of 1 lemon
A grind of black pepper

FOR THE BISCUITS
$1^1/2$ cups all-purpose flour
2 tablespoons sugar
$1^1/2$ teaspoons baking powder
$1/2$ teaspoon baking soda
$1/2$ teaspoon coarse salt
4 tablespoons ($1/2$ stick) cold unsalted butter, cut into small bits
$1/2$ cup cold baked sweet potato, peeled
$1/3$ cup buttermilk, or more as needed

Heat the oven to 375 degrees.

FOR THE TOPPING: Combine the almonds, brown sugar, and a few gratings of nutmeg in a small bowl.

FOR THE FRUIT: Put the berries in a large bowl and dust with the flour, sugar, lemon zest, and pepper. Toss lightly to coat the berries, then dump the mixture into a shallow 2-quart baking dish.

FOR THE BISCUITS: Stir the flour, sugar, baking powder, baking soda, and salt with a fork in a mixing bowl. Drop in the butter and toss it in the flour. Using the fork or your fingers, work the butter into the flour until it resembles oatmeal.

Whip the sweet potato with a fork until it's very smooth, then add it to the bowl. Work it in lightly but thoroughly with your fingertips. Add enough buttermilk to make a smooth and only slightly sticky dough.

Dump the dough onto a floured surface and knead it two or three times. Flatten it out to ½ inch thick—you don't need a rolling pin to do this—and cut out biscuits with a 2-inch cutter. Arrange the biscuits on top of the fruit, leaving ½ inch or so between each. Gather the biscuit scraps together and cut out more biscuits if needed to cover the fruit. Brush the tops of the biscuits with buttermilk. Sprinkle on the almond topping.

Bake until the biscuits are well browned and the fruit is bubbling up between them, about 40 minutes.

Serve in deep dessert bowls with some biscuit topping on each one. A big splat of whipped cream or scoop of vanilla ice cream would not be unwelcome.

SPICY SUMMER FRUIT SLUMP

These tender sweet potato dumplings are steamed on top of summer fruits that have been poached in spiced red wine. The syrup bubbles up between the dumplings and stains the edges a pretty purple. This is an old-timey stovetop dessert (kin to a grunt), but the flavors are current. Use a combination of whatever's most delicious in the market to make up the fruit. What you use is pretty much up to you—just avoid apples and pears.

You can poach the fruit before dinner. Then, if you have the ingredients for the dumplings ready, it will just take about 15 minutes for you to bring a hot dessert to the table.

2 cups dry red wine (a Côtes du Rhône if you have it)
1 cup sugar
1 star anise
One 2-inch piece of cinnamon stick
2 or 3 grinds of black pepper
2 strips orange zest (as wide as your peeler and about 2 inches long)
3–4 pounds summer fruit (such as a combination of halved apricots and plums, pitted cherries, peeled and quartered peaches, and quartered nectarines)

FOR THE DUMPLINGS
1 1/2 cups all-purpose flour
1 teaspoon baking powder
1 teaspoon baking soda
2 tablespoons sugar
1/4 teaspoon coarse salt
Heaping 1/3 cup mashed sweet potato
3/4 cup milk
tablespoons unsweetened butter, melted

Pour the wine into a wide nonreactive saucepan and add the sugar, star anise, cinnamon, pepper, and zest. Bring to a boil, stirring to dissolve the sugar, then reduce to a gentle simmer and cook for 15 minutes.

Turn up the heat to medium and begin adding the fruit, starting with the ones that will take longest to cook. Let the fruits cook until they are barely tender. Now you can let this sit until you're ready to make the dumplings and finish the slump.

FOR THE DUMPLINGS: Sift the flour, baking powder, baking soda, sugar, and salt into a bowl. Whisk or stir with a fork a few times.

Put the sweet potato, milk, and butter in a small bowl and beat with a fork until smooth. Add the potato mix to the flour and stir with a fork. You don't want clumps of dry ingredients, but you shouldn't overwork this, or the dumplings will end up leaden.

Bring the fruit back to a simmer and drop the dumplings by the spoonful over the top; you'll need to nestle them together pretty closely. Cover and simmer quietly until the dumplings are cooked through, about 8 minutes. Serve this right from the pan.

SWEET POTATO SEMIFREDDO

SERVES 8

Not a classic ice cream, this is a frozen dessert that's very sweet and light. The bitter chocolate sauce is optional, but I find that it cuts the sweetness just enough.

You can vary your presentation on this, from the simplest—scooping it from the dish you froze it in—to fancier—freezing it in a rectangular mold, then unmolding and cutting it into slices—to the fanciest—using elegant molds for individual servings.

1 large (about 1 pound) sweet potato, scrubbed
2 tablespoons Grand Marnier or other orange liqueur
1 cup heavy cream, well chilled
1 cup sugar
1 tablespoon light corn syrup
5 large egg whites, at room temperature
Bitter Chocolate Sauce (page 570)

Heat the oven to 400 degrees.

Prick the potato all over with the tip of a knife or a fork, place it on a double layer of aluminum foil, and bake it for 1 hour 45 minutes. Yes, that's a long time, but you want the potato to really caramelize. Juices will bubble from the pricks and cook to a dark caramel, and the flesh will be creamy and sweet.

Put the potato on a rack until it's cool enough to handle, then peel it and place the flesh in a small bowl. Scrape any caramelized flesh off the skin into the bowl, spoon in the Grand Marnier, and beat the potato with a fork until it's smooth.

Beat the heavy cream until it holds soft peaks, then cover it and refrigerate.

Put the sugar in a small deep saucepan (with a pouring spout, if you have one). Drizzle the syrup over it, then pour in ⅓ cup cold water. Use your finger to make an X in the sugar (this just makes sure it all gets moistened), then

ONE POTATO, TWO POTATO

bring to a boil over medium-low heat. Once the syrup is boiling, increase the heat to medium, stick a candy thermometer in the pan, and start beating the egg whites in a large bowl with an electric mixer on medium speed.

By the time the whites have reached the soft-peak stage, the syrup should be at 240 degrees. Increase the speed to medium-high and carefully pour the syrup into the whites. Be careful not to burn yourself when you do this. Now increase the speed to high and continue beating until the bowl is cool, another 4 to 5 minutes. You'll have a very thick meringue.

Transfer the meringue to a larger bowl and fold in the sweet potato thoroughly. Give the cream a whisk or two, then fold it in. Spoon the mixture into a 3-quart soufflé dish or into individual molds. Wrap first with plastic, then with aluminum foil, and freeze for at least 3 hours.

Serve with a pitcher of the chocolate sauce.

BITTER CHOCOLATE SAUCE

This keeps for at least a week. To reheat, scoop out what you need and put it in a metal bowl over just-simmering water. Stir it a few times as it melts.

¾ cup heavy cream
2 tablespoons light corn syrup
½ pound bittersweet chocolate, finely chopped
1 ounce unsweetened chocolate, finely chopped
2 tablespoons bourbon (or 2 teaspoons vanilla extract)
Coarse salt

Bring the cream and corn syrup to a boil in a saucepan. Turn off the heat. Add the chocolate and shake the pan so all the chocolate is covered with cream. Let it sit for a few minutes to melt the chocolate, then stir until it's smooth. Add the bourbon and a pinch of salt.

The sauce should be warm, so reheat it over simmering water if it cools down before dessert or if you've refrigerated it in the ubiquitous covered container.

CHOCOLATE COCONUT MACAROONS

MAKES ABOUT 40 CANDIES

These little things are every bit as addictive as the Almond Joys they so closely resemble.

Most recipes for this candy call for paraffin in the chocolate, which makes the coating more stable and dipping a bit easier. I don't find these stay around long enough for storage to be a problem and I'm not big on eating wax, but if you want, melt ⅓ bar of paraffin along with the chocolate and stir well.

3/4 pound russet potato, peeled and cut into chunks
Coarse salt
1 (1-pound) box confectioners' sugar
4 tablespoons (½ stick) unsalted butter, melted and cooled
14 ounces sweetened flaked coconut
2 teaspoons vanilla extract
About 3 ounces almonds or hazelnuts
½ pound semisweet chocolate, chopped
2 ounces unsweetened chocolate, chopped

Put the potato in a saucepan, cover with cold water by at least an inch, add a pinch of salt, and bring to a boil. Lower the heat to medium and cook until the potato is tender. Drain well, then push the potato through a strainer or through a ricer. Let it cool completely.

Combine the potato, confectioners' sugar, butter, coconut, vanilla, and a pinch of salt. Your hands are the best tool for this, but you can use a sturdy spoon. Cover with plastic and chill for at least an hour, until it's firm enough to shape (you can leave it overnight if you want).

Line a baking sheet with parchment or waxed paper. Shape the mixture into balls, using about 1 tablespoon for each. Stick each with an almond and put the candy on the baking sheet.

Melt the chocolates together in a bowl set over simmering water (or use the microwave). Dip the candies into the chocolate. I cover the top and most of the sides, and then let the chocolate drip down. Put the candies back on the sheet as you dip them. Refrigerate until set, at least an hour.

ANDERSON, JEAN. *The American Century Cookbook*. New York: Potter, 1997.

——. *Jean Anderson Cooks*. New York: Morrow, 1982.

BAKALAR, RUTH. *The Complete Potato Cookbook*. New Jersey: Prentice-Hall, 1969.

BARR, NANCY VERDE. *We Called It Macaroni*. New York: Knopf, 1991.

BEARD, JAMES. *The Fireside Cookbook*. New York: Simon & Schuster, 1949.

——. *James Beard's Menus for Entertaining*. New York: Delacorte Press, 1965.

BEROLZHEIMER, RUTH. *The United States Regional Cookbook*. Halcyon House, 1947.

BOCUSE, PAUL. *Paul Bocuse's French Cooking*. New York: Pantheon, 1977.

CASAS, PENELOPE. *¡Delicioso! The Regional Cooking of Spain*. New York: Knopf, 1996.

COLICCHIO, TOM. *Think Like a Chef*. New York: Potter, 2000.

CORRIHER, SHIRLEY. *CookWise*. New York: Morrow, 1997.

DAVID, ELIZABETH. *French Provincial Cooking*. New York: Penguin Books, 1970.

DERECSKEY, SUSAN. *The Hungarian Cookbook*. New York: Perennial Library, 1972.

FIELD, CAROL. *The Italian Baker*. New York: Harper Collins, 1985.

FOBEL, JIM. *Jim Fobel's Big Flavors*. New York: Potter, 1995.

——. *Jim Fobel's Casseroles*. New York: Potter, 1997.

HAZAN, MARCELLA. *Essentials of Classic Italian Cooking*. New York: Knopf, 1993.

HAZELTON, NIKA. *The Unabridged Vegetable Cookbook*. New York: M. Evans and Company, 1976.

JOHNSTON, MIREILLE. *Cuisine of the Sun*. New York: Fireside, 1990.

KENNEDY, DIANA. *My Mexico*. New York: Potter, 1998.

MADISON, DEBORAH. *Vegetarian Cooking for Everyone*. New York: Broadway Books, 1997.

MARSHALL, LYDIE. *A Passion for Potatoes*. New York: HarperCollins, 1992.

MILLER, ASHLEY. *The Potato Harvest Cookbook*. Connecticut: Taunton Press, 1998.

NATHAN, JOAN. *Jewish Cooking in America*. New York: Knopf, 1998.

NEAL, BILL. *Biscuits, Spoonbread, and Sweet Potato Pie*. New York: Knopf, 1991.

NICHOLS, ANNIE. *Potatoes: From Pancakes to Pommes Frites*. New York: Rizzoli, 1998.

OLNEY, RICHARD. *Simple French Food*. New York: Atheneum, 1983.

ROJAS-LOMBARDI, FELIPE. *The Art of South American Cooking*. New York: HarperCollins, 1991.

SAX, RICHARD, WITH SANDRA GLUCK. *From the Farmers' Market*. New York: Harper & Row, 1986.

STEWART, MARTHA. *The Martha Stewart Cookbook*. New York: Potter, 1995.

TANNAHILL, REAY. *Food in History*. New York: Crown Trade Paperbacks, 1998, 1973.

TASCA LANZA, ANNA. *The Flavors of Sicily*. New York: Potter, 1996.

TAYLOR, JOHN MARTIN. *Hoppin' John's Charleston, Beaufort & Savannah*. New York: Potter, 1997.

————. *The New Southern Cook*. New York: Bantam Books, 1995.

Vegetables in "The Good Cook" series, Time Life Cooks. New York, 1979.

VON BREMZEN, ANYA, AND JOHN WELCHMAN. *Please to the Table: The Russian Cookbook*. New York: Workman, 1990.

The Wise Encyclopedia of Cookery. New York: Wm. H. Wise & Co., 1949.

WOLFERT, PAULA. *Paula Wolfert's World of Food*. New York: Harper & Row, 1988.

ZUCKERMAN, LARRY. *The Potato: How the Humble Spud Rescued the Western World*. Boston: Faber & Faber, 1998.

INDEX